The East Turkestan Independence Movement

The East Turkestan Independence Movement

1930s–1940s

Wang Ke

TRANSLATED BY
Carissa Fletcher

The Chinese University Press

The East Turkestan Independence Movement: 1930s–1940s
   By Wang Ke
   Translated by Carissa Fletcher

© The Chinese University of Hong Kong 2018

All rights reserved. No part of this publication may
be reproduced or transmitted in any form or by any
means, electronic or mechanical, including photocopying,
recording, or any information storage and retrieval
system, without permission in writing from
The Chinese University of Hong Kong.

ISBN: 978-962-996-769-7

The Chinese University Press
The Chinese University of Hong Kong
Sha Tin, N.T., Hong Kong
Fax: +852 2603 7355
Email: cup@cuhk.edu.hk
Website: www.chineseupress.com

Printed in Hong Kong

This publication has been sponsored by the Suntory Foundation
under its Support for Overseas Publication program.

For my professor
Yamauchi Masayuki

Contents

List of Figures and Tables   /   xi
Map   /   xiii
Introduction   /   xv

Chapter 1
The "*Ummah*" and "China":
The Qing Dynasty's Rule over Uyghur Society in Xinjiang 1
1.1 The "New Borderland" (*Xinjiang*) of the Qing Dynasty 2
1.2 The People of the Manchu Emperor under Segregated Rule 9
1.3 From "*Jihad*" by the Kashgar Khoja Clan to the Founding of the
    Province of Xinjiang 17
    Summary 25

Chapter 2
Origins of the East Turkestan Independence Movement:
Social Context and Shape of the Movement 27
2.1 Ideology of the East Turkestan Independence Movement 27
2.2 The First Independence Movement 32
2.3 Ethnic Oppression in Xinjiang 36
2.4 Xinjiang's Dual Social Structure and the Public Administrative System
    for Uyghur Communities 40
    Summary 46

Chapter 3
The Anti-Japanese, Pro-Soviet Agenda: Surface and Substance—Sheng Shicai's Political Agenda and Ethnic Problems in Xinjiang 49
3.1 Japan's Infiltration of Xinjiang in the Early Modern Era 50
3.2 Sheng Shicai's Anti-Japanese, Pro-Soviet Policies 59
Summary 71

Chapter 4
The Dual Power Structure and Ethnic Problems: The Political Agenda and Ethnic Policies under Sheng Shicai's Regime 73
4.1 Soviet Support and the Establishment of Sheng Shicai's System of Governance 74
4.2 The Formation of a Dual Power Structure in Xinjiang Province 81
4.3 Sheng Shicai's Political Repositioning 94
Summary 104

Chapter 5
Soviet-Backed "Jihad" by the Turkic-Islamic Peoples of China: The Rise of the Second Independence Movement and the Ghulja Uprising 107
5.1 Nationalist Secret Societies and Their Political Views 108
5.2 Secret Rebel Organizations and Guerrilla Forces Formed by the Turkic-Islamic Peoples 119
5.3 The Ghulja Uprising 128
5.4 Victory in the Ghulja Uprising and Soviet Support 134
Summary 141

Chapter 6
Authority and Power: Political Structure of the East Turkestan Republic in Wartime 143
6.1 Legitimacy Founded Upon Traditional Authority 143
6.2 Intellectuals and Political Power in the Republic 151
6.3 Formation of an Intertwined Power Structure 161
Summary 170

Chapter 7
The Meeting Point of Nationalism and Communism:
Soviet Backdrop to the Expansion of the East Turkestan Republic 173

7.1 The Establishment of a "Three-Front War," "Residence No. 1," and "Residence No. 2" 175

7.2 The "Liberation of Tarbagatay District" and the "Imir Command Post"...181

7.3 The "Liberation of Altay District," the "White House," and the "Blue House" 185

Summary.. 194

Chapter 8
International Politics and the Tragedy of the Republic:
Behind the Scenes of the Xinjiang Peace Talks 197

8.1 Soviet Objectives in Supporting the National Independence Movement... 198

8.2 The Shift in Soviet Policy 203

8.3 The Soviet Union and the Xinjiang Peace Talks 212

Summary.. 221

Chapter 9
"National Independence" or "National Liberation":
The Fall of the East Turkestan Republic 225

9.1 A Schism over the Objective of "National Revolution" 226

9.2 From the "Revolutionary Youth League" to the "Revolutionary Party" ...232

9.3 Fall of the Republic... 244

Summary.. 251

Chapter 10
Ideals Versus Reality: A Detailed Analysis of
the Second East Turkestan Independence Movement........................... 253

10.1 The Will of the Soviet Union and the Undemocratic Political System.. 254

10.2 Conflict between Modern Objectives and Traditional Society............ 259

10.3 Uyghur-Centrism in the Republic... 263

10.4 Economy of the East Turkestan Republic.. 269

10.5 The Historical Significance of the East Turkestan Republic............... 275

Postscript   / 281

Timeline of Important Events   / 285

Notes   / 291

List of Figures and Tables

Figures

2.1 Structural Diagram of Xinjiang Society 41
4.1 Xinjiang's Dual Power Structure (1934–1942) 90
5.1 Street Map of Ghulja 129
5.2 Coalition of East Turkestan Nationalist Forces in Ili District 137
6.1 Organizational Chart of the East Turkestan Republic 153
6.2 Diagram of the Intertwined Political Forces within the East Turkestan Republic 163
7.1 Relational Diagram between the Imir Command Post and the Secret Rebel Organizations of Tarbagatay 185
7.2 Evolutionary Flowchart of the Kazakh Rebel Forces in Altay 191
9.1 Organizational Structure of the "East Turkestan Revolutionary Youth League" 234

Tables

4.1 Evolution of the Xinjiang Provincial Police Organization under Sheng Shicai 86
4.2 Evolutionary Chart of the Ethnic Affairs Department under the Police Organizations in Sheng Shicai's Era 92
5.1 Comparison of "Why Are We Fighting?" and "Why We Must Fight" ... 110
5.2 Leaders of the Ghulja National Freedom Group 119

6.1 Members of the Interim Government Council of the East Turkestan Republic 150
6.2 References to Military Matters in the Resolutions of the Interim Government Council of the East Turkestan Republic (to March 1945) 158
7.1 Founding Members of the National Revolutionary Interim Government of Altay 192
8.1 1946 Budget Statement for Separately Budgeted Organizations, Formulated by the Planning Bureau of the Ministry of Finance 211
8.2 Expenditures of the East Turkestan Republic under the 1946 Annual Budget..211
9.1 Members of the Central Executive Committee under the First Session of the "East Turkestan Revolutionary Youth League"................235
9.2 Principal Members of the Central Executive Committee of the East Turkestan Revolutionary Party 241
10.1 Population of the East Turkestan Republic and Regional Representation of the Kazakh and Uyghur Peoples 265
10.2 Interim Government Council Members Appointed after November 12, 1944 265
10.3 Revenue Items in the 1946 Budget of the East Turkestan Republic 270

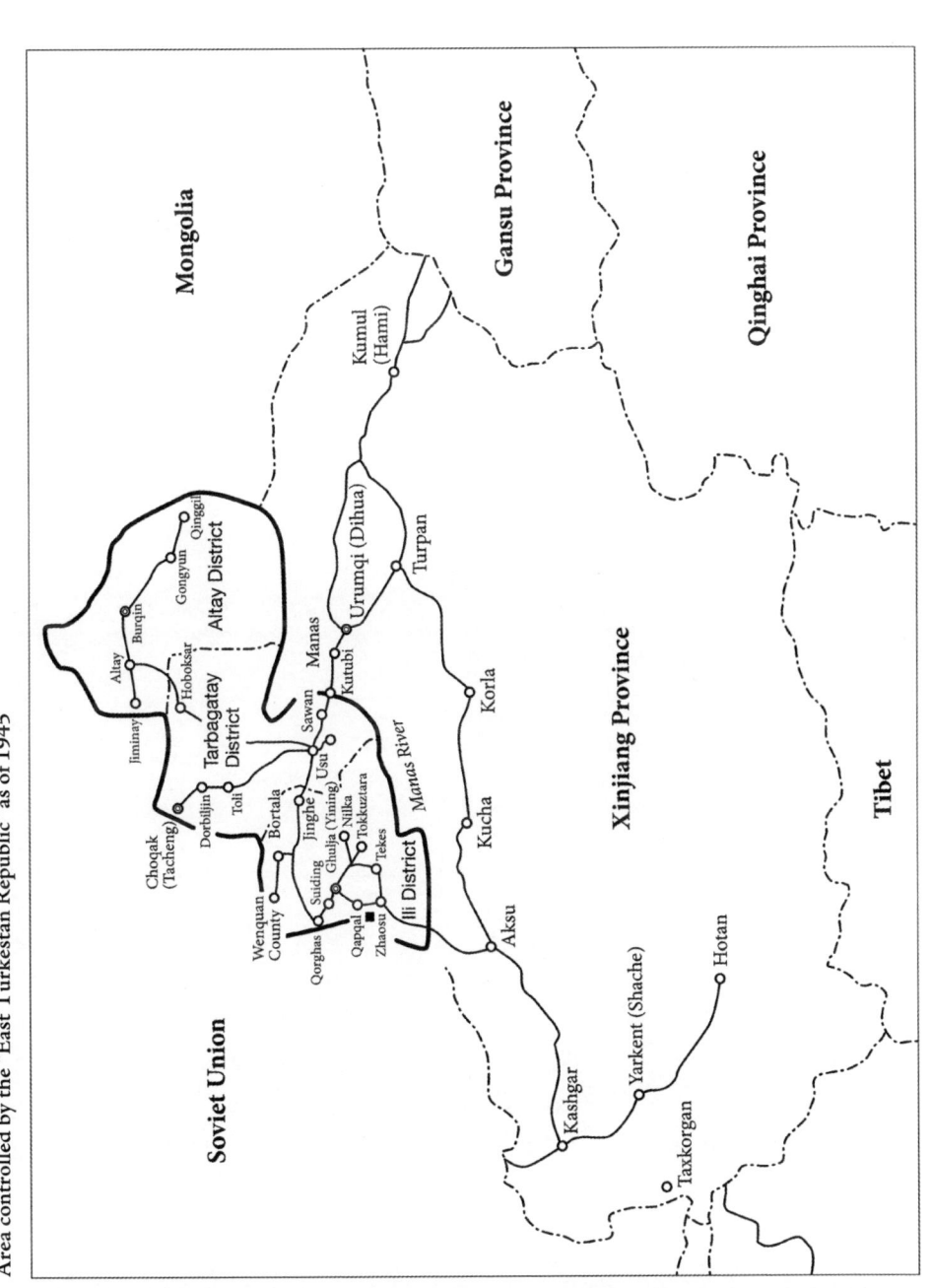

Introduction

On July 5, 2009, Urumqi, the capital city of the Xinjiang Uyghur Autonomous Region, was shocked by violent civil unrest, triggered by a deadly brawl at a toy factory in faraway Guangdong Province during which at least two Uyghurs were murdered by a Han Chinese mob. Infuriated by the lack of a police response, hundreds of Uyghur protesters converged upon Urumqi's central market square. The initially peaceful protest took a violent turn as protesters began attacking Han Chinese passers-by, as well as Hui Muslims and other minorities with Han features, clubbing and stoning them to death. According to Chinese government statistics, 197 people were killed during the riots, including 134 unarmed Han Chinese, 11 Hui Muslims, and 1 Manchu; nearly 2,000 people were wounded. More than 1,000 Uyghur suspects were arrested in the following days, and several were later sentenced to execution. Although official sources claimed that "these grave and violent crimes of assault, looting and arson were meticulously planned and organized by a 'trifecta' of domestic and international groups," there is no doubt that these events were triggered by widespread inter-ethnic hatred. The brutality of the riots left many wondering how such events could occur against the backdrop of China's meteoric rise in the early 21st century, and prompted many to ponder the following chain of questions: Were the Chinese government's minority policies problematic? If not, why would the Xinjiang region's Uyghur inhabitants bear such enmity toward their Han Chinese neighbors, with whom they normally coexisted peacefully? If so, what were the key problems, and how could they be resolved?

The cities of Kashgar and Ghulja (Yining) had in fact previously been witness to similar incidents provoked by racial hatred. On October 30, 1981, a Han Chinese shop clerk in Kashgar entered into a dispute with a Uyghur farmer and beat him to death with a hunting rifle off the store shelf. Uyghur protesters stormed the city, attacking Han civilians; 2 people were killed on the scene, and 262 were wounded. In 1997, riots spread across Ghulja between February 5 and 7 in response to rumors that a number of Uyghur religious worshippers had been arrested by the Chinese government during Ramadan; 7 Han Chinese civilians were killed during the riots, and a number of protesters were killed or wounded as the crowds were dispersed by police. These two incidents are both similar in nature to the 2009 Urumqi riots, though dissimilar in scale. This congruence suggests that the events in Urumqi were in many ways linked to the circumstances of Uyghur communities in other regions of Xinjiang, including the southern region where Kashgar is located. Thus, in order to truly understand the nature of the Urumqi riots, we must also first explore the motivations behind the incidents that occurred in Kashgar and Ghulja.

The reason is in fact quite simple: Kashgar and Ghulja historically served as the birthplace and base of operations for the first and second East Turkestan independence movements respectively. To understand the ethnic tensions between Uyghurs and Han Chinese in Xinjiang today, we must start by understanding the nature of the East Turkestan independence movement.

The aim of the East Turkestan independence movement was to establish a Uyghur nation-state in Xinjiang. The First East Turkestan Independence Movement began in Kashgar in southern Xinjiang in 1933, and the "Islamic Republic of East Turkestan" was founded in Kashgar on November 12 in the same year. However, the Islamic Republic collapsed a mere 85 days after its founding, before its government and system of state power could be fully formed. The independence movement experienced a resurgence in 1944, and the "East Turkestan Republic" was established on November 12 of that year in the city of Ghulja (Yining) in northern Xinjiang. Compared to the first movement, the Second East Turkestan Independence Movement was of broader scale and longer duration; it played a part in the global war against fascism, and impacted the post-war reconstruction of the international order. However, the movement was dependent on the support of the Soviet

Union to escape the yoke of the Chinese Nationalist government, which was then in power, and its proponents ultimately bowed to Soviet pressure to abandon their calls for independence. The movement was later subsumed under the banner of the Chinese Communist Party, and in the post-1949 era, it was referred to in China as the "Three Districts Revolution."[1] However, this appellation is based solely on the movement's final outcome, and does not reflect either its origins or its nature.

The ideas of the East Turkestan independence movement still survive today in the Xinjiang region, despite the passage of more than eighty years since it first came into being. For self-evident reasons, the independence movement went underground during the Mao Zedong era, but the idea of independence for East Turkestan has experienced a revival since the 1980s, against the backdrop of China's overcorrection of policies from the Mao era, the rise of a global Islamic renaissance, as well as the liberation of the Central Asian countries following the failure of perestroika and the collapse of the Soviet Union. The ideas of the East Turkestan independence movement have steadily gained in momentum. In October 1989, the Uyghur author Turgun Almas published a book entitled *The Uyghur People* (Uygurlar), in which he proposed the radical theory that the Uyghur people have been living nears the oases of the Tarim Basin for eight thousand years.[2]

The East Turkestan independence movement is not only the tie that binds modern Uyghur history from the 20th century onward; it is also a crucial page in the history of China in the modern and contemporary eras. Faithfully reconstructing the true circumstances of the East Turkestan independence movement and, in particular, accurately understanding and evaluating the nature of the Second East Turkestan Independence Movement can help provide insights into the simmering ethnic tensions that have given rise to events such as the 2009 Urumqi riots, and could also have profound significance in the efforts to chart China's future as a multi-ethnic state. Regrettably, few studies on the East Turkestan independence movement have been published.

Works that make relatively detailed references to the first and second East Turkestan independence movements include *A Concise History of Xinjiang* (Xinjiang jianshi), Volume 3, published by the Xinjiang Academy of Social Sciences; *Warlords and Muslims in Chinese Central Asia: A*

Political History of Republican Sinkiang 1911–1949 (Cambridge: Cambridge University Press, 1986), by Andrew D. W. Forbes; and *Seventy Years of Upheaval in Xinjiang* (Xinjiang fengbao qishi nian) (Taipei: Lanxi chuban youxian gongsi, 1980), by the Taiwanese author Zhang Dajun. However, these works all describe the movement from the perspective of the political history of China and Xinjiang, and do not explore the East Turkestan independence movement itself in any great depth.

In the author's view, the monograph *Seventy Years of Upheaval in Xin-jiang* provides the most detailed narrative of Xinjiang's political history in the early modern era. It is based on a previous work by Zhang Dajun published in 1954, entitled *Overview of the Last Forty Years of Upheaval in Xinjiang* (Xinjiang jin sishi nian bianluan jilüe) (Taipei: Zhongyang wenwu gongyingshe, 1954), so it addresses more attention to the two East Turkestan independence movements of the 1930s and 1940s. The Japanese author Nakada Yoshinobu also published an article which could be described as a revised summary of Zhang Dajun's *Overview of the Last Forty Years of Upheaval in Xinjiang*, entitled "The I-Ning Affair and the National Movement in Sinkiang" (Inei jihen to Shinkyō no minzoku undō).[3] However, Zhang Dajun, who served as a deputy regiment commander in the Chinese Nationalist army in 1945, had no means of discovering the political developments which underpinned the East Turkestan Republic; his narrative of the facts is therefore unavoidably error-ridden, and his analysis of the nature of the events is highly colored by emotional factors.

In 1990, Linda K. Benson published *The Ili Rebellion: The Moslem Challenge to Chinese Authority in Xinjiang, 1944–1949* (Armonk, London: M.E. Sharpe, Inc., 1990) in the United States. This work was praised at the time as "the sole scholarly work in the world to date that discusses the Three Districts Revolution."[4] However, its content on the Second East Turkestan Independence Movement and the political mechanisms of the East Turkestan Republic was limited to a few scanty pages in Chapter 4, "The Establishment of the East Turkestan Republic" (*The Ili Rebellion*, pp. 42–66), still focusing primarily on the political and military countermeasures taken by the Nationalist government and the provincial authorities in Xinjiang. Benson was aware of the limitations of her work: in 1991, she requested an interview with the son of Ahmatjan Kasimi, the then-deceased leader of the East Turkestan Republic in its later stages, but the request was denied.

In the 1990s and thereafter, a number of works on Xinjiang in the modern era were published in mainland China, including: Bai Zhensheng and Koibuchi Shin'ichi (eds.), *Outline of Xinjiang's Modern Sociopolitical History* (Xinjiang xiandai zhengzhi shehui shilüe) (Beijing: Zhongguo shehui kexue chubanshe, 1992); Xinjiang Three Districts Revolution History Editing Committee, *History of the Xinjiang Three Districts Revolution* (Xinjiang san qu geming shi) (Beijing: Minzu chubanshe, 1998); Huang Jianhua, *A Study of Nationalist Government Policies on Xinjiang* (Guomindang zhengfu de Xinjiang zhengce yanjiu) (Beijing: Minzu chubanshe, 2003); Miao Pusheng and Tian Weijiang (eds.), *Historical Survey of Xinjiang* (Xinjiang shigang) (Urumqi: Xinjiang renmin chubanshe, 2004); Li Sheng (ed.), *The History and Current Conditions of Xinjiang, China* (Zhongguo Xinjiang lishi yu xianzhuang) (Urumqi: Xinjiang renmin chubanshe, 2006), and so on. Although these works are chiefly characterized as historical overviews, two served as important references with respect to the historical sources and research methods used in this book. The first is the *History of the Xinjiang Three Districts Revolution*, which minutely plots out the course of the Second East Turkestan Independence Movement; however, because the movement is viewed through the lens of the revolutionary conception of history, a number of issues are not fully explored. The second is *The History and Current Conditions of Xinjiang, China* by Li Sheng: although this work is also a survey history, Chapter 3, which discusses the history of Xinjiang prior to the Second East Turkestan Independence Movement, and Chapters 4 and 5, which narrate the course of the movement, offer a great deal of useful information; its references to the existence of Russian-language archives are particularly invaluable. Regrettably, perhaps owing to political considerations, Russia later refused to authorize the release of the archival materials, and even today, the scholars who reviewed these materials are still unable to provide detailed descriptions of their contents, which remain an unfathomable mystery.

The scarcity of prior research on this subject, and in particular the lack of studies from an ethnonational perspective or from the perspective of the movement's political mechanisms, is due first to the lack of sources, and secondly to the diversity of those sources that are available. For a truly thorough study, it is necessary to address sources in a wide variety of languages, including Chinese, Uyghur, Kazakh, Russian, English, and

Japanese, a prospect which deters many scholars. In the course of writing this book, I reviewed hundreds of important sources, including the official documents of the East Turkestan Republic in the period from 1944 to 1946, the constitutions of the "East Turkestan Revolutionary Youth League" and the "East Turkestan Revolutionary Party," as well as speeches, essays and letters by leading figures in the East Turkestan Republic. I also read the memoirs and diaries of Sheng Shicai and Wu Zhongxin, the former governors of Xinjiang, and collected a number of memoirs written in Uyghur, Kazakh and Chinese by figures involved in the Second East Turkestan Independence Movement. Other sources included Japanese and American diplomatic documents related to Xinjiang. I was also fortunate to have the opportunity to interview a number of Uyghur, Kazakh and Sibe figures with special ties to the leadership of the East Turkestan Republic in that period. These collections served as the fundamental source materials for this book.

This book primarily relied on the first-hand sources described above in attempting to reconstruct the East Turkestan independence movement and the political evolution of the East Turkestan Republic from four perspectives: social structure in Xinjiang and within the region's Turkic-Islamic communities; the origins and evolution of the idea of national revolution; the principles underpinning the internal coherence of the East Turkestan independence movement, and power structures in the East Turkestan Republic; and international relations and politics surrounding the Xinjiang region. These perspectives served as the foundation in exploring the nature of the East Turkestan independence movement.

In terms of its content, this book can be divided into five sections. **Chapters 1 and 2** provide context for the social transitions in the premodern and early modern eras, examining the characteristics, successes and failings of the Qing Dynasty's policies on Xinjiang during the era of traditional rule; the grim international situation faced by Xinjiang during its period of transition; the social status of Islam in Uyghur communities, and its changing circumstances; the influence of pan-Turkism and pan-Islamism in early modern Uyghur society; and social structure in Xinjiang and within Uyghur communities, to analyze and explore the motivations that propelled the rise of the East Turkestan independence movement. **Chapters 3 and 4** analyze politics and ethnic minority policies under the regime of the Han ruler Sheng Shicai, revealing how he was able to suppress the First East Turkestan Independence Movement and the Islamic Republic of East Turkestan, at the cost of ultimately exacerbating ethnic conflict in the region. **Chapters 5, 6 and 7** seek to reconstruct the events behind the rise of the Second East Turkestan Independence Movement, the founding of the East Turkestan Republic, and the expansion of the republic's sphere of influence in each of its three districts, to serve as a basis for exploring the characteristics of power structures in the East Turkestan Republic. **Chapters 8 and 9** reconstruct the political developments behind the Xinjiang Peace Talks and the fall of the East Turkestan Republic, exploring the underlying causes for the republic's collapse from the external perspective of international politics, as well as the internal perspective of the inherent contradictions within the national movement. **Chapter 10**, which serves as the conclusion to this book, analyzes the nature of the East Turkestan Republic from the perspective of its political systems, social structure, inter-ethnic relations, and economic conditions, and explores the significance of the Second East Turkestan Independence Movement and the East Turkestan Republic in the history of the Uyghur people, the Xinjiang region, and early modern China.

Chapter 1

The "Ummah" and "China"
The Qing Dynasty's Rule over Uyghur Society in Xinjiang

Of all China's historic dynasties, the Qing Dynasty ruled over the largest number of ethnic groups. After the collapse of China's traditional dynastic system, the domain of the Qing Dynasty was inherited by the Republic of China. However, a lingering question remains: Why did the border regions once ruled by the Qing Dynasty, in particular Mongolia, Tibet, and the Uyghur regions of Xinjiang, persistently experience ethnic independence movements during the era of the Republic of China? An exploration of the relationship between "state" and "ethnicity" in China since the early modern era and analysis of the policies adopted by the Qing Dynasty in these regions bears important significance with respect to this issue.

The Qing Dynasty gained direct control over the Islamic communities residing near the oases of the Tarim Basin through conquest: this area is known today as the Uyghur region, and some scholars believe that it is contextually defined by a sense of old borders inherited from previous dynasties. The region was once under the rule of the Dzungar Khanate, which paid tribute as a vassal of the Qing Dynasty.[1] This chapter will chiefly examine the policies through which the Qing Dynasty governed Uyghur society and the Uyghurs' response, and analyze the policy objectives of the Qing Dynasty in its rule over Uyghur society, to gain perspective on the ethnic and state structures built by the Qing Dynasty, and the ethnic, religious and national identities that these accorded to the Uyghur people. It must first be clarified that, although the unified ethnonym "Uyghur" did not come into use among the inhabitants of this region until the 1930s, this chapter will use the term "Uyghur" for the sake of narrative convenience.²

1.1 The "New Borderland" (*Xinjiang*) of the Qing Dynasty

From Vassalage to Subjugation

In 1755 (20th Year of the Qianlong Reign), the nomadic empire of the Dzungar Khanate located in the northern Tianshan Mountains fell into civil unrest, and the Qing Dynasty seized this opportunity to dispatch troops to eliminate the Khanate. Although the Dzungar had long paid tribute as a vassal of the Qing Dynasty, the Khanate had also repeatedly invaded the Khalkha Mongols, an important ally of the Qing Dynasty; thus, eradicating the Dzungar Khanate had been a long-cherished desire of the Qing Dynasty since the Kangxi era (1661–1722). The territorial expansion was at first limited to the direct results of subjugating the Dzungar: however, as the Qianlong Emperor expressed in his poem, "The Western Frontier" (*Xichui*), "The affair strayed far from Our intentions." The Qing Dynasty's original objective had been merely to "recruit vassals" among the other ethnic groups in neighboring regions once governed by the Dzungar, and allow them to acknowledge the Qing Dynasty as their suzerain.

The Qing Dynasty apparently had no intention at first of directly occupying regions other than the Dzungar. This is clearly evidenced in the Qianlong Emperor's appointment of the commander of the Dzungar Expeditionary Force under the title of the "General for Border Determination" (*dingbian jiangjun* 定邊將軍). The Qing Dynasty referred to the Kazakhs and the Bulut (Kyrgyz), who "requested to serve as vassals and sent envoys to pay tribute," as "protective screens outside the borders," or extraterritorial vassal states: "Only the two tribes of the Kazakhs and the Bulut shield the territories for Us."³ Similarly, in the region of the southern Tianshan Mountains inhabited by the Turkic Muslim Uyghurs,⁴ although the Qing Dynasty ultimately captured the region directly through military subjugation, it should be noted that this was not the Qing Dynasty's original intention.

Prior to the Qing occupation, the Uyghur community was in fact controlled by the White Mountain and Black Mountain factions under the

Naqshbandi Sufi order of Islam (al-Tariqah al-Naqshiban-diyyah). The Naqshbandi order is a Sufi order that emerged in the Central Asian region of Samarkand. The founder of the Naqshbandi order, Makhdumi Azam, died in 1542, and his sons experienced a schism due to a dispute over control of the order. His eldest son Ishan-i-Kalan and his followers founded the "White Mountain" (Aq-taghlyq) sect, while his seventh son Ishaq (a younger half-brother of Ishan-i-Kalan) and his followers founded the "Black Mountain" (Qara-taghlyq) sect. In the late 16th and early 17th centuries, the Black Mountaineers spread from Samarkand into the southern Tianshan mountains, and, with the support of the then-ruler of the Yarkent Khanate, gradually became a powerful force centered on the Yarkent region with influence over the regime of the Yarkent Khanate as well as Uyghur society. In the mid-17th century, the eldest son of Ishan-i-Kalan, Yusup Khoja, also left Samarkand and made his way through the southern Tianshan Mountains to the Kashgar region, where he established a base to build up his own forces. The Black Mountaineers and the White Mountaineers not only wielded enormous influence over the populace, but also collaborated with political powers, sparking intense conflict. Since both sects were led by self-professed "Khoja" (*Hoja, Khwaja*, "descendants of the prophet," referring to the descendants of the Prophet Muhammad), and were both active in the region centering on Kashgar, they are generally referred to as the "Kashgar Khoja."

The White Mountaineers were in a disadvantaged position due to their late arrival to the region; their leader Afaq Khoja therefore reached out through the Dalai Lama of Tibet to request support from Galdan Khan of the Dzungar Khanate. In 1678, Galdan sent soldiers to the southern Tianshan Mountains to eliminate the Yarkent Khanate, supporting Afaq Khoja as a puppet ruler over the Uyghur population. After Galdan's death, his nephew Tsewang Rabtan (also written Tsewang Araptan) succeeded him to the throne. Tsewang Rabtan sought to exploit the Black Mountain Khoja to exert his rule over Uyghur society; the White Mountain Khojas were captured and detained in Ghulja, the capital of the Dzungar Khanate (modern-day Yining).

When the Qing Dynasty launched its assault against the Dzungar Khanate, the White Mountain Khojas detained in Ghulja, including Mahmat Khoja, the grandson of Afaq Khoja, as well as his two sons born in captivity, Burhan al-Din and Khoja Jihan, sought out the Qing armies to express their allegiance.[5] Since the Qing Dynasty originally had no intention of directly ruling over the Uyghur population, Burhan al-Din was released in the southern Tianshan Mountains as part of a ploy to "recruit vassals" among the Uyghurs.[6] Zhao Hui, the General for Border Determination, dispatched Deputy Governor-General Amindao to accompany Burhan al-Din southward on a mission to "offer amnesty and recruitment";[7] in the "Imperial College Inscription by Gaozong, Emperor Chun, on Achieving the Pacification of the Muslim Regions" (*Gaozong Chun huangdi pingding Huibu gaocheng Taixue beiwen*), the mission was also referred to as "official negotiations." In sum, it is quite clear that the Qing Dynasty initially sought only to exercise indirect control over Uyghur society via the Khoja brothers.

Burhan al-Din's younger brother Khoja Jihan was held in Ghulja for some time to assist the Qing Dynasty in pacifying the local Muslim community. However, Jihan's aim was to achieve complete independence for Uyghur society, and he instead joined the armed rebellion led by the Dzungar prince Amursana. After the rebellion was suppressed, he fled to the southern Tianshan Mountains, where he convinced his brother Burhan al-Din to assassinate Amindao and his entourage of one hundred Qing soldiers in 1757 (22nd Year of the Qianlong Reign), and openly raise the banner of rebellion against the Qing Dynasty. The Khoja brothers, who had suffered under the tyranny of the Dzungar until being liberated from their long imprisonment by the Qing Dynasty, which recognized their status and released them into the Uyghur community, thus "met kindness with enmity," inciting the wrath of the Qianlong Emperor. The "Engraved Yarkent Inscription by Gaozong, Emperor Chun, on the Pacification of the Muslim Regions" (*Gaozong Chun huangdi pingding Huibu leiming Ye'erqiang beiwen*) states: "The Dzungar barbarians . . . ravaged their people and brutalized the populace, treating the Muslims as sheep. . . . Two tribal chieftains were detained on the shores of the Ili. The four great Muslim cities conveyed *tangga* as contributions for the land tax, to provide for the defenses. The dreaded levies could not be endured by the valleys; how was this to be borne in facing one's inner heart? The Dzungar have now been pacified, and all the Muslims can see the heavens. It was said that from this day forth, they could be well-fed and sleep in comfort. Their chieftain was sent to nurture the lands and his kindred; how could any change have been suspected? His mind suddenly turned to enmity, and he aided our rebel borderlands in killing the envoy's retinue; for this reason, troops were dispatched in a punitive expedition to condemn their misdeeds."[8] The Qianlong Emperor therefore appointed the "General for Quelling of Rebellions" (*jingni jiangjun* 靖逆將軍) in May 1758, and dispatched troops to handle the armed "rebels" and quash resistance by the Khoja forces. The Uyghur communities in the southern Tianshan Mountains were conquered in August 1759.[9]

The above transition from "recruiting vassals" to subjugation had an enormous impact on the policies later formulated by the Qing Dynasty to rule over its new borderland (*xinjiang* 新疆), particularly with respect to governance over the Uyghur communities.

Divide and Conquer: The Beg System of Uyghur Society

After gaining sovereignty over the Dzungar region in the northern Tianshan Mountains and the Uyghur region in the southern Tianshan Mountains, the Qing Dynasty renamed the area Xinjiang, in keeping with its significance of "new borderland." It is worth noting that the Qing Dynasty had also bestowed the name "new borderland" upon other regions it had conquered in the past, even though these were regions historically included in the domain of the Chinese empire.[10] In other words, the term *xinjiang* or "new borderland" did not signify "new territories," but rather the area most recently acquired by the Qing Dynasty. Since the Qing Dynasty did not acquire sovereignty over any other new regions after gaining control over the Tianshan Mountains, the term *xinjiang* became set as the exclusive name of this region. In official documents, the Qing Dynasty continued to refer to the Dzungar region as Ili, the Dzungar tribal region (*zhunbu* 准部), or the Northern Circuit (*beilu* 北路), while referring to the Uyghur people as "Muslims" (*Huizi* 回子) or else as "turbaned Muslims" (*chantou Hui* 纏頭回: Muslims who wrapped their heads in turbans), to distinguish them from other Islamic peoples. With respect to the Uyghur region of the southern Tianshan Mountains, the term "Muslim borderland" (*Huijiang* 回疆) was used in a regional sense; the term "Muslim tribal region" (*Huibu* 回部) was used in an ethnonational sense; and the term "Southern Circuit" (*nanlu* 南路) was used in a geographical sense.

In 1762 (27th Year of the Qianlong Reign), the Qianlong Emperor appointed the "Governor-General of Ili and Other Areas" (*zongtong Ili deng chu jiangjun* 總統伊犁等處將軍, generally referred to as *Ili jiangjun* 伊犁將軍, the "Ili General) to begin gradually establishing a "military protectorate system" (*junfu zhidu* 軍府制度), transforming Xinjiang into a military colony. The Ili General had command over all Qing troops stationed across the Northern Circuit, Southern Circuit, and Eastern Circuit (encompassing the Kumul and Turpan regions of eastern Xinjiang, which were already under the rule of the Qing Dynasty), and was also the highest-ranking civil official in the Xinjiang region. Below this rank, ministerial attachés, ministers of affairs, or ministerial leaders were installed in each of the major cities in the Northern and Southern circuits, depending on their size, while a governor-general was installed at Dihua (modern-day Urumqi): these figures commanded the garrison troops, and were responsible for regional defenses. The Qing Dynasty stationed a total of 39,726 soldiers in Xinjiang, though only 5,185 were stationed in the Southern Circuit: the majority of the forces were sent to the Northern Circuit and the Urumqi region.[11] The differing sizes of the garrisons may have been informed by the need to take precautions against Russia, or they may have been determined out of consideration for the former status of the Northern Circuit as the center of Dzungar influence, or to handle conflicts that could arise with the neighboring Kazakhs and Kyrgyz.[12] On this point, the Qing Dynasty clearly differed from the westward-oriented policies of previous Chinese dynasties, which had always been centered on the Southern Circuit.

In terms of its governing policies, the Qing government implemented three separate administrative and bureaucratic systems in the Xinjiang region. First, the Eastern Circuit, including Urumqi, was incorporated into the county system used in China's interior, and divided into precincts, protectorates, prefectures and counties in 1759 (24th Year of the Qianlong Reign). There were three key reasons for implementing the county system in this region: (1) The county system had previously been implemented in that area under the auspices of the Chinese government during the Tang Dynasty; (2) Geographically speaking, the region bordered on China's interior provinces, and was inhabited by a large number of Han Chinese as well as Chinese-speaking followers of Islam, namely Hui Muslims; (3) In terms of military strategy, the region was a transportation hub between the

Northern and Southern circuits and China's interior, and implementing direct governance would aid in controlling this region. In terms of the outcome, after being incorporated into the county system during the Qing Dynasty, this region experienced livelier immigration patterns, predominated by Han Chinese and Hui Muslims, who accounted for approximately 70% of the region's total population by the early 20th century.

Second, the jasagh system was implemented among the nomadic Mongol herders of the Northern Circuit and the Uyghur communities in the Kumul and Turpan regions of the Eastern Circuit. After the Manchu Qing Dynasty formed its alliance with the Mongols, the Mongol people had been divided and reorganized into "banner" units, with the jasagh as the "banner leader." The jasaghs formed a military protectorate system with the greatest autonomy ever granted to subjugated peoples in Chinese history. Because Abdullah Beg of the Kumul and Emin Khoja of the Turpan had professed their allegiance to the Qing Dynasty and had been granted the title of jasagh as early as the Kangxi and Yongzheng reigns (1662–1722, 1723–1735), and since their peoples actively aided the Qing Dynasty in conquering the Uyghur communities of the southern Tianshan Mountains (or the Southern Circuit), the Qianlong Emperor continued to recognize their special status in formulating the overall policy for governance of Xinjiang.

Third, the beg system was adopted amongst the Uyghur communities of the Southern Circuit—the "Muslim borderland." In the Turkic family of languages, "beg" or "bek" means "chief," and was once the title for the ruling class. The Qing Dynasty interpreted "beg" as "official," bestowing this title upon the traditional leaders of the Uyghur communities and forming a hierarchy of official ranks (from Grades 3 to 7), thus transforming the Uyghur communities into a bureaucracy under Qing rule; the Qing Dynasty referred to this policy as "bringing order to customs without changing laws."

The begs were divided into different categories: the Hakim beg was responsible for the civil administration of communities in a given region; the Ishihana beg served the Hakim beg in a position akin to a deputy; the Ghazanachi beg was responsible for taxation; the Mirab beg managed irrigation works; the Qazi beg served as an Islamic judge, and so on. Aside from external military affairs and defenses, which fell under the administration of the Qing military, the Uyghur begs represented the Qing government in managing local civil administration, public order, judgments, taxation, agriculture, industry and commerce, education and religious affairs in Uyghur communities; in addition, each beg was assigned a troop of "Muslim soldiers" (*Huibing* 回兵) in order to maintain public order. The Qing Dynasty not only granted political privileges to the begs, but also bestowed emoluments upon them in the form of "official fields" (*zhifentian* 職分田) as well as *yanqi* (燕齊), or exclusive tenant farmers. For instance, a Grade 3 beg received 200 *mu* of land and 100 households of *yanqi*; in addition, 800 *tangga* (騰格) in copper cash was disbursed by the National Treasury to the Hakim beg each year as an "official salary" (*yanglian* 養廉), and 300 *tangga* was disbursed to the Ishihana beg.[13]

After conquering the "Muslim borderland," the Qing Dynasty gave preference to members of the Uyghur community who had sworn allegiance of their own volition, especially Uyghurs originating from Kumul and Turpan, as well as former begs and other members of the local social elite. There were initially only 20 categories of begs in the Muslim borderland;[14] later, this number gradually increased to 32. The Qing Dynasty divided the Muslim borderland into a total of 31 regions including 4 metropolitan cities, 4 medium cities, and 23 small cities, appointing between 5 and 30 begs to each region depending on its size.[15]

As the Qing Dynasty's conquest of the Muslim region was not based on economic considerations, it was initially determined that funding for the governance of this region would primarily be reallocated from the interior provinces. Aside from stationing troops in Xinjiang, the Qing also appointed 1,400 administrative officials. Their salaries and administrative expenses amounted to 688,900 taels annually; this included around 610,000 taels disbursed by the central government. The remaining 71,790 taels was collected locally, primarily through the operation of official inns and the sale of tea leaves to the soldiers.[16] To be sure, the Qing Dynasty established a system of taxes and levies immediately after its conquest of the Muslim borderland, and among the various categories of begs, many had duties involving the collection of taxes. However, the levy of approximately 600,000 *dan* of grains collected from land-owning Uyghur peasants each year merely served to fill the grain rations of the Qing armies stationed in the area. Even in its waning years, when the Qing Dynasty faced extreme financial straits, tax levies upon the Uyghurs were not significantly increased.[17]

There are few detailed historical records on the Uyghur population: one source places the population at 262,078 in 1766 (31st Year of the Qianlong Reign),[18] while another gives the population as 200,277 in the 1770s, and 282,619 in the 1840s.[19] Aside from trade and the handicrafts industry, the primary source of income for Uyghur communities in that era was traditional oasis agriculture. After the Qing conquest, Uyghur farming villages contained at least three types of farmers: land-owning peasants who tilled their own land; hired farmhands who cultivated "expropriated lands" (*ruguan di* 入官地) owned by the Qing government (lands belonging to Khojas or fugitives, which were confiscated by the Qing government); and the *yanqi*, who were bestowed upon the begs along with the "official fields" by the Qing government as a form of salary. The Qing government did not collect taxes from the *yanqi*, but a tax in the amount of one tenth of crop yields was levied upon hired farmhands, and one half of crop yields was collected from the farmhands tilling "expropriated lands."[20] The governing policies adopted by the Qing Dynasty not only allowed many begs to acquire a degree of power and influence, but also led some to develop a sense of "indebtedness" (*enyi* 恩義) toward the Qing Dynasty. This sense of "indebtedness" and gratitude induced at least some of the Uyghur elite to acknowledge the legitimacy of the Qing Dynasty's rule.[21]

1.2 The People of the Manchu Emperor under Segregated Rule

Uyghur Communities in Isolation from the Dominant Chinese Culture

One important characteristic of the Qing Dynasty's policies for governance of Uyghur communities was the segregation of different races, in particular the severing of all contact between Uyghurs and Han Chinese, to prevent the Uyghurs from being influenced by Chinese culture.

The Qing Dynasty implemented a garrison system in the Tianshan Northern Circuit, but in the Southern Circuit, a relief garrison system was adopted. Garrison troops were allowed to bring their families, and were not transferred between different stations; relief garrison troops could not bring their dependents, and were regularly transferred from station to station. In each region of the Tianshan Southern Circuit, the Qing Dynasty prohibited soldiers from interacting or intermarrying with Uyghurs.[22] Apart from the "Muslim cities" (*Huicheng* 回城) inhabited by the Uyghurs, the Qing Dynasty also established eighteen "Han cities" (*Hancheng* 漢城) scattered across the region, to provide quarters for the ministers and troops stationed in the area. This policy did indeed have the effect of preventing the troops from harassing the local populace, as well as preventing local residents from assaulting or harming the stationed troops. However, given that the Qing garrison in the Tianshan Southern Circuit was primarily composed of ethnic Han Chinese under the Green Banner (with only 349 soldiers under the Manchu Eight Banners), all of whom were relief troops, it is clear that the Qing Dynasty had formulated careful arrangements to prevent interaction between the Uyghurs and Han Chinese in the "Muslim borderland."[23]

Han Chinese from the interior provinces were prohibited from entering the Muslim borderland, and severe restrictions in the form of a permit system were implemented for Han merchants requesting entry into the region. In 1764 (29th Year of the Qianlong Reign), they were "ordered to conduct trade only at the garrisons"; thereafter, merchants were permitted to establish bazaars midway between the "Han cities" and "Muslim cities" to engage in trade.[24] To subsidize the expenses of the garrisoned troops, the Qing Dynasty organized a number of *tuntian* (屯田) or "station fields" across Xinjiang. The *tuntian* were divided into different categories, including *bingtun* (兵屯, "soldier stations," composed of Qing troops); *huitun* (回屯, "Muslim stations," composed of Uyghur Muslims migrating from Ili); *hutun* (戶屯, "household stations," composed of immigrants from the interior provinces); *qitun* (旗屯, "banner stations," composed of Eight Banners troops and their families); and *fantun* (犯屯, "criminal stations," also known as *qiantun* 遣屯, "exile stations," composed of criminals primarily originating from the interior provinces). However, it is worth noting that, after the Qing Dynasty instituted its rule over Xinjiang in the Qianlong Reign, it began establishing "soldier stations" and "banner stations" on a massive scale in the Tianshan Northern Circuit, as well as "household stations" and "criminal stations" for the large numbers of farmers and criminals migrating from the interior. Yet in the Southern Circuit, until the late Jiaqing

Reign (1796–1820), there were very few "soldier stations," and only one solitary *mintun* (民屯, "civilian station"), primarily composed of ethnic Han farmers, was established on the easternmost edge of the Southern Circuit in Karasahr.[25] "Civilian stations" did not begin appearing in the central regions of the Muslim borderland until after 1831.[26]

In fact, in 1760 (25th Year of the Qianlong Reign), or the second year after the Qing Dynasty's conquest of Xinjiang, the Qianlong Emperor had declared that, "Manchu generals and high officials shall be stationed here." The Ili General and the Governor-General of Urumqi were designated as "banner vacancies" (*qique* 旗缺, referring to official positions that could only be held by members of the predominantly Manchu Eight Banners). Although there were 23 ministers in total stationed across the Tianshan Southern Circuit, these ministerial positions were all held by people of Manchu and Mongol ethnicity.[27] This system of governance, characterized by ethnic discrimination, arose not out of consideration for national border defenses, but rather from the Qing Dynasty's need to maintain its own rule over China as a non-Han regime, thus carving out a special place for the Xinjiang region within the Qing's overall governing policies.

The Qing Army comprised more than 800,000 soldiers scattered across the empire, but the Eight Banners forces in fact numbered less than 200,000. Given the vast size of its territories, the Qing Dynasty was compelled to install defenses only at key positions, assigning its most trusted Eight Banners armies to the regions with important military significance.[28] However, at the point when the Qing Dynasty extended its rule to Xinjiang, 115 years after its invasion of China, there were few Eight Banners forces at its disposal. Nevertheless, the Qing Dynasty still stationed 20,990 Eight Banners soldiers in Xinjiang, amounting to more than half of the total Qing military forces assigned to the area. This demonstrates that the Qing Dynasty regarded Xinjiang as a military dominion under the rule of the Manchus. The Qing Dynasty installed 14 garrison generals in important regions across its empire, but compared to the other generals, the Ili General held jurisdiction over vaster territories and commanded greater numbers of soldiers, while also boasting an annual official salary of more than 1,000 taels.[29]

As a dynasty founded by an ethnic minority, for the Qing to rule over China, the question of how to absorb non-Han ethnic forces into its own

A Uyghur beg wearing Qing court dress

camp, so as to contain the massive population of Han Chinese, was in fact of supreme importance. It is clear that the Qing Dynasty's great efforts to prevent contact between the Uyghurs and the Han Chinese were informed by this very motive. In 1761 (26th Year of the Qianlong Reign), the Qing central government uniformly manufactured official seals for the Hakim begs, the content of which was written "concurrently in Manchu script, Mongol script, and Muslim script" (namely in the Manchurian, Mongolian and Uyghur languages). The Chinese language was notably absent.[30] The Qing Dynasty also discouraged the Eight Banners troops stationed in Xinjiang from learning Chinese, yet the children of the Uyghur begs were actively encouraged to learn the Manchu language.[31] In addition, while the Han Chinese had been forced to shave their heads and plait their hair in the Manchu-style queue, the Qing only allowed high-ranking begs to wear the queue, with an air of granting a favor. The Qing Dynasty's prohibition against contact between the Uyghur communities and the interior provinces was also reflected in the financial policies instituted in Xinjiang, where the Qing circulated a special currency known as *pul* (普爾) cast with Uyghur script, in contrast with currency of the same value circulated in China's interior.[32] Even under circumstances such as court visits by the begs to pay their respects, the Qing often made careful arrangements to prevent them from entering ethnic Han regions in the interior, instead granting them passage through the northern Mongol regions to pay court to the emperor at Chengde, which still fell in Mongol territories at the time.[33] These court visits consisted of "interviews" (*jiejian* 接見) with the Uyghur begs and the Mongol jasaghs, for the purpose of affirming their political relationship with the Manchus, with strong overtones of forging an "alliance."

The True Purpose of the "Board for the Administration of Outlying Regions"

The Qing Dynasty's policies for governance of China did not seek the homogenization of the border regions and the interior, but instead deliberately created a distinction between the interior provinces and the peripheral outlying regions of Mongolia, Tibet and the "Muslim borderland." However, the "outlands" (*fan* 藩) of the Qing Dynasty differed from the "outlands" as understood under previous Chinese dynasties, and should more accurately be described as a political alliance between the Manchus and the various ethnic groups of the northwestern regions. The Qing Dynasty's purpose in dividing its territories into the "interior" and the "outlands" was to institute the segregation of the Han Chinese and other ethnic groups. The implementation of the jasagh system in the Mongol territories, the establishment of a theocratic system in Tibet led by the Dalai lama, and the importation of the beg system into the Muslim borderland allowed the Qing Dynasty to lean on elite figures in local ethnic communities to exert indirect rule over local regions, while also evoking a sense of ethnonational kinship with the Manchus. The Qing Dynasty's ultimate objective was to make the ethnic groups of the outlying regions the allies of the Manchus, and use them to contain the massive population of Han Chinese in the interior provinces. Thus, structurally speaking, the Qing Dynasty's rule over China was not simply divided in two territorially, but in fact exhibited a dual nature: in a national sense, the Qing Dynasty was a Chinese empire, but from the perspective of its relationships with other ethnic minorities, it was an ethnic regime that remained perpetually on guard against the Han Chinese, while seeking political alliances with other ethnic groups.[34]

The management of these ethnic political alliances fell under the province of the Mongol Yamen, established in 1636 (Founding Year of the Shunde Reign) and later renamed as the Board for the Administration of Outlying Regions (*Lifan yuan* 理藩院); the Board was a central organ of the government with status equal to the Six Ministries of Personnel, Revenue, Rites, War, Justice, and Works. As the Kangxi Emperor once declared, "The Board for the Administration of Outlying Regions holds sole charge over the affairs of outlying regions, and bears heavy responsibilities."[35] The existence of the Board for the Administration of Outlying Regions had extremely important significance within the framework of Qing rule over China.

Chinese history contains several examples of diplomatic positions or institutions for the reception of envoys from neighboring ethnic groups, such as the "Commissioner for State Visits" (*Dahonglu* 大鴻臚) of the Han

Dynasty and the "Court of State Receptions" (*Honglusi* 鴻臚寺) of the Tang Dynasty; the Yuan Dynasty featured the "Court for the Spread of Governance" (*Xuanzheng yuan* 宣政院), an organ of the central government which handled relations with Tibet. However, the Board for the Administration of Outlying Regions of the Qing Dynasty was the first central institution that directly managed plural minority ethnic groups. Aside from one position for adjunct assistant minister (an auxiliary deputy outside the normal complement of personnel) reserved for the appointment of Mongols, the other leading positions (minister, assistant minister) at the Board for the Administration of Outlying Regions were designated as "banner vacancies," and were filled by Manchus. After the reforms of the Shunzhi (1644–1661), Kangxi, and Qianlong reigns, in 1761 (26th Year of the Qianlong Reign), the Board for the Administration of Outlying Regions established the Border Reception Bureau for exclusive management of the "Muslim borderland," transforming itself into a central institution composed of six departments, including the Border Reception Bureau, the Inner Mongolian Bureau, the Inner Mongolian Reception Bureau, the Outer Mongolian Bureau, Outer Mongolian Reception Bureau, and the Judicial Bureau, bolstered by the promulgation of corresponding laws, such as the *Imperial Legal Code of Mongolia* (*Qinding Menggu lüli*, 1741, 6th Year of the Qianlong Reign), the *Imperial Code of the Board for the Administration of Outlying Regions* (*Qinding Lifanyuan zeli*, 1814, 19th Year of the Jiaqing Reign), and the *Imperial Code of the Muslim Borderland* (*Qinding Huibu zeli*, 1814).

In order to contain the Han Chinese population in the interior provinces, the Qing Dynasty felt it necessary to retain the "Muslim borderland" as the dominion of the Manchu people. However, the comprehensive ban on interactions and exchanges between the Han Chinese and the Uyghurs and the governing policies allowing their direct submission to the Manchu Qing emperor did not signify that the Qing Dynasty trusted the Uyghurs. The Qing government carefully crafted its policies to forestall opposition among the Uyghurs. Two of the most important elements involved the stationing of senior ministers to supervise the begs, and the implementation of a policy for thorough separation of religion and government.

In 1758 (23rd Year of the Qianlong Reign), the Qianlong Emperor, who had already made the determination to conquer the "Muslim borderland," declared: "We believe it unnecessary to appoint Muslims as garrison commanders, but shall continue to follow the old system, whereby a chief is installed in each city, and united under the general stationed in Ili."[36] In other words, even in the very early stages, the Qing Dynasty had already decided not to establish an integrated administrative system for the Uyghur communities, leaving each region mutually unaffiliated, and rendering the Hakim begs directly subordinate to the Ili General. Although the ministers stationed in each region did not directly interfere in local administration, the system for supervision of the local begs by the ministers appointed to a given region imposed a certain degree of restriction on the begs' authority.

To prevent the begs from exploiting the populace, the Qing Dynasty adopted the following measures to limit their local influence: (1) The traditional system of hereditary begs was abolished, and a new system was installed whereby the appointed ministers determined the candidates for a beg's replacement, to be appointed by the Qing court; (2) A system of avoidance was established, whereby high-ranking begs of Grades 3 or 4 were not selected from among the local populace, and it was not permitted for begs of Grades 5, 6, or 7 to be appointed to local positions; (3) The power of the Hakim begs was diluted by the Ishihana begs; (4) A system was established for begs to visit court for imperial audiences; (5) Untrusted begs and Khojas were taken to reside in Beijing.[37]

After the conquest of Xinjiang, the Qing Dynasty sought to "accommodate the religion without changing the customs," acknowledging the *akhund* (阿訇), or religious scholars, as the spiritual leaders as well as the arbiters of culture and education for the Uyghur people, allowing the local Muslims to engage in their daily religious activities, and renovating the Khojas' tombs (*mazar*, 麻扎). However, the Qing Dynasty believed that the existence of the Khoja clan was the fundamental cause of political unrest among the Uyghur communities, thus its first thought was to restrict the clan's power and influence. Many among the White Mountain Khojas fled to the Khanate of Kokand, as the Qing Dynasty relocated the remaining White Mountain Khojas to Beijing, isolating them from the Uyghur community. The Black Mountain Khojas were treated in similar fashion: although the Qing Dynasty appointed them as begs and granted them special privileges, they were also separated from their ancestral homes and thus removed from their traditional power base, and the order was prohibited from conducting group worship activities. In order to weaken the

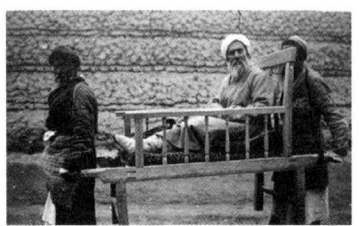
An Islamic religious teacher (mullah)

economic strength of Islam, the Qing Dynasty deliberately refused to recognize the legality of the religious taxes levied by mosques, *mazars*, and religious schools (*madrasa*), and incorporated the *yanqi* tilling *waqf* lands (瓦哈甫地, lands donated by the faithful to mosques and religious schools) into the general household registration system, thus converting them into taxpayers of the Qing Dynasty. The Qing government also instituted a system whereby the begs recommended and sponsored new candidates for *akhund* at the mosques, for appointment by the stationed ministers.

The Qing Dynasty implemented a principle of thorough separation of religion and government in the "Muslim borderland." In 1760 (25th Year of the Qianlong Reign), the Qianlong Emperor gave instruction that the begs appointed by the Qing government were to be held accountable only to the Qing Dynasty; the Khojas and *akhund* were strictly prohibited from interfering in administrative governance, and stripped of their right to criticize the begs. The Qing government repeatedly emphasized its prohibitions against the appointment of *akhund* as begs, and against begs concurrently serving as *akhund*, and even banned private interactions between the stationed Qing ministers and the *akhund*. One Hakim beg was put under investigation for tacitly allowing his wife to "read forbidden canons"—that is, participate in the activities of the Sufi order.[38] Although the Qing Dynasty recognized the authority of Islamic judges (Qazi beg) in civil judgements—mediating civil disputes, determining inheritance shares, officiating over marriage procedures, and so on, handling criminal cases under Islamic (Sharia) law was strictly prohibited. During the Xianfeng Reign (1850–1861), the imperial clansman Yingyun (1810–1881), the ministerial attaché to Yarkent, was convicted under Sharia law, but was instead sentenced with banishment.

The Qing government also prohibited contact between the Uyghurs and neighboring states. The primary reason was that the White Mountaineers, namely the Kashgar Khoja clan, were utilizing the Khanate of Kokand as a base for their anti-Qing, restorationist activities. The Naqshbandi order also wielded great influence in the Kokand region. Due to the congruency between their religious beliefs and lifestyles, contemporary Uyghurs recognized little distinction between themselves and the people of Kokand, and the peoples of the two regions had long enjoyed unfettered interactions as well as economic exchanges. However, since the Kashgar Khojas who fled to the Khanate of Kokand after the conquest of Xinjiang continued to exert great influence over their followers, the Qing Dynasty had to constantly remain on guard against their restorationist activities. The once unconstrained interactions between the Uyghurs and the Khanate of Kokand were therefore banned beginning in the Qianlong era; by the Jiaqing era, even correspondence between the Hakim begs and other states (including Kokand) was prohibited.[39]

In order to support their claim to being an orthodox Chinese dynasty and maintain their rule over the Chinese people, the Manchu rulers of the Qing Dynasty granted political and economic privileges to the Uyghur people, especially the elite of Uyghur society; however, they also instituted a policy of ethnic segregation, thoroughly isolating them from the Han Chinese populace. Moreover, the Qing Dynasty perpetually remained on the alert against the emergence of separatist ideas among the Uyghurs: in particular, a number of restrictions on were imposed on various Islamic activities, preventing Uyghur society from functioning as a purely Islamic community, or *Ummah* (烏瑪). Under the Qing Dynasty's rule, the Uyghur communities were neither a part of "China," nor fully a part of the "Mohammedan *Ummah*."

1.3 From *"Jihad"* by the Kashgar Khoja Clan to the Founding of the Province of Xinjiang

A Challenge from Islam

In 1765 (30th Year of the Qianlong Reign), only six years after the Qing conquest of Xinjiang, the Uyghur inhabitants of the Uqturpan region staged a large-scale rebellion in reaction against their oppression at the hands of Hakim beg Abdullah and the Qing minister Sucheng. A major flaw in the Qing Dynasty's policies for governing the "Muslim borderland" thus came to light: the conditions of severe class antagonism in Uyghur society created by the begs.

The *Imperial Code of the Muslim Borderland* (1814) imposed a number of prohibitions on the begs. The detailed content tells us that these provisions were formulated by the Qing Dynasty in response to the begs' repeated misuse of their authority to exploit the Uyghur populace. Other Qing texts reveal that the begs frequently seized their subjects' wives, daughters and lands, monopolized agricultural water, and wantonly conscripted additional *yanqi*. Although the Qing Dynasty reduced taxes after its conquest of the "Muslim borderland," exploitation by the begs rendered the financial burdens on the Uyghur people even heavier than before. Despite the saying that "The people should respect not officials but rather those who rule over them,"[40] the ministers stationed in Xinjiang, who were of Manchu origin and wielded the great power of the Qing government to select, promote and supervise begs and *akhund*, also sought to exploit the Uyghur people via the begs, and even perpetrated the rape of Uyghur women.

In the 19th century, the Qing Dynasty gradually became more careless in the selection and appointment of high ministers: increasing numbers of ministers whose sole aim was to exploit the region for material wealth were stationed in the "Muslim borderland," and incidents of unlawful conduct among the ministers grew more severe. Under these conditions, the Qing Dynasty's rule over the Uyghur communities began to suffer challenges from *jihads* (holy wars) incited by the Kashgar Khoja clan from their base in the Kokand region.

The Kashgar Khojas' ability to incite *jihad* was inseparable from the support granted to them by the Khanate of Kokand. After the Qing conquest of Xinjiang, the Kokand regime formed a tributary relationship with the Qing Dynasty, and nominally became a vassal of the Qing. During this period, the Qing Dynasty allocated a certain amount of funds each year to the Kokand regime: in return, Kokand was to monitor the Kashgar Khoja clan. However, after the turn of the century, Kokand gradually grew more powerful, and in 1817, the khanate began issuing ceaseless demands to the Qing Dynasty, insisting that the Qing agree to exempt Kokand merchants from customs duties on entering Xinjiang, and allow the khanate to install *Aq-saqal* (elders) in Xinjiang to independently levy taxes on Kokand merchants and exercise other trading privileges; if the Qing were to refuse, Kokand threatened to release the Kashgar Khojas. When its demands were rejected by the Qing Dynasty, the Khanate of Kokand adopted a new approach, and began supporting the return of the Kashgar Khojas to the Kashgar region. The Kashgar Khojas incited eight *jihads*, in 1820, 1824, 1826, 1828, 1830, 1847, 1852, and 1857, with the aim of restoring their rule over Xinjiang. The four *jihads* incited by Jahangir Khoja (the grandson of Burhan al-Din) between 1820 and 1828, which became known as the "Jahangir Rebellion" (*Zhangge'er zhi luan* 張格爾之亂), spanned the longest period of time, and were the most widespread. The Qing Dynasty spent a total of ten million silver taels and invested 36,000 troops in seven years of conflict before finally stamping out the armed rebellion; Jahangir Khoja was ultimately captured and sent to Beijing for execution.[41]

It should be noted that, in 1826, Jahangir Khoja led a force of only five hundred from Kokand, but upon entering the Kashgar region, his troops immediately swelled to ten thousand with the addition of the local Uyghur inhabitants. This demonstrates that, although the Qing Dynasty had imposed severe restrictions on every aspect of Islam, within the Uyghur communities, Islam still retained immense power and influence. Of course, the reason why the *jihads* attracted the support of the local Uyghurs, aside from their faith in the Khoja clan, was the dip in prestige suffered by the Qing Dynasty due to corruption among the stationed ministers and the Hakim begs.

The series of *jihads* incited by the Kashgar Khojas were ultimately unsuccessful, due not only to the absolute superiority of the Qing forces, but also to the fact that, upon entering the Uyghur regions, the Kashgar Khojas abused and massacred local Black Mountain followers, thereby losing the support of the local Uyghur inhabitants; this was an important factor in their defeat. However, after the failure of each *jihad*, many White Mountain followers among the Uyghurs retreated alongside the Khojas to the Khanate of Kokand. By the 1850s, approximately fifty thousand Uyghur households had resettled in Kokand, thus forming a base of support for the Kashgar Khoja forces.[42]

In 1828, Nayancheng (1764–1833), the Governor-General of Zhili, who was sent to the "Muslim borderland" in the office of Imperial Commissioner to formulate policies in the aftermath of the "Jahangir Rebellion," returned to Beijing to report to the Qing central government on the many unlawful practices of the stationed ministers and the begs. Based on his recommendations, the Qing government decided to strengthen supervision over the ministers, while also increasing their official salaries to reduce the temptation for exploitation. However, the unlawful practices of the ministers were, by and large, perpetrated via the hands of the Uyghur begs, and in comparing the exploitative actions committed by these rulers of two different ethnicities, the begs in fact exhibited more cruelty toward the Uyghur populace.[43] Nevertheless, the Qing Dynasty did not adopt any particularly severe punishments or supervisory measures with respect to the begs. After the "Jahangir Rebellion," the Qing government instead adjusted the division of tasks amongst the begs to strengthen their rule over rural Uyghur areas. Rural areas were first partitioned into sections, and then the official powers of low- and mid-ranking begs in a given section were ascribed to a single individual, who would oversee tax collection, irrigation works, and other matters for a given area, rather than sharing these tasks amongst other begs.[44] In other words, in an era of intensifying class antagonism, the Qing Dynasty perversely concentrated more power in the hands of individual begs.

However, the *jihads* of the Kashgar Khojas also caused the Qing Dynasty to reconsider the policy of ethnic segregation that had been implemented in the "Muslim borderland." The Qing came to the conclusion that the relief garrison system of the Southern Circuit, which had been designed to achieve the aim of ethnic segregation, was one factor in its failure to prevent the uprisings. After the "Rebellion of Yusup Khoja" (*Yusupu hezhuo panluan* 玉素普和卓叛亂) in 1830, the Qing Dynasty transferred 3,000 cavalry from Ili and 4,000 foot soldiers from the interior provinces to supplement the forces in the "Muslim borderland" and form a new military system.[45]

Although the Qing government had reduced military expenditure in all provinces to raise the funds needed to suppress the "Jahangir Rebellion," this was ultimately only a stopgap measure. As other parts of the empire were also experiencing financial difficulties, in an attempt to increase local fiscal revenue, the Qing confiscated the family property of *jihad* supporters, increased taxes on trade, and minted a new batch of *pul* currency. However, due to the erosion of the local population, the above measures had no significant effects. The Qing Dynasty therefore granted permission for farmers from the interior provinces to migrate into southern Xinjiang, and in 1832, a "household station" (*hutun*) was established at Barchuk. The Qing later decided to abandon the station fields out of consideration for the interests of the Uyghur population; however, due to financial difficulties, this decision was reversed two years later, and "household stations" for inland farmers (of Han Chinese and Hui ethnicity) were established across the "Muslim borderland."

Rebuilding the System of Governance for Uyghur Society

On June 4, 1864, Hui soldiers among the Qing forces stationed in Kucha, Xinjiang, incited a preemptive rebellion in the belief that the Qing Dynasty planned to massacre them to prevent the "Northwestern Muslim rebellion" (*Xibei Hui luan* 西北回亂) from gradually spreading across Xinjiang. The Uyghur inhabitants of Kucha seized this opportunity to stage their own rebellion, electing an Islamic cleric as "Khoja" to serve as their leader. The event rapidly evolved into a *jihad* targeting *kafir* ("non-believers"): within a few days' time, they had stormed the walls of Sayram Town and Bay Town; this was followed by the capture of two of the larger cities in the Muslim borderland, Aksu and Uqturpan.

The incidents in Kucha were the flashpoint for a series of Muslim revolts across Xinjiang. Unlike in Kucha, the participants began targeting *kafir* from the outset, giving their rebellions overtones of an Islamic *jihad*. In terms of their organizational characteristics, the *jihads* that arose across Xinjiang can be divided into three categories: (1) Rebellions launched by the Hui; (2) Uprisings led by the begs; (3) Uprisings led by Islamic clerics. By November, the Uyghur inhabitants in the Ili region of the Northern Circuit, where the Ili General was stationed, had already risen up and captured Ghulja. The Qing Dynasty's system of governance in Xinjiang thus experienced an utter collapse.

The class oppression and exploitation fomented by the beg system was another motivation for the Uyghur populace to participate in the 1864 uprisings.[46] However, the Uyghurs were not a simple class group: in that era, only Islam could unite all of Uyghur society, and the influence of Islam permeated the value system, ethics, and identity of the Uyghur people. It was for this very reason that each of the uprisings across Xinjiang evolved into a *jihad* or holy war; and it was in the name of *jihad* that the 1864 uprisings were able to gather so many supporters so quickly, and achieve such immense victories in such a short period of time. This was an inescapable reality of Uyghur society in the mid-19th century.

However, it was also woven into the nature of these uprisings that, once the Qing system of governance collapsed and the object of the *jihads* evaporated, Uyghur society began to fracture into different factions. After a series of internecine struggles amongst the different factions, the Khoja regime of Kucha captured the Kucha, Aksu and Yarkent regions, Sidik Beg gained control over the Kashgar region, and Habib Ghaji seized the Hotan region, establishing separate rule over these respective regions. This point demonstrates that the Uyghur communities, which resided around isolated oases and followed different Islamic orders, had no independent, unified system of administration, and had not yet formed a national consciousness that could unify all the Uyghur peoples.

In January 1865, Buzurg Khan Khoja of the Kashgar Khoja clan returned from Kokand to Xinjiang; one theory is that he was coerced into making this journey by the Kokand general Yaqub Beg.[47] Yaqub Beg, who combined the titles of commander and Khoja in one, had always been a figure of strong political ambitions. Taking advantage of the chaos to invade Kashgar, Yaqub Beg made use of his unique military skills and diabolical knack for politics to first thoroughly exterminate the residual Qing forces in Xinjiang, and then massacre or drive out all remaining members of the Kashgar Khojas, led by Buzurg Khan. By December 1866, Yaqub Beg had destroyed the regime of Habib Ghaji in Hotan; and by June 1867, he had crushed the Khoja regime in Kucha and massacred its leaders, finally establishing his own regime to rule over the *Yette Xeher* or "Seven Cities" of the Xinjiang region.[48]

Yaqub Beg

Yaqub Beg himself was not Uyghur: the main reason why he was able to rule over Uyghur society for ten years rested in his policies on Islam.

Yaqub Beg often feigned to be a devout Muslim, and it was said that he "did not take a step without making an obeisance." When visiting different regions, he was sure to donate cash or clothing to the students at Islamic schools or the *akhund* at mosques, and even during an invasion, he would not forget to worship at the *mazar* (tomb) of the local saint; he even renovated the *mazar* of the Kashgar Khoja clan, whom he had destroyed. In addition, Yaqub Beg established religious tribunals across the land, improving the social status of the *akhund*.[49] The purpose of these actions was to use Islam as a conduit to erase the Uyghurs' distrust and antipathy towards him. His methods achieved a certain degree of success, and some *akhund* in the Uyghur communities ultimately became zealous supporters of the Yakub Beg regime. However, Yaqub Beg had employed despicable methods during his war of conquest, eliminating the Khoja clan, which had been active in Uyghur society for three hundred years, and brutally slaughtering the local Uyghur people.[50] Moreover, nearly all the important positions in his regime were filled by his own people from the Khanate of Kokand, all of which provoked intense resentment amongst the local Uyghur populace.

Yaqub Beg's rule over Uyghur society also coincided with the period when imperial Russian and British forces began encroaching upon Xinjiang. When Xinjiang had been under the rule of the Qing Dynasty, the region had in fact served as a buffer zone between these two great imperial powers. However, when Xinjiang reverted to an independent political entity after the Muslim uprisings of 1864, Russia and Britain both seized the opportunity to make strides into the region. To gain legitimacy for his rule over the Uyghur communities, Yaqub Beg sought support from the Ottoman Empire on the one hand, and attempted to approach British forces in northern India on the other. In 1870 and 1873, the British colonial government in India sent diplomatic missions led by T. D. Forsyth to Kashgar, and agreed to provide military aid to Yaqub Beg; Britain was consequently able to sign a treaty with the Yaqub Beg regime in 1874, acquiring free trade rights, settlement rights, most-favored-nation status and extraterritoriality in the southern Tianshan region. In the meantime, Russia destroyed the Muslim regime in the Ili region in May 1871, in the name of "restoring the rule of the Qing Dynasty." After capturing the Ili River Valley, in 1872, Russia sent a diplomatic mission led by Baron Alexander Vasilyevich Kaulbars to sign a treaty with Yaqub Beg, finally acquiring free trade rights in the southern Tianshan region, which had been Russia's long-cherished wish, as well as low customs duties and the right to station trade representatives.[51]

On one occasion, the British even attempted to use diplomatic channels to force the Qing Dynasty to recognize the Yaqub Beg regime.[52] During this same period, the Qing Dynasty was also dealing with the Japanese invasion of Taiwan in 1874. The encroachment by the Western powers and the aggression of its smaller neighbor to the east, Japan, dealt a great blow to the Qing Dynasty, and many voices within the government began calling for China's southeastern coastal defenses to be strengthened. However, due to the need to pay wartime reparations to the foreign powers, as well as frequent domestic military skirmishes, the Qing Dynasty had sunk into a deep financial crisis. In the midst of this predicament, the inner circle of the Qing government stirred up a great controversy over whether or not Xinjiang should be reconquered, in what was known as the "Debate of Coastal Defenses versus Border Pass Defenses" (*Haifang saifang lunzheng* 海防・塞防論爭).

Notably, this debate revolved almost wholly around the threat that the invasion and penetration of Xinjiang by the European powers could pose to China. Li Hongzhang, the Governor-General of Zhili, argued that it was geographically impossible for Xinjiang to escape imperilment by Russia and Britain, therefore it was not worthwhile for the Qing government to spend several million taels of silver annually to defend this vast desert region. Li maintained that, "If Xinjiang is not recovered, the vitality of the body and limbs shall be unaffected; if the coast is not defended, the harm to the vital organs shall grow ever more dire."[53]

In response to such views, Zuo Zongtang, Governor-General of Shaanxi and Gansu, and other figures argued that the land defenses in the northwestern border region should be equally as valued as the coastal defenses: they stressed that, in China's relations with Russia, Britain, or other, even more perilous countries, "If we withdraw from the line of defense, retreating an inch will allow the enemy to advance a mile . . . only by retaking Xinjiang can Mongolia be protected, and only by protecting Mongolia can the capital be defended."[54] The Qing Emperor ultimately acceded to the recommendations of Zuo Zongtang and his cohort, and in 1876 (2nd Year of the Guangxu Reign), the Qing armies entered the battle to retake Xinjiang, under the command of Zuo Zongtang. By December 1877, the Qing forces had already recaptured all of Xinjiang apart from the Ili region, and Yaqub Beg had committed suicide.[55] Once the military action to retake the territories of the Yaqub Beg regime had concluded, the

Qing government entered into lengthy negotiations with Russia to recover the Ili River Valley, which it achieved in 1881 after paying reparations.

After reviewing its earlier failed policies for the governance of Xinjiang, in 1884, the Qing Dynasty introduced the provincial system used in the interior to the Xinjiang region. Concurrent with the implementation of this system, as the territories of Xinjiang were carved up into the same precincts, protectorates, prefectures and counties seen in the interior provinces, the Qing Dynasty abolished the traditional governing systems, including the beg system. However, the significance of "founding the province of Xinjiang" was not limited to the above considerations: this political move also demonstrated that, given the grim global circumstances and international environment, the Qing Dynasty could no longer afford to regard Xinjiang as merely a domestic matter. The Qing government was therefore compelled to abandon its old system of thought and the political systems derived therefrom, including the dual ethnic and national political structure that had been instituted in Xinjiang, the segregation of the Han Chinese and the border ethnic groups, and the policy of mutual containment by the Han Chinese residents of the interior provinces and the ethnic peoples of the border regions, so that the dynasty could better rule the whole of China.

Summary

The system of governance established by the Qing Dynasty in Xinjiang was designed not only to rule over Xinjiang, but also to cater to the practical circumstances of a non-Han ethnic group ruling over all of China. Its most fundamental characteristic was thus a prohibition against interaction between the local Uyghurs, who were regarded as the subjects of the Manchu rulers, and the Han population; the home of the Uyghur population, the "Muslim borderland," was treated as the sovereign territory of the Manchus, and Han Chinese were forbidden to migrate to the area, consistent with the dynasty's intention of incorporating the Uyghur populace into an outlands system established to contain the Han Chinese population of the interior provinces. The Qing Dynasty therefore instituted provisions expressly forbidding local residents from learning Chinese, and strictly prohibited the spread of Chinese civilization into the region. Its every institution was designed to suggest or declare to the local ethnic groups that they were not like the Han Chinese, and were instead part of a community of interest alongside the Manchus. Although the complex collection of policies and systems instituted by the Qing Dynasty to contain the Han Chinese populace of the interior provinces was an important factor enabling it to rule over China for nearly 270 years, it is undeniable that these same systems and policies left the Uyghur population caught in the interstices between the Islamic "*Ummah*" and "China," while also firmly preventing the Uyghur people from developing a Chinese identity or sense of Chinese nationalism.

The establishment of "Xinjiang Province" redefined Xinjiang, formerly the military dominion of the Manchus, as part of Chinese national territories. Han Chinese bureaucrats were thereafter permitted to serve in the highest-ranking civil and military positions in Xinjiang, and a number of Han bureaucrats were dispatched to the area by the Qing Dynasty; the government also actively encouraged Han Chinese farmers from the interior to resettle in regions across Xinjiang, including the "Muslim borderland." The nature of the Uyghurs and other local ethnic groups in Xinjiang thus shifted from "subjects of the Manchu emperor," to people of the Chinese state. In order to cultivate a sense of Chinese identity among the local ethnic groups, the Qing Dynasty established free government-run schools and mandated that the Uyghurs learn Chinese; thus began the process of Xinjiang's transformation into a heartland province, and the Uyghur population's transformation into Chinese citizens.

CHAPTER 2

Origins of the East Turkestan Independence Movement
Social Context and Shape of the Movement

The East Turkestan Independence Movement first began to take shape in 1933. Every historical event has its elements of chance, but how was the unprecedented East Turkestan Independence Movement able to so quickly mobilize the population, and erupt ubiquitously and simultaneously across the territory of Xinjiang? These circumstances indicate that early modern Xinjiang society harbored simmering ethnic problems.

This chapter focuses on social structure in early modern Xinjiang, analyzing the social, political and economic causes for the latent East Turkestan Independence Movement, to discover the ideological starting point for the independence movement and explore the ideological system that sustained it, as well as analyzing the organizational characteristics of the First East Turkestan Independence Movement, to reveal the nature of the movement.

2.1 Ideology of the East Turkestan Independence Movement

"East Turkestan"
As is well known, "Turkestan" signifies "Land of the Turks": it is generally divided into East Turkestan, which falls within Chinese territories, and West Turkestan, which falls within the territories of the former Soviet Union. However, the significance of the term "East Turkestan," which once expressed a geographical concept, is in fact unclear, both in a temporal and in a spatial sense.

The spatial ambiguity is due to the fact that the term "East Turkestan" has been used at various times in reference to southern Xinjiang (the Tarim Basin and the surrounding region), in reference to the region of eastern Xinjiang containing the Hami Basin, and even in reference to the entire territory of Xinjiang. The temporal ambiguity is based on the lack of definite hypotheses regarding the point when the term "East Turkestan" (*Xarh Turkestan*) emerged in the Uyghur language: some sources refer to Xinjiang as "East Turkestan" even prior to the in-migration of the Turkic peoples.

Although *The Life of Yakoob Beg*, written by Demetrius Charles Boulger and published in London in 1878, refers to southern Xinjiang as "Eastern or Chinese Turkestan,"[1] it should be noted that *Tārīkh-i Khāmīdī* (History of Hāmīdī), written by the Uyghur historian Molla Musa Sayrami and completed in 1908, still refers to the region as "Mogulistan Yurti yaki Yette Xeher" (Mogulistan, or the Land of the Seven Cities).[2] Other sources show that, even in the early 1920s, the Uyghur people still did not refer to the region as "East Turkestan." In a 1934 essay entitled "Xinjiang Legislators in the Era of the Beijing Government," which criticizes the Uyghur parliamentarians under the Republic of China, the original Uyghur author refers to himself as a "resident of southern Xinjiang" (*nan Jiang ren* 南疆人).[3] These sources demonstrate that, even among local Uyghurs, the place name "East Turkestan" was a loanword that was not accepted until the early modern era.

It was not until the 1930s that Uyghurs began broadly utilizing the term "East Turkestan": this was likely linked to the nascent "East Turkestan Independence Movement," which first began to take shape in that era. As related by the Japanese scholar Yasushi Shinmen, in September 1933, the leaders of the Turpan Rebellion sent a letter to the British consulate in Kashgar, describing the contemporary conditions in "East Turkestan" and "West Turkestan."[4] Britain in fact played what some observers called a "dishonorable role"[5] in the rise of the East Turkestan Independence Movement: whether this is tied to the introduction of the English-language term "East Turkestan" into the Uyghur language bears further research. On November 16, 1933, the official newspaper of the government of the Islamic Republic of East Turkestan, *Independence* (*Istqlāl*) ran the statement: "Our slogan is, 'East Turkestan is the East Turkestan of every person in East Turkestan.' ... We do not use their [Chinese] language and place names."[6] The term "East Turkestan" finally permeated the Uyghur language as a place name after the First East Turkestan Independence Movement. The above passage shows that the significance of the term "East Turkestan" was initially based on condemnation of ethnic oppression, as well as advocacy for national consciousness and a sense of territoriality; the emergence of this national consciousness and territoriality was undoubtedly tied to changes in the self-identity of the Uyghur people. We can see also that the significance of "East Turkestan" was ideologically linked to the early modern "Uyghur Enlightenment."

The Early Modern "Uyghur Enlightenment" and "Pan-Turkism"

The 1880s witnessed the rapid expansion of trade between the Uyghur communities and Russia (Tatar merchants, to be specific): following the suppression of the Yaqub Beg regime, the Qing Dynasty had founded the province of Xinjiang and granted special trading privileges to Russian merchants, including complete exemption from taxes in the region of Xinjiang, as well as permission to "exchange goods" and "pay debts in kind with sundry goods," leading to the rise of an industrial capitalist class of *bāy* (the "wealthy"), who enriched themselves through industry as well as, and especially, trade.[7] At the same time, as exchanges between the Uyghurs and the outside world, particularly foreign states, gradually increased, Uyghur society quietly birthed an early modern cultural enlightenment.

The Uyghur Enlightenment was a movement centering on a "new class of intelligentsia" who were "beginning to have a profound sense of crisis regarding their own ethnic identity," as well as "certain religious figures" who launched a new-style, universal school education movement (known as *usul ul-jadid*, or "new method," also referred to as Jadidism)—aside from Islamic education, these schools also taught history, geography, mathematics, chemistry, and other modern sciences.[8] The economic backers for this movement were the wealthy industrialists of the new Uyghur capitalist class, the *bāy*.

The Uyghur Enlightenment first arose in the Kashgar region, the cultural and economic center of Uyghur society in the southern Tianshan Mountains. According to the recollections of a Uyhgur elder, the famous industrialist brothers Husayn Musabayow and Bawadun Musabayow sponsored the establishment of Uyghur society's first Jadidist school in 1883, at Iksak Township in Atush County, 20 kilometers north of the city of Kashgar. The Uyghur Enlightenment reached its peak in the 1910s. In one example, the well-known *akhund* Abdukadir Damulla, who went on pilgrimage to Mecca and passed through Ottoman Turkey to return to Kashgar, founded the first Jadidist school in the city of Kashgar in 1912.[9] During this period, Jadidist schools were founded in Ili, Turpan, Qitai (Guchung), Hami (Kumul), Kucha, Aksu and other Uyghur cities.[10]

According to many Uyghur scholarly sources, as well as recollections by the older generation of Uyghurs, the most noteworthy aspects of the Uyghur Enlightenment were the popular trends of "studying abroad" and "inviting foreign teachers." In point of fact, the foreign countries involved in these trends were essentially limited to Ottoman Turkey and Russia. It should also be noted that the Uyghurs' experiences in studying "abroad" were fairly limited. The Uyghurs who traveled to study in Russia were not exposed to the influence of the proletariat revolution in Russia's urban centers; instead, they were concentrated in the city of Kazan, today the capital of the Tatarstan region of Russia, and the teachers invited to Xinjiang were also Tatars from Kazan.[11]

Since most of the instructors initially hired to teach at the Jadidist school in Iksak had a background at traditional religious schools and were unable to meet the requirements of a Jadidist education, the Musabayow brothers decided to send seven young Uyghurs to study abroad in the city of Kazan, with which they had trade relations. When these figures returned to Iksak, they broadened the scope of education at the school, and redesigned the teaching content based on the curricula of schools in Kazan and Istanbul in Ottoman Turkey. By 1892, the Musabayow brothers had reportedly sent more than 50 individuals to study in Russia and Ottoman Turkey. The Musabayow family paid for the entire cost of these trips out of pocket.[12]

Yamauchi Masayuki, a Japanese scholar well-known for his research on Islamic studies and ethnic issues in the former Soviet Union, notes that: "In 19th and early 20th-century Tatar society, reforms to school education were a matter of life or death." Due to these reforms, "After the Revolution of 1905, [Kazan] became the center of Muslim politics and culture, and it played a role in the Islamic world in no way secondary to that of Istanbul,

Cairo, or Beirut."[13] This has important significance in understanding the nature of the early modern Uyghur Enlightenment. The Uyghurs' efforts to deepen their connections to Tatar society were based on their shared identity as "subjugated ethnic groups" seeking a way forward for their people. The Tatars, who had achieved a measure of success in this respect, therefore served as a ready-made role model for the Uyghur people.

As the only independent state ruled by a Turkic people, Ottoman Turkey also played an important role in the Uyghur Enlightenment. The Jadidist schools in southern Xinjiang engaged a number of Turkish teachers; this is corroborated by many Uyghur memoirs. The Uyghurs who studied abroad in Ottoman Turkey were also extremely active in the Enlightenment.[14] To improve the quality of education at his school, Bawadun Musabayow invited Ababakil, Ahmet Kamal, Abudu Rahim, Mukal and other Turkish figures to teach at the school. After Ababakil returned to his home country in 1905, Ahmet Kamal became a central figure. At the request of Bawadun Musabayow, Ahmet Kamal founded Uyghur society's first normal school for teachers at Iksak in 1907.[15] However, other accounts state that Ahmet Kamal did not arrive in the Kashgar region until March 1913, at the invitation of the Musabayow family. At the time, there had been plans to found a normal school in the city of Kashgar, but due to opposition by conservative forces, the school was moved to Iksak, and opened its doors on April 19, 1913.[16]

At the normal school in Iksak, Ahmet Kamal taught students that the sultan of the Ottoman Empire was their true leader; he also taught them to sing Turkish marches, and the content of his lessons showed a strong inclination toward pan-Islamism and pan-Turkism. Kamal's actions were informed by the rise of the First World War: he hoped to arouse the "Turkic" consciousness of the local Uyghur population through his teachings, and inspire in them a sense of responsibility as "Turkish compatriots" to support the Ottoman Empire as the "leader of the global Islamic alliance."[17] Mas'ut Sabri of

The city of Kashgar in the 1930s

Ili, who studied abroad in Ottoman Turkey, also taught his students at the Jadidist school that, "Our ancestors are Turks."[18]

The ideological origins of the Uyghur Enlightenment can undeniably be traced back to both Ottoman Turkey and Kazan Tatar society: "The Tatar Turks and Ottoman Turkey both served as wellsprings of early modern Turkic nationalism."[19] Here, "early modern Turkic nationalism" is another term for "pan-Turkism." The version of pan-Turkism that arose in Tatar society sought to strengthen the unity of the Turkic peoples, so that the "subjugated" Turkish ethnic groups could continue to survive and develop within early modern international society.[20] Many Uyghurs adopted pan-Islamism and became strongly influenced by pan-Turkism after experiencing exchanges with these two regions.

When the First East Turkestan Independence Movement arose in 1933, teachers at the Jadidist schools in Atush who had studied abroad in Turkey mobilized their students to support the movement.[21] These circumstances demonstrate the web of connections between the Uyghur intellectuals who traveled to Ottoman Turkey, the Uyghur Enlightenment, and the East Turkestan Independence Movement. In particular, many of the principal actors in the Uyghur Enlightenment later became the leaders of the East Turkestan Independence Movement, revealing the ideological ties between the two movements.

2.2 The First Independence Movement

Origins of the Independence Movement

The "Kumul Rebellion" (referred to in Chinese as the *Hami qiyi* 哈密起義 or "Hami Rebellion") of March 1931 set the scene for the First East Turkestan Independence Movement. The fuse for the Kumul Rebellion was the proposal by Jin Shuren, then the warlord governor of the Xinjiang provincial government, to "abolish hereditary chieftancy and institute centralized governance" (*gaitu guiliu* 改土歸流), for the sake of expanding his own power. This move signaled the removal of the hereditary Kumulik Uyghur "princes" (*wang* 王) of the semi-autonomous Kumul Khanate formerly appointed by the Qing government, channeling the Uyghur farmers under the jurisdiction of the khanate into local administrative districts under the governance of regular bureaucrats. The Uyghur farmers had previously staged two uprisings seeking the abolishment of the Kumul Khanate (also referred to as the *Hami wangzhi* 哈密王制 or "Hami Principality"), thus Jin Shuren's actions initially seemed to be aligned with the farmers' demands. However, the reforms did not simply result in a loss of political privileges for the people connected to the khanate: the government also sent in troops to squeeze the local populace, while rising Han Chinese immigration threatened the stability of ordinary Uyghur farmers,[22] thus inciting universal discontent amongst the Uyghur elite as well as the general population.

It is arguable that the Kumul Rebellion carried "anti-Han" overtones from its inception: the rebels sought to massacre all Han immigrants who had settled down in the region. Participants in the uprising noted in their memoirs that the leaders of the rebellion were all figures connected to the old khanate: the fact that two different social classes with divergent objectives were able to unite in a struggle against the Han Chinese demonstrates that ethnic conflict was a more salient and more compelling force than internecine class antagonism within contemporary Uyghur society.[23]

Amidst the surging ethnic movement of the Uyghur peoples in the 1930s, from the earliest Kumul Rebellion to the movement's gradual spread into the southern Tianshan Mountains, the term "East Turkestan" never made an appearance. As noted above, the Kumul or Hami region was at times not even included in the concept of "East Turkestan." This region was situated between the Chinese interior and the Uyghur communities of southern Xinjiang, and its geographical location allowed for frequent exchanges with the interior Chinese provinces; the region also undoubtedly experienced a higher influx of Han Chinese immigrants in comparison to other areas.[24] Given this historical and social context, the extent to which the contemporary Uyghur residents of the Kumul region subscribed to the concept of "East Turkestan" is questionable.

However, in comparison with the Kumul region, southern Xinjiang was essentially populated by homogeneous Uyghur communities. Proponents of the movement held that, "Turkestan is the birthplace of the Turks, and must naturally become the land of the Turks,"[25] and declared that the Han Chinese "who have contaminated our land for many long years" would be "driven back to their old homes." These fiery slogans of independence demonstrate that the rise of the East Turkestan Independence Movement was linked to a strong sense of territoriality among some Uyghurs.[26] It is clear that the fundamental aims of the East Turkestan Independence Movement were to "overthrow China's rule" and strive to "liberate ethnic territories," while the movement's most essential characteristic involved attacking and purging everything that symbolized "China."

Organizational Characteristics of the Movement

The First East Turkestan Independence Movement succumbed not to enemy invasion, but rather to conflict among the movement's elite. In May 1934, Hoja Niyaz, the president of the Islamic Republic of East Turkestan, reached an agreement with the government of Xinjiang Province to detain and hand over Prime Minister Sabit (Sawut) Damulla as well as the republic's Minister for Judicial Affairs, leading to the collapse of the Islamic Republic before the provincial government forces even reached Kashgar. In this sense, it was Hoja Niyaz who buried the First East Turkestan Independence Movement.

It is worth noting that, although Hoja Niyaz and Sabit Damulla were both heads of state in the Islamic Republic of East Turkestan, they in fact commanded two different factions. As the leader of the Kumul Rebellion, Hoja Niyaz led forces composed of rebels from the Kumul and Turpan regions in eastern Xinjiang, who had gradually retreated westward toward Kashgar, while Sabit Damulla headed a nationalist group that had been active in the region between Hotan in the southern Tarim Basin and Kashgar, with the aim of establishing an independent ethnic regime. Sabit Damulla was in fact the spiritual leader of the First East Turkestan Independence Movement.

Since both factions featured residents of the Turpan region as well as Islamic religious figures, they cannot be fully differentiated on either a regional or a religious basis. Sabit Damulla was born in Atush in the Kashgar region: he was a religious figure as well as a Uyghur intellectual, having studied abroad in Turkey and "received a modern education and a political baptism."[27] Many of his followers were reported to be "youths who had studied abroad in foreign countries."[28] Damulla's faction therefore arguably centered on a core group of Uyghur intellectuals with modern education. The role of Uyghur intellectuals as proponents and participants was the first important organizational characteristic of the East Turkestan

Independence Movement; it also reflects the lineal relationship between the independence movement and the Uyghur Enlightenment of the early modern era.

Sabit Damulla, who is referred to as the father of the Islamic Republic of East Turkestan, once candidly acknowledged in a letter to an Indian Islamic youth organization that Uyghur society had fallen far behind international society.[29] The Islamic Republic of East Turkestan was organized in the form of a republic, and operated under a directorial system of governance: these positions were inscribed in the "Founding Principles" of East Turkestan, which was formally established on November 12, 1933, in Kashgar.[30] However, the new republic's "Founding Principles" also stated that: "Persons undertaking government duties must be conversant with the Quran and with modern science,"[31] demonstrating that the so-called "Islamic Republic" did not seek to institute secularism. The "Founding Principles" also show that, in terms of its political ideology, while the First East Turkestan Independence Movement advocated an end to ethnic oppression at the hands of Han Chinese dictators along with separation from China, it also promoted the modernization of Uyghur society. This again marks the Independence Movement as the ideological heir to the Uyghur Enlightenment.

Inspired by the Kumul Rebellion, southern Xinjiang erupted in a series of uprisings. Religious figures played a clear role in forwarding these uprisings, and the concept of "Islamic *jihad*" had an inspiring effect on the rebels. One figure who served at a command post for the rebellions recalled that, during the "Turpan Rebellion," everyone from the commanding personnel to the ordinary rebels was filled with religious fervor.[32] Sabit Damulla reportedly utilized the theory of "Islamic *jihad*" to mobilize Uyghurs in the Hotan region prior to the "Hotan Uprising."[33] The injunction to "carefully abide by the Quran" was also explicitly written into the "Founding Principles" of the Islamic Republic of East Turkestan.[34] Though its time was short, it was the association with Islam that led the rebel forces in different regions to briefly unite under the "republic"; this is an undeniable fact.

The efforts of the Islamic Republic of East Turkestan to achieve unity through the rallying cry of "Islamic *jihad*" were informed by the fact that the participants in the uprisings stemmed from different social classes and different regions: although they were able to find common ground in opposing ethnic oppression, rebels of different socioeconomic classes diverged sharply in terms of their motivations and their objectives. Since most of the inhabitants of a given region were engaged in the natural economy of self-sufficient oasis agriculture, conflicts over oases had given rise to a deep-seated sense of territorialism within Uyghur communities.[35] In addition, the fingerprints of Uzbek figures from the Soviet Union and Afghanistan could also be discerned in many of the local uprisings. Calling upon the "righteous cause" of "Islamic *jihad*" was therefore necessary to achieve complete cohesion in the political unification of diverse interest groups from different regions and different social classes; this was entirely a reflection of the practical circumstances of contemporary Uyghur society. Popular mobilization in the name of Islam was the second important organizational characteristic of the East Turkestan Independence Movement. The organizers of the First East Turkestan Independence Movement, as well as its successor movements, used "Islamic *jihad*" as a rallying cry to mobilize mass participation, treating Islam as a conduit to unify the various political forces participating in the independence movements.

2.3 Ethnic Oppression in Xinjiang

Political Inequality

The progression from the Uyghur Enlightenment to the East Turkestan Independence Movement shows that a sense of ethnic crisis among Uyghur intellectuals, who had been exposed to the influence of modern international thought as well as pan-Turkism and pan-Islamism, was the primary motivating force for the germination of the independence movements. This sense of ethnic crisis stemmed from contemporary social conditions in Xinjiang, and the ethnic oppression experienced by Xinjiang communities in the first half of the 20th century was the most direct cause for the rise of the East Turkestan Independence Movement.

Hai Weiliang defines the relationship between Uyghur communities and the central government prior to the latter half of the 19th century as "the relationship of a tributary state and a suzerain."[36] This definition is not entirely apt, but there is no doubt that the Qing government granted a certain degree of autonomy to Uyghur communities. However, after the

Qing Dynasty recaptured the territory of Xinjiang, and particularly after it founded the province of "Xinjiang" in 1884, the Uyghurs' unique bureaucratic system—the "beg" system—was abolished, and the Uyghur population was absorbed under the direct administration of the central government. Thereafter, a large influx of Han Chinese bureaucrats, immigrants, and other figures began flowing into Xinjiang, including the Uyghur region.[37]

According to a 1928 national survey by the Ministry of the Interior of the Republic of China, at the time, Xinjiang had a total population of 2,551,741; Uyghurs comprised 70% of the population, while the Han Chinese population represented less than 10%.[38] However, the Uyghur population may have been even larger in actuality. The estimates by Japanese scholar Hori Sunao place the total Uyghur population at 2,941,000 in 1940. Extrapolating from the figures provided by Hori, the Han Chinese population at that time would have only been around 234,715.[39] Regardless of whether or not these calculations are accurate, it is an incontestable fact that the Han Chinese population in Xinjiang was extremely small in that era. Yet many of these Han Chinese inhabitants were bureaucrats, soldiers and merchants, who maintained a tight grasp on real political, military and economic power in Xinjiang.[40]

During the era of the Republic of China, political power in Xinjiang was concentrated in the hands of the Han Chinese: this is clear from the contemporary administrative structure and the ethnic composition of officials. From the founding of the Republic of China in 1911 to the mid-1940s, a series of warlords and dictators of Han Chinese background had ruled over Xinjiang, concurrently serving as the chief administrator (provincial governor) and the highest-ranking military officer (governor-general), and espousing "closed-door" policies. The senior officials of the organs of the provincial government (including the Department of Civil Affairs, Department of Finance, Department of Education, Department of Works, and the Foreign Affairs Office) were also all of Han Chinese ethnicity.[41] Having been converted into a "utopia" that was almost wholly isolated from the central government and the interior provinces,[42] turnover of Xinjiang's highest-ranking leaders was achieved only by means of assassinations and regime changes. Yet the Uyghur people were unable to play any kind of role amidst this farce of rapidly changing regimes.

Within the local administrative system (comprising 8 administrative districts and 59 counties), people of local ethnic background were similarly nowhere to be seen. In southern Xinjiang, although Uyghurs represented nearly 95% of the local resident population,[43] the period from 1912–1922 witnessed only one figure of Uyghur background amongst the senior administrators and county magistrates.[44] "Who has the right to say that a people should be subject to wicked oppression by a minority? Who can admit that a people should not struggle for its survival? From the vantage point of the entire Republic of China, in the spirit of Mr. Sun Yat-sen's Three People's Principles for founding the state, there are no advantages to Xinjiang separating itself from China and seeking independence for the people of Xinjiang, yet the facts tell us, we cannot begrudge this to the people of Xinjiang." As noted in the passage above by two intellectuals recalling the course of the First East Turkestan Independence Movement, in analyzing the causes for the rise of the independence movement, the political inequality between ethnic groups in that era cannot be overlooked.[45] According to the essay "Xinjiang Legislators in the Era of the Beijing Government," cited above, among the 20 parliamentarians elected in Xinjiang in 1921, only 3 were Uyghurs; moreover, they were all puppets hand-picked by the Provincial Governor Yang Zengxin, and their ability to represent the Uyghurs' interests and wield any personal political power was naturally viewed as suspect by the local Uyghur populace.[46] Even more surprisingly, the 40 parliamentary representatives elected in Xinjiang in 1915 did not include a single person of Uyghur ethnicity.[47] These facts illustrate how the Uyghurs, despite being the majority ethnic group in the region, were completely excluded from legislative bodies and the policymaking process in contemporary Xinjiang society.

Economic Extortion and Policies for Cultural Assimilation

However, the Han Chinese elite who wielded political hegemony in the region of Xinjiang did not play any active role in local socioeconomic development. During the Republican era, economic conditions in Xinjiang experienced little change in comparison with the late Qing era: the region saw no advancements in modern industry and transportation,[48] and depended on foreign imports for the vast majority of manufactured goods.[49] A Uyghur intellectual offered the following critique of the ruling authorities in 1921: "Upon entering the Republican age, the biggest change in Xinjiang was writing such-and-such year, such-and-such month of the Republic of China in letters, and even that, we Uyghurs learned from the Han Chinese."[50]

During the era of the Qing Dynasty, the central government had annually disbursed around 3 million taels in funding or "interprovincial assistance" (*xiexiang* 協餉) to the Xinjiang provincial government.[51] However, in the Republican era, even this type of funding was discontinued. In response to a severe financial crisis, the first provincial governor of Xinjiang, Yang Zengxin, adopted measures for increased taxes, paper rationing, revitalization of industry and commerce, wasteland reclamation, and so on.[52] However, Yang's "revitalization" of industry and commerce achieved little to no results,[53] and he ultimately resorted to extortion of the local populace to mitigate the crisis. Between 1912 and 1915, Xinjiang issued 6,232,800 taels of paper currency not backed by reserves.[54] In comparison with 1884, the year the province was founded, by 1915, agricultural taxes in Xinjiang had risen sharply: taxes on wheat had increased by a factor of 2–3, and taxes on corn had increased by a factor of 2–5, while taxes on grass fodder had soared by a factor of 19.[55]

Local bureaucrats abusing their privileges to plunder the Uyghur inhabitants was a common occurrence.[56] The surprising phenomenon of ministers of the provincial government seeking demotions to the level of county magistrate was a reflection of the opportunities such direct administrative positions offered for exploitation of the populace.[57] The memoirs of bureaucrats from that era record many strategies for pillaging via taxation.[58] County magistrate positions in Kucha, Aksu, Yarkent, Kargilik, and other regions in southern Xinjiang with a high concentration of Uyghurs were regarded as particularly "lucrative positions" (*feique* 肥缺). It is therefore easy to imagine the scale on which Han Chinese bureaucrats plundered the local Uyghur population.

Until 1933, the Xinjiang provincial government had enforced a policy mandating that Uyghurs receive an education at Chinese-language schools (academies). The original purpose of this policy, dating back to the Qing Dynasty, was to induce Uyghurs to abandon their traditional customs and instead adopt Chinese customs; the policy thus carried an implicit bias against Uyghur culture.[59] Such ethnically biased policies encouraged a sense of ethnic superiority amongst the Han Chinese inhabitants of Xinjiang. A 1930s report on Xinjiang by an observer from the Soviet Union notes that, even after living in a Uyghur region for 50 years, one Han Chinese elder was completely unable to speak the Uyghur language.[60] The Han Chinese residents of Xinjiang also disdained the Islamic taboo on idolatry, building Buddhist temples, Confucian temples, and shrines to General Guan Yu in the seat of every county government, and carving out their own ethnic communities within Uyghur territories.[61]

The acute ethnic discrimination and oppression that informed every sphere, from politics and the economy to culture and society, naturally gave rise to ethnic hatred for the Han Chinese amongst the Uyghur inhabitants. Many Uyghurs "feel that the Han bureaucrats who rule over them know only the demons of exploitation and butchery, and that the Han people are all demons too."[62] The Uyghurs' ethnic enmity toward the Han Chinese thus took shape as the primary source of social conflict in contemporary Xinjiang.

2.4 Xinjiang's Dual Social Structure and the Public Administrative System for Uyghur Communities

The Dual Structure of Regional and Ethnic Communities

Many of the counties in southern Xinjiang were established around an oasis. The county magistrate held supreme authority over taxation, the construction of cities and roads, the police and public security forces, the judicial system, and so on.[63] However, the contemporary system of bureaucratic appointments by the provincial government only extended as far as the county level. County governments thus became the link between the national bureaucratic system and Uyghur communities, while relying on local Uyghur figures for administrative operations and public management below the county level. The local public administrative system for Uyghur communities was further divided into grassroots-level administrative organizations, water management organizations, religious tribunals, and so on.

Given that only around 3,000 Han Chinese had migrated into southern Xinjiang during this time period,[64] we can speculate that the traditional structure of Uyghur society had not yet suffered much erosion. However,

Figure 2.1 Structural Diagram of Xinjiang Society

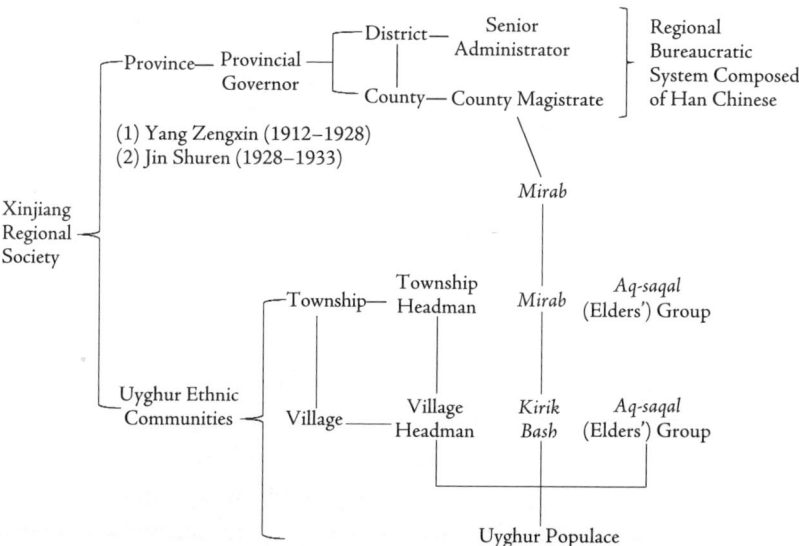

Source: Compiled by the author.

as shown in Figure 2.1, since the Han Chinese controlled nearly all regional administrative resources, the Uyghurs were in fact situated within a dual social structure, consisting of regional Xinjiang society and the Uyghur communities.

There is little extant information that can offer us a better understanding of Uyghur social structure in the period from the early 1900s to the 1930s. The following attempt to restore the rural Uyghur social systems of the early 20th century is based primarily on information from a survey of the Kashgar region by a Soviet observer in the early 1930s and a second survey completed in the 1950s, as well as the first-hand recollections of Uyghur inhabitants.

During this time period, 90% of the Uyghur population was engaged in agriculture. There were numerous permutations of the local titles, but various sources confirm the existence of the beg (also known as *Ming bash*, or "leader of a thousand households"), the village headman (*xiangyue* 鄉約, also known as *Yuz bash*, or "leader of a hundred households"), the *Mirab* (who supervised water and irrigation works), the *Kirik bash* (or "leader of forty households"), the *Qazi* (a judge), the *Alim* (a scholar), the *Rais* (a law-enforcement official) and other positions and titles. These positions were further subdivided under the administrative, water management and judicial systems, which together comprised the public administrative system for rural Uyghur communities.

In administrative terms, the beg was the administrative leader of a township, while the village headman was the administrative leader of a village: their duties primarily involved maintaining social order and collecting taxes.

To manage irrigation works and the distribution of agricultural water, counties and townships also installed a *mirab*, while villages installed one or two *kirik bash*. However, the county *mirab* was responsible for appointing the township *mirab*, who was in turn responsible for appointing the *kirik bash*, thus creating a water management system independent of the administration.[65] This structural feature of the public administrative system arose due to the importance of water to the Uyghurs as an "irrigated agricultural society."[66]

"The criminal matters heard by the county magistrate include homicide, crimes endangering the state, malfeasance, political offences, and so on."[67] All other civil matters, including marriage, inheritance, property, land transactions, and so on were entrusted to Islamic tribunals or *Mahkima Sharia*, which held trial and issued judgment in accordance with Islamic Sharia law. The *Mahkima Sharia* in Toguzak Township, Kashgar, was composed of three *Qazi*, one *akhund*, and 16 *Rais*.[68] This court also presided over civil disputes between Uyghurs and Han Chinese merchants. Some Han merchants complained that any judgments issued by the court would surely benefit the Uyghurs.[69] It is clear that Islam played an undeniable role in unifying the Uyghur people.

Interestingly, although the Qing Dynasty formally abolished the beg system in December 1885, county-level administrative leaders were still popularly referred to as "begs." In addition, the water management systems presided over by the *mirab* had been in existence since the 16th century.[70] It is evident that, even after the founding of the Republic of China, the traditional Uyghur community management systems and old social production relationships continued to be perpetuated in Uyghur villages.

Another special feature of rural Uyghur society was the "equal parts land rent system" (*dengfen zhi dizu zhidu* 等分制地租制度): under this system, the rent paid by tenant farmers to their landowner consisted of grain and labor in equal parts.[71] The purpose of the system was to ensure the landowner's supply of labor, while also allowing landowners to directly manage a greater expanse of farmland. The reason why landowners preferred to gain direct control over more farmland rather than collecting rent from tenant farmers was due to the problems with water for irrigation in oasis farming.

Quotas for irrigation water based on one's holdings as a proportion of the total amount of farmland fed by a single river, determined through negotiations with the local water management system: they were first issued to each village, and then distributed by the villages amongst the farming households. However, in Asa Village, Guma County (Pishan County), landowners holding 35.4% of the village's total land laid claim to 47.37% of its agricultural water.[72] Land with a guaranteed supply of water naturally yielded a better harvest than water-starved land. In other words, the "equal parts land rent system" prevailing in rural Uyghur society was in fact a sort of privilege system allowing the land-owning class to guarantee their means of production. Since a variety of taxes, including the land tax and other miscellaneous taxes, were set on the basis of agricultural water usage, it is generally believed that landowners' water usage as tabulated by townships and villages may have been much lower than their actual water usage.[73] These examples reflect the degree to which the land-owning class in that era was able to intervene directly in public administrative affairs in rural Uyghur communities.

Previous studies have argued that this type of intervention arose due to collusion amongst the ruling class. However, this simple classist interpretation may obscure the unique characteristics of rural Uyghur society. A 1956 survey of No. 3 Township of District 1, Kashgar Kona Xahar County (Shufu County), revealed

A Uyghur farmer plowing a field

that, among the 11 county-level *aq-saqal*, 10 were landowners who "rented land to others and personally collected rent."[74] These circumstances show that the ability of the land-owning class to intervene in public administrative affairs in rural Uyghur society in fact stemmed from the Uyghurs' unique "*aq-saqal* system."

The Aq-Saqal *System and Ethnic Crisis*

In Turkic languages, *aq-saqal* originally meant "white-beard," or "elder." The social authority of the *aq-saqal* was based on social conventions, and could either be "inherited" or bestowed on an individual.[75] The records show that, aside from the 11 county-level *aq-saqal* in No. 3 Township of District 1, Kashgar Kona Xahar County, each village also had between 4 and 5 *aq-saqal*: in other words, townships and villages each had separate cliques of *aq-saqal*.

The roles filled by the *aq-saqal* in contemporary rural Uyghur society included: recommending candidates for various public offices under the leadership of the begs; distributing the township and village tax and labor quotas amongst the villages or amongst individual households; presiding over criminal cases; sanctioning marriage, divorce, inheritance, succession and other civil administrative matters; and overseeing land transactions.[76] Despite regulations stipulating that candidates for public office, whether for administration, water management, or tax collection, were to be elected by the people before being appointed by the senior administrator, the candidates were in fact nominated by the *aq-saqal* cliques. In many cases, when one *aq-saqal* was appointed to a certain position, other *aq-saqal* would serve as assistants. The custom whereby candidates for beg and village headman had to be approved through internal discussion by the *aq-saqal* cliques prior to their appointment is also clearly reflected in the records of a survey report on rural Kashgar in the early 1930s by an observer from the Soviet Union.[77] These records confirm that the *aq-saqal* had become a powerful interest group in rural Uyghur society, with a monopoly over all public offices.

The majority of the *aq-saqal* were landowners. The monopoly that *aq-saqal* cliques held over public offices and the exercising of public authority thus not only bestowed legitimacy upon their control over rural Uyghur society, but also guaranteed the privileges of the land-owning class in monopolizing the means of production. Although the public administrative system in rural Uyghur society was composed of three separate systems for administration, water management, and the judiciary, since the *aq-saqal* operated as a bloc, these systems were unable to achieve a complete separation of powers. This allowed individual *aq-saqal* to expand their existing powers, and created the conditions for a segment of landowners to oppress and exploit the populace.

Within this public administrative system, collusion between Islamic functionaries and the *aq-saqal* was also particularly in evidence. In the No. 3 Township of District 2, Aksu County, administrative rights over approximately 42.4% of the township's total *waqf* lands (lands donated by Muslims to mosques) had been handed over to 41 households of landowners, representing less than 4% of the entire township population.[78] On a local, community level, Islam thus became a vehicle for amassing the Uyghurs' discontent with Han Chinese control over public authority; but at the same time, within ethnic communities, it also served as a tool for preserving the vested interests of the land-owning class.

Another survey shows that, among the 24 households of landowners in the No. 5 Township of District 1, Aksu County, 19 households believed that their economic status had changed after joining an *aq-saqal* clique, enabling them to become landowners.[79] It is therefore arguable that the Uyghur public administrative system, centering on the *aq-saqal*, in fact spurred class differentiation in rural Uyghur society. When the People's Republic of China was founded, in regions with relatively heavy land use, nearly 72.4% of all land was held by the land-owning class, which represented only 7.1% of the total population.[80] Furthermore, due to loss of territory, many farmers had become long-term hired hands, "lacking even the right to speak with others as equals"; there were even cases in which they were forced to sell themselves as slaves.[81] In some regions, the illiteracy rate was as high as 96%.[82] As economy disparity widened under feudal production relationships, the Uyghur people sank into a profound crisis.

The first to sense this ethnic crisis were the "new intellectual class" of Uyghur society, along with certain religious figures. In addition, it should be noted that the emerging industrial capitalists, who found themselves at odds with traditional Uyghur society, also supported the early modern Uyghur Enlightenment initiated by intellectual and religious figures, demonstrating that the Uyghur Enlightenment largely arose out of discontent and resentment directed at traditional Uyghur social structures.

Due to a lack of data, it is not possible to comprehend the true circumstances of the Uyghur industrial capitalist class in the early 20th century. According to several Uyghur memoirs, the emerging industrial capitalists began gathering in cities like Kashgar, Turpan, Ili, and Urumqi (Dihua) in the late 19th century. Intriguingly, the Musabayow family, which originated from Atush in the Kashgar region, used the border city of Ili as an important stronghold for their primary economic pursuit of exporting agricultural products (mainly cotton) produced in southern Xinjiang, and importing foreign industrial products. This contact with the outside world not only opened their eyes to the backward state of Uyghur society, but also granted them the opportunity to establish ties with Ottoman Turkey and the Tatar communities of Kazan, Russia. These connections brought exposure to the influence of pan-Turkism and pan-Islamism, establishing an ideological foundation for the Uyghur Enlightenment as well as the subsequent East Turkestan Independence Movement.[83]

Summary

The ideological underpinnings of the East Turkestan Independence Movement can be traced back to the ideas of pan-Turkism and pan-Islamism that arose in Ottoman Turkey and the Tatar communities of Kazan, Russia. These concepts flourished in the cradle of Uyghur society due to the Uyghur Enlightenment, which was again highly influenced by Ottoman Turkey and the Tatars. The motivations that led to the Enlightenment movement arose out of a sense of ethnic crisis among the nascent Uyghur intellectual class, certain religious figures, and the emerging industrial capitalists. Under the unique dual structure of contemporary Xinjiang society, ethnic oppression and discrimination intensified on a regional scale; under the public administrative system of traditional Uyghur society, class differentiation within local ethnic communities grew ever more severe, thus giving rise to an ethnic crisis.

As the ideological heir to the Uyghur Enlightenment, the East Turkestan Independence Movement was also highly influenced by pan-Turkism and pan-Islamism: the basic aims of the movement were to "overthrow

China's rule" and strive to "liberate ethnic territories," while its most fundamental characteristic involved attacking and purging everything symbolic of "China." One important organizational characteristic of the independence movement was the role of Uyghur intellectuals as its primary proponents and participants; these circumstances emerged due to the lineal relationship between the Uyghur Enlightenment and the East Turkestan Independence Movement. Another important organizational characteristic of the movement was the use of "Islamic *jihad*" as a rallying cry to attract the support of the Uyghur populace. This facet of the independence movement was influenced in part by the concept of pan-Islamism, but it was also a reflection of the reality of contemporary Uyghur society: only the "righteous cause" of Islam could serve as a vehicle to achieve political unity between different regions and across the diverse classes and interest groups of Xinjiang society.

CHAPTER 3

The Anti-Japanese, Pro-Soviet Agenda: Surface and Substance

Sheng Shicai's Political Agenda and Ethnic Problems in Xinjiang

On April 12, 1933, Xinjiang's provincial capital of Urumqi (Dihua) witnessed another coup d'état. As a result of the coup, Sheng Shicai supplanted Jin Shuren as the leader of Xinjiang. During Sheng's time in power, he advocated and promoted his personally drafted "Six-Point Policy": anti-imperialism, pro-Sovietism, ethnic equality, integrity, peace, and construction. Although Sheng Shicai maintained in his "Lectures on the Six-Point Policy" that the policies were all interrelated,[1] anti-imperialism and pro-Sovietism represented a distinctly ideological political agenda; in contrast, the other four policies represented more concrete social measures, and substantively speaking, the issues they addressed were not on the same level as the political elements of the policy slate. A reporter for *Dagong Daily* (*Dagong bao* 大公報) who developed a favorable impression of Sheng Shicai's policies while touring Xinjiang in 1937 described the relationships within the "Six-Point Policy" thusly: "Anti-imperialism and pro-Sovietism are like a person's head; ethnic equality and integrity are like the body; and peace and construction are like the feet. Each has its own place, and each has its own purpose."[2]

As China began to suffer from Japanese imperialist aggression in the 1930s, "anti-imperialism" morphed into "anti-Japanese sentiment." Given its great distance from Japan, why would Xinjiang raise the banner of resistance against Japan? Why was it necessary for the anti-Japanese agenda to be tied to a pro-Soviet agenda? To answer these questions, this chapter draws on the diplomatic files of the Japanese Foreign Ministry, currently held in the Diplomatic Archives of the Ministry of Foreign Affairs of Japan, to analyze the relationship between Xinjiang and Japan in that era, while also examining the reasons and purpose behind Sheng Shicai's formulation of his "anti-imperialist" and "pro-Soviet" policies, against the backdrop of the political situations in China and in Xinjiang from 1933 to 1937.

3.1 Japan's Infiltration of Xinjiang in the Early Modern Era

Japan's Objectives in Infiltrating Xinjiang

What was the likelihood of Xinjiang suffering threats or encroachment by Japan? What was the nature and substance of Japanese policy on Xinjiang in that era? To answer these questions, we must first examine the historical relationship between Japan and Xinjiang.

The Japanese first began to take notice of Xinjiang in the later Meiji period. During the Meiji era, the following Japanese figures visited the Xinjiang region: (1) Nishi Tokujirō, Japanese envoy to Russia (1880);[3] (2) The Ōtani expeditions, led by Ōtani Kōzui and Tachibana Zuicho (1902, 1908, and 1910);[4] (3) Hatano Yōsaku, Hayashide Kenjirō, and Sakurai Yoshiyuki, among the second class of students at Toa Dobunshoin University in Shanghai (1905);[5] (4) Hino Tsutomu and Uehara Taichi, officers of the General Staff (1906).[6]

Of the above, only the members of the Ōtani expeditions had cultural aims; the remaining figures all in fact entered Xinjiang in the service of the Japanese Foreign Ministry and the Army General Staff to gather information. For instance, Kaneko Tamio, author of *The Japanese in Central Asia*, speculates that Hino Tsutomu compiled his three travelogues on the Xinjiang region as reports to be presented to the General Staff upon returning to Japan.[7]

Uehara Taichi made his way into Xinjiang around the same time as Hino Tsutomu.[8] The public archives in Japan do not contain any records of Uehara, but Chinese sources show that, in 1907, when the Qing Ili General Chang Geng established the Army Expedited Martial Studies Academy (*Lujun wubei sucheng xuetang* 陸軍武備速成學堂) in Ghulja (Yining), the seat of the general's mansion, the "Japanese person Hara Takashi" was appointed as a military instructor. We may thus infer that Uehara Taichi used the name Hara Takashi, or Yuan Shangzhi in Chinese, to gain a position as a military instructor in Ghulja.[9]

However, whilst bearing the title of an instructor at the Qing military academy, Uehara in fact served as an intelligence officer for the Japanese Army. Among the documents in the Diplomatic Archives of the Ministry of Foreign Affairs, I discovered a telegram sent by Major-General Saitō Suejirō, Assistant Military Attaché to the Japanese legation in Beijing, to General Hasegawa Yoshimichi, Chief of the Army General Staff.[10] The telegram contains the line: "According to the telegram sent by Uehara Taichi from Ili, we have learned that the Ili General is dead, and the purpose of Russia's actions in the region are to gain power by lending funds." The upper left corner of the telegram is marked with the words, "Army," "Classified," and "Print Publication Prohibited."[11] This document confirms that Uehara Taichi was engaged in intelligence-gathering work in Ghulja, and used a radio communications device to continually send reports to the Japanese military. In addition, the telegram refers to the death of the Ili General during the Ili Rebellion in January 1912,[12] allowing us to infer that Uehara Taichi remained in the city of Ghulja near the Sino-Russian border for at least six years, from 1906 to 1912.

A common thread appears in the intelligence-gathering work of the above figures: each of them evinced a close interest in the expansion of Russian influence in Xinjiang, and focused their efforts on discovering the extent and purpose of said expansion. During his trip to Xinjiang in 1880, Nishi Tokujirō visited only the Ili region.[13] At the time, Ili was still occupied by the Imperial Russian Army. The survey of Xinjiang by Hatano and his companions proceeded on the basis of negotiations between the Japanese Foreign Ministry and the British Foreign Office: "The alliance established between Britain and Japan to oppose Russia's seizure of China and the neighboring regions was thus manifested."[14] Hino Tsutomu traveled through northern and southern Xinjiang along the edge of the Tianshan Mountains, finally returning to Japan via India. Uehara Taichi laid plans to secretly slip into Russia, but was caught and detained.[15] In addition, between 1916 and 1917, at the beginning of the Taishō era, Corporal Sata Shigeharu of the Japanese Army Reserves disguised himself as an employee of Mitsui & Co., and was stationed in Urumqi in the name of conducting a commercial survey. He was in fact dispatched by the Japanese Army General Staff to engage in espionage.[16] The three Japanese geisha under his command resided for a period of time in Tacheng, another city along the border between China and Russia.[17]

In short, the Japanese first entered Xinjiang in connection with the expansion of Russian forces in the region. In other words, fear of Russian expansionism in Xinjiang was the primary reason for Japanese infiltration of Xinjiang.

Xinjiang and Japan's "Special Interests" in Manchuria and Mongolia

Japan was opposed to the expansion of Russian influence in Xinjiang due to its efforts to absorb the regions of "Manchuria and Mongolia," which geographically neighbored on Xinjiang, into its own sphere of influence; Russia's expansion into Xinjiang would have negatively impacted Japan's plans in this regard.

Following the Russo-Japanese War of 1904–1905, as Japan extended its reach further into the mainland, the Japanese Army General Staff drafted a secret report entitled "Russian Operations in Manchuria, Mongolia and Xinjiang, No. 1."[18] This report, written on June 12, 1912 (Meiji 45) and currently held in the Diplomatic Archives of the Ministry of Foreign Affairs, was compiled on the basis of the latest intelligence reports on Russia's activities in northeastern China and eastern Inner Mongolia (or the regions of "Manchuria and Mongolia," as referred to by Japan at the time). As indicated by the title, from the perspective of the Japanese military, Russia's efforts to expand its power in Xinjiang were linked to its efforts to extend control over Manchuria and Mongolia.

However, at the time, the Japanese government, particularly the Japanese military, regarded Manchuria and Mongolia as belonging to its own sphere of influence. In fact, starting in the later Meiji period, especially after the Sino-Japanese War of 1894–1895, both the Japanese government and the military began actively pursuing a "special position" and "special interests" in the Chinese regions of Manchuria and Mongolia.[19] Given that the General Staff began compiling secret reports similar to the above and sending intelligence officers into the Xinjiang region around the same time period, it is clear that the Japanese military believed that Russian forces in

Xinjiang threatened Japan's "special position" and "special interests" in Manchuria and Mongolia.

During this era, the Japanese government espoused the view that Japan's so-called "special position" and "special interests" in Manchuria and Mongolia consisted of "the total sum of the special interests held by Japan in said region on the basis of treaties, in addition to the natural outcome of its neighboring status and geographical location, as well as sundry negotiations up to the present day."[20] These interests specifically referred to: leasing rights over the Kwantung Territory, including Lüshun and Dalian; interests related to the Manchuria Railway, as well as garrison rights and administrative rights in the region bordering on the Manchuria Railway; freedom for Japanese citizens to reside, travel to and fro, and engage in various pursuits in "Southern Manchuria"; the right for Japanese citizens to commercially lease land in "Southern Manchuria," and engage in cooperative agriculture in eastern Mongolia; mining concessions at designated mines and in designated regions in "Southern Manchuria"; and extraterritoriality for Japanese citizens.[21] In fact, these rights and interests had largely been wrested from Russia following Japan's victory in the Russo-Japanese War. It is therefore not difficult to imagine that Japan's most important concern in preserving these interests was to prevent Russian forces from staging a comeback in the region.

What was the connection between the "special interests" Japan claimed in northeastern China and its efforts to prevent the expansion of Russian influence in Xinjiang? The answer to this question may be found in the "Summary of Policies on China (Manchuria–Mongolia) Drafted by Director Abe of the Political Affairs Bureau · Outline of Diplomatic Policies on China · Drafted in Taishō 1," in the archive *Directives of Foreign Minister Uchida to Ambassador Ijuin Regarding Policies on China (Manchuria–Mongolia)* held in the Diplomatic Archives of the Ministry of Foreign Affairs. This policy outline begins by noting that, "It is often argued that the means of effecting a resolution to the Manchuria–Mongolia question is to seize territory, and that the Empire ought to carve away southern Manchuria and neighboring eastern Inner Mongolia, thus resolving this question." However, the "Outline" notes further that, "arbitrary use of force" would not only incur opposition by China and other countries, leading to financial difficulties for Japan, but would also give rise to the following concerns:

This would occasion tremendous burdens and inconveniences for the Empire:

(1) It would not only arouse resistance by the Chinese military and civilians, but would also incite agitation within China to boycott Japanese goods. . . . This would not only impede our economic activities in China and their development; there would even be concerns that our industry's notion of treating China as its primary market would suffer a heavy impact.

(2) In our diplomatic affairs, not only would this be a breach of promise in China, it might also deepen the misgivings of our allies . . . and would certainly cause Japan to meet with greater inconveniences with respect to the matter of exercising its discursive rights in China.

(3) . . . in commencing the partitioning of China, there is a concern that this would ultimately cause several powerful countries to be entrenched in the mainland, which is separated only by a narrow strip of water.

(4) . . . If the Empire carves away southern Manchuria and eastern Inner Mongolia, this would inevitably cause Russian forces to push forward, potentially even uniting western Inner Mongolia with Outer Mongolia; northern Manchuria would naturally go without saying, and they would even peer toward Xinjiang, Gansu, Shaanxi, and Shanxi. If China were driven out of Manchuria and Mongolia, the result would be direct contact between the two countries of Japan and Russia in Manchuria and Mongolia, thus aggravating the conflict of interests between the two countries.

The Japanese government therefore decided with respect to its diplomatic policies on China that it would "not harbor intentions to obtain new territory in Manchuria and Mongolia."[22]

The reason why the Japanese government cabinets in that period—including the second Saionji cabinet (August 30, 1911–December 21, 1912), the third Katsura cabinet (December 21, 1912–February 20, 1913), and the Yamamoto Gonbee cabinet (February 20, 1913–April 16, 1914) held such a cautious attitude with respect to the question of Manchuria and Mongolia is because they were forced to consider Japan's strength relative to the international community. However, if Russia were able to absorb Xinjiang into its sphere of influence and expand eastward, it would come into direct contact with the Japanese forces in the Manchurian and Mongolian regions, and conflict would inevitably ensue. If this were to occur, Japan's "special interests" and "special position" in Manchuria and Mongolia would be threatened. Japan's concerns in this regard and the tensions that informed its opposition to the advent and expansion of Russian influence in Xinjiang are clearly reflected in the above "Outline."[23]

Even after Russia's October Revolution in 1917, Japan did not alter its policy of monitoring the activities of Soviet Russian forces in Xinjiang. In May 1918, the "Mutual Defense Agreement of the Japanese and Chinese Armies" was concluded between Japan and the Beiyang government. Chinese and Japanese records differ with respect to the actions taken by the two countries under the auspices of this agreement. Chinese sources record that, in 1918, six Japanese figures, including Oniwatazumi Taikichi and Ōta Toyo, conducted an inspection of the defenses on the Sino-Russian border in Xinjiang, accompanied by Cheng Yuchen, an officer of the Chinese Army General Staff.[24] In contrast, Japanese sources record that eight Japanese officers, including Major Narita Tetsuo, Captain Nagamine Kamesuke, Captain Tajima Eijirō, and Captain Aiba Shigeo, entered Xinjiang in 1919 to engage in intelligence-gathering activities in Urumqi and cities near the border with Russia, including Ghulja, Tacheng, and Kashgar.[25]

In short, prior to the Shōwa period (1926–1989), Japan did not evince any direct territorial ambitions with respect to Xinjiang, but it did continuously monitor the region, due to its concerns that the expansion of Tsarist and later Soviet Russian forces in the Xinjiang region would threaten Japan's "special interests" and "special position" in Manchuria and Mongolia.

Xinjiang and the War of Resistance Against Japan

At the start of the Shōwa period, "Shidehara diplomacy," which supported the preservation of the Washington system and opposed interference in China's internal affairs, came under assault on two sides by Japanese political and military circles. In June 1927, the newly formed Tanaka cabinet convened the "Far East Conference" to formulate a new diplomatic policy on China: its key content included the decision to adopt "resolute defensive measures" to uphold Japan's interests in China, by separating the regions of Manchuria and Mongolia from the territories of China proper, and placing them under Japan's sphere of influence; Japan would assume responsibility for maintaining order in the region. By the late 1920s, the idea of "using Manchuria and Mongolia as a breakthrough point to resolve Japan's economic difficulties" had come to be regarded as Japan's "lifeline."[26]

As Manchuria and Mongolia came increasingly under the spotlight, the Xinjiang region also began attracting greater attention from Japan. In the Diplomatic Archives of the Ministry of Foreign Affairs, records on Xinjiang dating to the Meiji and Taishō periods are scarce, and scattered amongst different files. In contrast, there is an immense quantity of archives from the Shōwa period, with more than ten separate bound volumes.[27]

These materials include a secret report sent by Minami Jirō, Ambassador Extraordinary and Plenipotentiary to Manchukuo (and Commander of the Kwantung Army), to Foreign Minister Hirota Kōki on October 24, 1935. This report, formulated by the Kwantung Army General Staff and entitled, "On the Situation of the Soviet Union's Red-ification of Xinjiang," contains the following passage in its introduction:

> We are currently targeting Outer Mongolia through various direct efforts; in addition, the forces of Japan and Manchukuo are advancing through Inner Mongolia, Suihua and Ningxia to threaten the Soviet hinterlands from the direction of Xinjiang, and efforts are being launched to contend against Soviet red-ification forces entering China's Central Plains through Mongolia and the Xinjiang region, turning Mongolia, Xinjiang and northwestern China into battlegrounds; in the future, this will continue to grow in intensity. With respect to the Soviet Union's various efforts in Xinjiang, these should be regarded as connected to the mobilization of the Chinese Red Army and Chiang Kai-shek's United Front Policy for alignment with the Communists, or to the Muslim problems, and must not be dismissed as "a fire burning on the other side of the river."[28]

During this period, Japan's objective in Xinjiang continued to be forestalling the southward advance of Soviet forces, paired with considerations for how to present a threat to the Soviet Union. However, in order to advance "through Inner Mongolia, Suihua and Ningxia to threaten the Soviet hinterlands from the direction of Xinjiang," it would be necessary to draw Xinjiang into its own sphere of influence. Although this report does not offer any specific prescriptions, it clearly reveals the scheming by certain individuals in the Japanese military to absorb Xinjiang into Japan's sphere of influence.

However, the intelligence reports on Xinjiang gathered by the Japanese Foreign Ministry in the period from 1933 to 1935 were all collected from outside the region, consisting of information from local news coverage and press agencies compiled by Japanese embassies and consulates, particularly those stationed in Afghanistan, India, and the Soviet Union. In 1934, the Soviet Union began controlling news reports on Xinjiang, and foreigners were prohibited from traveling to any of the Central Asian republics aligned with the Soviet Union that bordered on Xinjiang, greatly impeding the efforts of the Japanese embassies and consulates in the Soviet Union to gather intelligence on Xinjiang.[29] In response to this situation, on December 1, 1935, the Japanese consulate in Novosibirsk sent a proposal to the Foreign Ministry on its "Recommendations for a Field Survey of Xinjiang." This document, which is currently held in the Diplomatic Archives, forcefully advocated for the Foreign Ministry and the Ministry of War to form a joint survey team, which would clandestinely enter Xinjiang through either the Chinese interior or Afghanistan.[30]

In 1933, a Japanese individual gained entry to Xinjiang in the train of the Hui warlord Ma Zhongying, who launched an invasion of Xinjiang from his base in Gansu. Sheng Shicai, then the sovereign ruler of Xinjiang under the title of Xinjiang Frontier Defense Commissioner (*Xinjiang bianfang duban* 新疆邊防督辦), used this as a pretext to accuse Japan of instigating Ma Zhongying's invasion of Xinjiang. The individual denounced by Sheng Shicai as a "Japanese spy" was named Ōnishi Tadashi (operating under the Chinese alias of Yu Huating).[31] According to the recollections of Staff Major Yang Boqing of Militia Division 36 of Ma Zhongying's army, Ōnishi was a mysterious, unidentified Japanese individual with the ability to decipher coded telegrams. Ōnishi did not serve in Ma's army, but rather had been captured by Ma Zhongying while en route to Xinjiang; thus the two arrived in Xinjiang together.[32] However, Ōnishi was again captured and detained by Sheng Shicai's forces not long after Ma Zhongying crossed into Xinjiang.

Moreover, according to Wu Zhiping, who also served in Ma Zhongying's army and claimed to have secretly searched Ōnishi Tadashi's luggage, Ōnishi was carrying a large number of Japanese documents and a card (perhaps a "calling card"?) on which was written the name of a White Russian General residing in Xinjiang; on the strength of this name (which was not specified in Wu's memoirs), Wu speculated that Ōnishi had come to Xinjiang to make contact with this individual.[33] However, no firsthand materials verifying Ōnishi Tadashi's identity have been found as yet amongst the historical records held at the Diplomatic Archives of the Ministry of Foreign Affairs, the National Institute for Defense Studies of the Ministry of Defense, or other locations.

In 1935, Japanese forces began penetrating northern China. The Swedish explorer Sven Anders Hedin, who traveled through Xinjiang in 1933–1934, offered the following characterization of the positions of China, Soviet Union, and Japan in the region: "The situation has changed very much since 1934 and 1935. Since then the Japanese have conquered Chahar, Sui-yuan and Shansi [Shanxi]—the provinces of Northern China in which the great trade and caravan routes to Sinkiang [Xinjiang] start. If the Japanese refurnishing in Asia proceeds in the same direction as now and at the same pace, Sinkiang may become a bone of contention between Japan and Russia."[34]

From Japan's perspective, if Soviet forces entered northwestern China, including the Xinjiang region, this would threaten Japan's monopoly over the region of Manchuria and Mongolia; this would also signify that, if total war broke out between China and Japan, China would be able to receive foreign aid via these regions, particularly from the Soviet Union, and would thus be able to stage a long, drawn-out resistance.

By 1935, Chiang Kai-shek had realized that, in the case of total war between China and Japan, China's coastline would be subject to a Japanese blockade. In that scenario, the Soviet Union would likely be the only country able to provide arms and ammunition to China, since the Soviet Union geographically bordered on Xinjiang. At the end of that year, Chiang Kai-shek sent Chen Lifu to the Soviet Union to sound out its attitude toward the establishment of a Sino-Soviet military agreement.[35] In fact, in the initial stages of the Sino-Japanese War, the Soviet Union was the only member of the international community willing to provide aid to China. Soong Mei-ling, the wife of Chiang Kai-shek, confirmed this point in comments made in Washington in 1940: "As an honest intellectual, I'm afraid I must say that the aid received from the Soviet Union over the last three years of China's War of Resistance in fact exceeds the British and Americans put together, many times over."[36] The Soviet Union had in fact actively supported China in its War of Resistance against Japan since the early stages of the war, leading to the gradual fusion of the "anti-Japanese" sentiments of the Chinese people with "pro-Soviet" ideas.

After the conference of 1937, China and the Soviet Union determined that Soviet matériel would be transported to the Chinese interior along two different routes. However, the Ulaanbaatar–Erenhot–Lanzhou route, which primarily passed through the region of Mongolia, was in fact never used, as it approached too closely to the Japanese-controlled region of Manchuria and Mongolia. The Almaty–Ili–Urumqi–Hami–Lanzhou route, which passed through Kazakhstan, Xinjiang and Gansu, therefore became the sole passage leading from the Soviet Union to China. In the space of just one year between 1937 and the summer of 1938, approximately 6,000 tons of material aid (arms, ammunition, medicines, gasoline, and so on) from the Soviet Union were transported to the Chinese interior through Xinjiang.[37]

Due to the existence of the Xinjiang passage, Japan's "operation to cut off aid to Chiang via the Burma passage," initiated in 1938 with the objective of applying pressure to the Nationalist government to force Chiang Kai-shek to change his policy of resistance against Japan, ended in failure. In this sense, from China's perspective, Xinjiang was a "lifeline" and "an important base area for the resurgence of the Chinese people," during the early stages of the Sino-Japanese War.[38] If Xinjiang had been unable to play this role during that era, China's War of Resistance might have progressed differently.

3.2 Sheng Shicai's Anti-Japanese, Pro-Soviet Policies

The Origins of Sheng Shicai's Anti-Japanese Ideas

Xinjiang's inhabitants largely belonged to Turkic Muslim ethnic groups, and it was geographically situated far from Japan, thus the policies of the Xinjiang government, which were formulated and implemented by the Han warlord Sheng Shicai, were the most important reason why Xinjiang was able to play such an enormously positive role in China's War of Resistance against Japan. Although Sheng Shicai stood in political opposition to the Nationalist government in Nanjing at the time, he unhesitatingly expended manpower, financial resources and materials to support the front lines in the War of Resistance.[39]

Eric Teichman, a consular officer at the British Embassy in China, offered the following opinion on Sheng Shicai's reasons for actively supporting the War of Resistance against Japan after meeting with Sheng in October 1935: "As he himself was a Manchurian . . . Sheng *Tupan* and these Manchurian troops . . . were, like all other Chinese from Manchuria, particularly incensed against Japan; a circumstance which led them to accept all the more readily the assistance proffered by the Soviet."[40] Teichman's analysis could perhaps explain the general anti-Japanese sentiments amongst the inhabitants of northeastern China, but this argument is overly simplistic when applied to Sheng Shicai.

In fact, Sheng Shicai had deep-seated connections with Japan: during his youth, he studied abroad in Japan on three occasions. On the first occasion, in 1917, Sheng reportedly studied political economics at Meiji University.[41] In 1918 and early 1919, Chinese exchange students in Japan launched a large-scale repatriation movement to protest the signing of the "Mutual Defense Agreement of the Japanese and Chinese Armies" and the acknowledgement of the transfer of former German interests in China to Japan at the Versailles Peace Conference.[42] Sheng Shicai also expressed strong anti-Japanese ideas during this movement. In 1938, Du Zhongyuan, who studied abroad with Sheng Shicai during that period and claimed that the two had "become friends at that time," offered the following description of Sheng's actions during the movement:

> His national consciousness was extremely strong, and he was rich in revolutionary spirit. During the time in Tokyo, every time a conflict arose over a problem between China and Japan, he was always a part of it. I also recall that, at the time of the Paris Peace Conference, China opposed the acknowledgement of the Twenty-One Demands; the exchange students in Tokyo held several meetings and decided to all return to China, in a show of resistance. In the middle there were some weak-willed fellow students who would rather blindly continue studying, and were unwilling to discontinue their studies halfway through. Mr. Sheng took a big cudgel in his hand to act as the enforcer. Anyone who was unwilling to return home would have to eat his cudgel.[43]

At the time, Sheng Shicai was selected as the representative for the exchange students' repatriation petition.[44] Furthermore, after returning to China, he did not immediately return to Japan, but instead enrolled at the Shaozhou Branch of the Yunnan Military Academy. According to Du

Zhongyuan, Sheng was motivated by a revelation that the transformation of China had to begin with the military. Sheng Shicai reportedly joined military service because he was keenly moved by China's circumstances at the time, with "great powers prowling across the country, seeking opportunities to attack."[45]

Sheng Shicai made his second trip to Japan after being recommended by General Guo Songling of China's Northeastern Army to study military affairs at the Army War College in Japan. Sheng's encounter with Guo Songling changed the course of his life. The works *Sheng Shicai and New Xinjiang* by Du Zhongyuan and *A Bird's-Eye View of Xinjiang* by Chen Jiying both record how Sheng Shicai gained recognition and rose in the ranks under Guo's command; Guo even personally officiated at his wedding, and later recommended him to study abroad at the Army War College in Japan.[46] Moreover, according to Zhou Dongjiao, who was Sheng Shicai's closest friend prior to his ingress into Xinjiang, Guo Songling regarded Sheng as a son due to having no children of his own, and even granted Sheng his adopted daughter's hand in marriage, and allowed the pair to travel together to study abroad in Japan.[47] In other words, the childless General Guo Songling brought Sheng into his own family as the husband of his adopted daughter, clearly revealing the high degree of recognition which he had been granted.[48]

Sheng Shicai (1897–1970).
The inscription reads:
"With Compliments to Dr. He.
Sheng Shicai,
October 17, 1934."

The May Thirtieth Movement erupted in 1925. Triggered by an incident occurring on May 30 in which Shanghai police fired on protesting civilians in the International Settlement, a wave of democratic, anti-imperialist, and patriotic movements swept across the country. Guo Songling, who was caught up in the fervor of the national patriotic movement, launched a revolt on November 25 in response to northeastern warlord Zhang Zuolin's collusion with Japan's Kwantung Army. Sheng Shicai interrupted his studies to answer Guo Songling's call to return home and join the campaign against Zhang Zuolin.[49] The revolt incited by Guo Songling ultimately failed, and

Guo himself was assassinated by Zhang Zuolin. However, there is a great deal of evidence indicating that Guo Songling's failure was due to intervention by Japan.⁵⁰ Sheng Shicai, who had regarded Guo Songling and his wife as his "parents," and who had experienced this chain of events first-hand, naturally developed a deep antipathy toward Japan following Guo's downfall and assassination.⁵¹

After the failure of the campaign against Zhang Zuolin, Sheng Shicai had no choice but to return to Japan. However, Zhang Zuolin threw up obstacles to disrupt his studies at the Army War College. According to Chen Jiying, Sheng Shicai was stripped of his student status; however, Du Zhongyuan states that Sheng retained his student status, but lost his government scholarship. Both scholars note Sheng's predicament following the "suspension of government funding, with no means to borrow money." In the end, Sheng was reportedly able to complete his studies with the economic support of Sun Chuanfang, Feng Yuxiang, and Chiang Kai-shek. The poverty Sheng suffered on this, his third trip to Japan, may have also been due to collusion between Zhang Zuolin and the Japanese. Sheng Shicai reportedly had no further contact with any Japanese individuals following his return to China. It is clear that Sheng Shicai's three trips to study abroad in Japan failed to cultivate any pro-Japanese sentiments in him: instead, against the backdrop of Sino-Japanese relations in the early modern era, these experiences served to reinforce Sheng Shicai's anti-Japanese sentiments and ideas with respect to his sense of nationalism and his political stance.⁵²

One reason why Japan was ultimately stirred to plot against Guo Songling's revolt was that the Japanese had reportedly learned of a secret agreement between Guo and the northwestern warlord General Feng Yuxiang, which revealed Guo's intentions to work against Japan.⁵³ In fact, one month before Guo Songling launched his revolt, Japan had obtained the content of a secret treaty between Feng Yuxiang and Lev Karakhan, the Deputy People's Commissar for Foreign Affairs of the Soviet Union. The key points of the treaty included: the institution of a federal system in northwestern China; acknowledgement of residency for Soviet citizens and freedom to engage in ideological propaganda in the region; cooperation between China, the Soviet Union and Mongolia to expel Japanese and British political forces from the regions of Xinjiang and Inner Mongolia; and so on.⁵⁴ Japan was naturally loath to see General Guo Songling—a fiercely anti-Japanese and pro-Soviet partisan, and an ally of Feng Yuxiang—become the "King of the Northeast."

However, General Guo Songling's trusted subordinate Sheng Shicai did become the "King of Xinjiang" seven years later.⁵⁵ Sheng also appointed Guo Songling's younger brother Guo Daming to serve a long term as the secretary-general of the Xinjiang Provincial Government.⁵⁶ Although no direct evidence of this has been discovered to date, based on the similarity of their political views, in particular the linking of "pro-Soviet" and "anti-Japanese" ideas, it is apparent that Sheng Shicai was influenced by the thinking of Guo Songling and Feng Yuxiang in formulating his policies.

The "April 12" Coup and Sheng Shicai's Crisis of Legitimacy

In reviewing the state of society and the political process in Xinjiang in the period from 1933 to 1934, it is clear that Sheng Shicai's implementation of "anti-imperialist," "pro-Soviet" policies on the Xinjiang stage was in fact related to the contemporary social conditions and political trends in Xinjiang.

A number of figures, including Chen Zhong, the head of the General Staff Department, Urumqi Mayor Tao Mingyue, and Li Xiaotian, President of the Aviation College, were behind the plot for the "April 12" coup of 1933 in Urumqi (Dihua), and the coup itself was staged by the White Russian "Naturalized Army" (*guihua jun* 歸化軍).⁵⁷ Sheng Shicai in fact had no advance knowledge of the coup,⁵⁸ and his name does not appear in the list of the 50 members of the "Provisional Preservation Committee" formed by the instigators of the coup on April 12.⁵⁹

However, following a counterattack launched on the 13th by forces under the command of Yang Zhengzhong, who stood on the side of Jin Shuren, then the provincial governor and the Xinjiang Frontier Defense Commissioner, the coup's backers suddenly found themselves in a disadvantaged position.⁶⁰ Sheng Shicai, who commanded "the strongest army in Xinjiang Province," stationed in Ulanbay, an outer suburb of Urumqi, thus became a key deciding force.⁶¹ The coup's supporters and Jin Shuren's supporters both sent delegates to win over Sheng Shicai, in the hope of gaining the backing of his troops.⁶² However, Sheng Shicai ultimately decided to commit his forces to the coup's supporters, leading to the demise of Jin Shuren's regime. At the second emergency meeting of the Provisional Preservation Committee held on April 14, Sheng Shicai, backed by a powerful army, was thus elected as the Provisional Governor-General, becoming the sovereign leader of the Urumqi regime.[63] Chen Zhong, Tao Mingyue, and the other instigators of the coup, who were not appointed to any positions of real power, were left to stew in resentment against Sheng Shicai for "reaping the rewards of others."[64]

The Nationalist Government in Nanjing did not immediately recognize Sheng Shicai's position as the Xinjiang Frontier Defense Commissioner. Several high-ranking officials began actively working to take advantage of the opportunity offered by the coup to restore the central government's direct rule over Xinjiang. On June 1, the central government dispatched Huang Musong, the Deputy Chief of Staff, to serve as "Pacification Commissioner" (*xuanwei shi* 宣慰使), leading a train of bureaucrats, party officials and experts to Urumqi. Upon his arrival, Huang Musong established the "Pacification Commissioner's Office" which made frequent contact with all elements of Xinjiang society, building a framework to take over the regime.[65] In their frustration, the anti-Sheng faction within the Urumqi regime ultimately decided to join hands with the Nationalist Party, and the Han Chinese officials in Xinjiang Province also began slowly gravitating toward the side of the Pacification Commissioner.[66]

However, several memoirs from this period show that Sheng Shicai had harbored strong political ambitions since he first arrived in Xinjiang.[67] Sheng was therefore unlikely to lightly abandon power once it came into his hands; and the Pacification Commissioner and the Xinjiang officials hovering around the periphery of these events certainly presented a threat. During this period, Sheng had led troops north of the city to counter the resistance led by the Hui warlord Ma Zhongying. He returned to Urumqi from the front lines on June 19; on the following day, he assassinated Chen Zhong, Tao Mingyue, Li Xiaotian and other figures on the spot at a meeting of the Preservation Committee, and put the Pacification Commissioner under house arrest, thus eradicating the forces opposing his regime at one stroke.[68]

Huang Musong (1883–1937)

However, consolidating his position as the sovereign leader of the Urumqi regime was not equivalent to seizing control over all of Xinjiang. The motivating factor for the April 12 coup had been the fracturing of Xinjiang society caused by the Kumul Rebellion and other independence movements. By 1933, as anti-government factions within various ethnic groups became increasingly active, the Urumqi regime had in fact already lost its authority over Xinjiang society.[69]

In southern Xinjiang, where the forces of the East Turkestan Independence Movement were concentrated, as early as January 1933, the Uyghur inhabitants had begun participating in a series of insurrections spread across Kucha, Aksu, Hotan, Kashgar and other areas; the region was no longer under the control of the Xinjiang provincial government.[70] Responding to the call of the Kumul Uyghur leader Yulbars Khan, troops under the command of the Hui warlord Ma Zhongying moved into the region of eastern Xinjiang in late January, initially to take up arms against Jin Shuren. Supported by the region's Hui inhabitants, Ma's forces also absorbed Uyghur rebel contingents from the Kumul and Turpan regions into their ranks. Ma achieved a series of victories in pursuing his plan of attack, the aim of which was to directly seize the provincial capital of Urumqi, and soon advanced into the city's outlying districts.[71] In the Altay region of northern Xinjiang, Kazakh nomads launched their own rebellion. By April, contact between Urumqi and the surrounding regions had already been severed, and the only territory over which the authorities of the Xinjiang provincial government actually retained control was Urumqi itself, along with some of its outlying districts. Rumors even circulated in Beijing that Ma Zhongying had captured Urumqi.[72]

Yulbars Khan (1889–1971)

Ma Zhongying (c. 1912–c. 1937)

These ethnic conflicts certainly were not to be pacified by a change of leadership at the provincial government's seat in Urumqi. Ma Zhongying in fact regarded the coup as an opportunity to personally seize control as the sovereign leader of Xinjiang, and therefore redoubled his efforts to capture Urumqi. However, at the Battle of Ziniquan in June 1933, the Uyghur forces led by Hoja Niyaz, a commander in Ma Zhongying's camp, suddenly withdrew due to "the extraordinary good luck of an unusual weather event," and Sheng Shicai was able to repulse the attack by Ma Zhongying's troops.[73] This victory notwithstanding, Sheng Shicai's army at the time numbered less than 6,000, while Ma Zhongying's troops numbered around 10,000.[74] In an era when conflict could often be resolved only by resorting to arms, of the internal and external challenges faced by Sheng Shicai and his regime at Urumqi, Xinjiang's ethnic unrest represented the most important and yet the most insoluble of difficulties.

To resolve these ethnic problems, it was absolutely essential for Sheng Shicai to obtain outside support. Yet despite having been formally appointed as Xinjiang Frontier Defense Commissioner by the Nationalist government of the Republic of China on August 1, Sheng did not even consider requesting aid from the Nationalists. The reason was the central government's ambivalent attitude: it looked on, apparently "unconcerned," as Sheng Shicai struggled in victory and in defeat,[75] whilst seizing every opportunity to subjugate him. The collection of the Institute of History of the Xinjiang Academy of Social Sciences contains a telegram sent by Zhang Peiyuan (Commander of the Ili Border Reclamation Garrison, both a high-ranking administrative official and Commander of the 8th Division of the Nationalist Army) to Yan Huiqing, the Chinese Ambassador to the Soviet Union, on December 16, 1933. The telegram reveals that Luo Wengan, Special Envoy of the Nationalist Government and Minister of Foreign Affairs, had come to Xinjiang to preside over the swearing-in ceremonies of Liu Wenlong (Provincial Governor of Xinjiang), Sheng Shicai, and Zhang Peiyuan; yet even on such an occasion, Luo was pursuing plans for an alliance with Ma Zhongying and Zhang Peiyuan to overthrow Sheng Shicai.[76] Given these circumstances, it is no exaggeration to say that Sheng Shicai's only option for resolving Xinjiang's ethnic problems and maintaining his own rule was to seek the support of Xinjiang's neighbor, the Soviet Union.

Adoption of an "Anti-Japanese," "Pro-Soviet" Agenda and Pacification of Xinjiang's Ethnic Unrest

The immediate reason why Sheng Shicai, who had long subscribed to anti-Japanese ideas, ultimately decided to adopt a pro-Soviet agenda was likely his own vulnerability. From the perspective of the contemporary international situation, the combination of an anti-Japanese, pro-Soviet platform was also a historical inevitability. Sheng Shicai himself stressed that, "To rejuvenate the Chinese people, we must first topple imperialism, particularly Japanese imperialism. To topple Japanese imperialism, as the Premier [Sun Yat-sen] said, we must unite the world to treat our people equally, and fight alongside us. When we ask who in the world has truly treated our people equally, aside from the Soviet Union, who is there?"[77] The above passage demonstrates the link between Sheng Shicai's anti-Japanese and pro-Soviet agendas, as well as the rationale behind his adoption of such policies.

However, it should be noted that Sheng Shicai's motivations in adopting a pro-Soviet agenda in Xinjiang were not solely to defend the interests of the Chinese people. Sheng himself stated that, in formulating the "Six-Point Policy," his thinking graduated from "ethnic equality," to "anti-imperialism," to "pro-Sovietism." Sheng also once said to Chen Jibao, "If the imperialist powers someday enter Xinjiang, there is a danger that Xinjiang's ethnic groups will become divided and alienated; and if the region of Xinjiang someday becomes unstable, there is a possibility that the territories of Xinjiang will be carved up."[78] The above passages show that, from the outset, Sheng Shicai's slogan of "anti-imperialism" was directed toward the resolution of Xinjiang's ethnic problems.

Huang Fensheng, the author of *A Study of Border Politics and Religion* (1946), theorized that "anti-imperialism" and "pro-Sovietism" meant borrowing the strength of the Soviet Union to repel the Japanese and British forces.[79] It should be noted that, under the policies formulated by Sheng Shicai, anti-government factions among Xinjiang's Islamic ethnic groups were also regarded as "imperialist forces." "Certain imperialists agitate for the independence of southern Xinjiang, and Japanese imperialists undertake to aid the turbaned Muslims,[80] to establish a Muslim state. If we do not give them a sharp warning and strike a cutting blow against them, putting each of the ethnic groups throughout the borderland on the alert, then all government decrees will be impacted."[81] In other words, the nascent Islamic Republic of East Turkestan was already regarded as the puppet of "certain imperialists," while the Muslim leader Ma Zhongying was regarded as the "running dog" of the Japanese imperialists. Sheng's descriptions of anti-government factions among the Turkic Islamic peoples of Xinjiang as the "running dogs" and "puppets" of the Japanese and other imperialist forces allowed him to openly enlist the aid of the Soviet Union in suppressing the opposing ethnic groups. In other words, Sheng Shicai's anti-Japanese and pro-Soviet political agenda largely grew out of his need to address the ethnic unrest in Xinjiang.

However, from a policy perspective, Sheng Shicai's pursuit of an "anti-Japanese" and "Pro-Soviet" agenda was undoubtedly his best option. His anti-Japanese position comported with the patriotic fervor of the Chinese people in that era, and made a favorable impression on Soviet Russia, which had been locked in a struggle against the expansion of Japanese forces since the early modern era; his pro-Soviet position suited China's need to resist the expansion of Japanese imperialist forces, while also conforming to international trends since the 1930s. Of course, for Sheng Shicai, the most important consequence of expressing anti-Japanese and pro-Soviet slogans was obtaining aid from the Soviet Union, and drawing on said aid to impressively crush the ethnic resistance, thus cementing and preserving his newly gained position as the ruler of Xinjiang.

Sheng Shicai's "anti-Japanese" and "pro-Soviet" policies soon yielded results. In December 1933, Ma Zhongying's forces advanced on Urumqi from the direction of Turpan in the southeast, as Zhang Peiyuan's forces approached from the direction of Ili in the northwest. However, before Zhang's vanguard reached Urumqi, Soviet cavalry swept into the Ili region, isolating Zhang's forces from their base of operations; Zhang Peiyuan himself was forced to commit suicide.[82] In the meantime, Ma Zhongying's troops had encircled Urumqi: on January 15, they were met at Toutunhe in the western suburbs of Urumqi by troops led by "General Zhao," belonging to the self-professed "Altay Naturalized Army" and "Tarbagatay Naturalized Army."[83] After an intense series of clashes, Ma Zhongying's forces were ultimately defeated on February 10 in a decisive battle against an army equipped with fighter planes, tanks, armored cars and artillery; Ma was forced to withdraw from Urumqi and retreat to southern Xinjiang.[84]

In his *Memoir of a Decade in Xinjiang*, Sheng Shicai claims that the Soviet consul general informed him about the "naturalized armies" only after their arrival in Urumqi, and that the armies were composed of former Soviet troops.[85] However, this is an obvious lie. Burhan Shahidi, who then served as the Altay Pacification Commissioner under Sheng Shicai's regime, confirmed in his own memoirs, *Fifty Years in Xinjiang*, that Sheng Shicai instructed him to meet a detachment of ten to twenty thousand soldiers from the Soviet Red Army at the Sino-Soviet border near Tarbagatay, provide them with Chinese uniforms, and then guide them to Urumqi, under the nominal command of Zhao Deshou, the senior administrator of the Tarbagatay District.[86] It is clear that the Soviet Army dispatched troops to Xinjiang to provide aid to Sheng Shicai, at Sheng's behest.

The Uyghur leader Hoja Niyaz also reached a compromise with Sheng Shicai through the mediation of the Soviet Army, and withdrew to southern Xinjiang after being granted the title of "Garrison Commander" (*jingbei siling* 警備司令) for the region.[87] Although Hoja Niyaz had been appointed as president of the Islamic Republic of East Turkestan, under pressure from the Soviet Union, he dared not accept the post: soon after returning to southern Xinjiang, he arrested Prime Minister Sabit Damulla, the "father of the Islamic Republic of East Turkestan," and sent him to Urumqi under escort to be handed over to Sheng Shicai.[88] As for the Uyghur leader Yulbars Khan, who also came to terms with Sheng Shicai and withdrew to the Kumul region, under advisement from the Soviet Union, Sheng appointed him as Garrison Commander of Hami (Kumul) District.[89]

Hoja Niyaz (1889–1938)

Photograph of Ma Zhongying on horseback

In April 1934, Ma Zhongying retreated to the regions of Kashgar and Hotan under pursuit by the Soviet Army, and took control of the area after sweeping away the surviving forces of the Islamic Republic of East Turkestan. Ma Zhongying thereafter reached an agreement with Sheng Shicai through the mediation of the Soviet consul in Kashgar, under which Sheng agreed that Ma's troops could be stationed in the Hotan and Shache (formerly Yarkent) regions.[90] Ma Zhongying later enrolled at a Soviet military academy and was refused permission to return to China, living out his remaining years in the Soviet Union.[91]

During this same period, Burhan Shahidi succeeding in persuading the Kazakh rebel forces of northern Xinjiang to cooperate with the new government, under the rallying cry of "pro-Sovietism" and "anti-imperialism."[92] The Kazakhs were subsequently granted arms and support by the Soviet Union, and with the cooperation of the Soviet Red Army, they annihilated those remnants of Ma Zhongying's forces still active in the Kazakh region of northern Xinjiang under the command of Ma Heying.[93]

Sven Hedin, who personally witnessed the flight of Ma's forces, offered the following description of their defeat: "It was the Russians who defeated the Tungans, not Sheng Shih-tsai. Without Russian help the war between the Chinese and Tungans would have taken quite a different course."[94] Sheng Shicai himself admitted that the initial establishment of his rule and the resolution of Xinjiang's ethnic unrest were derived wholly from the aid of the Soviet Union. In 1935, Sheng stated to Eric Teichman during his visit to Xinjiang that, "He owed nothing to Nanking, but much to Moscow, for the assistance which had enabled him to triumph over Ma Chung-ying."[95] Of course, while Teichman was ostensibly traveling through Xinjiang to return to England via the overland route, the real reason for his visit was the British government's fear that the advent and development of Soviet Russian influence would turn Xinjiang into a "second Manchukuo." The British government's apprehensions coincided with the views of the Nationalist government. Although Sheng Shicai attempted to block Teichman's visit with a series of excuses, such as ongoing brigandage and an outbreak of bubonic plague in southern Kashgar, he ultimately embarked on the journey with the strong support of the Nationalist government.[96]

Summary

Japan first began taking notice of Xinjiang in the later Meiji period. After the turn of the 20th century, Japan began maintaining a watch on the expansion of Russian influence in Xinjiang to defend its interests in the regions of "Mongolia and Manchuria." At the start of the Shōwa period, these considerations also led Japan to attempt to draw Xinjiang into its own sphere of influence, though it initially did not have a clear or specific plan for doing so. It should be noted that, regardless of the era, Japan's focus on the Central Asian region of Xinjiang, situated in the interior of the Asian continent, was informed by the contemporary relationship between China and Japan, and particularly by the antagonistic relationship between Japan and Russia, and later between Japan and the Soviet Union, regarding their conflicting interests in China. The events of the 1930s, as Japan perpetrated the Mukden Incident of September 18, 1931, and began accelerating its aggressions against China, brought home to China the legitimacy and necessity of strengthening its administration of its ethnic borderlands.

Sheng Shicai developed fierce anti-Japanese ideas due to his experiences in Japan during his youth. However, his most important objective in adopting an anti-Japanese, pro-Soviet political agenda was to resolve Xinjiang's ethnic problems, which presented the greatest threat to his regime. As the newly minted ruler of Xinjiang, Sheng Shicai's enactment of an anti-Japanese, pro-Soviet policy represented his best option for defending his interests. This policy allowed Sheng Shicai to obtain direct military aid from the Soviet Union to suppress the ethnic conflicts in Xinjiang, thus enabling him to consolidate his political power and status. Yet these choices foreshadowed the political unrest and social upheaval that Xinjiang was soon to face.

Chapter 4

The Dual Power Structure and Ethnic Problems
The Political Agenda and Ethnic Policies under Sheng Shicai's Regime

Sheng Shicai's reign over Xinjiang (April 1933–August 1944) coincided with the decline of the First East Turkestan Independence Movement (March 1931–April 1934) and the rise of the Second East Turkestan Independence Movement (August 1944–June 1946). Based on this timeframe, it would appear that the factors giving rise to large-scale ethnic antagonism and ethnic conflict in Xinjiang were gradually eliminated during the early period of Sheng's regime; however, the later stages of his regime planted the seeds for a new round of ethnic conflict in the 1940s.

As described in Chapter 3 of this book, ethnic conflict and ethnic antagonism were the most problematic issues encountered by Sheng Shicai as he sought to establish his rule over Xinjiang. Sheng was only able to resolve these problems by proposing "anti-Japanese," "pro-Soviet" slogans to elicit the Soviet Union's trust and support. Sheng Shicai therefore must have known that, in order to preserve his rule over Xinjiang, it would be necessary to forestall the rise of further ethnic conflict, while mitigating antagonism between ethnic groups. So why did Sheng Shicai ultimately lead Xinjiang society into another round of large-scale ethnic antagonism and conflict? This chapter explores the political scene during Sheng Shicai's regime, analyzes the impact of various political, social and diplomatic developments on Sheng's political actions and policy decisions, and examines how and why Sheng Shicai's regime compounded the ethnic problems in Xinjiang, to reveal the factors leading to the rise of the Second East Turkestan Independence Movement.

4.1 Soviet Support and the Establishment of Sheng Shicai's System of Governance

The Establishment of Political, Military and Economic Systems

In September 1933, Sheng Shicai placed Liu Wenlong, who had been appointed as provincial governor by the Chinese Nationalist government, under house arrest for "attempting to subvert the Xinjiang Provincial Government," and installed a hand-picked successor, thus establishing his own political dictatorship within the Xinjiang regime.[1] On April 12, 1934, Sheng Shicai convened the "First Xinjiang People's Congress," at which he unveiled his "Eight-Point Declaration." The content included: (1) Achieving ethnic equality; (2) Guaranteeing freedom of religion; (3) Implementing agricultural relief; (4) Reorganizing the financial administration; (5) Implementing clean and honest governance; (6) Expanding and improving education; (7) Implementing autonomous governance; and (8) Reforming the judicial system.

The content of the declaration reveals that, from the outset, Sheng Shicai's regime faced an array of challenges, from resolving ethnic, economic and fiscal problems, to reorganizing Xinjiang's political system. Given the circumstances in that era, in order to resolve these difficulties, it would be necessary for Sheng Shicai to install an improved military system, establish effective political institutions, rebuild Xinjiang's economic and fiscal systems, and eliminate antagonism between ethnic groups. Sheng arguably achieved each of the above objectives by drawing on the aid of the Soviet Union, in the name of resisting Japan.

The first task was to improve the military system. In 1935, Sheng Shicai renamed Xinjiang's Provincial Army (*shengjun* 省軍) as the "Anti-Imperialist Army" (*fandi jun* 反帝軍), characterizing the Anti-Imperialist Army as "forces opposing imperialism and opposing Japan," "forces supporting the Soviet Union," "forces supporting the Six-Point Policy," and "forces defending Xinjiang as the territory of China." The Anti-Imperialist Army was outfitted entirely with Soviet equipment, trained by Soviet advisors, and provided with an ideological education by representatives of Communist International.[2]

Sheng's "political institutions" were similarly modeled after the Soviet Union's political police.[3] These institutions were established in the name of guarding against Japanese spies, but in reality they had two main functions. The first was to eliminate political enemies within Xinjiang: this function was chiefly performed by a secret police organ known as the Administration for Political Supervision (*Zhengzhi jiancha zong guanli ju* 政治監察總管理局). The second function was to gather intelligence outside Xinjiang: this work was primarily performed by a secret intelligence organization known as the Border Affairs Office (*Bianwu chu* 邊務處). As will be discussed below, the Administration for Political Supervision and the Border Affairs Office were both established in 1936, at the Soviet Union's suggestion and with its assistance.

Xinjiang's civil war had exacerbated the shortage of material goods and accelerated the rise of commodity prices, leading to a severe economic collapse. The issuance of paper currency was arguably Sheng Shicai's only means of preserving the province's financial administration upon first gaining power.[4]

There were two main facets to the reconstruction of Xinjiang's economic system under Sheng Shicai's rule. First, the reconstruction plan was formulated by economic experts from the Soviet Union.[5] "A commission headed by Stalin's brother-in-law, Svanidze, was sent to Sinkiang to draw up a plan of reconstruction for the province."[6] Secondly, the regime was granted a massive amount of economic aid by the Soviet Union. Sheng Shicai had applied to the Nationalist government for economic aid as well, but his request was denied. Between May 1935 and October 1936, the Soviet Union provided two loans to Sheng Shicai's cash-strapped regime, for 5 million and 2 million gold rubles (at the time, 1 gold ruble was equal to 4.38 rubles), and granted permission for Xinjiang to provide agricultural and livestock products as repayment for the loans.[7] With the approval of the Soviet Union, Sheng Shicai also founded the "Abundant Xinjiang Native Products Company" (*Yu Xin tutechan gongsi* 裕新土特產公司) in the winter of 1934, which gradually established a monopoly over trade between Xinjiang and the Soviet Union, guaranteeing a rich source of revenue.[8]

Sheng Shicai was able to maintain Xinjiang's political independence from the central government by relying on military, political, and economic aid from the Soviet Union. The Xinjiang Provincial Government instituted an entry-exit visa system in the winter of 1934,[9] banning the entry of transport vehicles operated by the Chinese Xinsui Company, which handled trade between Xinjiang and China's interior provinces, into the region west of Kumul (Hami).[10] Although this policy was portrayed as a countermeasure for preventing the entry of Japanese spies into Xinjiang, "the home front for resistance against Japan,"[11] during the same year, Sheng Shicai also shut down the Xinjiang Province Committee of the Nationalist Party; forced the resignation of the heads of the Xinjiang Provincial Department of Civil Affairs and the Department of Works, who had been appointed by the Nationalist government;[12] and even released flyers vehemently condemning the Nationalist government's plans to build roads and railways to Xinjiang, depicting such ideas as plots to allow "the Japanese imperialists . . . to invade Sinkiang." Based on these actions, there is no doubt that Sheng Shicai's true objective, with the backing of the Soviet Union, was to drive out the forces of the central government and establish "complete autonomy" for himself in Xinjiang.[13]

"Ethnic Equality" and Mobilization for War

The large-scale ethnic conflict that had raged across Xinjiang was finally pacified in August 1934, when Sheng Shicai and Ma Zhongying reached a cease-fire agreement. However, after many years of war, real power was largely concentrated in the hands of Muslim ethnic leaders in many regions of Xinjiang. Although the First East Turkestan Independence Movement had failed, the movement's ideals of ethnic independence and the establishment of a nation-state had not been completely eradicated within Xinjiang's ethnic communities of Turkic Muslims. The Kashgar region, the birthplace of the East Turkestan Movement, experienced a resurgent trend for the founding of Jadidist schools, under the leadership of local luminaries. These activities in fact represented a form of introspection into the national character after the failure of the East Turkestan Independence Movement.[14]

The ubiquitous nationalist trends undoubtedly impeded Sheng Shicai's efforts to politically unify Xinjiang society. However, Sheng was unable to directly suppress these nationalist tendencies, for two reasons: (1) The ethnic Muslim leaders of this era leaned more toward the examples of Yunus (a leader of the national movement, known in Chinese as Yu Wenbin) and Abudulla Damolla (an *akhund*) of Kashgar, or Turdi Ahun (an industrial leader) of Ili, who had earned the trust of the local people, rather than the example of the Uyghur leaders Hoja Niyaz and Mahmut Muhiti of southern Xinjiang, Yulbars Khan of the Kumul region, or the Kazakh Sharif Khan of Altay, who commanded their own forces; (2) In pursuit of their own personal objectives, each of these ethnic leaders had already established or were endeavoring to establish a special relationship with the Soviet Union.[15] Because he was reliant on the Soviet Union's support to preserve his rule, Sheng Shicai was hesitant to contravene the Soviet Union's wishes by suppressing the ethnic leaders. At the same time, without the Soviet Union's military aid, Sheng Shicai would have been unable to subdue the expanding ethnic forces relying solely on his own military forces.

Faced with these circumstances, Sheng Shicai instead adopted a policy of amnesty and recruitment. He acknowledged the authority of the local ethnic leaders by appointing them as officials in the Xinjiang Provincial Government, thus absorbing them into the system and regaining local control. In the latter half of 1934, Sheng Shicai successively installed Hoja Niyaz as the Deputy Governor of the Xinjiang Provincial Government, Mahmut Muhiti as the Commander of the 6th Division of the Xinjiang Provincial Army, Yunus as the head of the Department of Agriculture and Mining, Sharif Khan as the senior administrator of the Altay Administrative Region, and Yulbars Khan as the Commander of the Kumul (Hami) Garrison. A number of ethnic leaders were also appointed to positions as deputy directors to various departments of the provincial government, public security chiefs for administrative regions, county magistrates, and so on.[16]

During this era, Chinese intellectuals concerned about the Xinjiang problem universally believed that, unless Sheng Shicai expended enormous efforts in the political sphere, it would be impossible to eliminate the danger of the reemergence of ethnic conflict between the Han Chinese and Islamic ethnic groups in Xinjiang society.[17] The policy of offering amnesty and recruitment to insuppressible hostile forces was a political tradition that had failed countless times over the many generations of Chinese history. Given his available forces and the circumstances in Xinjiang at the time, Sheng Shicai was unable to deviate from this "benevolent path." The difference was that, in recruiting the ethnic Muslim leaders, Sheng depicted this political stratagem as an effort to "achieve ethnic equality."

Sheng Shicai's advocacy of "ethnic equality" was supplied with a theoretical basis, systematized, and concretized with the aid of Communist International. In June 1935, Communist International sent another dozen members of Chinese nationality to aid Sheng Shicai in stabilizing his regime.[18] By this time, Communist International had already dispatched 25 of its members, all of whom held important posts in Xinjiang's political circles, the press, and education circles.[19] It should be particularly noted that these Comintern members simultaneously held key positions in the "Xinjiang People's Anti-Imperialist Federation" (abbreviated below as the "Anti-Imperialist Federation"). Sheng Shicai used this federation to mobilize and organize the populace.

The Anti-Imperialist Federation was founded in July 1934, and its members were initially all high-ranking officials in the provincial government. According to the memoirs of He Yuzhu, the first committee chairman of the Anti-Imperialist Federation, the federation's establishment and the compiling of its first members list proceeded in accordance with the instructions of Garegin Apresov, the Soviet Consul General in Urumqi (Dihua). To receive these instructions, He Yuzhu and the secretary-general of the Anti-Imperialist Federation were required to make weekly visits to the Soviet consulate in Urumqi.[20] The Anti-Imperialist Federation underwent its first reorganization in December 1935 once Communist International personnel arrived in Xinjiang, shifting from a committee system to a board of directors. Sheng Shicai personally served as the president of the federation, and chapter associations were established within provincial departments and offices, community organizations, military divisions, and local communities. The nature of the federation's work shifted toward ideological education within the given region or department, and the membership requirements became more stringent; some criteria were even analogous to those of a governing party.[21] The federation's secretary-general, the head of its Organization Department, and other figures of Chinese nationality sent to Xinjiang by Communist International were in fact responsible for the operations of the reorganized Anti-Imperialist Federation.

Unlike the many Soviet advisors who were directly appointed to various positions in the Xinjiang Provincial Government, the Chinese-born members of Communist International were more likely to be assigned to the Anti-Imperialist Federation. The intent was to emphasize the federation's nature as a Chinese organization. Targeting Xinjiang society, which, "like scattered sand, lacked a national spirit of unity,"[22] the Anti-Imperialist Federation proposed a series of slogans to "mobilize, spread propaganda, and educate the masses." "Xinjiang's fourteen ethnic groups, with a population of four million, shall unite with China's population of four hundred million to overthrow Japanese imperialism and achieve freedom and liberation for the Chinese people"; "In developing the northwest, reclaiming the northeast, opposing imperialism, and opposing fascism, we are primarily opposing Japanese imperialism."[23] Based on the activities of the Anti-Imperialist Federation, Sheng Shicai's aim was to bring about the following scenario: politically, he would rely on the support of the Soviet Union to escape the control of China's central government, and maintain political independence; from a social perspective, the efforts of the Anti-Imperialist Federation would instill a sense of Chinese nationalism in Xinjiang's various ethnic groups, including the Islamic peoples, thus developing Xinjiang's capacity for social mobilization.

Of the 25 members of Communist International sent to Xinjiang, the most important figure was Wang Shoucheng, who served as the secretary-general of the "Anti-Imperialist Federation." His greatest contribution to Sheng Shicai's Urumqi regime was the construction of a theoretical framework for Sheng's concept of "ethnic equality."[24]

Wang Shoucheng completed his cultural education plan, which was "shaped by ethnic culture, and based on the Six-Point Policy," for Sheng Shicai's regime in 1935.[25] Sheng's government sought to introduce unified cultural education for all ethnic groups in Xinjiang in order to seize control over the increasingly dynamic education system offered by ethnic communities, while increasing Chinese nationalist content within minority education. Sheng Shicai's tireless advocacy for "education with the aim of strengthening traditional ethnic culture" in fact resulted in a period of expansive development for minority schools between 1935 and 1938.[26]

Wang Shoucheng (an alias used by Yu Xiusong, 1899–1938)

At the "Xinjiang-Mongolia People's Representative Congress" in April 1937, Wang Shoucheng presented a "Report on the New Government's Ethnic Policies," which established a theoretical foundation for Sheng Shicai's ethnic politics, and created a more systematic and concrete ethnic policy program for Sheng's regime. Wang Shoucheng noted in his report that the key content of Sheng Shicai's ethnic policies included equal status for all ethnic groups, improvement of the economic situation and living conditions for all ethnic groups, development of traditional ethnic culture, respect for freedom of religion, and guarantees for the traditional status and privileges of the aristocratic elite, ethnic leaders, religious figures, lamas and monks. Wang went a step further in interpreting "ethnic equality" more specifically as both "political equality" (allowing and encouraging people of minority background to enter the political sphere) and "cultural equality" (allowing and encouraging ethnic education).[27]

Until the 1980s, Wang Shoucheng's report continued to be regarded as "good teaching materials for promoting the Marxist view on ethnic groups,"[28] and Wang himself was remembered as the "first [person] to systematically disseminate Marxist ethnic policy in Xinjiang." But in reality, his report was designed to propagandize Marxism. The report used a variety of data points, such as the proportion of people of minority background involved in politics or the development of school education, to highlight the concern that Sheng Shicai's regime showed for the local ethnic population, and praised the regime's achievements, stating that, apart from the Soviet Union, "only the post–'April Revolution' Xinjiang has implemented correct ethnic policies." In other words, the primary purpose of the report was to persuade Xinjiang inhabitants of ethnicities other than Han Chinese to accept the ethnic policies of Sheng Shicai's regime, and acknowledge Sheng's achievements with respect to ethnic liberation.

These policies, which recognized the political rights and cultural autonomy of local ethnic groups, undeniably represented the polar opposite of the oppressive and obscurantist policies visited upon minority ethnic groups under the regimes which preceded Sheng Shicai. However, it should be noted that "ethnic equality" was neither unconditional nor absolute during Sheng's rule: for instance, the people of minority background who entered politics were largely relegated to deputy positions; and in the spring of 1936, Sheng Shicai installed education bureaus in Kashgar, Aksu, Ili, Tarbagatay,

Altay and other minority regions to oversee ethnic education. Of the exchange students sent to the Soviet Union, 40% were Han Chinese, though the latter represented less than 10% of the total population. These and many other phenomena reveal the limitations of the ethnic policies instituted during Sheng Shicai's era.[29]

4.2 The Formation of a Dual Power Structure in Xinjiang Province

The Motivations behind the Soviet Union's Selection of Sheng Shicai

Many people from this era or people involved in these events have revealed in their memoirs that, before the Soviet Union decided to support Sheng Shicai, it was in contact with a number of different political factions in Xinjiang.

According to the Kumulik Uyghur leader Yulbars Khan, during the Kumul Rebellion of 1931, Soviet functionaries approached him in the hope of persuading him to accept Soviet backing.[30]

Hoja Niyaz, another Kumulik Uyghur leader who stood in opposition to Yulbars Khan, was similarly subject to the blandishments of the Soviet Union. Rumors were widely circulated that at least part of Hoja Niyaz's store of arms and ammunition was provided by the Soviet Union.[31]

In 1934, the Soviet Union also sent functionaries to treat with the Kyrgyz leader Osmanhal, another enemy of Hoja Niyaz, promising him that, "As long as you cooperate with us, we will recognize your status and grant you aid."[32]

Records also show that, in 1934, the Islamic Republic of East Turkestan sent a delegation to the Soviet Union to seek support; the delegation received a warm welcome in Tashkent.[33]

According to the memoirs of Li Huiying, the sister-in-law of Sheng Shicai's political opponent and former commander of the Ili Border Reclamation Garrison, Zhang Peiyuan, the Soviet Union also expressed its willingness to support Zhang Peiyuan in communications with him in 1934, but Zhang rejected these overtures.[34]

In sum, prior to its ultimate decision in November 1933 to support Sheng Shicai, and even after this support was extended, the Soviet Union continued to approach Xinjiang's various political factions to explore the possibility of aid and cooperation. These actions have important contextual significance in understanding the Soviet Union's policies on Xinjiang. From this perspective, the Soviet Union's involvement in Xinjiang was based not on ideology, but rather on national interests. It therefore sought to infiltrate Xinjiang through two channels simultaneously, cultivating a pro-Soviet political system by aiding the Han Chinese ruler of Xinjiang, while also fostering pro-Soviet social factions by offering encouragement and support to local ethnic movements, to facilitate Xinjiang's complete absorption into its sphere of influence.

So why did the Soviet Union ultimately abandon the local Islamic leaders and decide to support the Han Chinese ruler Sheng Shicai in 1930s Xinjiang? There are generally believed to be two reasons: first, Sheng Shicai stated to the Soviet consul-general in Urumqi (Dihua) in May 1933 that he was a Communist; and second, Sheng Shicai was a legitimate ruler selected by the Xinjiang regime, and appointed as the ranking leader of Xinjiang by the Chinese Nationalist government in July 1933.[35]

It is true that Sheng Shicai expressed his Communist leanings to the Soviet consul-general in Urumqi in May 1933, not long after he became the interim governor-general, while exploring the possibility of obtaining Soviet support. However, the newly appointed consul-general did not actually open negotiations with Sheng Shicai until November, after he was formally appointed as the "Xinjiang Frontier Defense Commissioner" by the Chinese Nationalist government in July.[36] In other words, the first presumed reason, i.e. Sheng Shicai's declared espousal of Communism, was not in fact part of the Soviet Union's criteria in deciding whom to support; rather, the most significant factor in the Soviet Union's ultimate decision to support Sheng Shicai was the Nationalist government's legitimization of Sheng's rule over Xinjiang.

It is likely that the Soviet Union's criteria in this decision were tied to the international situation in the Far East during this era. Japan invaded Rehe in February 1933, withdrew from the League of Nations in March, signed the Tanggu Truce in May and, through its military actions, had clearly signaled its intentions to expand from Manchuria into the Chinese interior and Mongolia. Japan was thus in the process of becoming the greatest threat to the Soviet Union in Asia. "During this era in the Far

East, the Soviet Union's greatest concern was to buy time through the Chinese people's movement to resist Japan."[37] At this point, the Soviet Union was naturally aware that supporting the minority ethnic residents of China's border regions in establishing an independent Islamic state in Xinjiang would give rise to anti-Soviet sentiment within the Nationalist government, which was gradually shifting toward resistance against Japan, while also threatening the cooperative relationship between the Soviet Union, Britain and the United States.

Many Chinese and international scholars believe that the objective behind the Soviet Union's actions in Xinjiang in the 1930s was not to "establish a Soviet Xinjiang in the manner of a second Republic of Outer Mongolia,"[38] but rather to "adopt a method similar to the approach used in Outer Mongolia—gradual transformation into an ally, to turn Xinjiang into a republic of the Soviet Union."[39] Sheng Shicai himself maintained in the 1950s that the Soviet Union's purpose in extending feelers into Xinjiang was to transform the region into a Soviet satellite state.[40] However, even Sheng Shicai was unable to offer conclusive evidence for his claim that the Soviet Union's policy during his rule was to separate Xinjiang from China.

According to Communist Party member Wen Feiran, who worked alongside Communist International personnel in Sheng Shicai's Urumqi regime, Stalin personally gave instructions to Wang Shoucheng and the other personnel prior to their entry into Xinjiang: "Think of Xinjiang as being supported by the Third International; it is a third political force falling under China. It is not part of the Nationalist Party, yet it is also separate from the Communist Party."[41] If this statement is true, it could confirm that Stalin's plan was to absorb Xinjiang into the Soviet sphere of influence by supporting Sheng Shicai's regime, but not to separate Xinjiang from the Chinese territories. The fact that Sheng Shicai defined the primary aim of the Anti-Imperialist Federation as "establish[ing] Xinjiang as a permanent territory of China,"[42] and at one point dared to openly deny the rumors published in Tianjin's *Dagong Daily* regarding Xinjiang's accession to the Soviet Union[43] only serves as circumstantial evidence regarding the nature of the Soviet Union's policies on Xinjiang in that era.

According to a theory by Ishikawa Tadao, the primary aims of the Soviet Union's policies on Xinjiang were to shore up security and pursue economic interests. "Regarding the former, there is no doubt that Xinjiang was treated as the front line of the Soviet Union's defenses in central Asia; regarding the latter, the development of Xinjiang's abundant underground resources would aid in the Soviet Union's economic construction."[44] Kasahara Masaaki also pointed out that, during the 1930s, the Soviet Union's specific motivations with respect to Xinjiang were to gain access to the region's agriculture, livestock and mineral resources, resolve the problem of the White Russians who fled to Xinjiang, influence the Islamic ethnic groups of West Turkestan within Soviet territories, and ensure its strategic position with respect to Japan, Britain and China.[45]

In sum, the objective of the Soviet Union's policies on Xinjiang during this era was to find a biddable faction to support that could maximally reflect its interests in the region, allowing it to draw Xinjiang into the Soviet sphere of influence. In pursuit of this objective, faced with a choice between the independence movement of Xinjiang's minority ethnic residents and the Han Chinese ruler appointed by the Nationalist government, the Soviet Union chose the latter.

A Separate Decision-Making System Operating on Direct Soviet Influence

The support of the Soviet Union was an important factor allowing Sheng Shicai to gradually establish control over Xinjiang society. However, given this context, it was natural that Soviet influence would soon deeply permeate every department and office of Sheng Shicai's regime.

Alexander Barmine, who was appointed as the Soviet Union's liaison to Xinjiang in 1934 and later fled to the United States, offered the following evidence of the extent to which Soviet influence had pervaded Xinjiang: "We had to equip 10,000 Sinkiang troops completely, from boots to Kuomintang insignia. Soviet advisors, who actually exercised the authority of ministers, were placed at the governor's elbow. My trust . . . was instructed to send engineers to build roads, airdromes and hangars all over Sinkiang. Sinkiang was soon a Soviet colony in all but name."[46]

Soviet advisors were assigned to every department of the Xinjiang Provincial Government. As witnessed by Eric Teichman, real power in each department was concentrated in the hands of the Soviet advisors.[47] For instance, decision-making powers at Xinjiang's newly created fiscal office, the Xinjiang Finance Commission, were monopolized by the Soviet advisors, and all proposals and budget expenditures had to be validated with an advisor's signature.[48] Sven Hedin also described the military advisor General Malikoff as "Sheng Tupan's right-hand man in military matters and a very powerful personage."[49]

Although it cannot be argued that these advisors outranked Sheng Shicai, the Soviet consul-general in Urumqi, who simultaneously served as the representative of Communist International as well as Sheng's chief advisor, did have the power to give orders to Sheng Shicai.[50] While Sheng Shicai was drafting his "Lectures on the Six-Point Policy" in 1936, the consul-general reportedly sent each chapter to Stalin for review as soon as it was completed.[51] The Communist International personnel who were sent to Xinjiang to serve in Sheng Shicai's Urumqi regime also received instructions from the consulate.[52] Xinjiang had in fact already developed a separate decision-making system operating on direct Soviet influence, to the exclusion of Sheng Shicai.

Among the departments under Soviet control, the most important were the Anti-Imperialist Federation and Xinjiang's secret police and intelligence organizations. As mentioned above, the Anti-Imperialist Federation was a system for political mobilization targeting Xinjiang's various ethnic groups, while serving in effect as a ruling party. The secret police and intelligence organizations included the Administration for Political Supervision of the Provincial Government, which was responsible for eliminating domestic political enemies, and the Border Affairs Office of the Xinjiang Frontier Defense Commissioner, which was responsible for gathering foreign intelligence; these organizations became important props sustaining Sheng Shicai's regime.

In each government department, Soviet functionaries served as advisors only. However, the secret police and intelligence organizations were directly controlled by representatives of the Soviet Union. The Administration for Political Supervision was renamed as the Provincial Security Office in October 1934, and later reorganized as the

Soviet Consulate in Urumqi (Dihua)

Provincial Public Security Administration in May 1936. As to its nature, Burhan Shahidi, who was then serving as the Deputy Director of the Population Department of the Anti-Imperialist Federation, offered the following description: "The Public Security Administration, along with its predecessor, the Administration for Political Supervision, was not in fact a spy organization for Sheng Shicai, but rather a political surveillance organization controlled by the Soviet Union. Sheng Shicai engaged in a secret struggle with the Soviet Union for many years to gain control over it."[53]

During the 1930s, the Japanese also decried the establishment of the Administration for Political Supervision of the Xinjiang Provincial Government as a "first move" by the Soviet Union to exert political control over Xinjiang.[54] The secret police organization was originally founded at the proposal of the Soviet Union, and was quickly commandeered by Zhang Yiwu, Wang Lixiang and other Soviet-trained Chinese members of Communist International, as well as Soviet personnel (Table 4.1).[55] After

Table 4.1 Evolution of the Xinjiang Provincial Police Organization under Sheng Shicai

Police Bureau of the Office of the Xinjiang Frontier Defense Commissioner: Established in June 1934 by Sheng Shicai at the suggestion of his Soviet advisors. Bureau Chief: Wang Yushu, Deputy Chief: Li Tingfu
Administration for Political Supervision of the Xinjiang Provincial Government: Reorganized in August 1934. Director: Sheng Shicai (concurrent), Proxy Director: Zhang Yiwu (Comintern member) Deputy Director: Alexander Barmine (a Soviet advisor, who returned to the Soviet Union in late 1934) Secretary-General: Wang Lixiang (a Chinese Comintern member, who returned to China in January 1935 at Sheng Shicai's invitation) Departments (8 in total): The Director of the General Affairs Department (Department 1), Deputy Director of the Political Department (Department 2), Deputy Director of the Military Affairs Department (Department 3), Deputy Director of the Ethnic Affairs Department (Department 4), and the Deputy Director of the Foreign Affairs Department (Department 5) were all Communist International personnel.
Xinjiang Provincial Security Office: Renamed in October 1934 with no changes to staff; branch offices were established in Kumul (Hami), Turpan, Ili, Tarbagatay, Kashgar, Aksu, Kucha and other minority regions, and intelligence agents were planted in local communities, schools, and army divisions.

the administration was established, a number of Communist International personnel of Chinese nationality or of Turkic ethnicity from Soviet Central Asia were also sent to Xinjiang. Together with the Soviet personnel, they established a spy network across Xinjiang modeled after the Soviet Union's State Political Directorate (GPU).[56]

The secret police soon became a symbol of political terrorism. "The Security Office existed for about one year and seven months, from October

Table 4.1 (continued)

Xinjiang Provincial Public Security Administration: Reorganized in May 1936. Absorbed the general police and established five subordinate departments, including the Security Department (Department 2), which took over the work of the former Security Office.
Director: Zhang Yiwu (Dismissed in summer 1937; later arrested and exiled to the Soviet Union)
Deputy Director, Director of the Security Department: Liu Xianchen (Comintern member; later dismissed at the same time as Zhang Yiwu, arrested and exiled to the Soviet Union)
In summer 1937, Zhao Jianfeng (Deputy Chief of the Office of the Xinjiang Frontier Defense Commissioner) was appointed as Administration Director; in spring 1938, he was transferred to the position of senior administrator of the Tarbagatay Administrative Region.
In spring 1938, Li Yingqi (Director of the Political Disciplinary Office of the Office of the Xinjiang Frontier Defense Commissioner) was appointed as Administration Director.
In September 1938, Hashim Ghaji (Comintern member) arrived in Xinjiang for the purpose of reestablishing the Ethnic Affairs Department.
In winter 1939, the "Inspection Office" for intelligence-gathering and analysis was established in order to isolate the Ethnic Affairs Department.
(In January 1943, the Xinjiang Party Branch of the Chinese Nationalist Party was revived.)
Xinjiang Provincial Police Division: Reorganized in July 1934, later merged with the "Inspection Office."
Chief: Li Yingqi
(In September 1944, Sheng Shicai left for Chongqing to serve as the Minister of Agriculture and Forestry in the Nationalist government, bringing an end to his reign.)

Source: Compiled by the author on the basis of Wen Feiran, "Xinjiang under the Control of Sheng Shicai's Secret Agents"; Zhao Jianfeng, "The Rise and Fall of the Xinjiang Provincial Public Security Administration," Selected Cultural and Historical Materials on Xinjiang, vol. 7 (1981).

1934 to May 1936, and it inspired fear and apprehension in the public as it penetrated every corner."[57] However, as revealed in a memo by Sheng Shicai censuring Wang Lixiang for disobeying his orders, Sheng was in fact unable to fully control the actions of the Security Office.[58]

Chen Peisheng, who served as Deputy Director of the Border Affairs Office and later as an advisor to the Ministry of State Security of the People's Republic of China after 1949, offered the following description of the nature of his office: "The Border Affairs Office was established in 1936 at the recommendation and with the assistance of the Soviet Union. Its tasks were to guarantee Xinjiang's security, and surveil hostile outside forces to gather intelligence. Its primary targets included: the warlord Ma Jiajun and the anti-Communist army of Chiang Kai-shek in the neighboring province to the east, and the military activities of the British imperialists in northern India and eastern Afghanistan, which neighbored on the Xinjiang region to the south. As the Border Affairs Office was highly classified, it was not included among the eight departments of the governor's office, but instead was directly run by Sheng Shicai. The Soviet Union sent a major-general to be an advisor and three colonels to be intelligence instructors, and there was also a radio specialist of German nationality. The telecommunications equipment needed by the Border Affairs Office and the large and small vehicles used for transportation were all provided by the Soviet Union, making it possible to rapidly establish and operationalize military intelligence services both inside and outside the province." Chen's account has certain discrepancies with the testimony of other involved parties, likely because he himself had been sent to Xinjiang by the Soviet Union. Li Guoqing, who began working at the Border Affairs Office in 1941 and was later promoted to Deputy Director, recalled that, "Although the Border Affairs Office was an intelligence organization run by Sheng Shicai, in essence it was a military intelligence organization under the Intelligence Bureau of Third International stationed in Xinjiang"; "At first, the funding for the Border Affairs Office was laid out in the annual plan by the office's Financial Affairs Department, and then, with the approval of the Deputy Director, it was given to the Soviet Union's chief instructor to hand over to the Soviet consulate in Dihua for disbursement. Later when Zhou Bin [Mao Zemin] was appointed as the director of the Department of Finance of the Xinjiang Provincial Government, the budget plan of the

Border Affairs Office was reviewed and approved by Director Zhou. The budget plan was classified, and aside from the director, the other personnel in the Department of Finance had no knowledge of it." Although the intelligence gathered by the Border Affairs Office was reported to Sheng Shicai, Sheng had no direct administrative powers over the office. The personnel working at the Border Affairs Office were subjected to strict controls, and were required to swear an oath in the presence of the major-general sent by the Soviet Union to serve as an advisor and chief instructor: "In my work at the international intelligence organization, I must strictly observe and fulfill all disciplinary regulations. For any transgressions, I shall willingly stand for a confidential trial before a closed military tribunal."

In 1938, a mechanized division of the Soviet Red Army (the 8th Regiment) was stationed in Kumul (Hami), the eastern gate to Xinjiang. The regiment's nominal missions were to prevent Japan from invading Xinjiang, and to protect the route for transporting material aid to China, but in reality, the Soviet Union seized this as an opportunity to assert control over the transportation hub between Xinjiang and China's interior provinces. A dual power structure comprised on the one hand of the political forces of the Chinese warlord Sheng Shicai and on the other of Soviet forces led by the Soviet consulate in Urumqi (Dihua) thus gradually took shape in Xinjiang (Figure 4.1).

Soviet Overtures to Local Ethnic Factions

In 1934, though Japan had revealed its plans to launch a full-scale war against China, its intentions with respect to a direct invasion of Xinjiang were still an enigma. Sheng Shicai was able to obtain a massive amount of aid from the Soviet Union on the strength of rumors to that effect. The Soviet Union in fact also relied on rumors of Japanese invasion to propose the ethnic liberation of Xinjiang, framed as a struggle against imperialism. This formulation obscured the contradictions between the Soviet Union's voiced support for ethnic equality and its actual support for the continued rule of a Han Chinese warlord in Xinjiang.

On May 2, 1934, an article entitled "China's Ethnic Problems" was published in issue no. 73 of *Struggle* (*Douzheng* 鬥爭), the official newspaper of the Chinese Communist Party. The author was unable to locate the original Chinese version, but the article was included in an investigative

Figure 4.1 Xinjiang's Dual Power Structure (1934–1942)

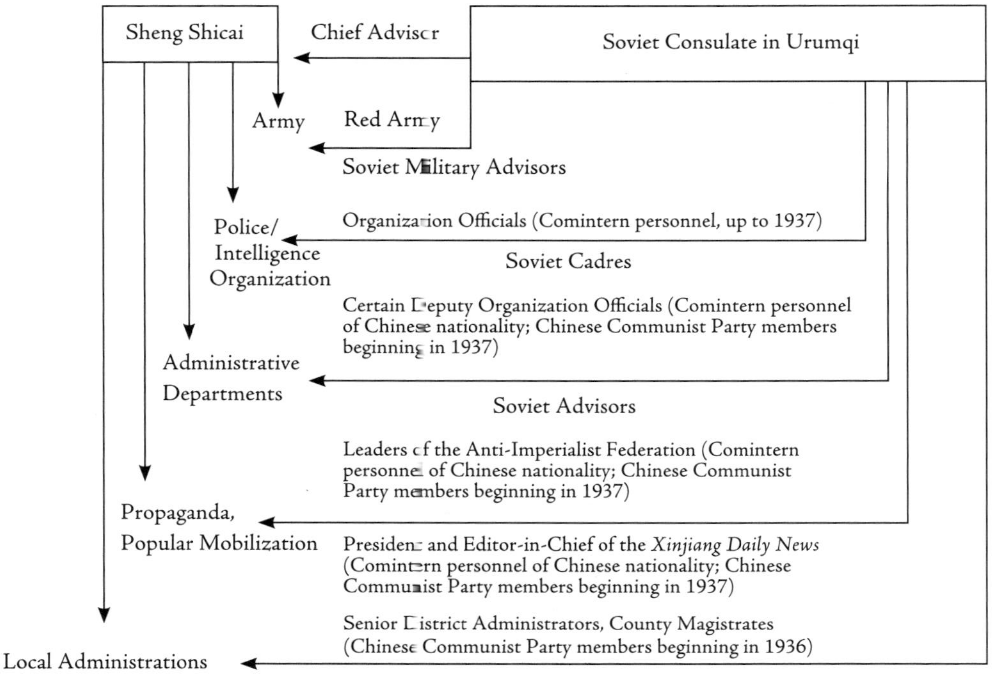

Source: Compiled by the author.

report produced by the Political Affairs Bureau of Japan's Asia Development Board. The article offered the following depiction of the potential role that Xinjiang could play in the fight against Japanese imperialism:

> Two thirds of the inhabitants of Xinjiang are Mongolians, Kazakhs and Dzungars belonging to the Uyghur and Oirat ethnic groups, etc., yet Xinjiang Province is a colony of the Han Chinese, governed by others on the basis of military feudalism and exploitation. . . . The Chinese Communist Party unconditionally acknowledges the right of Xinjiang's ethnic groups to freely establish an independent state.
>
> Yet now the elite and imperialist agents among the Han exploiters are utilizing the complexity of interethnic relations to sow dissension among the different ethnic groups, in order to pursue their own interests. British imperialists, the most active, are unceasingly plundering Xinjiang of its abundant oil, coal, and mineral resources, and exploiting the people's growing sense of resentment against Han oppression with the aim of turning Xinjiang into a source of instability on the borders of the eastern Soviet republics. The Japanese imperialists similarly hope to absorb Xinjiang into their territories, and it has already been incorporated into their plans for armed intervention. The Chinese Communist Party opposes the style of "national self-determination" for the ethnic peoples of Xinjiang. Under this style of "national self-determination," each ethnic group would continue to be subject to the rule of feudal parasites, becoming mutually oppressive accomplices to the imperialists, and engaging in dangerous activities. The Chinese Communist Party calls for Xinjiang's ethnic peoples to form a united front to oppose the imperialists and their agents, merging the struggle for ethnic liberation with the Chinese revolution, while also adopting an attitude of amity and good will toward the great nations that have achieved socialist construction.[59]

Given the relationship between the Chinese Communist Party and the Soviet Union at the time, we can infer that this passage was intended as a defense of the Soviet Union's policies on Xinjiang. However, the overall theme of the article also sends a message that supporting the Han Chinese rulers of Xinjiang does not necessarily mean abandoning support for its local inhabitants' struggle for ethnic liberation. In fact, under the dual structure of political power in Xinjiang, the Soviet Union continued to strengthen its ties with local ethnic forces.

As shown in Table 4.2, the Ethnic Affairs Department of the secret

Table 4.2 Evolutionary Chart of the Ethnic Affairs Department under the Police Organizations in Sheng Shicai's Era

Ethnic Affairs Department (Department 4) of the Administration for Political Supervision of the Xinjiang Provincial Government: Established in August 1934. Monitored, exposed and reported on the speech and actions of Xinjiang's ethnic inhabitants. Director: Li Shanwei Deputy Director: Kadir Ghaji (Comintern member from the Soviet Union)
Ethnic Affairs Department (Department 4) of the Xinjiang Provincial Security Office: Renamed in 1934. The Xinjiang Provincial Security Office established branch security offices across the region.
Ethnic Affairs Office (Department 2, Office 4) of the Xinjiang Provincial Public Security Administration: Reorganized in May 1936; responsible for overseeing the document processing, intelligence analysis, interrogation, and translation teams. Deputy Administration Director, Director of Department 2: Liu Xianchen (Comintern member from the Soviet Union) Deputy Department Director, Manager of Office 4: Sayyid Ghaji (Comintern member from the Soviet Union) 1st Deputy Office Manager: Yasavi 2nd Deputy Office Manager: Bazar Bay (Comintern member from the Soviet Union)
Ethnic Affairs Department (Department 6) of the Xinjiang Provincial Public Security Administration: Reorganized following the arrival of Comintern member Hashim Ghaji in Xinjiang in September 1938. This department was responsible for overseeing six offices: Office 1 focused on the Uyghur and Taranchi peoples, Office 2 focused on the Uzbek and Tatar peoples, and Office 3 focused on the Kazakh and Kyrgyz peoples; each of the former were responsible for intelligence-gathering and surveillance activities. Office 4 was responsible for examining mail; Office 5 was in charge of interrogations; and Office 6 handled translation. Manager of Office 1: Tursun Sabitow (Uyghur individual with experience studying abroad in the Soviet Union) Manager of Office 2: Tursun Tariyow (Uyghur individual with experience studying abroad in the Soviet Union) 2nd Manager of Office 2: Abijan (Appointed as Public Security Director of the Ili District of the East Turkestan Republic in 1946) Manager of Office 3: Bazar Bay (Comintern member from the Soviet Union) Manager of Office 4: Abdukirim (Uyghur individual with experience studying abroad in the Soviet Union)

Source: Compiled by the author on the basis of Zhao Jianfeng, "The Rise and Fall of the Xinjiang Provincial Public Security Administration."

police was controlled by Communist International members or figures who had studied abroad in the Soviet Union. In regions with a highly concentrated local minority population, such as the Kumul and Kashgar administrative regions, Communist International personnel from the Soviet Union monopolized the position of public security director, while the Soviet agent Mansur Apandi served as the director of the Society for the Promotion of Uyghur Culture. Both Mansur and Kadir Ghaji, the Kashgar Public Security Director, reportedly had a Turkic-Islamic ethnic background; both figures acted to spread the concept of "national revolution" amongst the Uyghurs, and recruited a number of intelligence agents.[60] Mansur later played a large role in the Second East Turkestan Independence Movement.

The increasingly close ties between the Soviet Union and local ethnic factions were naturally of great concern to Sheng Shicai. There were two reasons for this: first, a number of circumstances indicated that the Soviet Union apparently held certain expectations with respect to these local ethnic factions. After the Uyghur leader Hoja Niyaz ascended to the position of Deputy Governor of the Xinjiang Provincial Government through the mediation of the Soviet consul-general in Urumqi (Dihua), he was constantly surrounded by a bevy of Communist International personnel; the Soviet consulate in Urumqi also kept in close contact with Niyaz, and regularly instructed him on "revolutionary theory."[61] Second, the Hui warlord Ma Zhongying, who had retreated to southern Xinjiang with the Soviet army in pursuit, later improved his relationship with the Soviet Union with the aid of the Soviet consulate in Kashgar. In July 1934, Ma Zhongying traveled to the Soviet Union at the head of 280 military officers to study military command at the Soviet academy.[62] The forces commanded by Ma Zhongying and Hoja Niyaz were respectively stationed in the Hotan and Kashgar regions. There were rumors that Ma Zhongying joined in a discussion with ten Soviet military officers in the winter of 1935, addressing topics such as the geography of northwestern China, the deployment of the Nationalist government's armed forces, routes into Xinjiang that could be used by the Red Army, and so on.[63] Given these circumstances, Sheng Shicai could not lightly dismiss the possibility that the Soviet Union might abandon him, and install a Muslim ethnic leader in the Islamic region of Xinjiang.

4.3 Sheng Shicai's Political Repositioning

The First Great Purge of 1937

In 1967, Sheng Shicai claimed in his own defense that the ties he established with the Soviet Union in the 1930s were based on his espousal of Communism at the time.[64] However, this in fact was not the case.[65] When Sheng Shicai admitted Communist International personnel into Xinjiang, he reportedly made three demands of the Soviet Union: (1) Economic development and universal education were to be prioritized in Xinjiang, with no pursuit of class struggle; (2) The command of the armed forces and local administrative powers were to remain intact; and (3) Sheng would respect the views of the Communist Party, but would not permit the establishment of a Communist Party organization in Xinjiang.[66] In other words, Sheng Shicai drew on the support of the Soviet Union not due to his political beliefs, but rather to establish and preserve his own rule.[67]

However, the formation of a dual power structure in Xinjiang indicates that the Soviet Union similarly granted its support to Sheng Shicai not on the basis of ideology, but rather in the pursuit of national interests. As Soviet forces infiltrated the Xinjiang regime and established ties with ethnic leaders, the conflicts between the dual mechanisms of power controlled by Sheng Shicai and the Soviet Union were thus gradually revealed.

In December 1937, the Chinese Communist Party cadre Xu Mengqiu was persuaded by Sheng Shicai to remain in Xinjiang rather than traveling on to the Soviet Union; in January 1938, he was appointed as the Deputy Director of the Xinjiang Provincial Department of Education. Xu was the first CCP cadre to join Sheng Shicai's regime in Urumqi. At least 70 CCP cadres arrived in Xinjiang in 1938 and were appointed to positions in Sheng's regime.[68]

Several commentators have posited that Sheng Shicai's wide-scale purge of bureaucrats from the old regime prior to assuming power had resulted in a number of official vacancies, and that this was the reason why he began hiring CCP cadres in 1937.[69] The establishment of the "Xinjiang Province Political Cadre Personnel Training Class" in 1938 indicates that there may indeed have been a shortage of candidates for official positions. However, the purge of the old guard bureaucrats was not the only reason why Sheng began hiring CCP cadres. CCP forces had begun moving into Xinjiang as early as April 1937, with Sheng Shicai's approval, and had made certain contributions to the preservation of Sheng's rule.[70] After the Marco Polo Bridge Incident of July 7, the Chinese Communist Party also established the "Eighth Route Army Representatives Office" in Urumqi, forming a united national front to resist the Japanese alongside Sheng Shicai.[71] Furthermore, Sheng's purge of officials from the previous regime had in fact begun when he came to power in 1934. The theory that Sheng Shicai waited until November 1937 to begin appointing CCP cadres to the vacant positions that emerged due to his purge of the old guard bureaucrats thus appears to be inconsistent with the facts.

Sheng Shicai's invitation for CCP cadres to join his regime in Urumqi was reportedly extended after his meeting with Wang Ming, Kang Sheng and other leaders of the "International Faction" (*Guoji pai* 國際派) of the Chinese Communist Party as they returned from Moscow to Yan'an via Xinjiang in November 1937.[72] It is worth noting that this meeting came to light because Wang Ming and Kang Sheng used this opportunity to denounce Wang Shoucheng and the other members of Communist International to Sheng Shicai as "Trotskyites."[73] This incident reveals that the accession of the CCP cadres into Sheng's regime was connected in some way to the "Trotskyite clean-up" that Sheng launched in Xinjiang.

In 1937, Sheng Shicai claimed to have discovered an "international plot of rebellion": in August, a number of Han officials were arrested as "Han traitors"; in October, Hoja Niyaz and other local ethnic Islamic leaders were arrested as "Trotskyites," and in December, Wang Shoucheng, Wan Xianting, Zhang Yiwu, Liu Xianchen and other Comintern members of Chinese nationality were also arrested for the same charges.[74] Sheng Shicai's audacity in carrying out this series of political purges in the latter half of 1937 was in part rooted in the global upheaval and domestic turmoil in China occurring in 1937. Full-scale war against Japan broke out in July, allowing Sheng Shicai to legitimize his actions to stamp out dissidents in the name of "eliminating Japanese spies." Once the Sino-Soviet Non-Aggression Pact was signed on August 21, "Soviet Russia proceeded to build up the strength of the Chinese Nationalists as a counter against Japan."[75] This temporarily diverted Soviet attention away from Xinjiang, providing an excellent opportunity for Sheng Shicai's purges.

However, Sheng Shicai's primary objective in launching these political purges was to recapture real power in his regime. It is clear that Sheng's intentions did not extend beyond strengthening his own political dictatorship. The arrests of the Communist International personnel sent to join Sheng Shicai's regime did not necessarily arise due to personal discord between the Comintern members and Sheng Shicai, but these actions certainly represented an attempt by Sheng to wrest political power away from the Soviets. There is no doubt that Sheng Shicai's 1937 political purges were primarily motivated by his resentment of the dual structure of political power that had taken shape in Xinjiang due to the presence of Soviet forces. This thinking is also reflected in Sheng's demand, sent to Stalin in the same year, that Consul-General Apresov be recalled for harboring "Trotskyites" in Xinjiang.

Sheng Shicai had of course been aware of the threat posed by the dual power structure prior to the purges of 1937. For instance, Sheng had been locked in a struggle with Soviet forces for control of the secret police for many years. Sheng landed the first blow by repatriating the organization's Soviet-born deputy director in 1934; in November 1935, he also succeeding in banishing Wang Lixiang. Sheng thereafter employed various means to impose restrictions on the power of the secret police, ultimately reorganizing the Security Office as the Public Security Administration in 1936. By merging the ordinary police with the public security office, Sheng transformed the Soviet-controlled secret police into a general police force to maintain public order.[76]

Intriguingly, CCP cadres began joining Sheng's regime in large numbers after he began arresting the Chinese-born Comintern personnel in December 1937. Specifically, nearly all of the positions to which CCP cadres were appointed had been recently vacated by Comintern personnel, who had either been arrested or dismissed. This turn of events indicates that the CCP cadres were recruited by Sheng Shicai as replacements for the Chinese-born Communist International personnel.

However, during this era, the Chinese Communist Party was still a branch organization under the leadership of Communist International, and its actions were subject to the directives of the Soviet Union. So what were Sheng Shicai's motivations in substituting Chinese Communist Party members for representatives of Communist International? The only rational explanation is that, in 1937, although Sheng Shicai was plotting to wrest power away from the Soviet forces, he still did not wish to completely relinquish the support of the Soviet Union.[77]

Some historians have identified a link between Sheng Shicai's 1937 political purges and the purges launched by Stalin in 1936.[78] However, this connection is based solely on the use of similar political methods. Sheng Shicai did in fact draw lessons from Stalin's political purges, with respect both to methodology and in manufacturing pretexts for his actions, arbitrarily leveling the vague accusation of being a "Trotskyite" in order to persecute his personal enemies. By arresting Communist International personnel under these charges, Sheng avoided being perceived as a traitor to the Soviet Union, instead portraying himself as loyal to Stalin. At the same time, by installing cadres from the Chinese Communist Party in the positions vacated by the "Trotskyites," Sheng left the Soviet Union with even less space for doubting his "loyalty."

The Shift Toward Policies of Ethnic Oppression

In the spring of 1937, an uprising was sparked by Uyghur troops stationed in Kashgar under Division Commander Mahmut Muhiti, a subordinate of Hoja Niyaz; Ma Zhongying's deputy Ma Hushan, who was stationed in Hotan, also led the Hui forces under his command to join the rebellion. The Soviet Union swiftly gathered intelligence through the Border Affairs Office and unilaterally mobilized aircraft, tanks and a Kyrgyz cavalry brigade to suppress the uprising.[79]

The rebellion was in fact launched as cover for Division Commander Mahmut Muhiti's flight to India.[80] However, two questions remain unanswered with respect to the uprising and its suppression: First, why did Mahmut Muhiti want to flee the country? Second, given the good relationships that the Soviet Union had maintained with Hoja Niyaz and Ma Zhongying, Muhuti and Ma Hushan's respective commanders, why did it dispatch forces to suppress the uprising?

The revelation that Division Commander Muhiti had secretly sent representatives to Nanjing to make contact with the Nationalist government, drawing the ire of both the Soviet Union and Sheng Shicai, is the key to answering these questions.[81] Sheng sought to work against Muhiti and unravel his secret collaboration with the Nanjing Nationalist government by paying off his trusted followers.[82] In contrast, the Soviet Union massacred the rebel officers and soldiers, even those who had already surrendered, demonstrating the great umbrage felt by the Soviet Union at Muhiti's plot to introduce Nationalist forces into Xinjiang.[83]

The impact of the "Muhiti–Ma Hushan Rebellion" was not limited to the above: the uprising also made it impossible for the Soviet Union to continue openly dealing with Hoja Niyaz and other ethnic factions, and removed the possibility of using Niyaz and other local ethnic forces to contain Sheng Shicai. At the same time, Sheng Shicai's inducements to invite and permit ethnic leaders to join his regime in Urumqi vanished in the wake of the obliteration of the armed ethnic forces during the suppression of the uprising.

On October 12, 1937, Sheng Shicai abruptly arrested Hoja Niyaz.[84] This set the scene for the arrests of the Uyghur director of the Department of Agriculture and Mining of the Xinjiang Provincial Government, the Hui director of the Department of Civil Affairs, the Kazakh deputy director of the Department of Works, the Kazakh secretary-general of the Altay Administrative Region, a Mongolian advisor to the provincial government, and many other ethnic leaders who had joined the Urumqi regime in its early stages. Hoja Niyaz was arrested under the charges of secretly sending subordinates to make contact with spy agencies in Suiyuan Province and Japan, and attempting to establish an Islamic state in Xinjiang.[85] However, these charges were completely fabricated by Sheng Shicai.[86] From this point on, Sheng Shicai abandoned the policies designed to recruit ethnic leaders under the slogan of "ethnic equality," and instead turned toward the suppression of leading ethnic figures.

Hoja Niyaz had initially been persuaded by Soviet Consul-General Apresov to accept the position of Deputy Governor of the Xinjiang Provincial Government, and Apresov had promised to guarantee Niyaz's life and safety. However, one week after Sheng Shicai's arrest of Hoja Niyaz, Apresov still had not heard the news.[87] These events demonstrate that Sheng proceeded unilaterally in his purge of local ethnic forces, without consulting the Soviet Union.

Since 1934, the Xinjiang Provincial Government had annually sent one hundred Xinjiang youths to study abroad at the Soviet Union's National University of Central Asia; this program was abruptly suspended in 1937.[88]

It is clear that Sheng Shicai hoped to prevent Xinjiang's indigenous Islamic peoples from establishing personal ties with the Soviet Union. Sheng's decision to pursue the 1937 purges of Comintern personnel while simultaneously targeting ethnic leaders, with Hoja Niyaz chief among them, as well as the Soviet agents directed by Consul-General Apresov, was also based on such considerations. In other words, Sheng's opposition toward the gradually strengthening ties between Soviet forces and ethnic leaders under the dual structure of political power in Xinjiang was the primary motivating factor for the reshaping of ethnic policies in the region.

Objectives of the Political Purge of 1940

Despite these actions, Sheng Shicai still chose to visit Moscow in September 1938. While in Moscow, to express his loyalty to the Soviet Union, Sheng delivered his application to join the Communist Party of the Soviet Union directly into Stalin's hands.[89] Without Soviet aid, Sheng Shicai would have been unable to sustain Xinjiang's economy, let alone preserve his dictatorship over the region. For this reason, Sheng Shicai was still unwilling at the time to destroy his amicable ties to the Soviet Union.[90]

Sheng Shicai received a warm welcome during his visit to the Soviet Union, reflecting his success in cleverly disguising his persecution of Soviet personnel during the 1937 political purges. However, Sheng Shicai was unaware that he had been caught in his own web in this duplicitous performance for the Soviet Union.[91] Perhaps duped by Sheng Shicai's performance, Communist International sent another group of personnel to Xinjiang in September 1938. This time, Hashim Ghaji, a functionary of Turkic ethnicity originating from Soviet Central Asia, was sent to establish an Ethnic Affairs Department (Department 6) under the Provincial Public Security Administration. Through Kurban Niyaz, a Soviet-trained Uyghur and Deputy Director of the Public Security Administration, as well as other Comintern personnel of Turkic Central Asian background who were stationed across Xinjiang as the directors and deputy directors of local public security bureaus, Hashim re-formed an intelligence network to monitor and analyze the movements of ethnic peoples.[92] Despite having appointed himself as the director of the Provincial Public Security Administration after the 1937 purges, Sheng Shicai was unable to exert any control over this intelligence network, while authority over personnel matter at the Border Affairs Office remained in the hands of Chen Peisheng, leaving Sheng with no means of intervening in the affairs of the intelligence organizations.[93]

Sheng launched a counterattack in 1939, establishing an Inspection Office separate from the Public Security Administration to sever the link between the Ethnic Affairs Department and minority regions.[94] During this period, Sheng Shicai also began building up his personal secret intelligence organization, the "Six Star Agency" (*Liu xing she* 六星社).[95] However, the ties between Soviet forces and the Turkic-Islamic ethnic inhabitants of Xinjiang remained unbroken. After the 1937 purges, out of an instinct of self-preservation, many of Xinjiang's residents had acquired Soviet citizenship through the Soviet consulate general in Urumqi, as well as the consulates stationed in Kashgar, Ili, Altay, and Tarbagatay. Soviet delegations and survey teams frequently came into contact with local residents. Since an entry visa was not required for persons of Soviet nationality arriving in Xinjiang, members of Turkic-Islamic minority groups from the Soviet-controlled regions of Central Asia sought to deepen their ethnic, cultural and religious ties to Xinjiang's indigenous inhabitants, with whom they had much in common.[96]

In the spring of 1940, Sheng Shicai initiated a second round of political purges. He arrested Xaripkan, the Commissioner of the Altay District, and other Kazakh leaders under the charge of receiving support from Japanese imperialists for the establishment of a "Kazakh-Mongolian Republic" in northern Xinjiang. He also arrested Kurban Niyaz, the Deputy Director of the Public Security Administration; Hashim Ghaji, the Director of the Ethnic Affairs Department; Kurban Sayit, the Deputy Director of the Department of Finance; Abdulla Damolla, the Deputy Director of the Department of Works; and a number of other Uyghur leaders. In addition, Chen Peisheng, the Deputy Director of the Border Affairs Office, was arrested under charges of being a "Japanese imperialist spy."[97] The truth was that the alleged members of these three conspiratorial cliques fabricated by Sheng Shicai all had special ties to the Soviet Union. Sheng went so far as to send a report to Stalin, asserting that the acting Soviet consul-general in Urumqi had been an agent for the conspiracies behind the scenes.[98]

The purpose of the political purges of 1940 was to eliminate Soviet and pro-Soviet forces within the Urumqi regime, but they were also a symbol of Sheng Shicai's increasingly draconian policies of ethnic suppression. The Kyrgyz inhabitants of southern Xinjiang had been organized into a cavalry troop in 1937 at the suggestion of the Soviet Union, and had assisted in suppressing the "Muhiti–Ma Hushan Rebellion"; they therefore escaped Sheng Shicai's first round of political purges. In 1941, Sheng Shicai appointed their leader, Isakbek Munonow, as the director of Xinjiang's Society for the Promotion of Kazakh and Kyrgyz Culture; however, in April 1942, Munonow fled to the Soviet Union to avoid being arrested by Sheng Shicai.[99] Sheng Shicai also established the "Ammunition Confiscation Commission" (*Moshou qiangdan weiyuanhui* 沒收槍彈委員會) in the winter of 1939 to force ethnic minorities to hand over their ammunition; the commission placed a number of Kazakh, Kyrgyz, and Mongolian leaders under house arrest in Urumqi. Sheng Shicai's policies of ethnic suppression gave rise to ethnic resistance across the province. The Kazakh inhabitants of Altay rose up in rebellion in February 1940.[100]

Reasoning Behind the Suppression of Chinese Communist Party Forces

During the political purges of 1940, Du Zhongyuan, the President of Xinjiang College, was accused of being the mastermind behind the three conspiratorial cliques targeted by Sheng Shicai, and was arrested along with several of his students at the college.[101] Du Zhongyuan was a well-known intellectual who had come to Xinjiang at Sheng Shicai's personal invitation: at Xinjiang College, he defined the school spirit as "United, Alert, Sincere and Lively," closely patterned after the school motto ("United, Alert, Earnest and Lively") of the Anti-Japanese Military and Political University championed by Mao Zedong at Yan'an. This indicates that Du Zhongyuan had pro-CCP ideological leanings.[102] Several figures have therefore observed that Sheng Shicai's move to arrest Du Zhongyuan was, in essence, an attempt to destroy the Chinese Communist Party's social base in Xinjiang.[103] Why would Sheng Shicai take up arms against representatives of the Chinese Communist Party, whom he had personally invited into Xinjiang? The likely cause is that, between the two rounds of political purges in 1937 and 1940, he began to feel threatened by CCP influences within the Urumqi regime.

As discussed above, Chinese Communist Party cadres joined Sheng Shicai's regime in Urumqi in response to his cordial invitation. Sheng Shicai sent 20 trucks loaded with goods to Yan'an in early 1938 to express his gratitude for their acceptance.[104] Sheng initially expressed a highly favorable opinion of the CCP cadres: he appointed Mao Zemin, the younger brother of Mao Zedong, as the head of the Xinjiang Provincial Department of Finance; later, CCP cadres were installed in a number of important positions, including the head of the Department of Education, the head of the Accounting Office of the Office of the Commissioner of Border Defenses, the senior administrator of the Hami Administrative Region, the commander of the Hotan Administrative Region Garrison and senior administrator for the region, and so on.

Sheng Shicai also graciously admitted the CCP Red Army into Xinjiang.[105] According to the memoirs of Huang Huoqing, whom Sheng promoted from the Red Army to secretary-general of the Anti-Imperialist Federation and head of the secret interrogation committee, between 1937 and 1938, Sheng Shicai always consulted with the CCP cadres on every matter, accepted every one of their proposals, and met their demands to the best of his ability. Sheng even proposed the formation of a small committee consisting of the Xinjiang representative of the Chinese Communist Party, the Soviet consul-general in Urumqi, and Sheng Shicai himself. Chen Tanqiu, who became the CCP representative in Xinjiang in 1939, initially formed the impression that Sheng Shicai heeded Moscow's recommendations with respect to international matters, but listened to suggestions from Yan'an with respect to domestic issues.[106]

Sheng's alliance with the Chinese Communist Party was formed on the

Du Zhongyuan (1898–1943)   *Mao Zemin (1896–1943)*

"political foundation" of "pro-Sovietism" and particularly "mutual resistance against Japan."[107] By parading this political platform, Sheng Shicai was able to demonstrate the legitimacy of his regime in Xinjiang to Chinese society, while also gaining a pretext for mobilizing the local population; both of these factors played a relatively important role in Sheng Shicai's efforts to preserve his rule over Xinjiang. In early 1938, Xinjiang's Anti-Imperialist Federation underwent a second round of reorganization: its practical operations were entirely delegated to CCP cadres, and within two months, it had gained an additional 3,000 members.[108] The Xinjiang Student Federation and Xinjiang Women's Association, which had been established at the behest of Wang Shoucheng, were brought under the control of CCP cadres beginning in 1938.[109] The Xinjiang Student Movement, which included Uyghur students, focused on "promoting resistance against Japan."[110] Urumqi soon developed a reputation throughout China as the "second Yan'an." Between 1938 and 1939, a wave of well-known Chinese intellectuals, including Du Zhongyuan, Mao Dun, and Zhang Zhongshi, came to Xinjiang to join Sheng Shicai's regime in Urumqi, and praised Xinjiang under Sheng Shicai's rule before a national audience.

However, the kinship that Sheng Shicai expressed with the Chinese Communist Party was limited. When the CCP forces arrived in Xinjiang, they were obliged to establish a three-clause agreement with Sheng Shicai that they would "not propagandize Communism," "not publicize their status as Communist Party members," and "not mobilize the local people to join the Communist Party" in Xinjiang.[111] The Chinese Communist Party did not in fact recruit any new members in Xinjiang, but since Xinjiang was the sole passageway to the Soviet Union, the CCP sent heavyweight leaders to the region,[112] who actively devoted themselves to mobilizing the masses, promoting Marxism-Leninism, and increasing their influence.[113] For instance, during CCP cadre Lin Jilu's term as dean of Xinjiang College, many of the students at the college became adherents of Marxism. Lin Jilu also opposed flattery of Sheng Shicai.[114] After he was appointed as the secretary-general of the 3rd Xinjiang People's Representative Congress in October 1938, Lin published an unauthorized photograph of Mao Zedong in the congressional handbook, infuriating Sheng Shicai; he was demoted and sent to Altay to serve as the head of the regional Bureau of Education.[115]

The Chinese Communist Party cadres who came to Xinjiang nevertheless sought to form their own party organizations to organize activities.[116] At the same time, after the CCP cadres were absorbed into Sheng Shicai's regime in Urumqi, the Chinese Communist Party perpetuated the practice of adhering to the organizational principles prescribed by Communist International with respect to issues in Xinjiang. A secret agent who was tailing the CCP representatives in Xinjiang under Sheng Shicai's orders reported that, "The Yan'an representatives are frequently in contact with the Soviet consul; by my count, between May 7 and June 2 [1938], the delegation visited the Soviet consulate 11 times; the content of the discussions is unknown."[117]

In sum, the Chinese Communist Party's growing influence in Xinjiang after the purges of 1937 and its ties to the Soviet Union restored a system of political power excluding Sheng Shicai; this situation led Sheng Shicai to once more perceive a political threat.[118] In early 1939, Sheng Shicai began undermining Chinese Communist influence in the region: many CCP cadres were sent to Uyghur regions in southern Xinjiang, where they faced a language barrier.[119] In September, Sheng Shicai suggested to Zhou Enlai, who was passing through Xinjiang en route to the Soviet Union, that Deng Fa, the CCP representative in Xinjiang, should be recalled to Yan'an.[120] In August 1942, Sheng Shicai took advantage of Soviet setbacks in the war with Germany to break with both the Soviet Union and the Chinese Communist Party; he expelled all Soviet personnel from the region, arrested the CCP cadres,[121] and began actively gravitating toward the side of the Nationalist government.[122]

Summary

Politics during the era of Sheng Shicai's regime can be divided into three key stages. It is noteworthy that, based on the time periods, the changes to Sheng Shicai's political agenda coincided with his reversals on ethnic policy.

The first stage was from 1933 to summer 1937: it was during this period that Sheng Shicai first began implementing his pro-Soviet political agenda. However, his motivations for adopting an "anti-Japanese," "pro-Soviet" agenda were simply to draw on the Soviet Union's economic, political and especially military strength in order to consolidate his own rule over

Xinjiang, while his primary goal was to resolve the problems of ethnic antagonism and conflict in the region, which represented a grave threat to him.

In the second stage, from summer 1937 to spring 1940, Sheng Shicai gradually began rejecting Soviet influence; during this same time period, Sheng Shicai also shifted from an ethnic policy of amnesty and recruitment to a policy of suppression. The formation of a dual structure of political power within the Urumqi regime and the establishment of close ties between Soviet forces and ethnic leaders imperiled Sheng Shicai's dictatorship in Xinjiang. Sheng therefore embarked on changes to his political agenda, seizing the Soviet Union's domestic purges as an opportunity to launch his own series of political purges targeting pro-Soviet influences and ethnic factions within his regime.

The third stage was from spring 1940 to 1944: during this period, Sheng Shicai finally severed his ties to the Soviet Union, and began openly pursuing widespread suppression of Xinjiang's Islamic ethnic inhabitants. During this stage, Chinese Communist Party forces arrived in Xinjiang and began gradually shaping a new dual political power structure; the region's local Islamic residents also began resisting Sheng Shicai's rule. Despite facing these difficulties, Sheng Shicai nevertheless ultimately broke off relations with the Soviet Union, because he believed that Soviet assistance would no longer be of any avail in preserving his rule.

In sum, Sheng Shicai's political agenda and ethnic policies were interrelated. These circumstances arose due to Sheng's political ambitions, as well as the self-serving nature of the Soviet Union's policies on Xinjiang. The Soviet Union's actions in Xinjiang were fundamentally in service of its national interests. Thus, while supporting Sheng Shicai, the Soviet Union also pursued political power in Xinjiang, leading to the formation of a dual political power structure within the Urumqi regime; and it used this dual power structure to strengthen its ties to local ethnic forces. As a result, in deciding his political agenda, Sheng Shicai was necessarily obliged to consider it in conjunction with his ethnic policies.

Sheng's policy of ethnic suppression naturally gave rise to resistance, increasing the likelihood of ethnic conflict. At the same time, Sheng's decision to sever his ties to the Soviet Union, which had supported him in establishing and consolidating his rule, incurred a fierce backlash from the

Soviets. At this critical moment for the Han Chinese ruler Sheng Shicai, the Soviet Union abandoned its policy of supporting his regime, shifting toward support for the Turkic-Islamic national independence movement brewing in Xinjiang. This move would lead to the overthrow of Sheng Shicai's rule, allowing the Soviet Union to assert control over the Xinjiang region. In April 1942, Isakbek Munonow, the director of the Society for the Promotion of Kazakh and Kyrgyz Culture, fled to the Soviet Union; around this same time, a number of Uyghur, Kazakh, and Kyrgyz leaders disappeared from Xinjiang and resurfaced in the Soviet Union to receive training. With the support of Outer Mongolia and the Soviet Union, rebel Kazakh forces in the Altay region also gained in strength, as Xinjiang marched toward a period of resurgent and widespread ethnic conflict.

Chapter 5

Soviet-Backed "Jihad" by the Turkic-Islamic Peoples of China

The Rise of the Second Independence Movement and the Ghulja Uprising

The Second East Turkestan Independent Movement was set in motion in the Ili region in the summer of 1944.[1] The second independence movement was contemporarily referred to as the "November Revolution" by the Turkic-Islamic inhabitants of the region; today it is known in China as the "Three Districts Revolution" (*sanqu geming* 三區革命). Though both terms label the movement as a "revolution," each carries different significance. In a letter to Ahmatjan Kasimi, the leader of the "revolution," dated August 1949, Mao Zedong wrote: "Your many years of struggle are part of the democratic revolutionary movement of all the Chinese people," defining the independence movement as a "democratic revolution."[2] However, Ahmatjan Kasimi stated in 1946, "What we are pursuing is a national revolution," thus defining the nature of the Second East Turkestan Independence Movement as a "national revolution."[3]

Was the Second East Turkestan Independence Movement intrinsically a democratic revolution, or a national revolution? This chapter focuses on the insurgent activities of the Turkic-Islamic peoples of Xinjiang prior to the establishment of the Interim Government of the East Turkestan Republic, analyzing the political viewpoints and organizational efforts of the secret societies and armed rebel groups formed by Turkic Muslims in the Ili region—the birthplace of the Second East Turkestan Independence Movement, as well as the broader picture of their activities prior to the Ghulja Uprising, to explore the causes for the resurgence of the East Turkestan Independence Movement in 1944, as well as the nature of the "revolution." The supporting materials for this chapter primarily include leaflets produced by the secret societies, official documents of the Interim Government of the East Turkestan Republic, witnesses' memoirs, as well as the author's interviews with witnesses.

5.1 Nationalist Secret Societies and Their Political Views

"Why Are We Fighting?" and "Why We Must Fight"

Little to no research has been conducted on the nationalist secret societies founded by the Turkic-Islamic ethnic inhabitants of Xinjiang in the 1940s. This surprising state of affairs is a reflection of the lack of written sources and other difficulties posed to research. Given these circumstances, the report "Rebel Objectives in Sinkiang" compiled by the United States Consulate in Urumqi and sent to the U.S. Secretary of State on September 25, 1945, is particularly valuable.[4] Enclosed with the report were English translations of four leaflets produced by nationalist secret societies, along with translations of documents originating from the East Turkestan Republic. These included a document entitled "Why Are We Fighting?" signed by "The National Freedom Group."

The existence of these leaflets and the authenticity of their content is corroborated by the unpublished *Diary of Wu Zhongxin*.[5] In his entry for December 16, 1944, Wu Zhongxin, who was then the provincial governor of Xinjiang, included extracts from a document entitled "Why We Must Fight" (*Women weishenme yao fendou* 我們為什麼要奮鬥), signed by the "National Revolutionary Committee"; the document was supplied by Ping Rong, the newly appointed Ili Commissioner.[6] The extracts found in the diary are essentially consistent with the content of "Why Are We Fighting?" (Table 5.1). Wu Zhongxin's diary entry for January 11, 1945, also reveals that the United States Consulate in Urumqi sent an inquiry on that date to Wu Zhongxin regarding the status of the Ili Rebellion. The U.S. Consulate later also expressed an interest in using the media to draw international attention, and requested that Wu Zhongxin provide information on Xinjiang's political situation; this request was granted.[7] In sum, it is quite likely that the English text "Why Are We Fighting?" is a full translation of the original Uyghur document corresponding to "Why We Must

Fight," as it is rendered in Chinese.

The accounts given in the report and the diary differ in only one respect: "Why Are We Fighting?" is signed "The National Freedom Group," while "Why We Must Fight" is signed "The National Revolutionary Committee" (*Minzu geming weiyuanhui* 民族革命委員會). The discrepancy of "freedom" versus "revolutionary" may have been an error that transpired during the translation of the document from Uyghur into Chinese.

In fact, many Uyghur-language sources refer to the secret society formed by the Turkic-Islamic residents of the Ili region as *Azadlik Taxkilati* (the "Freedom Group"), with most omitting the term "National." To be sure, most of these Uyghur-language texts were written during the era of the People's Republic of China. After the founding of the P.R.C., the border peoples' struggle against their Han Chinese rulers for "national freedom" was recast as a struggle for class liberation; it is not inconceivable that such a movement could have also been described as a "revolution." This is mirrored in the general emulation of the People's Republic of China, whereby even the name "East Turkestan Republic" was rendered as the "East Turkestan People's Republic"; this recasting was widely adopted by many participants in the East Turkestan Independence Movement. Though various sources provide different formulations for the name of the secret society founded by Xinjiang's indigenous Turkic Muslims, the organization's formal name was in fact *Milli Azadlik Taxkilati* ("The National Freedom Group"). The society's name is noteworthy because it later became a core organization leading the Second East Turkestan Independence Movement.

Members of Azadlik Taxkilati *(the "Freedom Group")*

"Oppression" and "Savagery" under the Han Chinese Regime

With respect to its content, "Why Are We Fighting?" is composed of three main sections: Section 1 explains the motivations for the establishment of the National Freedom Group; Section 2 describes the objectives of the National Freedom Group, revolving around the ideal future society of East Turkestan and the nature of the state; Section 3 calls for the indigenous

Table 5.1 Comparison of "Why Are We Fighting?" and "Why We Must Fight"

"Why Are We Fighting?"	"Why We Must Fight" (*Women weishenme yao fendou*)
Divided into three sections: (1) Reasons for establishing the National Freedom Group (2) Objectives of the struggle by the National Freedom Group (3) Appeal for the people to join the organization	Divided into three sections: (1) Reasons for establishing the National Revolutionary Committee (2) Objectives of the struggle by the National Revolutionary Committee (3) Appeal for the people to join the organization
Reasons for Establishment: (1) East Turkestan is our homeland (2) The Turkic inhabitants of Kazakhstan, Kyrgyzstan, Uzbekistan, and Tatarstan are our compatriots (3) The Chinese people have invaded, pillaged and persecuted us, scornfully labeling us the "New Borderland" [Xinjiang] or "Western China," and many friends and relatives have died in the resistance (4) Since 1937, under the oppressive rule of Sheng Shicai, many ethnic leaders have been assassinated, chief among them being Hoja Niyaz and Sharif Khan (5) The Chinese rulers have sent a total of 1 million Chinese and Manchurian emigrants to the Xinjiang colony The secret society was established to wage resistance, in the name of "The National Freedom Group."	**Reasons for Establishment:** (1) East Turkestan is our homeland (2) The Turkic inhabitants of Kazakhstan, Kyrgyzstan, Uzbekistan, and Tatarstan are our compatriots (3) The Chinese people have invaded, pillaged and persecuted us, scornfully labeling us the "New Borderland" [Xinjiang] or "Western China," and many friends and relatives have died in the resistance (4) Since 1937, under the oppressive rule of Sheng Shicai, many ethnic leaders have been assassinated, chief among them being Hoja Niyaz and Sharif Khan (5) The Chinese rulers have sent a total of 1 million Chinese and Manchurian emigrants to the Xinjiang colony The secret society was established to wage resistance, in the name of "The National Revolutionary Committee."

Table 5.1 (continued)

"Why Are We Fighting?"	"Why We Must Fight" (Women weishenme yao fendou)
Objectives: (1) Cast off Chinese rule (2) Achieve ethnic equality (3) Establish a parliamentary democratic government (4) Implement elections for local administrators (5) Develop ethnic cultural education (6) Restore the various ethnic cultural associations (7) Abolish the police state (8) Achieve political freedoms (9) Establish friendly relations with the Soviet Union (10) Reduce taxes (11) Guarantee freedom of religion (12) Drive out the Chinese colonizers (13) Develop agriculture (14) Abolish unpaid labor	Objectives: (1) Cast off Chinese rule (2) Achieve ethnic equality (3) Establish a parliamentary democratic government (4) Implement elections for local administrators (5) Develop ethnic cultural education (6) Restore the various ethnic cultural associations (7) Abolish the police state (8) Achieve political freedoms (9) Establish friendly relations with the Soviet Union (10) Reduce taxes (11) Guarantee freedom of religion (12) Drive out the Chinese colonizers (13) Develop agriculture (14) Abolish unpaid labor
Source: Robert Ward, American Consul in Urumqi: "Rebel Objectives in Sinkiang" (September 25, 1945)	Source: Wu Zhongxin, Governor of the Xinjiang Provincial Government: *Diary of Wu Zhongxin* (December 16, 1944)

Source: Compiled by the author.

Turkic-Islamic inhabitants to attend to the life-or-death struggle in which their people were embroiled, and actively engage in the operations of the National Freedom Group.

In essence, "Why Are We Fighting?" serves as the political manifesto of the National Freedom Group. The most remarkable aspect of this manifesto is its particular emphasis on the ethnic and regional ties between the Turkic-Islamic peoples of "East Turkestan," from the Uyghurs and Kazakhs, to the Uzbeks, Kyrgyz, Tatars, and so on:

Our fathers and our fathers' fathers called the place where we are living "East Turkestan." From ancient time there have lived in this place Uighurs, *Taranchis*,[8] Kazaks, Uzbeks, and Tatars; at the present time also it is the place of their habitation. In this territory there are counted to be four million people; more than three million of them are of these nations (that we have named); for that reason the area—East Turkestan—was called the heart of the Turkish nations.... Our native place is East Turkestan; we are the eastern branch and part of the race ... the other parts of which lie within the Soviet Union....

The text maintains that there is an integral connection between a people and the land, essentially asserting the people's territorial rights. The term "native place" as provided in the English version of "Why Are We Fighting?" is likely a translation of the Uyghur word *watan*. *Watan* not only refers to a "native place," but also carries the significance of an "ancestral homeland." The leaflet argues that East Turkestan was the birthplace of the Uyghurs and the other Turkic-Islamic peoples, for the purpose of illustrating that sovereignty over this territory belongs solely to its Turkic ethnic inhabitants. It should be noted that this claim to territorial sovereignty is also founded upon recognition of "national independence": "Of the fourteen nations living in East Turkestan, the ten nations accounted the most numerous have had no national, racial, or cultural relationship nor any community of blood with the Chinese, nor did any ever exist." That is to say, China had no right to rule over this territory: put plainly, the text argues that this swathe of land and the Turkic-Islamic peoples who resided there should be independent of China.

In "Why Are We Fighting?," the term "East Turkestan" is used to refer to the entire territory of Xinjiang. After East Turkestan was captured by the Chinese, the text states, "Our territory was called 'West China' or 'Sinkiang.'" The idea that "East Turkestan" represented the whole of Xinjiang thus emerged for the first time in the East Turkestan independence movement; and unlike in the First East Turkestan Independence Movement, which drew only Uyghur participation, the leaflet also recognized the Kazakhs, Uzbeks, Kyrgyz, Tatars and other Turkic-Islamic peoples as part of the East Turkestan independence movement. The drafters of "Why Are We Fighting?" clearly understood that the inclusion of other Turkic-Islamic peoples apart from the Uyghurs would allow for the conceptual expansion of "East Turkestan," to encompass the entire region of Xinjiang.

To support the legitimacy of the independence movement, apart from highlighting territorial rights as the strongest claim to ethnic independence, "Why Are We Fighting?" also fiercely condemned China's oppressive rule over the society of East Turkestan:

> Through the sands of the desert from remote China there came Chinese to our East Turkistan. With the help of sabers and whips and taking advantage of our love of peace, the whiteness of our hearts, and our trustfulness, they took into their hands the control the whole government; they exacted from us heavy taxes and many kinds of contributions; they oppressed us until we had no more rights than animals. And they were at that time the least enlightened people in the world; they could not give to us brighter lives, they could not increase our knowledge or culture, they could not improve the ordinary living conditions of the people; instead they robbed us of light, held us in slavery, kept us illiterate and plunged us in darkness.

Here, the text describes not only political oppression but economic exploitation, with a particular emphasis on issues related to culture and education, indicating that a sense of crisis surrounding the decline of ethnic culture was among the many reasons prompting the rise of the independence movement. This passage mirrors the analysis of the causes of ethnic conflict offered by Urano Tatsuo in *Discourse on Ethnic Independence*: "The existence of ethnic minorities generally does not signify that ethnic conflict will necessarily ensue. If the 'minority' (ruled) ethnic group develops a sense of crisis vis-à-vis its ethnic extermination due to antagonistic and homogenizing policies of the 'majority' (ruling) ethnic group, leading to increased national self-awareness, it will demand equality with the 'majority' ethnic group, and will seek to restore its rights, autonomy and independence, thus giving rising to ethnic conflict."[9] The National Freedom Group and its offshoots were established in just such a context: "Our aim in forming the 'National Freedom Groups' is to free our people from enslavement to the savage Chinese and thereafter to make it so that these people, who have been oppressed by the Chinese, strangled by them, crushed down by them, may arise again as national races in possession of freedom, equality before the law, wealth, culture, and a fortunate life."

In a perpetuation of the ideals of the First East Turkestan Independence Movement, the Second East Turkestan Independence Movement thus gradually grew out of the fundamental aim of toppling Chinese rule over Xinjiang. However, the geographical heart of the movement had shifted from the southern Tianshan Mountains to the Ili region in the northern Tianshan Mountains, near the border between China and the Soviet Union.

From Sheng Shicai to Wu Zhongxin

Wu Zhongxin, the first provincial governor of Xinjiang to be appointed by the Chinese Nationalist government, arrived in Urumqi to take up his post on October 4, 1944.[10] However, the seat of Nilka (Gongha) County was captured by local Islamic guerrilla forces a mere three days later, on October 7. The fuse that sparked the Second East Turkestan Independence Movement was therefore undoubtedly lit during the regime of Wu's predecessor, Sheng Shicai.

As discussed in the previous chapter, Sheng Shicai's ethnic policies shifted from amnesty to suppression due to his resentment against the presence of Soviet forces, who had created a dual power structure within the Xinjiang regime. However, this dual political structure was not merely manifested within the government: it also extended into ethnic relations. Sheng Shicai's anti-Soviet policies thus not only harmed Soviet interests in Xinjiang: they also signaled calamity for all of the indigenous ethnic groups residing in the region.

The falling-out between Sheng Shicai and the Soviet Union prompted the Russians to halt their exports of industrial products to Xinjiang. This caused a shortage in the supply of commodity goods, bringing the Xinjiang economy to the brink of collapse. The indigenous Muslim peoples suffered greatly during the crisis, and were reportedly unable even to bury their dead: "Stocks of cheap manufactured cotton were soon exhausted. Islamic custom prescribes that a corpse be wound in a shroud, which requires up to twenty feet of cloth. Now there was nothing in which to bury the dead."[11]

Following efforts in 1942 to begin unifying the currencies of Xinjiang and the interior provinces, commodity prices in Xinjiang experienced

Wu Zhongxin (1884–1959)

a sharp rise in inflation. In the case of wheat flour, if the price index in 1940 were set as 100, by late 1942, it had risen to 865; by 1945, the index ballooned to 75,000, increasing by a factor of 750. According to contemporary accounts, the currency inflation rate reached 1,200% by 1944.[12] "Why Are We Fighting?" blames the Chinese government for the economic collapse: "There previously existed friendly trading relations between the people of East Turkestan and the Soviet Government; this relationship was disrupted by the Chinese administration; this cessation of trade worked great hardship in our lives." Of course, the "Soviets" should here be understood as referring more specifically to the region of Central Asia held by the Soviet Union.

Under these straitened economic circumstances, Sheng Shicai became even more ruthless in his plundering of the people. In 1943, Sheng ordered a levy of ten thousand war horses upon the nomadic peoples to support the formation of a new cavalry troop, further stirring up discontent within the population.[13]

In examining the political manifesto of the National Freedom Group, "Why Are We Fighting?," it is clear that Sheng Shicai's betrayal of his own "Six-Point Policy" and his repeated impositions upon the Turkic Muslim peoples directly instigated the rise of the Second East Turkestan Independence Movement.

> In the years 26 and 27 [1937–1938] the savage policies of Sheng Tupan [Governor Sheng] began to be put in operation, at the same time that fascism started.
>
> In the same way that fascism counts as its enemies all people who love peace and freedom, thus did Sheng Tupan and the savage Chinese who surrounded him count us, the native people of East Turkestan, as their enemies and as an inferior race. They oppressed us with every kind of cruelty. In 26 and 27 and the subsequent years Sheng Tupan arrested Ha Jeeneeyas [Hoja Niyaz], Sherif Jan [Sharif Khan], and over four thousand others of the vanguard. . . .
>
> Our fighters for the people's freedom will unite our forces in friendship and under right leadership to rise against the Chinese in order to destroy their savage mastery and power; therefore there have been formed in every locality the illegal "National Freedom Groups."[14]

It should be noted here that Abdulkerim Abbasow, the leader of the secret National Freedom Group in Ghulja (Yining), suffered direct harm as a result of Sheng Shicai's policies of ethnic suppression. Abbasow's father Hasim was arrested due to his relationship with Hoja Niyaz, and Abbasow himself was banished to Sawan (Shawan) County for being the "son of a traitor."[15]

In early 1943, the Nationalist government gradually began moving military, administrative, and party forces into Xinjiang, threatening Sheng Shicai's dictatorship in the region.[16] To defend his rule, Sheng launched the "August Coup" in 1944, arresting all of the personnel sent in by the Nationalist government, chief among them being Huang Rujin, the Secretary-General of the Nationalist Party in Xinjiang, and Lin Jiyong, head of the Provincial Department of Public Works.[17] The "Huang-Lin Incident" bolstered the Nationalist government's resolve to assume direct control over Xinjiang.[18] To ward off resistance on the part of Sheng Shicai, the central government massed its troops on Xinjiang's eastern border; and on August 29, a public declaration was released announcing that Sheng Shicai had been appointed as the Minister of Agriculture and Forestry, while Wu Zhongxin would take his place as the new governor of Xinjiang.[19] Lacking the erstwhile support of the Soviet Union, with military forces advancing on his borders and internal troubles brewing, Sheng Shicai was cast out of Xinjiang on September 11, bringing a close to his twelve-year dictatorship.

However, the arrival of Nationalist forces in Xinjiang did not represent an immediate end to the problems left behind by the Sheng regime. On the contrary, a campaign for Han Chinese from the interior provinces to emigrate to Xinjiang, the reinforcement of police organizations, and the establishment of provincial branch offices in Xinjiang for the Nationalist government's Central Statistics Bureau and Military Statistics Bureau— the Provincial Supervisory Department and Public Security Department No. 2, which were equivalent to secret police—fomented more discontent among the indigenous peoples.[20] Troops under the command of Zhu Shaoliang, the acting provincial governor and Commander of the 8th Military District, also took advantage of the difference in commodity prices between Xinjiang and China's interior provinces to engage in speculation and profiteering using military trucks and planes, negatively impacting price stability in the region.[21] In May 1944, a large contingent of the Central Army was dispatched to Xinjiang. The arrival of such a large contingent of troops exacerbated the economic chaos in the region,[22] as revealed in Wu Zhongxin's diary:

> On review, Xinjiang currently has four divisions of the Central Army, totaling 36,350 personnel. The monthly rice for each division is 400,000 kilograms; in all, more than 1,500,000 kilograms is required. Xinjiang truly lacks the capacity to shoulder this burden, and given the amount of the shortfall, it is necessary under the circumstances to ship in relief supplies from Gansu Province.[23]

After assuming the post of provincial governor of Xinjiang, Wu Zhongxin, who was on relatively friendly terms with Chiang Kai-shek, initiated a campaign promoting "justice," "national law," and "humanism," and proposed three concrete policies to address the most urgent priorities: "Cleaning up the jails" (releasing innocent prisoners); "pacifying localities" (explaining new government policies to the local ethnic inhabitants, and allaying their resentments); and "promoting friendly diplomatic relations" (restoring an amicable relationship with the Soviet Union).[24] As a result, many of the ethnic leaders imprisoned by Sheng Shicai were set free. In addition, Wu Zhongxin also established pacification committees composed of elite members of the various ethnic groups, which were hastily dispatched to different regions to subdue hostile sentiments among the ethnic inhabitants.

However, Wu Zhongxin, who had served since 1936 as the head of the Mongolian and Tibetan Affairs Commission—the highest organ of the Nationalist government for ethnic affairs—also extolled the idea of ethnic assimilation. According to Wu's secretary, Zeng Xiaolu, upon assuming his post as the governor of Xinjiang, Wu Zhongxin issued notice for repairs to be completed at Confucian and Guan Yu temples in the region, and created a regular schedule for worship. Wu Zhongxin also supported the Nationalist government's immigration policies, and encouraged Han Chinese farmers to emigrate to Xinjiang.[25] At the same time, he repeatedly asserted that the Turkic-Islamic peoples and the Han Chinese had ties of consanguinity. Wu made the following statements to local ethnic leaders across Xinjiang:

> In the past, many people have divided the Han and the Hui in two, believing that the Han and the Hui are two separate races. A careful study

of this view shows that it is in fact irrational. I can tell you plainly that our ancestors were all from a single race, a single bloodline."[26]

The Kazakhs are a branch of the Turkic peoples . . . and the ancestors of the Turks were the Huns, and the ancestor of the Huns was Yu the Great of the Xia Dynasty; as everyone knows, Yu the Great was also the ancestor of the Han.[27]

Historical research shows that the ancestors of the Uyghurs were the Huns, and the Huns are the descendants of Yu the Great of Xia, of the Chunwei. Thus it can be seen that Yu the Great was the ancestor of the Uyghurs. The ancestor of Yu the Great was Xuanyuan, the Yellow Emperor, thus the Uyghurs and the Han alike are the descendants of the Yellow Emperor . . . we therefore know that the Han and the Uyghurs have the same ancestry."[28]

It is clear that Wu Zhongxin hoped to convince both sides of their shared lineage, portraying the indigenous Turkic ethnic groups of Xinjiang as part of the Chinese race to bolster nationalist sentiment and suppress the possibility of calls for independence among the Turkic-Islamic peoples.

However, "Where the dominant race seeks to eliminate the factors of separation by emphasizing cohesion, it may perversely lead to the collapse of the multi-ethnic state."[29] The Nationalist government's efforts to attract a flood of emigrants from the interior provinces into Xinjiang to promote the assimilation of its Muslim inhabitants, along with other Han-centric policies, placed enormous psychological pressure on the indigenous Turkic-Islamic peoples. "Why Are We Fighting?," the political manifesto of the Ili National Freedom Group, denounced such policies: "The people of East Turkestan [Sinkiang] are like an orphaned child, without father or mother or anyone to heed its cries. The savage Chinese have torn the child from the mother that bore it (the Soviet Government) and seek to give it to a foster mother (the Three People's Principles) for the latter to trample it under foot." Without the original Uyghur text, it is difficult to say whether this translated passage is true to the original. Nevertheless, we can see that the members of the National Freedom Group were fundamentally unwilling to recognize any direct ties of consanguinity between themselves and China, and accused China of failing to care for the people of Xinjiang as her true-born children.

5.2 Secret Rebel Organizations and Guerrilla Forces Formed by the Turkic-Islamic Peoples

The Ghulja National Freedom Group

According to *Materials on the Three Districts Revolution in Ili Prefecture* and a number of other sources,[30] the leadership circle of the Ghulja National Freedom Group was composed of 12 members of Turkic-Islamic descent (Table 5.2). Its chairman, Ilhan Tora, was an Uzbek religious leader who fled to Ghulja from the Republic of Uzbekistan in Soviet Central Asia following the October Revolution of 1917.

Table 5.2 Leaders of the Ghulja National Freedom Group

Name	Ethnicity	Background
Ilhan Tora	Uzbek	Emigrated to Xinjiang from Soviet Central Asia at age 30; an influential religious figure
Abdulkerim Abbasow	Uyghur	Born in the Soviet Union; emigrated to Xinjiang around age 20, along with his family; graduated from the Affiliate High School of Xinjiang College
Kasimjan Kambiri	Uyghur	Poet, also believed to have been influenced by Marxism
Mahmautjan Mahsum	Uyghur	Born in the Soviet Union; emigrated to Xinjiang as a teenager, along with his family; intellectual
Jani Yoldaxup	Uyghur	Born in the Soviet Union, emigrated to Xinjiang around age 20
Rahimjan Sabir Ghaji	Uyghur	Member of the Sabir family of commercial capitalists in Ghulja
Abdurup Mahsum	Uyghur	Religious figure, commercial capitalist
Salman Bay	Uzbek	Born in the Soviet Union and later emigrated to Xinjiang; commercial capitalist and large landowner
Zunon Tayof	Tatar	Intellectual who studied abroad in the Soviet Union and held Soviet citizenship
Omarjan	Uyghur (?)	Unknown
Muhimdin	Uyghur (?)	Unknown
Nurdin Beg	Uyghur (?)	Unknown

Source: Compiled by the author on the basis of *Materials on the Three Districts Revolution in Ili Prefecture (1991) and other sources.*

Tora's background as a religious figure seems to be inconsistent with the image of the National Freedom Group portrayed in its manifesto, "Why Are We Fighting?" Though the Uyhgurs and the other Turkic peoples of Xinjiang were all Muslims, the tract explicitly guarantees freedom of religion, and makes no mention of the role that Islam would play in establishing the state of East Turkestan; the text also does not appear to have been written in an Islamic style. This indicates that the authors of "Why Are We Fighting?" were not Islamists.

The second section of "Why Are We Fighting?" clearly states that the National Freedom Group would fight "to establish anew strong and truly sincere relations of friendship with our great, freedom-loving friend and neighbor, the Soviet Union, and to develop wide and full trading relations between all our trading men and the Sovsintorg." This passage indicates that the authors of "Why Are We Fighting?," rather than being focused on Islam, instead harbored pronounced pro-Soviet inclinations.

In addition, in the passage, "Our nearest blood relations are Kazaks, Kirghiz, Uzbeks, and Tatars," the speakers seem to be Uyghur, indicating that the National Freedom Group was composed of a Uyghur majority.

The above analysis clearly suggests that Illian Tora, the chairman of the National Freedom Group, was not the author of the group's political manifesto, "Why Are We Fighting?," and potentially did not even play a role in determining its content. Contemporary sources, including memoirs by participants in these events, give differing accounts of the timeline for the founding of the National Freedom Group, and its founders. According to the account by Hakim Jappar, Abdulkerim Abbasow proposed the establishment of the National Freedom Group in 1943, and the group was founded by Abbasow and his comrades-in-arms.[31] However, the recollections of Anwar Hanbaba, the leader of a contemporary association of Uyghur intellectuals, indicate that Abbasow was not the founder of the National Freedom Group, as it had been formed before he emigrated from Sawan County, and that Abbasow did not join the group until after his arrival in Ghulja in 1942.[32]

These accounts are all somewhat problematic in that they conflate the National Freedom Group with its predecessors—secret organizations of Uyghur intellectuals. These organizations had all been established at some earlier date: the memoirs of first-hand observers confirm that they were already in existence prior to 1944. According to Saypidin Azizi, there were at least two underground associations of Uyghur intellectuals during this period. The first organization, led by Saydulla Saypullayow, was founded by students returning from study abroad in Tashkent, Uzbekistan, while the other, led by Anwar Hanbaba, was established by students returning from study abroad in Moscow.[33] Reports also point to a third secret organization, the "Marxist-Leninist Association," founded by Abdulkerim Abbasow.[34] None of these organizations were identified as the "National Freedom Group."

The account by Abilmit Hajiyow tallies most closely with the narrative provided in *Materials on the Three Districts Revolution in Ili Prefecture*: namely, that the National Freedom Group was founded on April 9, 1944, and Abdulkerim Abbasow was one of its founders.[35] Saypidin Azizi, another founder of the National Freedom Group, asserts that Abbasow united the Uyghur intellectual associations in Ghulja in early 1944: "Abbasow proposed to all of us the idea that we must establish a revolutionary organization with clear guiding principles and the right views." Abbasow repeatedly approached Ilhan Tora to persuade him to support this undertaking: the National Freedom Group was established with Tora's approval and aid, and Tora was installed as its chairman.[36]

In sum, the above sources allow us to conclude that: the Second East Turkestan Independence Movement was centered on Uyghur intellectuals residing in Ghulja, and began to take shape in late 1943; prior to the establishment of the National Freedom Group, Ghulja was already home to several secret associations of Uyghur intellectuals, which were the predecessors of the National Freedom Group; and Abdulkerim Abbasow played a significant role in founding the National Freedom Group in Ghulja, more so than its chairman, Ilhan Tora.

These facts indicate that, in comparison with the First East Turkestan Independence Movement, the second independence movement featured several new elements and characteristics. Although the Second East Turkestan Independence Movement was still dominated by Uyghur intellectuals, many of these figures had ties to the Soviet Union; the movement was also expanded to include other Turkic-Islamic peoples apart from the Uyghurs. Finally, "Why Are We Fighting?" was likely penned by these pro-Soviet Uyghur intellectuals, and was a reflection of their ideas.

As for the reasons why Abdulkerim Abbasow actively sought to recruit Ilhan Tora to form the National Freedom Group, Yasin Hudabardi, who participated in the East Turkestan Independence Movement in 1944, described this as "a strategy based on the trends at the time and the history of [East Turkestan] to mobilize the populace to achieve strategic revolutionary goals."[37] The National Freedom Group was founded for the purpose of achieving "national freedom,"[38] but the contemporary nature of Uyghur society meant that, without the aid of religious leaders, it would be impossible to marshal public support for a national revolution. Ilhan Tora, a "commanding" religious figure who was "lively in his speech and influential, with a certain power to inspire the people in a religious capacity," thus attracted the attention of the Uyghur intellectuals, who selected him as the chairman of the National Freedom Group.[39]

However, though Ilhan Tora was installed as the chairman, it was in fact Abdulkerim Abbasow who made nearly all the decisions on the activities of the National Freedom Group; Abbasow also presided over the meetings of the group's leadership circle.[40] Another important reason behind Tora's role in the organization, as noted in *History of the Xinjiang Three Districts Revolution*, was that the National Freedom Group was "directly controlled by Consul Dolbezhev and Vice Consul Borisov of the Soviet Consulate in Ghulja."[41] In other words, the National Freedom Group, established in April 1944, was actually led by Soviet agents and pro-Soviet Uyghur intellectuals: the imam Ilhan Tora was selected as a figurehead to broaden the organization's influence in Uyghur society.

Nilka Guerrillas

In mid-August 1944, Turkic-Islamic locals from Ulastay Tag in Nilka County in the Ili District formed a rebel guerrilla force (referred to below as the "Nilka guerrillas"). On August 17, the Nilka guerrillas raided the police station in Ulastay Tag, killing 10 police officers. On September 15, they repelled an incoming force of 300 soldiers and police officers. On October 6–7, guerrilla forces swept in from the north, west and south to capture Nilka County Town. By this point, the Nilka guerrillas had developed into a large contingent of over 800 fighters, divided into three large bands.[42]

The Nilka guerrillas were another group seeking independence for East

Turkestan. On October 14, Liu Bingde, the deputy chief of the Xinjiang Provincial Police Headquarters, who had been dispatched to the Ili District to scout out the movements of the local Turkic Muslims, sent the following report by telegram to Wu Zhongxin:

> On September 2 the bandits, led by the Soviet national Fatih and carrying weapons supplied by the Soviets, slipped into Ulastay Tag in Nilka to stir up riots, disseminating propaganda to sow dissension, and spreading discord amongst the other races to oppose the Han Chinese; they repeatedly bribed and corrupted the people with cotton and silks, tea and sugar, and furthermore they exchanged goods and cash to gather up livestock; thus at first they were no more than some thirty persons, occupying less than fifty square *li*, but within less than a month, they were able to tally a horde of six hundred seventy, capturing Nilka and raising the banner of the illegal state of East Turkestan, turning a single spark into a great conflagration.[43]

As Liu Bingde notes, Soviet support was an important factor in the growing strength of the Nilka guerrillas. Since the guerrillas left behind no written sources, it is unclear to what extent they were ideologically influenced by the Soviet Union: however, the group's formation and activities make evident its close ties to the Soviet Union.

The commanders of the guerrilla forces were all of Turkic-Islamic ethnicity. The key leaders included the Tatar Fatih Muslimow, the Kazakh brothers Akbar and Sayit, and the Uyghurs Jani, Hamit and Osman.[44] It is generally believed that the Nilka guerrillas were formed after the brothers Akbar and Sayit met Fatih and the other figures while seeking to obtain weapons from the Soviet Union, and that they were united by their shared desire to launch an armed resistance against the Chinese government.

However, it should be noted that Akbar and Sayit did not encounter Fatih in Xinjiang, but rather in the region near the Soviet border town of Iyintalga, which neighbored on Xinjiang.[45] Some accounts also claim that their meeting was organized by the Soviet border forces. According to the unpublished Chinese translation of *Memoirs on the Nilka Rebellion*, an officer from the Soviet border forces met with Akbar and Sayit as they sought to purchase weapons in the Soviet Union, and promised to send Fatih Muslimow and his organization to join them in the Ili region; they were also to be supplied with one pistol and one rifle for each guerrilla fighter.[46]

Based on the above sources, we may conclude that the Nilka rebel forces had indeed been supported by the Soviet Union since their inception.

However, other accounts indicate that the Nilka guerrillas merely purchased weapons from the Soviet border forces, while yet another account states that the Soviet border forces demanded that the brothers Akbar and Sayit bring horses from Xinjiang to exchange for the weapons, but that weapons were freely provided to Fatih Muslimow's organization.[47] In other words, the brothers Akbar and Sayit and Fatih Muslimow were initially part of two separate organizations, which received unequal treatment by the Soviet Union.

The brothers Akbar and Sayit had previously been arrested by the local Chinese government on multiple occasions for stealing livestock.[48] They reportedly escaped from jail in July 1944, and with no place to go, they decided to take up arms to resist the government.[49] That is to say, their motivations for following the path of armed resistance were not based on opposition to ethnic oppression, but rather arose purely out of consideration for their own personal situations. This is likely the reason why the Soviet Union reportedly withheld its support for the pair at first.

Due to the presence of Akbar and Sayit, the Nilka guerrillas were labeled by the government as the "Six Bandits." However, prior to 1943, Fatih Muslimow had served as the assistant manager of the Native Products Trading Company (*Yerlik Mehsulanlar Ix Baxkurux Oruni*) of the Nilka County government; he fled to the Soviet Union when he learned that the Sheng Shicai regime was planning to arrest him. Another account relates that Fatih Muslimow abruptly disappeared in early 1944 and secretly gained entry to the Soviet Union.[50] Yet another account states that Muslimow reached the Soviet Union as early as September 1943.[51] Though it fails to provide any concrete evidence, *History of the Xinjiang Three Districts Revolution* asserts that Fatih Muslimow and other figures began receiving military and political training from the Soviet Union in Almaty in the summer of 1943. After the training concluded in August 1944, Muslimow was sent back to mobilize an armed rebellion.[52]

Fatih Muslimow

In sum, we can affirmatively state that Fatih Muslimow, the commander-in-chief of the Nilka guerrillas, was a figure who had had close dealings with the Soviet Union. During his time in the Soviet Union, Muslimow was at the center of a group of Uyghurs who had secretly made their way from Xinjiang to the Soviet Union, including Hamit, Osman, Baychurin, Nur, and Uxur;[53] nearly all of these figures later became leaders of the Nilka guerrilla forces.

Communal Efforts to Topple Chinese Rule

The National Freedom Group of Ghulja had had ties to the Soviet Union since its founding, and was in fact established to serve as an "interim United Front organization";[54] it therefore sought to recruit members from all socioeconomic backgrounds. As shown in Table 5.2, the leaders of the National Freedom Group were composed of three different classes of people: pro-Soviet Uyghur intellectuals, led by Abdulkerim Abbasow; religious leaders, represented by Ilhan Tora; as well as commercial capitalists and large landowners, who also served as part of the Freedom Group's leadership.

The custom of reverence for elders, embodied in the class known as *aq-saqal* ("white beards"), pervaded every facet of Uyghur society. It is noteworthy, however, that despite being the youngest member of the National Freedom Group's leadership circle, Abdulkerim Abbasow was in fact the chief of the organization.[55] It is difficult to imagine that Abbasow could have commanded such political authority without some sort of behind-the-scenes support. A number of different sources indicate that Abbasow's power likely stemmed from his connections to the Soviet Union.

Abdulkerim Abbasow did not study abroad in the Soviet Union, but he did live in the Soviet Union until age 13. Prior to his arrival in Ghulja in 1942, he had also worked as a translator for a Soviet technician in Sawan County, and was in close contact with Soviet figures.[56] Even more surprisingly, Abbasow's first organization, the "Marxist-Leninist Association," admitted personnel from a Soviet intelligence agency. According to the memoirs of Wen Feiran, the head of the Ili District Office and a founding member of the Marxist-Leninist Association, apart from Yang Fengyi, Abbasow's Han Chinese lover, the association's earliest members included two Soviet consular personnel, one of whom—referred to as "Vasily"—was

Abdulkerim Abbasow
(1921–1949)

also an intelligence officer at the embassy. It should be noted that this "Vasily" later became a military advisor to the East Turkestan Republic,[57] and was given the rank of Colonel in the East Turkestan Army.[58] As discussed above, *History of the Xinjiang Three Districts Revolution* asserts that the National Freedom Group was directly controlled by Dobrezhev and Borisov, both officers of the Soviet consulate in Ghulja. However, the text cites no sources to support this claim, so it is not possible to confirm whether "Vasily" is a reference to one of these figures.[59]

The admission of Soviet intelligence officers into Abdulkerim Abbasow's Marxist-Leninist Association indicates that Abbasow had frequent contact with the Soviet consulate. It also suggests that Abbasow may have been acting in accordance with Soviet designs. According to Anwar Hanbaba, the division of tasks at the headquarters of the National Freedom Group left Abdulkerim Abbasow with the responsibility of "preparing for the revolution." Abbasow consequently made frequent secret trips to the Soviet Union.[60] Given these circumstances, it is clear that the Soviet Union had been playing an extremely important role in the activities of the National Freedom Group and its core group of Uyghur intellectuals since late 1943 and early 1944, contemporaneous with the resurgence of the East Turkestan Independence Movement. 1943 was also the year of the Soviet Union's victory in the Battle of Stalingrad in the war against Germany. The February victory was a key turning point which allowed the Soviet Union to once more turn its gaze eastward, channeling support to the forces of the East Turkestan Independence Movement in order to restore its influence in Xinjiang.

As a matter of fact, regardless of their ethnic background, socioeconomic status, or past ties to the Soviet Union, the vast majority of the participants in the secret rebel associations and armed groups established by Xinjiang's indigenous Turkic-Islamic peoples gladly accepted Soviet aid to achieve the mutual goal of overturning Chinese rule. In contrast with the First East Turkestan Independence Movement, which centered on southern Xinjiang, the acceptance of Soviet support was a salient characteristic of the Second East Turkestan Independence Movement, which erupted along the border between China and the Soviet Union.

In examining Soviet involvement in the Turkic-Islamic independence movement, the Soviet Union's willingness to render assistance was certainly an important factor; but why did the indigenous peoples of Xinjiang not turn toward Japan, Britain or the United States, rather than unilaterally seeking support from the Soviet Union as a means of toppling Chinese rule? There are three likely causes:

First, geographically speaking, the Soviet Union is Xinjiang's closest neighbor, and it was also most conveniently positioned for communications and transportation in and out of Xinjiang. As Sheng Shicai shifted toward policies of ethnic suppression, many minority leaders and elites, particularly Uyghur intellectuals who had studied abroad in the Soviet Union during Sheng Shicai's honeymoon period with the Soviets, or who had close ties to the Soviet Union, responded by gathering in the Chinese border town of Ghulja near the Soviet border.[61]

Second, this time period coincided with a falling-out between Sheng Shicai and the Soviet Union. As discussed above, Sheng Shicai's reversal on his ethnic policies was in fact conceived as a retaliation against the infiltration of Xinjiang's political and social spheres by Soviet agents. Given the circumstances, the enmity borne by the indigenous Turkic-Islamic peoples for Sheng Shicai was easily transformed into pro-Soviet sentiments.

The final and most important reason was that the Turkic-Islamic peoples of Xinjiang had ethnic and cultural ties to ethnic groups in Soviet Central Asia: this caused them to develop a strong interest in Soviet-style "national liberation," which involved the establishment of Soviet-aligned republics for different ethnic groups. This idea is clearly expressed in the political manifesto of the National Freedom Group, "Why Are We Fighting?": "Our [the Uyghurs'] nearest blood relations are Kazaks, Kirghiz, Uzbeks, and Tatars. In the Soviet Union each of these races has organized its own Government and its members are living free and joyful lives." Many of the Turkic-Islamic inhabitants of Xinjiang were deceived by the pseudo-state notion of an "aligned republic."

5.3 The Ghulja Uprising

Abdulkerim Abbasow and Ilhan Tora during the Rebellion

The Second East Turkestan Independence Movement reached high tide in October and November 1944. On October 6–7, the Nilka guerrillas stormed and captured Nilka County Town. The "Ghulja Uprising," which led into the Ili Rebellion, broke out on November 7. The East Turkestan Republic (*Xarkiy Turkistan Jumhuriyiti*) was founded soon after the uprising on November 12, in the city of Ghulja.

The Uyghur businessman Tarikat Musabayow reported the events of the Ghulja Uprising to the Xinjiang provincial governor, Wu Zhongxin:

> On November 5, Soviet soldiers and Nilka bandits appeared in Ghulja, in all some ten-odd persons; in the dark of night, they concealed themselves in friendly houses. On that day, the Nilka rebel bandits surrounded us, and on the 6th, the bandits swept in from the north; on the 7th, a horde of over one thousand bandits invaded Ghulja, working in concert with the bandits concealed within; thus began the incident.[62]

The groups involved in the Ghulja Uprising, which led to the high tide of the Second East Turkestan Independence Movement, included the National Freedom Group, referred to in the passage above as "concealed bandits"; as well as the Nilka guerrillas, referred to here as "rebel bandits."

Abdulkerim Abbasow was a key leader in the Ghulja Uprising. On November 2, Abbasow convened a meeting of the National Freedom Group near Qorghas (modern-day Huocheng County), where it was decided that the Ghulja Uprising would be launched on November 10. However, the plans were moved forward to November 7 after discovering that the government armed forces were building defensive emplacements around Ghulja. The Nilka guerrillas were sent into the area on November 4. On the evening of November 6, Abbasow led a group of more than 60 fighters across the Soviet border to secretly enter the city of Ghulja and set up a command post: "After consulting with the Ghulja Freedom Group, the uprising was set for November 7, the anniversary of the Soviet Union's October Revolution."[63] Abbasow had previously been in contact with the Nilka guerrillas regarding the timeframe for the uprising, so the purpose of his arrival on the 6th was likely to spread the word amongst the other members of the Freedom Group. On November 7, Abbasow led his forces to attack the police headquarters, as the Nilka guerrillas swept in from the outskirts of the city to lay siege to Ghulja.[64]

The events of the Ghulja Uprising appear to be fairly straightforward. After withstanding a series of attacks against their defensive positions near the local commissioner's office, police headquarters, telegraph office, and power station, the remaining government forces retreated northeast to the Hayranbaq region on November 12;[65] at this point, the city of Ghulja essentially fell under the control of the rebel forces (Figure 5.1). However,

Figure 5.1   Street Map of Ghulja

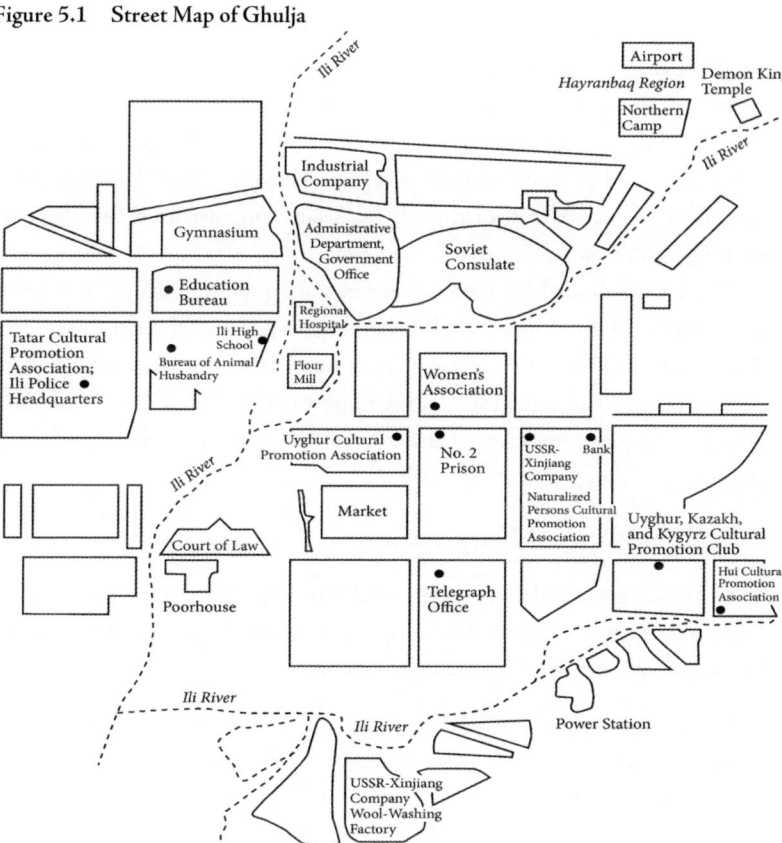

Source: Hand-drawn by the author on the basis of "Map of Chaos in the City Districts during the Ghulja Incident" (Zhang Dajun, Seventy Years of Upheaval in Xinjiang, p. 6311) and local surveys.

Ilhan Tora (1885–1976)

some questions remain: Did the city's Turkic-Islamic residents, who had no fighting experience, participate in the battle? If so, how were they organized and mobilized? Many of the facts surrounding the Ghulja Uprising remain elusive.

Apart from Abdulkerim Abbasow, the rebel command post was also overseen by Rahimjan Sabir Ghaji, a liaison officer in the National Freedom Group and a commercial capitalist based in Ghulja. Though this is not widely known, Ilhan Tora, the chairman of the National Freedom Group, was in fact also present at the command post during the uprising.

Ilhan Tora's role was to inspire religious animosity amongst the rebels. Ilhan Tora delivered the following speech in the dead of night at a meeting at the command post on November 6: "For the sake of holy Islam, we shall wage *Jihad* on the path shown to us by Allah. The sacrificed shall become martyrs, and the survivors shall become *Haji*."[66]

Ilhan Tora denied his involvement in the Ghulja Uprising.[67] However, the phrase, "The sacrificed shall become martyrs, and the survivors shall become *Haji*" (*Olsak xiet, Hayat kalsak hazi*) later became an important rallying cry for the rebellion.[68] This indicates that Ilhan Tora's religious authority unquestionably played a key role in mobilizing the populace to join the rebellion.

"Jihad" for National Independence

Ilhan Tora was elected as president of the Interim Government of the East Turkestan Republic. At the founding ceremony on November 12, he delivered a speech, part of which is extracted below:

> Arise! The time for rising up has come. Allah is our faith, Muhammad is our prophet, Islam is our religion, and East Turkestan is our fatherland. The time for rising up has come. . . . These bloodthirsty Han have perpetrated brutal oppression against all our people, and the people have endured extreme suffering. Under these circumstances, we truly could bear no more. Thus all our people, who had not the strength to live on, risked death in accordance with Allah's will to "punish the tyrants"; we believe in Allah's undeniable promise. We, the people of Ili, have united as one, rising

up with clubs, hammers and branches to rebel against a tyrannical regime. As the people of Ili unite, the strength of the masses shall be as the promise of the strength of Allah: when, in a very short time, the tyrannical Han regime has been overthrown, we shall found our Islamic government. We shall trample the banners of the bloody Han oppressors underfoot and turn them into dust. We shall raise the white flag passed down by our ancestors, emblazoned with the symbols of the crescent moon and star, on which is written the holy word Selflessness; we shall uphold the honor, dignity and solemnity of this sacred flag. To preserve these things, all Muslims and all soldiers shall reform our armies, take up arms, and as the Prophet Muhammad says, spare neither our lives nor our property to fight against the regime of tyranny. With Allah's guidance, we shall vanquish our enemies: to live with joy in this life and enter paradise in the next, we must realize these precious teachings.[69]

Efforts to highlight the Ghulja Uprising's connection to Islam were not limited to Ilhan Tora's speech. A number of sources and witness accounts assert that, on the day of the uprising, the rebels began carrying white flags bearing the phrase "There is no God but Allah, and Muhammad is the messenger of Allah" as an expression of their faith.[70] One participant in the Ghulja Uprising, who later served for an extended period as the commander of the Army Headquarters of the East Turkestan Republic, confirmed in an interview with the author that the rallying cry most frequently used during the rebellion was "Islam, arise" (*Islam azatlihi*).[71] There is no doubt that the rebel commanders deliberately drew upon Islamic symbolism to persuade the rebel fighters that they had joined a sacred "Islamic *jihad.*"

Another rebel candidly declared in his memoirs: "Denying that the Three Districts Revolution initially used slogans about independence like 'Found the East Turkestan Republic' [*Xarkiy Turkistan Jumuhuritini Kurux*], 'Fight for Independence' as well as slogans like 'The sacrificed shall become martyrs, and the survivors shall become *Haji*' is just covering up the true facts. These slogans were determined by the domestic and foreign circumstances and the historical conditions at the time; I think it was a strategy to mobilize the population to achieve strategic revolutionary goals."[72]

The slogan "Fight for Independence" (*Mustakkillik Uqun Kurax*) naturally refers to gaining independence from China. To strengthen the legitimacy of this "independence," Ilhan Tora fiercely condemned Chinese rule over the region of "East Turkestan" (Xinjiang) in his speech:

As for the fallacy that "Xinjiang is an inseparable part of the Chinese territories," the swindlers who manufactured this false history must listen clearly, and forever remember these facts: they must not forget that the heroic children of East Turkestan assailed them with clubs, and they could not withstand our attack. The bureaucrats and emperors of China built a Great Wall of three thousand five hundred kilometers for the sake of their own lands and power, and ran inside this Great Wall as does a rabbit who fears the hawk. Though these facts have been concealed by the historians of the Han government, the history of the entire world can testify to them. The sun cannot be covered by one's jacket sleeves. . . . The Han government had best abandon its ambitions for the territory of East Turkestan, and find a way to liberate its own Chinese territories from the iron heel of Japanese imperialism. It ought not hand over its richest and most beautiful lands, gardens, mountains and rivers to the Japanese imperialists, whilst oppressing the people of East Turkestan and invading the lands of East Turkestan.[73]

The pro-Soviet Uyghur intellectuals who led the movement were essentially erased from the events of the Ghulja Uprising. This is likely because these figures had little influence over Turkic-Islamic society in Xinjiang. The movement's leader, Abdulkerim Abbasow, was no more than 23 years of age; while Ilhan Tora, an authoritative religious figure who had stood on the front lines of the rebellion, embodied the nature of the Ghulja Uprising by "fighting to liberate the entire nation from the tyranny of Chinese rule over the fatherland of East Turkestan" and "performing the duties of a Muslim by waging *jihad*." It is evident that the rebel commanders made these arrangements to inspire Xinjiang's Turkic-Islamic inhabitants to join the rebellion in greater numbers. In fact, the rebellion rapidly expanded in scale and ultimately achieved victory due precisely to this strategy.

The Massacre of Han Civilians

However, these same factors caused the Ghulja Uprising to develop into a massacre of the Han "infidels." Likely owing to the bitter hatred directed toward the Sheng Shicai regime, emigrants from northeastern China (Sheng Shicai's place of origin) were reportedly targeted in mass slayings.[74] Many sources indicate that the rebels not only massacred the captured government soldiers, but also led great numbers of ordinary Han civilians to the same fate.[75]

Abdulkerim Abbasow, who was appointed as the Minister of Internal Affairs in the Interim Government of the East Turkestan Republic, made the following statement regarding the aftermath of the Ghulja Uprising: "We have made many mistakes. In the national liberation movement, we did not distinguish between the rulers and the ruled of the oppressor people, equating them [the ruled] with the Nationalist Party reactionaries."[76]

Ahmatjan Kasimi, another leader of the Interim Government, later declared: "With respect to ethnic problems, when our national liberation movement began—that is, when the national liberation movement entered the stage of armed insurrection—it cannot be said that we made no mistakes. Our people took up arms to join the battle, and as we overthrew the Nationalist Party regime and annihilated its armed forces in Ghulja, Suiding and other regions, the Han people were regarded as equal to the Nationalist Party reactionaries; we were unable to separate the Han population from the bureaucrats of the minority Nationalist government, the Nationalist armies who exploited the people, and the Nationalist police who oppressed the people, bearing the mistaken belief that all the Han Chinese were our enemies. The result was that we treated all the Han Chinese equally, not distinguishing between friend and foe, and wrongly attacking our friends—the Han people."[77]

Based on the above statements, we may conclude that the massacre of Han civilians during the Ghulja Uprising was not limited to the actions of a small number of the Turkic-Islamic rebels, but rather emerged from the consensus beliefs guiding the movement as a whole. Some of the Uyghur rebels involved in these events emphasized in their memoirs that the massacre of the Han population was motivated by the slaughter of the Turkic-Islamic peoples by police authorities. Before the police withdrew from the area surrounding Ghulja, they massacred a number of the local Turkic-Islamic residents, and threw their remains down the toilets and well at the police headquarters. The slaughter and the desecration of the remains provoked the enmity of the Turkic-Islamic population toward the Han Chinese, leading to the massacre of the Han residents.

Since more than one source refers to the slaughter and abuse of the region's Turkic-Islamic residents, these events are unlikely to have been fabricated. However, it should be noted that, though the authors of these memoirs were directly involved in the Ghulja Uprising, the accounts vary as to the locations where the remains were discovered and the number of bodies which were desecrated.

According to Yasin Hudabardi and Ismailow Mahmmut, the slaughter occurred at the Suiding County Police Bureau. However, Hudabardi states that 35 corpses were desecrated at the police bureau,[78] while Mahmmut places the number at 80;[79] the figures provided in these two accounts differ widely. In contrast, Saypidin Azizi states that the remains of nearly 100 people were discovered at the Ili District Police Headquarters.[80] In a work published in 1989, Sawdanow Zayir echoes Saypidin Azizi with respect to the location of the massacre, but reports the death toll as the very specific figure of 238.[81] Notably, another memoir published by Zayir in 1985 states that the remains were discovered at the Ghulja City Police Bureau, and gives the figure of 70 corpses.[82]

The variations in these accounts might easily lead one to believe that these events were invented or inflated by the Uyghur authors who participated in the Ghulja Uprising in an effort to justify the massacre of the Han population. Given that the Soviet military was also directly involved in the Ghulja Uprising, was it the police forces of the old regime, or could it have been the Soviet Red Army or even the rebels themselves who were responsible for the deaths of those 35 or 238 Turkic-Islamic civilians? The lack of definitive sources precludes us from lightly leaping to conclusions. However, the rebel headquarters immediately spread word about the massacre among the Uyghur population, and photographs of the dead were circulated among the public. It is clear that the rebel commanders seized upon these events to incite rancor among the Turkic-Islamic peoples and mobilize them to join the rebellion. In this light, the massacre of Han civilians during the Ghulja Uprising may be imputed to a certain extent to the actions of the rebel commanders.

5.4 Victory in the Ghulja Uprising and Soviet Support

The Soviet Union and the Planning of the Ghulja Uprising

Although both the Nilka guerrillas and the National Freedom Group in Ghulja were devoted to the East Turkestan Independence Movement, it is not clear that a leadership relationship was formed between the two groups prior to the uprising. To be sure, Sawdanow Zayir, who took part in the Ghulja Uprising and later became the secretary of the Political Department of the National Army of the East Turkestan Republic in April 1945, stated in his memoirs: "The peoples of Nilka, with the direct guidance and support of the National Freedom Group in Ghulja, as well as the guidance of Akbar and Fatih, rose up in rebellion to oppose the rule of the Nationalist Party reactionaries, and established an armed organization."[83] However, Zayir did not give any specific examples of the National Freedom Group's top-down "guidance" of the Nilka guerrillas.

The author interviewed several participants in the Second East Turkestan Independence Movement while visiting Urumqi. One of the interviewees stated that Zayir's memoirs were largely credible, but that he had concealed some of the facts with respect to the Soviet Union. Apart from Zayir's memoirs, there is no direct or circumstantial evidence to prove that there was any contact between the Nilka guerrillas and the National Freedom Group in Ghulja prior to the uprising. Since the two groups were established in different regions and had no members in common, it is more plausible that the coordination between the two sides during the Ghulja Uprising resulted through the mediation of an authoritative third party. The Nilka guerrillas, in particular, had no history of activity in the region of Ghulja.

Uyghur sources indicate that this mediator was in fact the Soviet Union. According to several written records, on November 4, 1944, three Soviet agents visited the camp of the Nilka guerrillas in Ulastay Tag. They handed over thirteen automatic rifles to Fatih Muslimow and "passed on the orders from the superior, which were that the Nilka guerrillas were to attack Ghulja. They also communicated that, while the fighters assaulted Ghulja from the east, the Ghulja revolutionaries would attack from the west."[84] *History of the Xinjiang Three Districts Revolution* gives a similar account, stating that the Soviet Consulate in Ghulja sent representatives to request that the guerrilla forces launch an attack on the city to coordinate with the rebellion led by the National Freedom Group.[85]

It should also be noted that pro-Soviet Russian expatriates had established an armed organization in the Lucaogou region in October 1944. On November 6, on the eve of the Ghulja Uprising, this armed group attacked the police headquarters in Lucaogou, severing the lines of communication between Urumqi and Ghulja, thus preventing the government armed forces from dispatching supporting troops to the Ili region. These three organizations stemmed from different origins, were formed independently of one another, and operated in different regions: absent a single unifying force with authority over all three groups to oversee the detailed planning and coordination, it is inconceivable that these disparate groups could have carried out such an intricate plan to launch the Ghulja Uprising (Figure 5.2).

In fact, there were signs as early as October 1944 that the Soviet Union was planning a major strategic move in Xinjiang. Around this time, the Kashgar District Police Bureau sent an intelligence report to Wu Zhongxin, who found the events detailed in the report to be quite curious:

> Before the Soviet consul in Kashgar returned to the Soviet Union, he warned the consulate personnel not to talk; when the new consul arrived to assume his post, he also said they must not talk overmuch, and within two months all would be well, etc. Given that both the new and old consuls made the same comments, the significance bears pondering.[86]

Based on the timeframe, these events appear to foreshadow the imminent Ghulja Uprising. First-hand accounts also indicate that Abdulkerim Abbasow entered the Soviet Union on multiple occasions prior to the uprising to purchase weapons.[87] The above statements and facts fully support the conjecture that the Soviet Union was involved in the planning stages of the Ghulja Uprising.

Soviet Military Intervention in the Ghulja Uprising

One element that remains unknown is the presence of Soviet figures within Abdulkerim Abbasow's forces. It is known that the commander-in-chief of the rebel headquarters in the Ghulja Uprising was in fact a Soviet national named Piotr Alexandrov. However, Abbasow reportedly led a group of only 66 fighters across the Soviet border and into Ghulja;[88] given the difficulty of slipping a larger contingent into Ghulja, which was closely guarded by the government armed forces, this figure is credible. Yet it is also unlikely that a group of only 66 fighters could have successfully launched the uprising. This naturally leads to the suggestion that Soviet forces may have been directly involved in military action on the side of the rebels.

The memoirs written by Turkic Muslims who lived through the Ghulja

Figure 5.2 Coalition of East Turkestan Nationalist Forces in Ili District

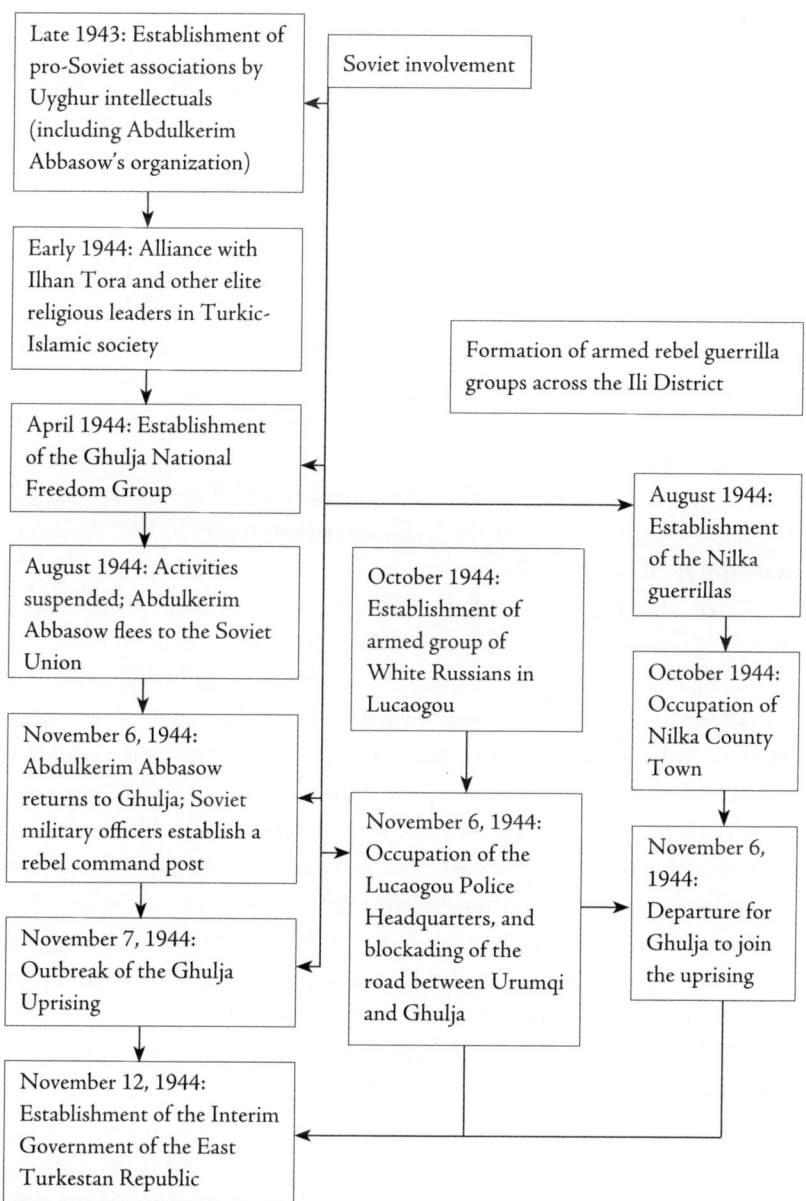

Source: Compiled by the author.

Uprising do not address the question of direct intervention by Soviet military forces. According to the views of certain officials in the era of the People's Republic of China, victory was achieved in the Ghulja Uprising because the government forces were too few, and the rebels overwhelmed them by force of numbers.[89] To clarify this issue, we must first compare the situations of the Turkic-Islamic fighters and government troops in the Ghulja region.

On September 12, 1944, the day after Sheng Shicai left Xinjiang, the acting provincial governor and military commander Zhu Shaoliang immediately dispatched Deputy Commander Du Defu of the 128th Division to Ili District, with orders to take direct command over military operations in the region. The government forces in Ghulja reportedly numbered more than 2,500 at the time.[90] It is true that a contingent was sent to subdue the Nilka guerrillas, but the distance from Ghulja to Nilka was only 100 kilometers, and these troops could have returned from Nilka at any time. At the same time, by request of Du Defu, a battalion from the 128th Division was already en route to reinforce Ghulja.[91]

What was the strength of the rebel forces at this time? As discussed above, in October, the Nilka guerrillas numbered more than 800 fighters; according to a report by Liu Bingde, the guerrilla forces had swelled to 1,500 by November 4, and were armed with 300 rifles.[92] Sawdanow Zayir states that the Nilka guerrillas numbered 1,500 by the time of their assault on Ghulja, but carried only 500 weapons.[93] Moreover, at the point when the Ghulja Uprising broke out, only the second band of the Nilka guerrillas had arrived at Ghulja as planned. This array of forces simply did not have the strength to overwhelm the government troops. Thus, if the uprising was indeed carried out independently by the Turkic Muslims in the region, the other key faction in the rebellion—the National Freedom Group of Ghulja—must have contributed a larger contingent of forces.

However, the fact is that the National Freedom Group had suspended all organizational activities in August, after the group's existence was discovered by the government. The clash between government armed forces and the Nilka guerrillas at Ulastay Tag on August 17 brought the Xinjiang provincial government's attention to the unchecked activities of the East Turkestan Independence Movement in the Ili region; as a result, Liu Bingde, the deputy chief of the Xinjiang Provincial Police Headquarters, was dispatched to Ghulja. Liu was of Hui ethnicity, had been born in Ili, and was fluent in the Uyghur language. Relying on his language skills and local contacts, Liu swiftly launched an investigation into the operations of the National Freedom Group. On discovering the threat, the National Freedom Group suspended all activities on the advice of Ilhan Tora. Many of its members fled to other regions of Xinjiang, while others, including Abdulkerim Abbasow, sought refuge in the Soviet Union.

When Wu Zhongxin arrived in Xinjiang in October 1944 and took up his position as governor, he sent Cao Riling, Chief of Staff of the 7th Reserve Division, to Ghulja as well. Cao Riling built defensive emplacements around Ghulja and arrested a number of rebel activists, rendering the atmosphere in Ghulja even more hostile for the National Freedom Group, and certainly precluding any secret activities. Thus, in comparison with the government forces, the rebels were indeed quite limited in strength; it simply was not possible for them to have independently achieved victory in the Ghulja Uprising.

In contrast with the Uyghur sources, the government military officers responsible for battle command at Ghulja all stated in their reports to Zhu Shaoliang, Commander of the 8th Military District, that the Soviet military was directly involved in the attack on Chinese government forces:

> November 9 [1944]. In the afternoon, the response [from the Chief of Staff] stated that an intelligence report had been received from Ghulja; partisans of dual nationality were discovered among the bandits in the region, with twenty new-style machine guns; they appeared to be of Soviet background, etc.[94]
>
> November 13. The rebels have ample ammunition, which could only have been supplied by the Soviet consulate. . . . There are a number of vehicles behind the offices, all hairy beasts [slang term for Russians].[95]

History of the Xinjiang Three Districts Revolution states, "As the battle reached its fiercest point, Polinov (a White Russian), who had once served as a military advisor to Sheng Shicai, led more than 60 armed fighters (all Russians) in two trucks from the Soviet Union to Ghulja to join the attack against the Nationalist army and police forces."[96] The actual number of Soviet nationals on the battlefield may have been even higher. On November 13, Jiang Xuanquan, the commander of the government armed forces, led his troops from Nilka back to Ghulja, where they encountered approximately 100 soldiers in Soviet military uniform behind the Soviet consulate. Both sides opened fire in an intense battle. Jiang Xuanquan wrote in a telegram to his superior: "This is not a bandit problem, but rather the beginning of a formal conflict between the Soviet Union and our army." On the same day, Cao Riling, the supreme commander of the government forces in the Ghulja region, wrote in a telegram to Zhu Shaoliang: "This is called bandit suppression, but it is in fact an international war. . . . The bandits in the city are all naturalized persons and Tatars, arrayed in the vicinity of the consulate, and all their weapons are of Soviet make." Cao's recommendation was therefore to, "Use diplomatic means to make a conciliatory request for friendly assistance, but do not allow Soviet Russia to send in its armed forces."[97]

With respect to direct Soviet intervention in military operations in the Ghulja Uprising, Wen Feiran, a Han Chinese associate of Abdulkerim Abbasow, affirmed that, "Abdulkerim Abbasow received the support of the Soviet Red Army to launch a revolution in Ghulja." Wen also recalled that Abbasow was concerned that his Han Chinese friend would suffer mischance during the massacre of Han civilians in Ghulja, and requested that the Soviet Red Army provide protection for Wen Feiran.[98]

The former commander of the East Turkestan Army Headquarters mentioned earlier in this chapter gave the following description of the Ghulja Uprising in an interview with the author in August 1991:

> The Ghulja Uprising was in fact a revolution with direct Soviet involvement. The Soviet Union not only provided aid in the form of personnel, weapons, and matériel, but also deployed its troops, and even directly committed artillery, tanks, aircraft, etc. to the battle. Because even pocket knives were confiscated during Sheng Shicai's era, it was simply impossible for the residents to have owned weapons. The Nationalist army had all the weapons.

The commander also detailed his own experiences during the uprising: "When the Ghulja Uprising broke out, there were many Russians in the rebel command post. The Soviet military personnel who came to Ghulja needed translators who understood Russian. Because I knew Russian, I was invited to join the revolution." Some Russian scholars argue that the Soviet

Union not only played a decisive organizational role in the Ghulja Uprising, but also provided key support with respect to matériel, tactical operations, and battle command, and that the victory achieved in the Ghulja Uprising was due to the proactive assistance offered by the Soviet Union. This conclusion does not seem to be an overreach.[99]

Summary

The date on which the Ghulja Uprising erupted, November 7, was the anniversary of Russia's October Revolution; even more coincidentally, the founding date of the Interim Government of the East Turkestan Republic was November 12, the same day on which the Islamic Republic of East Turkestan had been declared twelve years earlier during the First East Turkestan Independence Movement. The first of these dates held a special significance for the Soviet Union, while the second symbolized the history of the independence movement, thus crystallizing the two key elements of both the Ghulja Uprising and the Second East Turkestan Independence Movement.

Uyghur Saiman, the editor-in-chief of *Free East Turkestan* (*Azatlik Xarkiy Turkistan*), the official newspaper of the East Turkestan Republic, offered the following commentary on the relationship between the first and second East Turkestan independence movements: "In the two revolutions that broke out during the past decade, the aim was always national liberation. The targets of the revolutions were always the colonizers and dictators."[100] Ahmatjan Kasimi voiced high praise for the Islamic Republic of East Turkestan, which was founded during the First East Turkestan Independence Movement: "12 years ago, our province rose up in rebellion to liberate the Islamic people, calling for ethnic equality, integrity, construction and so on, to bring peace to our people."[101] The fundamental aim of the East Turkestan independence movements, which gradually took shape in the 1930s and 1940s, was to overthrow Chinese rule over East Turkestan; this goal was passed down after the first independence movement, and once again embodied in the Second East Turkestan Independence Movement.

Like the First East Turkestan Independence Movement, the Second East Turkestan Independence Movement held high the banner of Islamic *jihad*, drawing on the authority of religious leaders to mobilize more Turkic

Muslims to join the revolution. However, leadership by pro-Soviet Uyghur intellectuals and direct Soviet support for the later movement formed an important distinction between the first and second movements. From the outset, the Turkic-Islamic intellectual association represented by Abdulkerim Abbasow was granted Soviet aid, and worked in concert with the Soviet Union to plan the revolution. During the Ghulja Uprising, the Soviet Union directly committed troops to Chinese soil, deploying tanks, artillery and aircraft to strike a devastating blow against the local Chinese government forces. The Chinese scholar Li Sheng was able to confirm the following information held in the internal archives of the former Soviet Union: "A special operations unit was established under the guidance of the Soviet Union, led by General Ignarov of the Special Department of the People's Commissariat for Internal Affairs and his assistant Aleksandr Langfang, the head of the 4th Office of the First Directorate of the People's Commissariat for Internal Affairs. Command posts for this operations unit were established in Almaty and the border town of Qorghas. It also oversaw large-scale activities in southern Xinjiang from within the borders of Uzbekistan and Kyrgyzstan; the People's Commissariat for Internal Affairs of the Soviet Union launched operations there."[102] Given the above characteristics of the Second East Turkestan Independence Movement, it may feasibly be described as a Soviet-backed *jihad* carried out by the Turkic-Islamic ethnic inhabitants of China for the purpose of overthrowing Chinese rule.

CHAPTER 6

Authority and Power
Political Structure of the East Turkestan Republic in Wartime

On November 12, 1944, the Ghulja National Freedom Group shed the cloak of secrecy, holding a rally at the Uyghur, Kazakh & Kyrgyz Club in Ghulja to announce the founding of the Interim Government of the "East Turkestan Republic" (*Xarkiy Turkistan Jumhuriyiti*). The sphere of influence of the Interim Government of East Turkestan rapidly expanded, and by March 1945, the republic controlled nearly the entire territory of the Ili Administrative District. Concurrent with the expansion of its power base, the East Turkestan regime also sought to improve upon its existing systems, installing a number of new administrative bodies. On April 8, 1945, the armed rebel groups scattered across the region were reorganized into the army of the East Turkestan Republic—the "National Army" (*Milli Armiya*). Out of these efforts, a clear picture of the political structure of the East Turkestan Republic gradually emerged. This chapter focuses on the expanding sphere of influence of the East Turkestan Republic during this era, tracing political processes in the republic's early period, to analyze the characteristics of its political structure and the context for its formation.

6.1 Legitimacy Founded Upon Traditional Authority

The Two Versions of the "Nine Political Precepts"

As discussed in Chapter 5, many Uyghur texts written during the era of the People's Republic of China use the term "East Turkestan People's

Republic." But in fact, even in June 1946, as the republic's Interim Government stood on the precipice of annihilation, official documents continued to be issued in the name of *Xarkiy Turkistan Jumhuriyiti*, or the "East Turkestan Republic." In other words, the state founded in 1944 on the foundation of Xinjiang's Turkic-Islamic society was not in fact a "people's democratic dictatorship" like the People's Republic of China.

The "Nine Political Precepts" (*Tokkuz Maddlik Siyasiy Programma*, hereafter abbreviated as the "1944 Precepts") were announced at the rally for the founding of the republic's Interim Government on November 12, 1944; because the East Turkestan Republic never drafted a constitution, the 1944 Precepts in fact served as a proto-constitution. Their content is as follows:

> (1) Rooting out the tyranny of the Han Chinese; (2) Establishment of a democratic government; (3) Armed forces belonging to the people; (4) Equality for all ethnic groups; (5) Respect for religion; (6) Popular elections of government officials at all levels; (7) Implementation of pro-Soviet policies; (8) Development of education; (9) Adoption of the Uyghur script as the common written language of the Interim Government.[1]

However, the 1944 Precepts were soon revised. Under Resolution No. 4 of the Interim Government Council, the amended "Nine Political Precepts" (hereafter abbreviated as the "1945 Precepts") were released on January 5, 1945. The 1945 Precepts read:

> (1) The Han murderers in the national territories of the East Turkestan Republic shall be thoroughly exterminated;
>
> (2) A truly free and independent republic shall be established on the foundation of equality for all peoples within the borders of East Turkestan;
>
> (3) The economy of East Turkestan, including industry, agriculture, animal husbandry, private commerce, transportation, and other sectors shall be comprehensively developed, to improve the people's standard of living;
>
> (4) As the vast majority of the peoples living in East Turkestan are of Muslim faith, this religion shall be given special support. Freedom to follow other religions shall also be guaranteed;
>
> (5) The sectors of cultural education, sanitation and health care shall be developed;

(6) Political and economic ties shall be established with all the world's democratic nations, particularly the states neighboring on East Turkestan;

(7) In order to defend East Turkestan and defend peace, people from all ethnic groups must be recruited to establish a mighty army;

(8) Banks, the postal service, forests, and all underground deposits shall revert to state ownership;

(9) The pursuit of private interests, bureaucratism, narrow nationalism, bribe-taking and other bad practices shall be banned from state affairs.[2]

According to Saypidin Azizi, who was installed as Minister of Education of the Interim Government in March 1945, these revisions were implemented by the People's Congress, composed of the People's Representatives elected in each county, "upon the basis of the earlier political precepts formulated by the Interim Government."[3] However, to date, the author has not discovered any historical evidence indicating that a People's Congress was actually convened in January 1945. Since there were no major changes to the republic's leadership during this period, it may be supposed that the Interim Government Council was in fact responsible for instituting the revisions that resulted in the 1945 Precepts. Saypidin Azizi somewhat cryptically notes that the reason for the revisions was to correct "mistakes." So what were the mistakes to which Azizi referred? For that, it is necessary to compare the content of the two versions of the political precepts.

Both the 1944 Precepts and the 1945 Precepts expressed opposition to Chinese rule and established a fundamental political stance embracing pro-Soviet policies. However, the two versions do diverge, most notably in two respects. Firstly, the 1944 Precepts originally incorporated democratic concepts such as the establishment of a democratic government and a people's army, democratic elections for government officials, guaranteed ethnic equality, and educational development, all of which would serve to effectively safeguard citizens' political rights. However, the 1945 Precepts expunged the specific content on institutional protections for citizens' rights. Secondly, the 1944 Precepts stipulated that the Uyghur language would serve as the republic's official language; in the 1945 Precepts, this provision is again stricken from the text, and replaced with a proposal that the Interim Government of the East Turkestan Republic would grant "special support" to Islam, while also guaranteeing the "freedom to follow other religions."

The revisions are thus predominantly characterized by the elimination of content on democratic governance, and the granting of special status to Islam. In January 1945, the nascent government of the East Turkestan Republic lacked the will to open discussions regarding a democratic political system. Instead, the revisions to its political precepts primarily served as a vehicle to provide a legal basis for Islamic religious authority.

Building an Ethnic Community with a Shared Destiny

Saypidin Azizi claimed further in his memoirs that the "Nine Political Precepts" were revised in May 1945. In fact, the 1945 Precepts were formulated in January 1945; May 13 instead marked the announcement of two other important decrees passed by the Interim Government Council of the East Turkestan Republic: the *Provisional Regulations on Criminal Procedure of the East Turkestan Republic*, and the *Provisional Penal Code of the East Turkestan Republic*.

The *Provisional Regulations on Criminal Procedure of the East Turkestan Republic* codified the status of the "Nine Political Precepts" as the supreme law of the land, declaring that observance of the precepts was the duty of every citizen of the East Turkestan Republic. Article 7 of the regulations states, "Every citizen of the government shall support the Nine Declarations, which were ratified by the Interim Government Council, provisionally adopted by the government and proclaimed to all the people." Article 8 reads, "Any citizen who harms or contravenes the government's Nine Declarations shall be subject to punishment."

With the codification of Islamic religious authority under the supreme law of the land, accompanied by gradual changes to the rules of procedure within the Interim Government of the East Turkestan Republic, Ilhan Tora steadily gained in power.

The 1944 Precepts announced at the founding ceremony for the republic's Interim Government made no mention of the government's organizational structure. The members of the Interim Government Council were formally elected on November 12, 1944: on the same day, Hakimbek Hoja, the vice president of the Interim Government, convened and presided over a meeting to pass Resolution No. 1 of the Interim Government Council.

This resolution appointed several ministers and named a number of officials to the Ministry of Religion, along with the Chief Justice of the Supreme Court; it also included provisions on matters related to national finance and taxation.

Resolution No. 2 of the Interim Government Council was unveiled not long after. Excluding the language on national finance and taxation, Resolution No. 2 appears to be a simple reiteration of Resolution No. 1; the texts are even ordered in the same sequence. However, the two resolutions of the Interim Government Council do feature certain differences in terms of their format and content.

Firstly, the framing of Resolution No. 2 is entirely different from Resolution No. 1, the text of which launches directly into the decisions of the Interim Government Council. In contrast, Resolution No. 2 includes an opening statement, which reads: "2nd Assembly of the Interim Government Council of the East Turkestan Republic, presided over by Ilhan Tora, President of the Government. The assembly resolved as to the following matters. . . ." The resolution closes with the signature "Ilhan Tora, President of the Government." A review of later resolutions reveals that this wording became the official format for all resolutions of the Interim Government Council of the East Turkestan Republic.

Secondly, Resolution No. 2 also differs in some respects from Resolution No. 1 with regard to its content. In terms of the personnel appointments, although Resolution No. 2 appoints the same figures to the positions of Minister of Education, Minister of Animal Husbandry, Minister of Irrigation and Water Conservancy, and Chief Justice of the Supreme Court, it diverges from Resolution No. 1 by formally appointing the Interim Minister of Finance as the Minister of Finance, and by naming the Minister of Religious Affairs, a position which does not appear in Resolution No. 1. Resolution No. 1 further stipulates that the Interim Government shall hold final say over the administration of national finances and the furnishing of military uniforms; in Resolution No. 2 of the Interim Government Council, these powers are arrogated to the President of the Interim Government.

In other words, the significance of Resolution No. 2 lies not in its substantive reiteration of Resolution No. 1, but rather in the establishment of an official format, which in fact represents the birth of a system of power. Under this system of power, appointments to major positions and the formulation of important policies could only be decided by resolution of the Interim Government Council, under the aegis of the interim president; only the president had the ultimate authority to make decisions on major policy matters; and resolutions of the Interim Government Council were only valid once signed by the president. Although these changes appear on the surface to be no more than adjustments to the rules of procedure or policy decision-making process of the Interim Government Council, a closer examination reveals that these amended procedures provided institutional guarantees for Ilhan Tora's power as the President of the Interim Government.

However, by its nature, the East Turkestan Republic was a non-Islamic state at the time of its founding and thereafter. This finding is based on the fact that, firstly, neither version of the "Nine Political Precepts" explicitly stipulates as to the political status of Islam within the state system; and secondly, the principles of taxation articulated in Resolution No. 1 of the Interim Government Council for the East Turkestan Republic differ from those applied under an Islamic system.

The tax rates as provided under Resolution No. 1 of the Interim Government Council included a 5% commercial tax on the sale of goods, and a 3% agricultural tax on the value of agricultural products, with no discrimination between Muslims and non-Muslims. These rates were fundamentally inconsistent with the taxes applied under an Islamic legal code, including *ushr* (a 10% tax on harvests and merchandise) and *zakat* (a 2.5% tithe for Muslims). The resolution also stated that the "collection measures of the Chinese regime (era) would continue to be applied on a temporary basis" with respect to the freight tax and the residential property tax. It should be noted that Resolution No. 2, which was announced in Ilhan Tora's name, made no mention of national finance and taxation. Tora thus implicitly acknowledged the non-Islamic taxation measures provided under Resolution No. 1.

On the other hand, a crescent moon and star design in the color green, symbolizing Islam, was adopted for the national flag of the East Turkestan Republic.[4] The religious figure Ilhan Tora also steadily gained in political power after the founding of the republic. This indicates that, although the East Turkestan Republic was not an Islamic state, its leaders still hoped to politically exploit Tora's religious authority and social prestige, creating an image of the East Turkestan Republic as a champion of Islam for consumption by the Turkic-Islamic peoples of Xinjiang.

According to Saypidin Azizi, the leadership of the Interim Government had been predetermined at a meeting of the National Freedom Group on November 8, 1944. However, few representatives of the group's core demographic of Uyghur intellectuals actually sat on the Interim Government Council: instead, the council drew in a wide variety of elite figures from the Turkic-Islamic ethnic community, including not only religious figures but also begs, *ming bash* ("leaders of a thousand households"), powerful merchants, large landowners, and so on (Table 6.1). It is particularly noteworthy that many of the council members were not part of the National Freedom Group, and did not participate in the Ghulja Uprising. Hakimbek Hoja, a son-in-law of the administrator who had served as the last "Hakim beg" of Ili in the era of the Qing Dynasty, was even selected as the vice president of the Interim Government. In sum, from the day of its inception, the Interim Government of the East Turkestan Republic deliberately sought to win over the elite members of Turkic-Islamic society.

The broad composition of the government had two practical effects in the period after the founding of the East Turkestan Republic. Firstly, the inclusion of representatives from all social classes in the leadership rungs of the Interim Government allowed the republic to present itself to the people as an ethnic community with a shared destiny for all. Secondly, the presence of figures of religious authority, like President Ilhan Tora; political authority, like Vice President Hakimbek Hoja; or social authority based on economic status, like the Minister of Finance, Anwar Musabayow, served to strengthen the power and legitimacy of the Interim Government of the East Turkestan Republic. These two features of the government naturally had important significance with respect to popular mobilization as well as governance.

Table 6.1 Members of the Interim Government Council of the East Turkestan Republic

Name	Ethnicity	Position	Background
Ilhan Tora	Uzbek	President of the Interim Government	Chairman of the Ghulja National Freedom Group
Abdulkerim Abbasow	Uyghur	Minister of Internal Affairs; later served as Minister of Propaganda, Director of the Political Department of the National Army	Leader of the Ghulja National Freedom Group
Mahmautjan Mahsum	Uyghur	Chief Justice of the Supreme Court	Leader of the Ghulja National Freedom Group
Jani Yoldaxup	Uyghur	Director of the Supervisory Committee	Leader of the Ghulja National Freedom Group
Abdurup Mahsum	Uyghur	Secretary-General of the Interim Government	Leader of the Ghulja National Freedom Group
Rahimjan Sabir Ghaji	Uyghur	Vice Minister of Military Affairs; later served as Minister of Military Affairs, Minister of Internal Affairs	Leader of the Ghulja National Freedom Group
Salman Bay	Uzbek	Minister of Agriculture	Leader of the Ghulja National Freedom Group
Zunon Tayof	Tatar	Assistant Director of the Supervisory Committee; later served as Minister of Military Affairs, Deputy Commander of the National Army	Leader of the Ghulja National Freedom Group
Hakimbek Hoja	Uyghur	Vice President of the Interim Government	Son-in-law of the last Hakim beg (local administrator) of Ili in the Qing era
Anwar Musabayow	Uyghur	Minister of Finance	Member of the famous Musabayow family of commercial capitalists
Abulimiti Ali Halipa	Uyghur	Minister of Religious Affairs	Religious figure

Table 6.1 (continued)

Name	Ethnicity	Position	Background
Abdulla Heni	Uyghur	Chief Judge of Military Tribunals	Leader of the Nilka Guerrillas
Habib Yuqi	Tatar	Minister of Education	Intellectual with experience studying abroad in the Soviet Union
Ubulhari Tora	Kazakh	Minister of Nomadic Pasturing	
Piotr Alexandrov	Russian	Commander-in-Chief of the National Army, Minister of Military Affairs	Soviet commander of the Ghulja Uprising
Povel Maskolyov	Russian	Minister of Internal Affairs; later served as Chief of Staff of the National Army	White Russian residing in Ghulja
Puja Abal	Mongolian		Elite member of the Mongolian community

Source: Compiled by the author on the basis of official documents of the Interim Government of the East Turkestan Republic.

6.2 Intellectuals and Political Power in the Republic

Concentration of Intellectuals in the Ministries of Internal Affairs and Military Affairs

Saypidin Azizi, who served as Minister of Education in the Interim Government of the East Turkestan Republic, once quoted a Uyghur proverb to accuse Ilhan Tora of usurping the fruits of the rebellion by seizing the role of president: "Many become heroes after the city wall has been breached."[5] This sharp critique obliquely suggested that Abdulkerim Abbasow, who organized and led the Ghulja Uprising, was the only person fit to be president of the Interim Government.

Abdulkerim Abbasow, who had been a key figure among the pro-Soviet Uyghur intellectuals involved in the Second East Turkestan Independence

Movement, in fact held two extremely important positions in the Interim Government: government council member (*Hokumat Azasi*) and Minister of Internal Affairs (*Iqki Ixlar Nazariti*).

The Ministry of Internal Affairs of the Interim Government of East Turkestan was clearly modeled after the People's Commissariat for Internal Affairs (*Narodnyi Komissariat Vnutrennikh Del*, or NKVD) of the Soviet Union. Article 1 of the *Provisional Working Regulations of the Ministry of Internal Affairs of the East Turkestan Republic* stated: "The Ministry of Internal Affairs of East Turkestan shall undertake the tasks of ensuring the security of the state and the people, waging the struggle against all kinds of criminal acts, and resolving certain specific problems amongst the people. The Ministry of Internal Affairs shall also bear the task of imposing punishment on persons perpetrating any kind of political or criminal offense."[6] In other words, the Ministry of Internal Affairs was simultaneously equivalent to a law enforcement agency, the secret police, and a prosecutorial body, making it a key department wielding absolute power within the government of East Turkestan.

On January 16, 1945, the Interim Government Council "heard and approved the report of the Propaganda Bureau of the Central Ministry of Internal Affairs regarding its work in 1944."[7] This passage suggests that ideological control was another area under the purview of the Ministry of Internal Affairs. As the Minister of Internal Affairs, Abdulkerim Abbasow was thus simultaneously the director of law enforcement, the secret police, and criminal prosecution, as well as the supreme arbiter of ideological matters. Some therefore posit that Abbasow had a hand in writing nearly all of the republic's important documents.[8]

The personnel arrangements of the Interim Government reveal another feature of the East Turkestan Republic: important positions within the armed forces and the Ministry of Internal Affairs were all held by government council members identifying either as pro-Soviet intellectuals or as Soviet nationals.

Under the organizational structure of the Interim Government, the Ministry of Internal Affairs and the military belonged to separate systems (Figure 6.1). However, Resolution No. 46 of the Interim Government Council, dated April 29, 1945, explicitly states: "(3) The symbols of rank specified in Resolution No. 6 [which addressed the organization of the

Chapter 6: Authority and Power | 153

Figure 6.1 Organizational Chart of the East Turkestan Republic

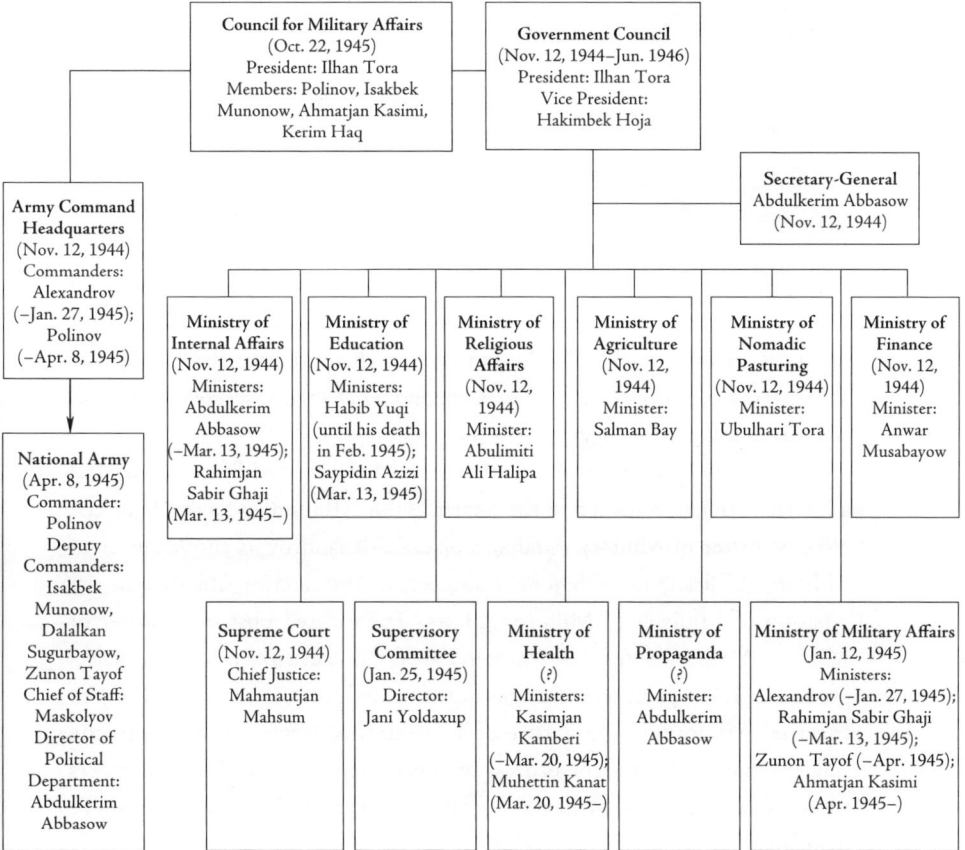

Source: Compiled by the author on the basis of official documents of the Interim Government of the East Turkestan Republic.

armed forces, military rank and uniform, and so on] of the Interim Government Council shall also apply to the Ministry of Internal Affairs. (4) Military insignias shall be used as insignias for the personnel of the Ministry of Internal Affairs." In addition, the *Provisional Working Regulations of the Ministry of Internal Affairs of the East Turkestan Republic*, issued in June 14 of the same year, declares plainly: "Article 1: All personnel of the Ministry

Rahimjan Sabir Ghaji

of Internal Affairs of the East Turkestan Republic shall, equivalent to personnel in the armed forces, be required to observe the disciplinary regulations of the Army of the East Turkestan Republic as well as the provisions of the Provisional Working Regulations. . . . Article 2: Compliance with the style of dress worn by officers of Army Garrison Command and the completion of military training are required." These regulations reveal that the Ministry of Internal Affairs adopted a militarized system of management, despite its administrative separation from the East Turkestan Army. This indicates that a relationship existed between the two bodies beyond what their discrete administrative structures would suggest.

In January 1945, Piotr Alexandrov, the Minister of Military Affairs and a Soviet national, returned to the Soviet Union.[9] Rahimjan Sabir Ghaji, the Vice Minister of Military Affairs, replaced Alexandrov as the Minister of Military Affairs. Sabir Ghaji later succeeded Abdulkerim Abbasow in the position of Minister of Military Affairs. The vacated post of Minister of Military Affairs was filled by Zunon Tayof, a Soviet citizen of Tatar background.[10] These personnel changes in the armed forces and the Ministry of Internal Affairs had the nature of a carousel of figures with ties to the Soviet Union, reducing the process of government personnel appointments to the Ministries of Military Affairs and Internal Affairs to a mere formality.

The military and the Ministry of Internal Affairs were undoubtedly the most important departments in the new government of East Turkestan, particularly in the early period of the regime. Within the Interim Government, only the ministers and vice ministers from the Ministries of Internal Affairs and Military Affairs concurrently served as members of the government council. In other words, although the pro-Soviet intellectuals and Soviet nationals serving on the Interim Government Council were few in number, their seats in the important departments of military affairs and internal affairs allowed them to grasp the reins of true power in the council.

The Military System and Soviet Influence

The Interim Government of the East Turkestan Republic was also staffed by a high number of Soviet Red Army officers, who were granted positions in the Ministries of Military Affairs and Internal Affairs. Both of these ministries, which stood within the inner circle of the East Turkestan regime, served as contact points for cooperation between pro-Soviet intellectuals and the Soviet Union. Piotr Alexandrov, who traveled alongside Abdulkerim Abbasow from the Soviet Union into Xinjiang, became the first commander-in-chief of East Turkestan's armed forces; when the Ministry of Military Affairs was established in January 1945, Alexandrov was appointed as its minister. At the time, the Vice Minister of Military Affairs was Rahimjan Sabir Ghaji, another of Abbasow and Alexandrov's comrades-in-arms, who helped organize the Ghulja Uprising.

The military initially did not form organizational ties to the government system, instead operating as an independent and autonomous unit. It was not until January 7, 1945, that the Interim Government Council decided in Resolution No. 5 to form a military branch of the government: the Ministry of Military Affairs. Resolution No. 6 of the Interim Government Council, dated January 12, reorganized the armed rebel groups scattered across the region as the regular armed forces of the East Turkestan Republic.[11] Piotr Alexandrov was responsible for undertaking both of these tasks, and under Resolution No. 7 of the Interim Government Council, dated January 15, he was granted the authority to confer military rank on subordinate officers.[12]

Resolution No. 26 of the Interim Government Council, dated March 1, 1945, announced the promotions of two colonels, two lieutenant colonels, and one major. Two Russian names appear on this list of appointments: Vasily Mogutnov, who was granted the rank of colonel; and Borderikov Ivanovich Keshken.[13] Based on this resolution, it can be concluded that Soviet nationals were able to directly obtain appointments as high-ranking officers within the military system of the East Turkestan Republic.

Rahimjan Sabir Ghaji, who had just been transferred from the position of Minister of Military Affairs to that of Minister of Internal Affairs, also appears on this list. However, his military rank was merely that of a lieutenant colonel.[14] Colonel Mogutnov's higher rank suggests that his contributions to the birth of the East Turkestan Republic were even greater than Sabir Ghaji's achievements, and if he had been a local Turkic Muslim, it is highly unlikely that his existence would have been entirely disregarded in later memoirs. Yet the fact is that no record of a "Colonel Vasily Mogutnov" appears in any of the memoirs written by the Uyghur intellectuals involved in these events. It is therefore certain that the Colonel was not an indigenous Turkic Muslim of Xinjiang; and it is quite possible that Mogutnov and the Soviet consular intelligence officer "Vasily," who joined the first incarnation of the National Freedom Group—the Marxist-Leninist Association—and later became a military advisor to the East Turkestan Republic, were one and the same.[15]

Materials on the Three Districts Revolution in Ili Prefecture (1991) reveals that, in mid-November 1944, not long after the Ghulja Uprising, General Kozlov of the Soviet Red Army assumed the position of chief military advisor to the "Guerrilla Army Headquarters of the East Turkestan Republic." In late November, a number of Soviet military advisors were accepted into the ranks of armed groups across the region.[16] In reality, these Soviet officers did not serve merely in an advisory capacity: they also took direct command over military operations as commanding officers. This is supported by the memoirs of a number of East Turkestan officers and soldiers: for instance, Colonel Mogutnov was the commander of the Suiding 1st Infantry Regiment.[17]

On April 8, 1945, the founding of the East Turkestan Republic's "National Army" (*Milli Armiya*) was proclaimed, and the armed groups scattered across the region were organized into seven regiments, four independent battalions, and one independent company.[18] The Soviet national Ivan Polinov (as named in Uyghur sources), who arrived in Xinjiang from the Soviet Union on November 16, 1944, was appointed as Commander-in-Chief of the National Army. The Chief of Staff was the White Russian Povel Maskolyov. A number of departments were established under the umbrella of the National Army Headquarters, including the Political Department, War Department, Military Administration Department, Cadre Department, Reconnaissance Department, and Logistics Department. Abdulkerim Abbasow served as the director of the Political Department, while an individual fluent in Russian took the position of director of the Reconnaissance Department.[19]

A former staff member of the National Army Headquarters stated in an interview with the author that not only were Soviet figures present at headquarters in large numbers, all the regiment and battalion commanders in the National Army were sent over from the Soviet Union; the Soviet Union even dispatched a deputy company commander to serve with each company. The interviewee listed a number of examples within the Ghulja Infantry Regiment, including Regiment Commander Baratsov, Chief of Staff Kirimsov, and Director Ahmatun of the Political Department, all of whom were sent over by the Soviet Union from the Red Army; Deputy Commander Kalman of the Jinghe Cavalry Company was also a Kazakh from Soviet Kazakhstan. In other words, even after the armed forces of the East Turkestan Republic were reorganized into the National Army, they remained under the direct control of Soviet forces.

The military's independence from the Interim Government was not solely expressed through personnel matters: it was even able to engage in military operations without consulting the Interim Government Council. Although the founding of the Interim Government of the East Turkestan Republic was proclaimed in Ghulja in November 1944, in late January 1945, pockets of Chinese government forces remained entrenched at the Northern Camp, Demon King Temple (*Guiwang miao* 鬼王廟) and the Hayranbaq Airfield near Ghulja. Contingents of Chinese soldiers were also scattered across the Ili region. The armed forces of East Turkestan launched a series of military operations across the region to eliminate the remaining Chinese forces; it took a full three months after the founding of the republic to sweep away the surviving stragglers.

However, the resolutions of the Interim Government Council in the period from November 12, 1944 to February 1945 make no mention of any relevant military activities. The omission suggests that these military operations proceeded without any address to the Interim Government Council. Among the 37 resolutions passed by the council between November 12, 1944 and the end of March 1945, a total of 18 resolutions make reference to the armed forces. However, the vast majority of these 18 resolutions are concerned with military logistics, supply, and support for the bereaved family members of fallen soldiers. In other words, the Interim Government Council's role with respect to military operations was limited to that of a logistics unit. See Table 6.2 for the council's resolutions on military matters.

Table 6.2   References to Military Matters in the Resolutions of the Interim Government Council of the East Turkestan Republic (to March 1945)

Date	Title of Resolution	Military-Related Content
Nov. 12, 1944	Resolution No. 1	Furnishing of military uniforms
Unknown	Resolution No. 2	Furnishing of military uniforms
Dec. 30, 1944	Resolution on the Establishment of a Quartermaster Depot	Decision to establish a Quartermaster Depot
Jan. 5, 1945	Resolution No. 3	Reference to the work of the Quartermaster Depot
Jan. 7, 1945	Resolution No. 5	Decision to establish a supreme military council within the government
Jan. 12, 1945	Resolution No. 6	Decision to establish the Ministry of Military Affairs and implement a system of military rank
Jan. 15, 1945	Resolution No. 7	Reference to officer promotions and military rank
Jan. 16, 1945	Resolution No. 8	Decision to build a convalescent hospital for wounded soldiers
Jan. 18, 1945	Resolution No. 10	Decision to establish a shelter and relief committee for the family members of wounded soldiers
Jan. 25, 1945	Resolution No. 12	Decision to expropriate all private motor vehicles to support the war efforts
Jan. 27, 1945	Resolution No. 13	Decision to dismiss Piotr Alexandrov from the position of Minister of Military Affairs
Jan. 28, 1945	Resolution No. 14	Decision to levy a religious tax to support *jihad*
Feb. 3, 1945	Resolution No. 18	Reference to aid for the family members of fallen soldiers
Feb. 3, 1945	Resolution No. 19	Announcement of a conscription system and the *Military Service Law*
Feb. 10, 1945	Resolution No. 21	Decision to expropriate horses and fodder for use by cavalry units
Feb. 24, 1945	Resolution No. 25	Decision on the conferral of the highest military decoration, the "Medal of Liberation"

Table 6.2 (continued)

Date	Title of Resolution	Military-Related Content
Mar. 1, 1945	Resolution No. 26	Conferral of military rank on seven officers
Mar. 13, 1945	Resolution No. 33	Reference to personnel changes for the Minister of Military Affairs and the Minister of Internal Affairs

Source: Compiled by the author on the basis of the resolutions of the Interim Government Council of the East Turkestan Republic.

Backlash Against Ilhan Tora as President of the Interim Government Council

The above analysis reveals that two political blocs were at work within the Interim Government of the East Turkestan Republic. The first consisted of social forces, embodied in religious leaders, represented by Ilhan Tora, and the elites of Turkic-Islamic society; the second was composed of Soviet forces, including pro-Soviet Uyghur and Tatar intellectuals, as well as Soviet nationals. The former were primarily concentrated in the Interim Government Council, while the latter were clustered in the military as well as the Ministry of Internal Affairs, which operated under a militarized system of management.

Within the Interim Government, political power did not seem to be directly linked to the number of seats on the council. Although Uyghur and Tatar intellectuals and Soviet nationals were in the minority in the Interim Government Council, their control of important positions such as minister and vice minister in the Ministries of Military Affairs and Internal Affairs, which were largely autonomous from the council, allowed them to hold more real power. For instance, at meetings of the Interim Government Council, "Abdulkerim Abbasow would explicitly state his political position frequently and without hesitation. If Ilhan Tora or any of the other council members raised a different opinion or made an error, he would be sure to sharply criticize them."[20] Abbasow in fact stood in opposition to Ilhan Tora, and his subordinates spread rumors that he never discussed anything with Tora.[21]

As President of the Interim Government, Ilhan Tora was incensed by the military's independence. The Uyghur merchant Talhat Musabayow of Ghulja, who had been sent as a representative of the East Turkestan Republic to persuade the Chinese government forces to surrender, instead defected to the Xinjiang Provincial Government. He later gave the following report in a letter to Governor Wu Zhongxin:

> The false president (chief council member) Alikhan Tora [Ilhan Tora] had a difference of opinion with Commander Alexandrov and Deputy Commander Fatih. Alikhan Tora had plans to organize his own armed forces to be commanded by Uyghurs to mount a resistance, and he repeatedly summoned Talhat for face-to-face meetings. On the afternoon of the 12th, in an interview with A. in the councilor's office, A. urged that 200 rifles be acquired from the Soviet Consulate to form a Uyghur army; after the prolonged discussion, there was no time that day to visit the consulate.[22]

It is likely that Ilhan Tora valued Talhat Musabayow for his financial resources and his influence owing to his position as the head of the Musabayow capitalist family of Ili, which had organized and supported a "Modern Uyghur Cultural Enlightenment Movement" in 1945. Of course, due to Talhat Musabayow's defection, Ilhan Tora's plans ultimately bore no fruit.[23] However, this account reveals that the sharp antagonism between Ilhan Tora and the military within the Interim Government was widely known.

Resolution No. 6 of the Interim Government Council, dated January 12, 1945, called for the establishment of a military department subordinate to the government: the Ministry of Military Affairs. This was likely an attempt by Ilhan Tora to preclude the autonomous operation of the military system, with the aim of instating government control over the armed forces, given that the first move in the skirmish was the dismissal of Deputy Commander Fatih from the Army Headquarters.[24] Resolution No. 13, dated January 27, moved to dismiss Commander Alexandrov from his position as Minister of Military Affairs: Alexandrov was swiftly removed from office and repatriated to the Soviet Union, and in February, Ilhan Tora himself became the Supreme Commander of the National Army.[25]

On the surface, Ilhan Tora appears to have gained the upper hand in this power struggle over command of the armed forces: however, "Supreme

Commander" was merely an honorific title, and it was Ivan Polinov, another Soviet national, who succeeded to the post of commander-in-chief and the position of real power.[26] Alexandrov also continued to hold official title as a member of the Interim Government Council, until he ceded his place to Polinov on August 9, 1945.[27] It may be inferred that, rather than representing a simple loss of status for a political figure, Alexandrov's dismissal and repatriation amounted to an internal restructuring of Soviet forces within the East Turkestan military in order to appease Ilhan Tora. Despite his efforts, Tora was unable to achieve his goal of seizing direct command of the military.

6.3 Formation of an Intertwined Power Structure

A System of Forced Coexistence

1944 was the year of expansion for Soviet forces in the East Turkestan Republic; but in 1945, Ilhan Tora succeeded in expanding his own power and influence. He began with the revision of the "Nine Political Precepts" on January 5 and the dismissal of Fatih and Alexandrov from the Army Headquarters, followed by the establishment of an Islamic court (Xariphan Ali Haji, who had served as the Minister of Religious Affairs under the Islamic Republic of East Turkestan in the First East Turkestan Independence Movement, was appointed as the presiding judge), and a general reform of the government in March. In the course of these reforms, Abdulkerim Abbasow was stripped of the position of Minister of Internal Affairs and demoted to Minister of Propaganda; the Ministry of Propaganda had formerly been no more than a subordinate department of the Ministry of Internal Affairs.

In April, around the time of the establishment of the National Army and Ilhan Tora's adoption of the honorific title of Supreme Commander of the National Army, the council decided by resolution that an *akhund* should be appointed to each government department to serve as a religious advisor; *akhunds* were also to be assigned to each regiment of the army as deputy regiment commanders. However, it should be noted that this did not constitute a total reversal in terms of power dynamics: Abdulkerim Abbasow's ally and kin relative Saypidin Azizi was promoted from Vice

Minister to Minister of Education during this same period,[28] and at the same time, Abdulkerim Abbasow was appointed as the Director of the Political Department of the National Army, becoming the highest political authority within the armed forces.

Although the Islamic deputy regiment commanders assigned to the army had no understanding of military matters and their positions quickly devolved into merely nominal titles,[29] they were still accorded high military rank. For instance, the Islamic deputy regiment commander of the Ili 2nd Infantry Regiment was given the rank of lieutenant colonel, and was reportedly the highest-ranking officer in the regiment.[30]

Unlike in the military, the religious advisors (*dinniy maslihatqisi*) assigned to the various ministries of the government held joint sway alongside the Soviet advisors (*Sowet itttpakqi maslihatqisi*). According to Saypidin Azizi, then Minister of Education, any order he gave had to be approved by both advisors.[31] However, one figure who served in the Ministry of Propaganda from 1945 to 1946 claimed that the Soviet advisor in his department was far more influential; Abdulkerim Abbasow allegedly told his staff they should defer to the decisions of the Soviet advisor in his absence.[32]

On May 13, 1945, the Interim Government Council promulgated the *Provisional Penal Code of the East Turkestan Republic*. The section on "Political Crimes" in the *Provisional Penal Code* contained the following passage: "Article 50, Clause 1: Assassination of important members of the government for the purpose of spying shall be prosecuted in accordance with Article 50, Clause 1 of the Penal Code, and capital punishment shall be imposed; Clause 2: Collusion among conspirators to assassinate important members of the government for the purpose of spying shall be prosecuted in accordance with Article 50, Clause 1 of the Penal Code, and capital punishment shall be imposed." This passage suggests that Ilhan Tora sought legal assurances for his life and safety.

The above developments reveal that, although both political factions continued to struggle over the distribution of power, based on their tactics, the Soviet forces seemingly were not bent on completely eliminating their opponents' power base. As the push and pull between the two factions wore on, by April and May 1945, an imbalanced power structure with two coexisting poles of power gradually developed within the Interim Government of the East Turkestan Republic (Figure 6.2). It should be noted that

Chapter 6: Authority and Power | 163

Figure 6.2 Diagram of the Intertwined Political Forces within the East Turkestan Republic

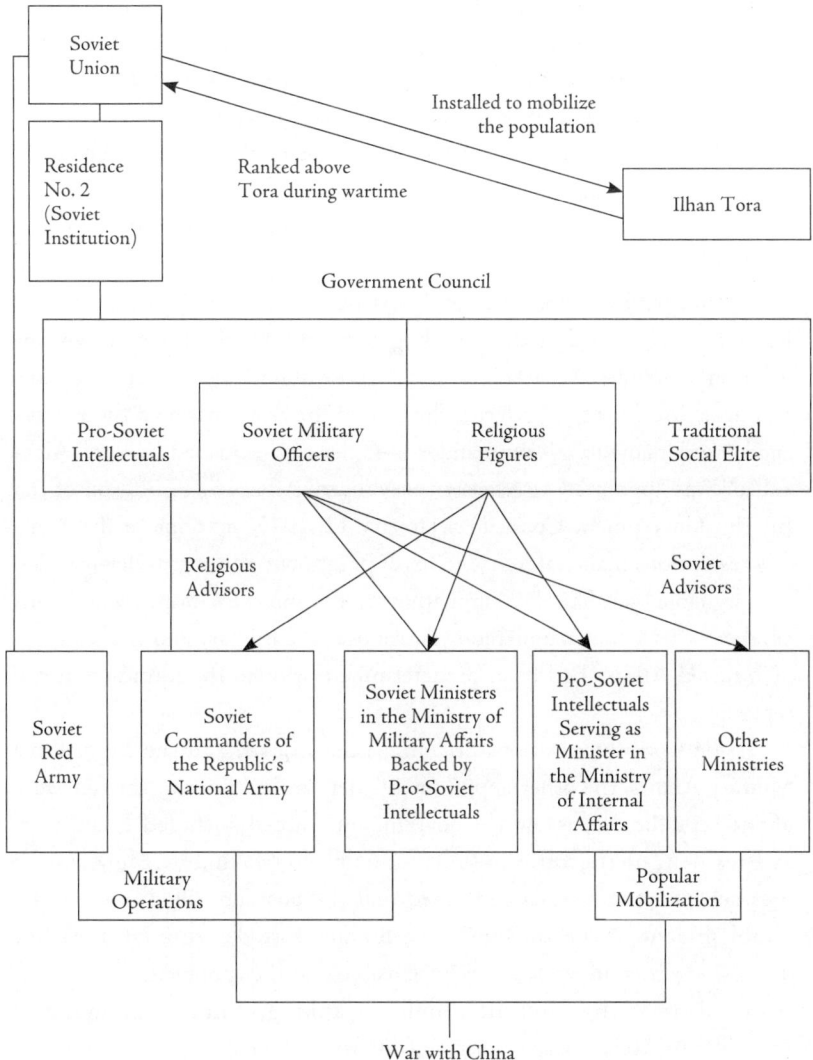

Source: Compiled by the author on the basis of official documents of the Interim Government Council of the East Turkestan Republic.

this intertwined structure did not form naturally with the passage of time, and that several signs of forced intervention are evident in the course of its development.

Unlike the Ministry of Military Affairs, which was separately established in January 1945, the Ministry of Internal Affairs was created alongside several other institutions of the central government on the day the republic was founded (November 12, 1944). However, it is noteworthy that, while the ministers of the other departments were appointed by resolution of the Interim Government Council, Abdulkerim Abbasow was not formally appointed by the government to the position of Minister of Internal Affairs.

The General Headquarters of the Armed Forces of the East Turkestan Republic was formed at the founding ceremony for the Interim Government on November 12, 1944, for the purpose of unifying the armed groups of Turkic Muslims spread across the region; the Soviet national Piotr Alexandrov was named as "Commander-in-Chief of the Armed Forces." Alexandrov was appointed as Minister of Military Affairs by resolution of the Interim Government Council on January 12, 1945, yet none of the council's resolutions make reference to his appointment as commander-in-chief. It is arguable that, like the nominations to the Interim Government Council, the Soviet Union's unilateral control over the military and the Ministry of Internal Affairs had been predetermined prior to the founding of the republic.

Aside from the positions of commander-in-chief and the Minister of Military Affairs, the other appointments determined prior to the founding of the republic, bypassing the government council, included Ilhan Tora as President of the Interim Government and Hakimbek Hoja as vice president. Saypidin Azizi confirmed that the positions filled prior to the establishment of the Interim Government were determined in earlier discussions. It is therefore entirely plausible that the appointments of Piotr Alexandrov as the republic's highest-ranking military commander, Abdulkerim Abbasow as Minister of Internal Affairs, Ilhan Tora as President of the Interim Government, and Hakimbek Hoja as vice president were all based on a prior agreement among the organizers of the Ghulja Uprising, including Ilhan Tora, before the uprising even occurred. In other words, the two political factions would have been cognizant from the outset of the necessity of building an intertwined power structure within the government of East Turkestan.

Soviet Support in the War with China

What was the import of this intertwined power structure for the pro-Soviet and traditional factions within the Interim Government? The answer to this question perhaps lies in a quote by Yasin Hudabardi: "Everything was for the war, for the front lines" (*Hamma piront uqun aldinki sap uqun*).[33] An analysis of the state of affairs in that period reveals that the newly founded East Turkestan Republic faced grim circumstances. For both Ilhan Tora and the pro-Soviet intellectual faction, winning the war was the most important and urgent task at hand.

On December 3, 1944, Chiang Kai-shek sent Director Bu Daoming of the West Asia Bureau under the Ministry of Foreign Affairs of the Nationalist government to Xinjiang to open negotiations at the Soviet Consulate in Urumqi. Chiang also asked Bu to deliver a personal letter to Wu Zhongxin, which read in part:

> If the current situation cannot be improved, our troops should take the following course of action: (1) Launch a vigorous attack on the forces gathered near Yining [Ghulja], with the aim of recapturing Yining and Suiding. If there are no other options, the long-term plan should be to spare no effort in making a stand at Yining. Even if a certain country interferes, there is no need to worry. . . . (3) Engage with Russia diplomatically on the ground, and if there is a ray of hope with respect to economic cooperation, all efforts must be exhausted to seek a compromise, with the aim of preserving our territory and sovereignty. As for the other territories of the border region as a whole, all political and military avenues and methods must be actively pursued to find a means of preserving them; this is most important.
>
> . . . Moreover, with respect to motor vehicles and gasoline, the Northwest Transportation Bureau and the Bureau of Logistics have been ordered to draft a comprehensive plan to provide material assistance, and prepare a separate detailed report.
>
> . . . With respect to finances and the economy in Xinjiang Province, the competent departments have been ordered to actively make preparations to avoid increasing the burden on Xinjiang, and all military expenditures shall be borne by the central government, so please do not concern yourself.[34]

It is clear that the Nationalist government planned to pursue all political, military, diplomatic and economic means in an exhaustive endeavor to recapture Ghulja and suppress the Second East Turkestan Independence Movement.

At Chiang Kai-shek's command, the Chinese government forces remaining at the Northern Camp, the Demon King Temple, and the Hayranbaq Airfield near Ghulja continued their desperate struggle to hold their positions; many of the soldiers ultimately died of starvation. Chinese reinforcements launched an assault on Ghulja on November 13, 1944, quickly capturing Ertai.[35] On November 15, Zhu Shaoliang, the Commander of the 8th Military District and the ranking military officer in Xinjiang, appointed Division Commander Li Yuxiang of the 7th Reserve Division as field commander: Li led a force composed primarily of the 7th Reserve Division and the newly formed 45th Division to "bring reinforcements to the battle at Yining [Ghulja] through Guozi Ravine."[36]

Faced with this assault, Soviet military support was indispensable in the defense of Ghulja. As stated in the memoirs of Zunon Tayof, who was appointed as a council member and Assistant Director of the Supervisory Committee when the East Turkestan Republic was first founded, and later went on to become Minister of Military Affairs, the Interim Government believed from the outset that maintaining friendly relations with the Soviet Union was the republic's most crucial task.[37]

Ilhan Tora was well aware of the perils faced by his fledgling nation. On November 24, 1944, Tora personally sent a request to the government of the Soviet Republic of Kazakhstan, pleading for aid to resolve a shortage of weapons.[38] The rebel forces associated with the East Turkestan Independence Movement fell far short of the strength required to defeat the Chinese government troops: this fact compelled Ilhan Tora to seek a compromise with the Soviet Union.

From November 1944 on, armed rebel groups massing at Pine Pass in the Guozi Ravine, Ertai, and other regions in the name of the East Turkestan Republic launched attacks day and night against the Chinese forces remaining in Hayranbaq, while also waging a fierce struggle against the government

Zunon Tayof

reinforcements. The rebel groups also sent forces farther afield into Ili District, capturing Zhaosu and Qapqal in mid- and late November, and Qorghas on November 20. East Turkestan forces seized Wenquan on December 20, Suiding on December 25, and Huiyuan on December 31; Tartala was captured on February 20, 1945, along with a number of other regions. In bureaucratic seats of the Nationalist government like Kunes, Tokkuztara, Tekes and other counties where no troops were stationed, Nationalist officials abandoned their posts as the rebel forces approached, fleeing across the mountains to Urumqi.

However, the armed forces of East Turkestan did not have the combat strength to wage such a large-scale war alone. In brief, aside from the worsening winter weather, the key factor in the defeat of the Chinese government troops was the direct intervention of the Soviet Red Army.

Wu Zhongxin wrote in his diary entry for November 28: "The position is very near to ours, within range of their six-inch guns. Henceforth aircraft can no longer land at that airfield. As for our reinforcements, due to the snowpack on the road along the route, many of the transport vehicles have been damaged; now we are waiting for a massed deployment at Jinghe to launch the general attack." The airfield Wu mentions in this passage likely refers to the Ghulja Hayranbaq Airfield; at this point, the defending forces were already isolated and cut off from all aid. On February 4, Division Commander Xie Yifeng, who returned to Urumqi from the front lines, reported to Wu Zhongxin: "Bitterly cold weather is ahead, and the soldiers are suffering many hardships. Half the men in the 1st Regiment of Xie Division have died of the cold or in combat. In addition, one battalion of soldiers launched an assault on a district some thirty *li* from Yining and were unfortunately led astray: they were surrounded by bandits and the entire unit perished, it is tragic to say. The bandits have a great many men, and their weapons are keen. Not only is their military planning and leadership entirely directed by a certain party, said party's regular troops have joined the battle, and their strength cannot be underestimated."[39]

One interviewee who personally joined in East Turkestan's attack on the Chinese government forces stationed in Hayranbaq confirmed to the author: "Two or three months after the last stronghold of the Nationalist army in Hayranbaq was surrounded, we were still unable to storm their defenses. So the Soviet Red Army went so far as to deploy its artillery.

Ghulja was no more than 70 kilometers from the Soviet border: the Soviets used trucks to come in overnight and leave at dawn, and the remains of the dead on the battlefield were all taken back to the Soviet Union."

After the plan to bring reinforcements to Ghulja via the Guozi Ravine failed on December 9, Zhu Shaoliang formulated a plan on December 26 for supporting troops to set out from Dengnus Dawan in southern Jinghe and approach Ghulja via the Ili river valley. Commander Li Tiejun of the 29th Regiment, Division Commander Xie Yifeng of the 45th Division, and other officers were appointed to lead their troops to the front lines by this route, but the operation ended in defeat. On January 31, 1945, the remaining Chinese government forces were forced to withdraw from the Hayranbaq region along with several thousand Han Chinese refugees, but all perished en route, resulting in the fall of Ghulja.[40] By March 1945, the front lines had been pulled back to Jinghe, and apart from the latter region, the whole of Ili District had been absorbed into the territories of the East Turkestan Republic.

Ilhan Tora's Religious Authority and Popular Mobilization for War

The interviewee mentioned above also stated that, "The majority of the weapons given to us by the Soviet Union were of German make (*Garmanika*)." The reason may be that the Soviet Union was loath to leave behind any evidence that could point to its interference in China's domestic affairs, and sought to conceal its association with the East Turkestan Independence Movement as far as possible. The formation of an intertwined power structure within the government of East Turkestan, with Soviet forces interspersed among religious leaders and elite members of Turkic-Islamic society, served as camouflage for the Soviet Union's active support of the East Turkestan Independence Movement. The fact that Ilhan Tora, the President of the Interim Government, was an Islamic religious leader was held up as an example to support claims that the East Turkestan Independence Movement was a "national revolution."

For the Soviet agents within the government of the East Turkestan Republic, the intertwined political system was most valuable in that it strengthened nationalist sentiment and the sense of a divine mission among the Turkic-Islamic peoples, mobilizing the population to join the war.

The materials enclosed in the report sent by the United States

Consulate in Urumqi to the U.S. Secretary of State, referenced in the previous chapter, included a bulletin circulated amongst the Turkic Muslim residents of Karasahr, Kucha, Korla and other regions in the name of Ilhan Tora as President of East Turkestan and Supreme Commander of the Army. The bulletin represents Tora's efforts to mobilize the local Muslim population:

> In the nearest future our Army marches forward toward you. You must stand ready. In this cause we will not be grudging either of our worldly goods or our mortal souls: to free ourselves from slavery, to defend our religion, to liberate our native country, we will struggle, we will wage open war! There should not be any kind of fear in us; if we die in this cause we shall be among the Elect of the Most High (who enter at once into the ultimate Paradise); if we are killed in this battle we become Martyrs for the Faith![41]

In late 1944 and the first half of 1945, Ilhan Tora traveled across the region delivering speeches; in each of these speeches, Tora fiercely denounced Chinese rule over Xinjiang, proclaiming, "The East Turkestan Republic is our fatherland."[42] On April 2, 1945, the Interim Government Council released Resolution No. 39, which declared the establishment of a "Tithe Collection Committee" to "support *jihad*." On April 8, at the founding ceremony for the National Army, Ilhan Tora personally presented the national flag to the Army, emblazoned with the symbol of the crescent moon and stars on a green background, carrying the slogan "Marching for the Independence of East Turkestan" along with a verse from Quranic scripture.[43]

The following passage written by Yasin Hudabardi serves to illustrate the enormous impact that Ilhan Tora had in mobilizing the population to join and support the war: "In the early stages of the revolution, due to the historical conditions and limitations of Xinjiang, religion was used as a tool as in other popular uprisings like the Taiping Heavenly Kingdom and the Boxer Rebellion, and the banner of religion was held high as a strategy to achieve popular mobilization and revolutionary objectives." Hudabardi also stated that, "In the early period of the revolution, the troops and the people were educated using the intertwined ideas of heroism and patriotism, which had a positive impact on victory in the revolution."[44] In this 1985 text, Hudabardi attempted to portray the East Turkestan revolution against the Nationalist government as part of the Chinese Communist Revolution. But in fact, the object of the people's patriotism in the East Turkestan Independence Movement was the East Turkestan Republic, not China.

The success of the East Turkestan Independence Movement did not end with the Ghulja Uprising: the East Turkestan Republic steadily expanded its sphere of influence from Ghulja to the entire Ili District, and further to the neighboring districts of Tarbagatay and Altay. These achievements may be attributed in large part to the intertwined system of complementary political factions that informed its Interim Government.

Summary

The two factions that controlled the government of the East Turkestan Republic consisted of religious leaders and elite members of Turkic-Islamic society, represented by Ilhan Tora, as well as Soviet forces composed of pro-Soviet intellectuals of Uyghur, Tatar or other ethnicities and Soviet nationals, represented by Abdulkerim Abbasow. The former were concentrated in the Interim Government Council, while the latter were clustered within the military and the Ministry of Internal Affairs. The most important feature of the internal political structure of the East Turkestan Republic was the intertwined, complementary system formed within the regime by these two political factions.

This intertwined system was formed through mutual agreement or tacit acknowledgement on the part of both factions, due to the political and social environment faced by the young republic and, in particular, to the exigencies of war. However, this codependent system undoubtedly had an impact on policy formulation in the Interim Government of East Turkestan. In this sense, the republic's intertwined political system is the key to understanding the nature of the policies issued by the Interim Government, as well as the nature of the government itself.

However, there were certain necessary preconditions for the formation and preservation of such a system. The Second East Turkestan Independence Movement was organized and led by pro-Soviet intellectuals: as a result, important organs of the government, such as the Ministry of Military Affairs and the Ministry of Internal Affairs, were controlled by intellectuals and other Soviet forces. This imbalance of power was in fact a prerequisite for the formation and perpetuation of East Turkestan's bipolar system. Ilhan Tora's faction was well aware that any attempt to upend this imbalance would result in their complete expulsion from the regime's inner circle.

Secondly, this codependent system was formed in the early stages of the revolution to meet the needs of the struggle to overthrow Chinese rule, creating a kind of circular logic: The intertwined system that formed to overthrow Chinese rule needed China as a common enemy in order to perpetuate itself, but the system could only survive and have value if it continuously faced new, external enemies; thus the purpose of its existence became the condition for its survival. This was one of the motivating factors in the continuous outward expansion of the East Turkestan Independence Movement and its namesake republic following the Ghulja Uprising.

The fundamental disagreements between the two factions in terms of political ideology meant that the loss of an external object would naturally result in the evaporation of the internal forces that held the system together. The collapse of the system was a definite possibility, as the military strength of the East Turkestan Republic was dependent on the Soviet Union's willingness to continue providing aid; this aid could be revoked at any time due to changes in the Soviet Union's international political needs or its attitude toward East Turkestan. Later developments proved this point: The East Turkestan Republic and the Second East Turkestan Independence Movement imploded at the very moment that its intertwined political system lost its raison d'être.

CHAPTER 7

THE MEETING POINT OF NATIONALISM AND COMMUNISM

Soviet Backdrop to the Expansion of the East Turkestan Republic

As the East Turkestan Republic expanded across Ili District, by July 1945, its armed forces had settled into a "Three-Front War," advancing into the territories of Xinjiang on three separate fronts. On the Northern Front, the East Turkestan army marched forward into Tarbagatay District, successively capturing Toli County, Dorbiljin County, and Choqak County (modern-day Tacheng), the seat of the district government.[1] By late August, the East Turkestan forces had advanced into Altay District,[2] capturing Kaba County and Burqin County on September 2, and seizing Chenghua County (modern-day Altay City), the seat of the Altay District Government, on September 7. On the Central Front, the republic's forces captured the bridgehead at Chepaizi near Usu Town on September 1; on the 8th, they stormed Usu, Jinghe and other important strongholds of the Nationalist forces, reaching the western shore of the Manas River. On the Southern Front, the East Turkestan army crossed the Tianshan Mountains in July, capturing Bay Town on August 14, Kurgan on August 25, and Aksu Old Town on September 6, and massing below the walls of Aksu City, the administrative seat of Aksu District.[3]

In this series of battles, the forces of the East Turkestan Republic defeated 12 regiments and 2 battalions of the Chinese Nationalist army, as well as the 2nd Army Headquarters Company and the 45th Division Headquarters Company;[4] Guo Qi, the commanding officer at the front lines in Jinghe, Division Commander Wan Lingyun, and Altay District Commissioner Gao Boyu were captured, along with 6,000 other officers and soldiers of the Nationalist army.⁵ By September, the republic controlled the entire territory of Ili District, Tarbagatay District, and Altay District.

The brilliant successes achieved by the East Turkestan Republic may of course be ascribed to its formidable military and weaponry. For instance, in the battles at Usu and Jinghe, although the Nationalist forces had deployed mines and built up fortifications around their position, digging a three-meter trench and flooding it with water, the National Army of East Turkestan was equipped with armored vehicles, artillery and other heavy weaponry, and was even able to scramble three bomber planes. The East Turkestan army thus defeated the Chinese government forces with superior weaponry,⁶ achieving a major victory referred to as "the greatest battle in the history of the National Army."⁷

As the superior forces of the East Turkestan Republic advanced on all fronts, the Nationalist army was prevented from providing support to its forces; this was another major factor in the republic's victories. Anti-Nationalist guerrilla groups formed by local Turkic Muslims were already present in the Tarbagatay and Altay districts: as the regular forces of East Turkestan fought on the front lines, a rebel group of Kazakh nomads led a series of attacks against Hoboksar Town in Hoboksar County, Tarbagatay District. In eastern Xinjiang, a group of Kazakh guerrillas cut off the Nationalist government's supply lines between Urumqi and the Altay District.⁸ Kazakh nomads residing near Urumqi also provided support to the guerrilla operations of rebel groups in Altay District.⁹ In Taxkorgan County in southern Xinjiang, a Kyrgyz guerrilla organization rose up in open rebellion against the Chinese government.¹⁰

As the East Turkestan Republic continued the push to expand its national borders, the war developed into a duel between rebel guerrillas and the Nationalist government forces. However, it is clear that, without the support of the armed forces of the republic in Ghulja, the rebel groups would have been unable to muster the military strength, organizational capabilities, leadership, and economic resources to engage in such a large-scale war.

This chapter traces the path of East Turkestan's military expansion from Ili District into the Tarbagatay and Altay districts and elucidates the history of the national movement as well as the characteristics and history of nationalist groups in the latter two districts, exploring the organization of Turkic Muslims in each district and their integration into the forces of the East Turkestan Republic, and analyzing the objective factors that allowed the republic to successfully expand its sphere of influence.

7.1 The Establishment of a "Three-Front War," "Residence No. 1," and "Residence No. 2"

Soviet Red Army Troops in the Ranks of the National Army

The war plan for the expansion of East Turkestan's zone of control was formulated not long after the establishment of the National Army. Saypidin Azizi described this as an enormously far-reaching plan of operations, advancing on the northern, central and southern fronts from Ili District into other regions of Xinjiang, to achieve the ultimate objective of capturing the provincial capital of Urumqi.[11]

However, the objectives listed in the "Three-Front War Plan" were impossible to achieve relying solely on the military strength of the East Turkestan Republic. At the point when the armed groups scattered across East Turkestan were reorganized into the "National Army," on April 8, 1945, the army's total strength numbered less than 15,000. The republic's war footing also meant that 5,500 troops had to be constantly held in reserve to defend the capital of Ghulja.[12]

In order to "resolve the most pressing issue of the war," the Interim Government of the East Turkestan Republic instituted a draft on June 19, 1945. Under the *Military Service Law* released by the Interim Government on February 3, 1945, men between the ages of 20 and 22 were required to serve in the military for a minimum of three years (when necessary, the age limit could be raised to 45). However, the draft resulted in only 500 recruits, despite being instituted in 10 counties.[13] According to the 1944 census, the population of Ili District at the time was 471,686. The fact that the draft drew such a small number of recruits, even under imminent threat of war, suggests that those meeting the conditions had already been mobilized, and no men of suitable age remained within the civilian population.

Even if the republic had been able to conscript more soldiers, it is unlikely that these raw, untrained recruits would have been directly committed to the battlefield. An officer academy at which National Army officers could be trained by Soviet Red Army officers and White Russian military instructors was established in Ghulja, but it should be noted that this academy was not founded until after the general war began in July 1945.[14] Thus, at the point when the East Turkestan Republic launched its "Three-Front War," it was able to mobilize no more than 10,000 troops.

In contrast, the Nationalist government had a force of approximately 60,000 stationed in Xinjiang at the time.[15] Another 5,618 men were drawn from the forces of the Hui warlord Ma Bufang in Qinghai Province to form the 5th Cavalry Army as reinforcements for Xinjiang.[16] When this news reached the East Turkestan Republic, Ilhan Tora reportedly wrote a letter to Ma Bufang, dated February 12, declaring that "We hold the same faith," and appealing to Ma not to send troops to oppress Muslims.[17] The 5th Cavalry Army nevertheless reached Xinjiang in June 1945.[18] In other words, East Turkestan's "Three-Front War" was launched in full knowledge that the 5th Cavalry Army and other forces had been deployed to Xinjiang.

Given the clear disparity between the forces of the two parties to the conflict, it is likely that East Turkestan's three-front battle plan relied on other forces in addition to its National Army. According to the memoirs of people who lived through the war, a contingent known as the "Isakbek Cavalry Brigade" was highly active on the northern and central fronts.[19] However, no such unit appeared in the lists of the National Army until April 1945 at the earliest. According to statements by prisoners of war captured by the Chinese government forces, the most effective unit fighting for East Turkestan was a cavalry troop of approximately 3,000 riders composed of Kazakhs, Kyrgyz and Uzbeks from Soviet Central Asia, led by a man referred to in Chinese sources as *Su-ka-u-bo* (斯喀乌伯).[20] The pronunciation of this transliteration is remarkably close to the name Isakbek, which is written in Chinese as *Isu-hak-bek* (伊斯哈克别克). As no other units of similar name have been discovered, it may be inferred that the "Su-ka-u-bo Troop" refers to the "Isakbek Cavalry Brigade." In other words, it is highly likely that the indigenous Turkic-Islamic inhabitants of Xinjiang played no part in this unit claiming the name of "Isakbek Cavalry Brigade": rather, it was formed by Kazakhs, Kyrgyz and Uzbeks originating from Soviet Central Asia.

The unit's name in fact referred to Isakbek Munonow. Munonow was of Kyrgyz ethnicity, and was born in Ulughqat in southern Xinjiang; at the time, he was the First Deputy Commander of the National Army of East Turkestan.²¹ According to a contemporary theory espoused by Republic of China officials, Munonow led the Isakbek Cavalry Brigade from Taxkorgan in southern Xinjiang onto the battlefield by way of Soviet territories.²² However, this simplistic explanation disregards the complete lack of evidence that the Isakbek Brigade was ever in southern Xinjiang, or that Munonow had formed an alliance with local rebels prior to the founding of the East Turkestan Republic, and it is otherwise difficult to believe

Isakbek Munonow
(1902–1949)

that this could have been achieved, both from a communications and from a transportation standpoint. Isakbek Munonow arrived in Ghulja on November 16, only nine days after the Ghulja Uprising, yet Taxkorgan is more than one thousand kilometers away from Ghulja. It would have been nigh impossible for Munonow to hear of the Ghulja Uprising and then lead a force of 3,000 from Taxkorgan to Ghulja in such a short period of time, considering the contemporary state of Xinjiang's roads and communications systems. It is worth noting that Isakbek Munonow arrived in Ghulja in the company of the Soviet national Ivan Polinov. These circumstances point to the conclusion that the arrival and mobilization of the Isakbek Cavalry Brigade were clearly arranged by the hand of the Soviet Union.

On the question of the involvement of Soviet forces in the "Three-Front War Plan," the scholar Li Sheng of the Borderland History and Geography Research Center at the Chinese Academy of Social Sciences offers a compelling argument based on his discoveries in the archives of the former Soviet Union. Li notes that, in June 1945, the Politburo of the Soviet Communist Party issued a resolution to send 500 officers and 2,000 noncommissioned officers and soldiers of the Soviet Red Army to reinforce the armies of the East Turkestan Republic. At the same time, a steady stream of artillery and munitions, transport vehicles, communications equipment to support military liaison and command operations, a massive amount of weaponry and other matériel was being moved into Xinjiang. Several important operations plans were also formulated by Soviet agents in conjunction with the Interim Government of East Turkestan.²³

Aside from question of military forces, the East Turkestan Republic also lacked the financial resources to support the war. In May 1945, the Interim Government of East Turkestan began forcibly relocating the Han residents of the Ili District to settlements.[24] The Han residents of Kunes and other counties were relocated to Qapqal County, while Han Chinese people in Qapqal County were removed to Huiyuan in Qorghas County. On August 6, the Ministry of Finance and the Ministry of Agricultural Land and Water Resources issued a joint statement declaring that the crops left behind by the Han residents would be harvested under the auspices of the Ministry of Agriculture, their fields and orchards would be put up for auction, and the remaining land would be leased to tenant farmers.[25] The alleged need to "implement centralized administration of Han residents" was in fact a ploy to seize the property of Han Chinese residents to aid in the war efforts.

The National Army reportedly drew on government coffers to pay for 70% of its supplies, while the remainder was allegedly funded through the confiscation of assets from banks and trading companies formed under the previous regime, as well as public contributions. There is insufficient evidence to support this claim, but it is also inconceivable that, in a region with a population of only 470,000, the newly founded Interim Government of East Turkestan could have amassed the resources in a few short months to support a large-scale, modernized war through normal fiscal revenue. It is also telling that, in 1945, a Soviet national was appointed as the head of the National Army's Supply and Logistics Department, overseeing efforts to establish military supply depots across the region to ensure the supply of provisions and other matériel for the National Army.[26]

In sum, East Turkestan was reliant upon the Soviet Union in many respects in waging its "Three-Front War." It is therefore highly likely that those responsible for formulating the detailed battle plan for the deployment of forces and supply chain logistics were none other than Soviet agents.

The Supreme Soviet Organs in Ghulja: "Residence No. 1" and "Residence No. 2"

The Soviet personnel connected to the East Turkestan Republic were primarily divided into three groups, including advisors to the Interim Government, officers in the National Army, and the staff of the Soviet

Consulate. Soviet advisors were installed in each ministry of the Interim Government. Saypidin Azizi confirmed in his memoirs that a Soviet advisor by the name of Muhshin hovered near Ilhan Tora.[27] Azizi expressed concerns that Muhshin would amass enough power to coopt Ilhan Tora's expanded authority, allowing the Soviet advisors installed within East Turkestan's Interim Government to participate directly in policy-making and the exercise of authority.

The author Zhang Dajun states that Ivan Polinov was the ranking leader of the Soviet agents in the East Turkestan Republic.[28] Polinov indeed wielded a great deal of power, serving as the Commander-in-Chief of the National Army up until June 1946. Though the Minister of Military Affairs merely held the rank of lieutenant colonel, Polinov was elevated to the rank of lieutenant general, and until October 1945, he was the only lieutenant general in the East Turkestan Republic.[29] However, Polinov by no means served as the vice president of East Turkestan, as Zhang Dajun claims. According to Resolution No. 79 of the Interim Government, dated August 9, 1945, we can see that Polinov was merely a government council member.[30] During the march into Tarbagatay District and the attack on Usu, Polinov also served in an actual command position at the very front lines;[31] this suggests that Polinov was not in fact the highest authority among the Soviet personnel within the East Turkestan Republic.

The Soviet Consulate in Ghulja was originally installed on the basis of diplomatic relations with China, but the Soviet Union did not move to abandon its consular offices in Ghulja upon the founding of the East Turkestan Republic. A telegram sent by Chinese Communist Party representative Deng Liqun to the Central Committee of the Chinese Communist Party upon his arrival in Ghulja in August 1949 confirms that the Soviet Consulate in Ghulja was a major voice among the forces involved in the East Turkestan Independence Movement.[32] However, this telegram was sent after the Soviet Union had implemented significant changes with respect to its policies on the East Turkestan Independence Movement, so it does not provide a completely reliable picture of the composition of Soviet forces in the East Turkestan Republic prior to 1946.

Saypidin Azizi's memoirs indicate that a Soviet official responsible for the question of the East Turkestan Republic was stationed in Ghulja. Azizi also asserts that a group of intellectuals led by Abdulkerim Abbasow sought to establish an "East Turkestan Revolutionary Party" in 1946, but were met with strong opposition by a Soviet advisor: "We decided to open a direct dialogue with the Communist Party of the Soviet Union. At the time, there was a person regularly going to and fro between Moscow and Ghulja due to the Three Districts Revolution. On one occasion when this person arrived in Ghulja, I accompanied Abdulkerim Abbasow to pay a visit to him, and unreservedly described our situation to him. After hearing about our current situation and our hopes, he agreed with our idea, and replied, 'Good, continue on in this way. . . . I know of your wishes, and that is to say Moscow knows as well.'"[33] Regrettably, Azizi speaks evasively in his memoirs with regard to the physical appearance of this figure and the nature of his work in Ghulja, and provides no concrete description.

In interviews with the author, many of the participants in the Second East Turkestan Independence Movement made reference to a Soviet institution known as "Residence No. 2," which existed in Ghulja during the period of the East Turkestan Republic. This residence was located by the Baishan River in Ghulja city proper, near the Ili District Police Headquarters of the old regime. The denizen of this residence was a figure known as the "No. 2" (второй). This figure was extremely mysterious: he rarely came in contact with the outside world, so few ever saw him, and even fewer knew his name; he was often referred to by the nickname "White-Hair." An analysis of this appellation suggests that the "white-haired" man known as "No. 2" may well have been the person to whom Saypidin Azizi referred in his memoirs: the chief agent in charge of Soviet affairs with relation to the East Turkestan Independence Movement.

Due to the characteristics of this expression in the Uyghur language, many of the interviewees believed that "No. 2" may have referred to an actual street number. However, given that Ivan Polinov was referred to within the East Turkestan Independence Movement as "No. 3," it is unlikely that "No. 2" is a street address. Although some of the interviewees who spoke with the author suggested that Polinov's appellation as "No. 3" was merely another nickname, it is clear that the "white-haired" man held superior authority over Polinov. In other words, the nickname "No. 3" was likely bestowed upon Polinov because he ranked just below the denizen of "Residence No. 2" within the command system of the Soviet forces in the East Turkestan Republic.

As to the question of whether there was a "No. 1" Soviet agent in East Turkestan, the interviewees all replied in the negative. However, *History of the Xinjiang Three Districts Revolution* contains the following passage: "In late November, the Interim Government invited two delegations of military advisors led by Vladimir Kozlov and Vladimir Stepanovich to Ghulja: under the code names "Residence No. 1" and "Residence No. 2," they participated in drafting and implementing the major political and military policy decisions of the Interim Government."[34] But why would two delegations of military advisors be sent at the same time? And if this account is factual, what was the relationship between these two delegations? There are still many ambiguities regarding the organizational structure of the Soviet forces within East Turkestan, but one point can be affirmed: East Turkestan's daring plan to advance simultaneously on three fronts to expand from Ili District to the entire territory of Xinjiang proceeded with the approval and support of the Soviet Union. Though no concrete evidence is provided, *History of the Xinjiang Three Districts Revolution* clearly states that the war plan "was drafted with the assistance of the delegations of Soviet military advisors."[35]

7.2 The "Liberation of Tarbagatay District" and the "Imir Command Post"

Mansur Apandi and the Secret Nationalist Organizations

The Chinese Nationalist government initially expected that East Turkestan's armed forces would strike out toward Xinjiang's provincial capital of Urumqi: Jinghe and Usu were therefore heavily guarded as key defensive points along the primary route between Ili District and Urumqi.[36] However, the East Turkestan army's first attack was not directed eastward toward Jinghe and Usu: instead, the army marched northeast toward the Tarbagatay and Altay districts. The Chinese army's defensive positions in northern Xinjiang were soon completely overrun, while Jinghe and Usu, which the Chinese military regarded as key to both recapturing Ili and defending Urumqi, were encircled by East Turkestan forces.[37] On September 7, the National Army finally launched its attack on Usu, "reinforced by a fair number of Soviet Red Army infantry troops, artillery, armored cars and aircraft"; on the 8th, Jinghe was captured "with the aid of Soviet military personnel."[38]

The decision to first march on the Tarbagatay and Altay districts was likely motivated by the prospect of easy victory. Two non-military members of the Government Council—Supreme Court Justice Mahmautjan Mahsum and Minister of Education Saypidin Azizi—accompanied the East Turkestan armed forces as they advanced into Tarbagatay District. Their task was to prepare for the establishment of a new government and administrative system in the soon-to-be liberated districts of Tarbagatay and Altay.[39] The presence of a civilian delegation demonstrates that the government of East Turkestan anticipated certain victory in its military operations in the Tarbagatay and Altay districts.

Compared to the situation at Jinghe and Usu, these two districts promised easy conquest, for a simple reason: few Chinese government forces were deployed in Tarbagatay and Altay, and they were countered by powerful groups of armed nationalist rebels. More significantly, like Ili, both Tarbagatay and Altay shared a border with the Soviet Republic of Kazakhstan and played host to Soviet consulates. This naturally begs the question: Did the minority ethnic rebel forces in Tarbagatay and Altay, like the Ghulja National Freedom Group and Nilka Guerrillas of the Ili District, also have a special relationship with the Soviet Union?

During this era, Tarbagatay District was divided into six counties: Choqak, Dorbiljin, Hoboksar, Chagantokay, Sawan, and Usu. According to the 1944 census conducted by the Xinjiang Department of Civil Affairs, the district had a total population of 170,422, including 103,180 Kazakhs and 10,515 Uyghurs.[40]

Several armed rebel groups came into being in the Tarbagatay District in 1944. On July 18, a group of approximately 800 fighters stormed Hoboksar Town. Hoboksar was a key fortification on the route between the Tarbagatay and Altay districts: Sheng Shicai, who still clung to power at this point as the ruler of Xinjiang, was forced to send troops to reinforce the garrison at Hoboksar in response. In mid-July, anti-government leaflets were discovered in Dorbiljin. The "rioters," as they were labeled, were all of Kazakh and Mongol ethnicity; and according to Zhang Dajun, they were supported behind the scenes by the Soviet Union.[41]

Wu Zhongxin's diary entry for December 20, 1944, contains the following account of the unrest in Tarbagatay District: "The Soviet Union sent Mansur to Tacheng [Tarbagatay] District to establish an armed organization, revealing its ambitions to expand to the whole of Xinjiang." Based on this passage, Wu Zhongxin believed that the rise of armed rebel groups in Tarbagatay District was instigated by the Soviet Union. Was this truly so? To determine the relationship between nationalist organizations in Tarbagatay District and the Soviet Union, we must first examine the figure "Mansur," whom Wu Zhongxin identifies as a bridge between the two sides.

A Soviet-born Uyghur, Mansur Roziyow was known amongst the minority ethnic leaders of Xinjiang as Mansur Apandi (Mr. Mansur).[42] Although previous studies have overlooked his significance, there is no doubt that Mansur played a key role in the modern political history of Xinjiang and the East Turkestan Independence Movement. As discussed in Chapter 4, Mansur served as both a Soviet political consultant and the director of the Society for the Promotion of Uyghur Culture during the Sheng Shicai regime; he reportedly instructed Hoja Niyaz, the leader of the First East Turkestan Independence Movement, on the "theory of national revolution."[43] He was later imprisoned after drawing the ire of Sheng Shicai, but was released and repatriated to the Soviet Union in 1942 through the intervention of the Soviet consulate.[44]

After returning to the Soviet Union, Mansur continued to promote the nationalist movement in Xinjiang. One of his associates at the time was Abilmit Hajiyow, who was later appointed as Secretary-General of the Tarbagatay District Government. Haziyow's memoirs contain a detailed account of Mansur's connections to the secret rebel nationalist organizations in Tarbagatay.[45] Mansur was allegedly "active in the Chinese-Soviet border region under the pseudonym of Abla Remzanov, to aid the people of Xinjiang who sought to overthrow the reactionary Xinjiang government." In May 1944, alongside the Uyghur Qasimahun Ismayilnov, who fled from Tarbagatay to the Soviet Union, Mansur founded the "Imir Command Post" within Soviet territory.[46]

The Soviet-Based "Imir Command Post"

Aside from the Soviet-born Uyghur Mansur, the Imir Command Post also boasted a Russian advisor.[47] The command post organized and guided the secret activities of nationalist organizations in the Tarbagatay District, and played an important role in the expansion of East Turkestan armed forces into the district.

The first secret nationalist organization in Tarbagatay District was founded by a Uyghur intellectual who had studied abroad in the Soviet Union, known by the locals as the "Man of Tashkent." This organization is believed to be a product of the Soviet consulate's efforts to implement its policies in the region.[48] A number of other secret organizations, all of which had ties to the Imir Command Post, were founded by Uyghurs, Kazakhs, Uzbeks, Tatars and other ethnic groups in the Tarbagatay District in 1944. Under Mansur's instructions, Abilmit Hajiyow made contact with these organizations in July 1944 and forged an alliance to found the "Organization of Fighters for Liberation" (*Azadilik Uqun Kuresh Kilish Texkilati*).[49]

In order to receive instructions from the Imir Command Post, liaisons from the Fighters for Liberation made around 100 trips to the command post between July and November 1944.[50] Notably, this occurred on the eve of the Ghulja Uprising. The Fighters for Liberation were reportedly in close contact with the armed organizations in the Ili and Altay districts, and in February 1945, they formed a secret armed branch within Tarbagatay:[51] a rebel guerrilla force based in the region of Ebi Lake. The Ebi Lake guerrillas later repelled an attack by Chinese government forces and established a stronghold to serve as their base of operations; the weapons and ammunition used by the guerrillas were provided by the Soviet Union.[52]

The activities of the Imir Command Post attracted the attention of the Xinjiang Provincial Government, and fortifications were established near the border for surveillance. However, the Imir Command Post called in assistance from the Soviet Red Army to slip across the border and destroy the watch post.[53] This incident demonstrates that the Imir Command Post was by no means spontaneously formed by the Turkic-Islamic inhabitants of Soviet Central Asia (Figure 7.1).

The Imir Command Post was the most important factor leading to the alliance between the nationalist rebels of the Tarbagatay District and the forces of the East Turkestan Republic. The Imir Command Post and the Fighters for Liberation reportedly sent a letter to the National Army in early July 1945 requesting the invasion of Tarbagatay District, and instructed the armed groups under their purview to actively cooperate with the National Army's military operations.[54]

Figure 7.1 Relational Diagram between the Imir Command Post and the Secret Rebel Organizations of Tarbagatay

Source: Compiled by the author.

On July 31, 1945, a contingent of National Army forces spearheaded by the 3rd Cavalry Regiment (led by Regiment Commander Leskan, a pro-Soviet White Russian), under the command of the Soviet commander-in-chief Polinov, captured Tarbagatay District's capital city of Choqak; on the following day, Mansur led the Uyghurs of the Imir Command Post from the Soviet Union into Tarbagatay District.[55] Mansur was appointed as the First Deputy Commissioner of Tarbagatay District, while Qasimahun Ismayilnov was appointed as the Second Deputy Commissioner; under their leadership, nearly all the Uyghur members of the Imir Command Post received appointments to administrative departments of the East Turkestan Interim Government in Tarbagatay District.[56] These appointments were a form of reward acknowledging the Imir Command Post's achievements in directing the activities of nationalist rebel organizations in Tarbagatay District during the three-year period from 1943 to 1945.

7.3 The "Liberation of Altay District," the "White House," and the "Blue House"

The Kazakh Rebel Movement in the Altay District

As the forces of the East Turkestan Republic advanced into Tarbagatay

District, armed Kazakh groups took action to support their military operations. A Mongol representative sent to request the surrender of a Chinese military fortification delivered the following statement on behalf of the East Turkestan Republic to the Chinese regiment commander: "The troops coming from Ili number more than 2,000, and all officers above the noncommissioned ranks are Russians or naturalized citizens. In addition, more than 1,000 bandits have come from Jiminay County [in Altay District], in all exceeding 3,500 men."[57] This joint military operation demonstrates that the forces led to war by the East Turkestan Republic had evolved into an alliance of Turkic Muslim rebels from across Xinjiang under the leadership of the Soviet military, to stand united against the Chinese government forces.

Beginning in late July, the region-wide war efforts were expanded. On July 29, by order of Resolution No. 79 of the Interim Government, Commander Ivan Polinov and Deputy Commander Isakbek Munonow, the two ranking leaders of the National Army, were respectively appointed as a Government Council member and alternate. In August, the forces deployed to the Northern Front were increased from one regiment to three.[58] On August 5, under the "No. 16 Directive to All Departments and Organizations," the Interim Government ordered the mobilization and enlistment of all government personnel, though in families with two brothers, only one was to be recruited. However, after seizing control of Tarbagatay District, Polinov pulled back from the Northern Front, leading two regiments to the Central Front to meet up with Munonow at Usu. This meant that only one regiment remained at the Northern Front: the task of capturing Altay District was largely entrusted to an armed rebel group of Altay-born Kazakh nomads led by Osman Islam and Dalalkan Sugurbayow.

Dalalkan Sugurbayow

"The Altay guerrilla force of more than 1,000 fighters, commanded by Dalalkan, and 50-odd military personnel from the Mongolian People's Republic" launched an attack on the Altay District Capital of Chenghua (modern-day Altay City),[59] and on September 7, 1945, Chenghua was captured by the National Army. The "Resolution of the Interim Government of the East

Turkestan Republic Regarding Altay District," dated September 23, opens with the declaration that "Altay District is part of the East Turkestan Republic." However, Resolution No. 85, which addressed the "issuance of Victory Bonds," designated an amount for circulation in Altay District, despite having been released a month prior to the region's annexation, on August 22.[60] This seemingly premature announcement was likely predicated on the fact that Kazakh rebel forces had already captured four of the seven counties in Altay District by July 1945.[61] However, at the time, the rebel groups in Altay had not made a final determination as to whether their district would join the East Turkestan Republic. In an interview with the author, Patihan Sugurbayow, the son of the Altay Kazakh rebel leader Dalalkan Sugurbayow, stated that, "The armed Kazakh rebel groups were capable of liberating Altay District, even if not a single regiment of the National Army came."[62]

The antagonism between the nomadic Kazakh herders and the Xinjiang Provincial Government can be traced back to the early 1930s. In 1931, a number of Kazakh nomads participated in the Kumul Rebellion initiated by the Uyghur leader Hoja Niyaz;[63] many of the Kazakh herders in Altay District later threw their support behind Sheng Shicai's enemy Ma Zhongying.[64] During the period from 1933 to 1939, a total of 11,680 Kazakh nomads from Barköl County in eastern Xinjiang migrated to Gansu to escape the chaos of war and ethnic oppression under Sheng Shicai's regime.[65]

The second wave of migration to Gansu, which occurred in 1939, was triggered by the policies of ethnic oppression implemented by Sheng Shicai's regime, as well as a program for the confiscation of bullets.[66] This program also became the impetus for the "Koktokay Rebellion" (*Koktokay Kozgilingi*) launched by Kazakh nomads in Altay District.[67] The Koktokay Rebellion erupted in two spates of violence in 1940 and 1941 before terms were finally reached with the Sheng Shicai regime.[68] Although Kazakh nomads accounted for 85% of the total population in all seven counties of the Altay District,[69] the Koktokay Rebellion was limited to a "resistance movement to defend [Kazakhs'] lives and interests," and did not develop into a war for national independence.[70]

From the "Altay Kazakh National Restoration Committee" to the "National Revolutionary Interim Government of Altay"

During the Koktokay Rebellion in 1941, two Kazakh leaders had rejected the terms of compromise reached with the Sheng Shicai regime: one was Osman Islam, who led several dozen fighters into the Dzungarian Basin of the Gobi Desert; the other was Dalalkan Sugurbayow, then the Deputy Magistrate of Chenghua County.[71] These two figures utterly transformed the Kazakh rebel movement in the Altay District.

Sheng Shicai arrested Osman's family and made several attempts to force his surrender, but was repelled each time by Osman.[72] On July 14, 1942, Osman circulated a bulletin in the region, declaring to the Kazakh nomads that, "Since we fell into the hands of the Han Chinese, they have taken away our blood, our lives, and our land; to prevent the Han Chinese from drawing near to us and to rescue our Kazakh brothers and sisters from suffering, we must seize control of our own land."

In mid-December 1943, Osman established the "Altay Kazakh National Restoration Committee" at his base near the upper reaches of the Burqin River in Qinggil County; the committee had 25 members, and Osman himself served as the chairman. The committee's political positions were summarized in the following eight points:

(1) Fighting for freedom, and rescuing the Kazakhs from crisis;

(2) Kazakh self-administration of the counties in eastern Altay District;

(3) Formation of a Kazakh militia in Altay District;

(4) Release of prisoners;

(5) Banning arbitrary government expropriation of herders' livestock;

(6) Abolishing exorbitant taxes and levies;

(7) Banning Han Chinese immigration to Altay District and the stationing of Han military forces;

(8) We shall continue to exchange local products for cloth from the neighboring countries with whom we formerly had good relations; this shall be rapidly transported to the region, and traders shall be permitted to engage in trade.[73]

By early 1944, Osman had seized control of Qinggil County, Koktokay County, and Burultokay County. This was the state of affairs when

Dalalkan Sugurbayow returned from Mongolia to Qinggil in June 1944 and formed an alliance with Osman; between July and September, uprisings were launched across the neighboring counties, and the rebels seized control of large swathes of Altay District, including Burqin County.[74] The "National Revolutionary Interim Government of Altay" was founded in Qinggil in October 1944;[75] Osman was appointed president, while Sugurbayow was appointed as vice president and commander of the armed forces. The

Osman Islam (?–1951)

nature of the Altay Kazakh rebel movement was thus rapidly transformed from resistance against oppression and exploitation to a national movement to oppose Han Chinese rule.

The Soviet Union and the Mongolian People's Republic played an active role in promoting the Kazakh national movement as it was transformed under Osman and Sugurbayow's leadership. Dalalkan Sugurbayow's disappearance in 1941 was in fact a plot engineered by the Soviet Union's deputy consul in Altay, allowing Sugurbayow to receive political and military training in the Soviet Union.[76] In 1943, Osman was able to "buy" weapons from the Soviet Union, and the Mongolian People's Republic sent delegates extending an offer for friendly relations with Osman and support in the form of weapons and ammunition. The Mongolian People's Republic provided Osman's forces with a place of refuge and a base for training, and offered grazing lands to the Kazakh nomads under his authority. Osman therefore used the China–Mongolia border region as a base of operations for his dealings as well as his clashes with Chinese government forces.[77] *History of the Xinjiang Three Districts Revolution* even notes that, in late April 1944, Prime Minister Khorloogiin Choibalsan and other military and political leaders of the Mongolian People's Republic met with Osman near the border between Mongolia and China, promising enthusiastic support in the form of rifles and ammunition, communications equipment, and advisors.[78]

"With the assistance of the Soviet Union and the Mongolian People's Republic, the armed forces led by Osman and Dalalkan grew ever more powerful."[79] The hands of both the Soviet Union and the Mongolian People's Republic can be seen in each of the three stages of the expanding alliances that gave shape to the national movement in the Altay District (Figure 7.2). The first stage was the alliance between Osman Islam and Dalalkan Sugurbayow, prompted by their shared experience in receiving support from the Soviet Union and Mongolia. When Sugurbayow arrived at Osman's base of operations in Qinggil in June 1944, he brought 14 Soviet and Mongolian advisors in train.[80] The Soviet advisors were referred to using the code name "people of the White House" (*Ak Uyning Adamliri*), while the Mongolian advisors were referred to as the "people of the Blue House" (*Kok Uyning Adamliri*).[81]

The second stage involved an alliance between the armed forces in Qinggil and another armed faction in Jiminay. The two organizations were both part of the origins of the Altay national movement, but each had different characteristics in terms of their operations. The rebels active in Qinggil and the surrounding area primarily relied on tribal structures to mobilize the local Kazakh nomads,[82] but this mobilization strategy was not used by the armed organization in Jiminay. This disparity arose from the different backgrounds of the organizations' leaders. In the Qinggil rebel group, political power was concentrated in the hands of Osman, Sugurbayow and other Kazakh figures, while the political leader of the Jiminay faction was the Uyghur Molla Islam Ismayil. Although Kazakhs and Uyghurs shared an identity as Turkic Muslims, the two ethnic groups had completely different lifestyles and social structures, as the predominantly agricultural Uyghur society was not organized into tribes. Though a great many members of the Jiminay rebel group were Kazakh, their leader Ismayil did not have a tribal background.

However, like Qinggil County, which shared a border with the Mongolian People's Republic, Jiminay County neighbored on the Soviet Union, with easy routes across the border.[83] Molla Islam Ismayil, the Uyghur leader of the Jiminay guerrillas, was a former member of the Soviet-based Imir Command Post;[84] after the rebels suffered defeat in an attack on Jiminay Town in August 1944, the group organized the local nomadic herders in Jiminay to temporarily relocate across the Soviet border.[85] During this period, both the Soviet Union and the Mongolian People's Republic unconditionally opened their borders to Altay's armed rebel organizations.

Molla Islam Ismayil of the Jiminay guerrillas ultimately became part of the National Revolutionary Interim Government of Altay; the Soviet

Figure 7.2   Evolutionary Flowchart of the Kazakh Rebel Forces in Altay

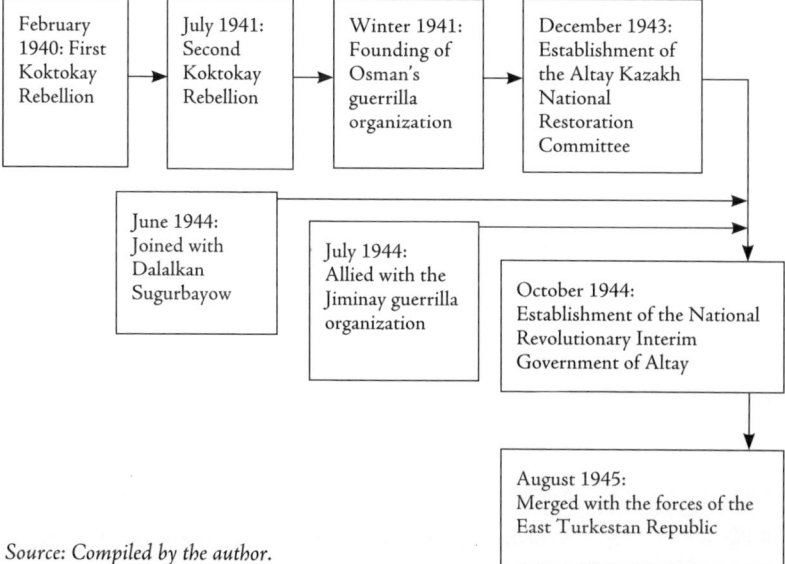

Source: Compiled by the author.

advisors of the "White House" and the Mongolian advisors of the "Blue House" were also present at the founding ceremony for the Altay Interim Government, which was held in October 1944 (Table 7.1).[86] This again demonstrates that the Soviet Union, alongside the Mongolian People's Republic, played an active role both in promoting the alliance between Altay's guerrilla organizations and in supporting the establishment of the Altay Interim Government.

Joining the Sphere of Influence of the East Turkestan Republic

Prior to the Altay District government's absorption into the East Turkestan Republic in September 1945, the general rallying cry of "Independence for East Turkestan" was entirely absent from the Altay national movement. One reason for this is encapsulated in a statement made to the author by Patihan Sugurbayow, the son of rebel leader Dalalkan Sugurbayow: "We, the Kazakh people, had no such concept as East Turkestan in our minds." The other reason is that the guerrilla organizations of the Altay District

Table 7.1 Founding Members of the National Revolutionary Interim Government of Altay

Name	Ethnicity	Position	Represented Region
Osman Islam	Kazakh	President	
Dalalkan Sugurbayow	Kazakh	Vice President, Military Commander-in-Chief	
Latip Musutapa	Kazakh		Qinggil County
Koksagan Chakow	Kazakh	Chief Court Justice	Qinggil County
Watkan Amur	Kazakh		Qinggil County
Adilkan	Kazakh		Koktokay County
Kamal	Kazakh		Koktokay County
Ashat Makay	Kazakh		Chenghua County
Kilis	Kazakh		Unknown
Kalip	Kazakh	Security Minister	Burultokay County
Ramazan	Kazakh		Jiminay County
Molla Islam Ismayil	Uyghur	Leader of the Jiminay Guerrillas	Jiminay County

Source: Compiled by the author on the basis of "On the Founding of the 'Revolutionary Interim Government' of Altay and Other Matters" (Yingi Junggo Kurux Yolida Kurban Bolganlar [Dedicated to building New China], Urumqi: Xinjiang Halik Naxiryatip), p. 179.

carried out their rebel operations in complete isolation, and had no direct contact with the forces of the East Turkestan Independence Movement in Ili District prior to mid-August 1945. In fact, the Kazakh national movement in Altay District was set in motion before the East Turkestan Independence Movement, and the National Revolutionary Interim Government of Altay was even founded earlier than the Interim Government of the East Turkestan Republic (October 1944 versus November 1944). Furthermore, before they were subsumed under the aegis of the East Turkestan Republic in September 1945, the Altay rebel organizations had already achieved a great deal of momentum: by the summer of 1945, forces under the command of Osman Islam and Dalalkan Sugurbayow had captured four counties in eastern Altay and had launched several attacks on Chenghua Town, the seat of the Chinese government in Altay.[87]

In August 1945, the Jiminay guerrillas encountered East Turkestan troops marching in from Tarbagatay District to take Jiminay County. The Kazakh witnesses to this event profoundly memorialized it as the "first contact between the Altay Revolutionary Army and the Ili Revolutionary Army on arriving in the Altay District." On September 3, the East Turkestan troops made contact with forces under the command of Dalalkan Sugurbayow, who were then staging an attack on Chenghua Town. However, Kazakh sources insist that the East Turkestan contingent only numbered between 195 and 200 soldiers at the time.[88]

Ahmatjan Kasimi, a leader of the East Turkestan Independence Movement in its later stages, acknowledged that the Kazakh national movement in Altay District emerged prior to the East Turkestan movement in Ili District, and that the two movements arose from different origins. "We truly started a national revolution, and this revolution first erupted in the Altay District. Owing to the brutal actions of despotic rulers who drank from the blood of the people, revolution broke out in Ili District as well, and the people of Tarbagatay District joined in. The national armies of the two regions of Ili and Altay ultimately joined forces."[89]

In September 1946, accompanied by Ahmatjan Kasimi and Soviet advisors, President Ilhan Tora of the East Turkestan Republic made his first visit to the Altay District and convened a meeting of the republic's Interim Government Council at Chenghua, declaring that "Altay is a part of the East Turkestan Republic," and announcing personnel appointments for the Altay District Government.[90] The Kazakh people, who observed a lifestyle and social structure different from the Uyghurs, and had no notion even of the state of East Turkestan, were thus united under the banner of the East Turkestan Republic, despite having launched their national revolution prior to the founding of the republic, and having even founded their own interim government.

Unlike the first and second stages of the Altay national movement, which centered on alliances between different Kazakh groups, the third stage involved the absorption of the Kazakh rebel movement in Altay by the Uyghur-centric East Turkestan Republic. This later became one of the driving forces for the schisms that arose within the East Turkestan Republic. There is no doubt that such a complex alliance was only achieved through the efforts of the Soviet Union, which served as the uniting factor for each of these disparate forces. Similar to the personnel model employed in the Tarbagatay District Government, the First Deputy Commissioner of the Altay District, Arupbay Alimjan, was originally a "White House" advisor. In other words, Alimjan was a Soviet advisor with long experience in guiding the operations of the local armed nationalist organizations.[91]

Summary

The analysis in this chapter confirms the existence of "Residence No. 1" and "Residence No. 2," the "Imir Command Post," and the "White House" and "Blue House," as well as the important role that each of these institutions played in the East Turkestan Independence Movement, rebel activities in Tarbagatay District, and guerrilla operations in the Altay District national movement, respectively. The development of the rebel movements in the Tarbagatay and Altay districts and the expansion of the East Turkestan Republic into these two regions were achieved by exploiting their geographical locations along the border zone to obtain organized guidance and support from the Soviet Union in the form of personnel, military matériel, and financial resources.

Each of these regional guerrilla nationalist movements was in fact peopled by a number of former students who had studied abroad in the Soviet Union. However, none of the movements' leaders, including those who had lived abroad in the Soviet Union, espoused Communist views, and by nature, the organizations they founded can at most be characterized as rebel or nationalist groups. Although the rebel and nationalist movements that sprouted across the region did not necessarily endorse the Soviet Union's political ideology and system of governance, foreign support was indispensable to their efforts to mount an armed resistance against Chinese rule and achieve other movement objectives. Therein lies the reason why each of these movements accepted Soviet leadership, and even actively sought Soviet aid.

However, in tracing the face of the East Turkestan Republic in each stage of its development, the degree to which the Soviet Union penetrated

Dalalkan Sugurbayow with members of the Altay Revolutionary Army

Xinjiang's Turkic-Islamic national movements is surprising. It is arguable that, without the Soviet Union's guidance, the disparate movements across the region would never have formed an alliance; and that, without the Soviet Union's support, the East Turkestan Independence Movement could never have expanded its sphere of influence. As the historian Li Sheng pointed out, "The victories of the armed forces of the East Turkestan Republic were ensured by the forces of the Soviet Union."[92] It should be noted that Sheng Shicai, who had thoroughly dismantled the Soviet Union's painstakingly constructed hold on Xinjiang, had already left the region by this time. The Soviet Union's objective in supporting the national movements in Xinjiang was thus not simply to destroy Sheng Shicai's erstwhile regime, but rather, more broadly, to overthrow the Chinese Nationalist government's rule over Xinjiang.

However, although the national organizations formed by the Turkish Muslims of Xinjiang found common ground with the Communist Soviet Union with respect to the political objective of toppling the Chinese government in Xinjiang, the important contributions that the Soviet Union made and the great influence that it wielded in pursuit of this goal meant that Soviet forces held an inescapable grip over the nature of the East Turkestan Independence Movement, the policy decisions of the East Turkestan Republic, and even the fate of the fledgling nation-state; this was ultimately the fatal flaw of the Second East Turkestan Independence Movement.

CHAPTER 8

INTERNATIONAL POLITICS AND THE TRAGEDY OF THE REPUBLIC

Behind the Scenes of the Xinjiang Peace Talks

In September 1945, the East Turkestan Republic experienced a major policy shift. The East Turkestan armed forces suddenly halted their advance at the western bank of Manas River, only 137 kilometers away from Xinjiang's provincial capital of Urumqi, and settled into a stalemate with the Chinese government forces. In October 1945, representatives of the government of the East Turkestan Republic opened peace negotiations with the Chinese government in the name of the "People of the Insurrectionary Districts of Xinjiang," and a peace accord was signed in January 1946. However, this chain of events, from the ceasefire to the abandonment of the name of "East Turkestan Republic," the opening of peace talks and ultimately the conclusion of a peace agreement, was clearly contrary to the original aims of the East Turkestan Independence Movement. Moreover, hardly a month prior to the talks, the forces of the East Turkestan Republic had been actively engaged in the Three-Front War, racing forward with violent momentum on all fronts and threatening to seize the whole of Xinjiang in one stroke. Yet as the stymied Chinese Nationalist government floundered for a response, the East Turkestan Republic executed a 180-degree reversal.

The policy reversal implemented by the East Turkestan Republic is perplexing in many ways. What was the reason for this shift? Did the forces behind the East Turkestan independence movement abandon their own aspirations in response to a directive by another interested party? If so, why did they willingly accept a directive occasioning such a major policy reversal? Finally, what internal political processes did the Interim Government of the East Turkestan Republic undergo after accepting this directive?

1945 was a year of dramatic changes across the globe. Against a backdrop of drastically shifting international circumstances, the relationship between the Chinese Nationalist government and the Soviet Union was improved through the mediation of Britain and the United States, and Soviet policy toward China also experienced major changes. The question is: Given the East Turkestan Republic's close relationship with the Soviet Union, was the republic's own policy reversal tied to the transformation of Soviet policy on China? This chapter traces the political processes within the East Turkestan Republic leading to the ceasefire and the signing of the peace accord, exploring the impact of the Soviet Union's policy transformation on politics in the East Turkestan Republic, from the perspective of internal trends within the republic's Interim Government as well as the changing face of international politics.

8.1 Soviet Objectives in Supporting the National Independence Movement

Sino-Soviet Diplomacy Revolving Around the East Turkestan Republic

Following the deterioration of relations with Sheng Shicai in 1942, the Soviet Union had been forced to temporarily withdraw from the political stage in Xinjiang Province. The United States and Britain established consulates in Urumqi soon after, in March and September 1943, respectively.[1] Xinjiang became a new convergence point for collaboration between China, the United States and Britain, with the aim of restraining Soviet influence; for the Soviet Union, which regarded Xinjiang as belonging to its own sphere of influence, this was naturally an unacceptable state of affairs.[2]

In June 1943, as the Soviet Union condemned Sheng Shicai for taking hostile actions, it also disclosed a secret agreement concluded between the Soviets and Sheng Shicai in 1942 to the Nationalist government in Chongqing, with the aim of sowing discord between Sheng Shicai and the Chinese central government.[3] This was also the precise time period when the Soviet Union began supporting the East Turkestan Independence Movement, in an effort to restore its influence over Xinjiang through another channel.[4]

In August 1944, Sheng Shicai launched his "August Coup" to remove Nationalist figures from his government, and separately made an attempt to restore friendly relations with the Soviet Union, but his overtures were rejected.[5] The Soviet Union's repudiation of Sheng Shicai was professedly based on the belief that Sheng was not acting in good faith. However, we cannot overlook the fact that the Soviet-backed "National Revolutionary Government of Altay" had already been founded at this point, while the Turkic Muslim peoples of Ili District and Tarbagatay District were already forming secret nationalist organizations and armed rebel groups. It is therefore conceivable that the Soviet Union's rebuff of Sheng Shicai was in fact based on a shift in Soviet policies on Xinjiang away from its erstwhile support for the leader of the orthodox regime, and toward support for the rebel forces of the East Turkestan independence movement.[6]

The Chinese Nationalist government was naturally aware of the Soviet Union's behind-the-scenes support for the East Turkestan independence movement. In November 1944, as Wu Zhongxin urged the Nationalist government to step in and engineer a resolution to the East Turkestan independence movement, he remarked to Foreign Minister Soong Tze-ven (also known as T. V. Soong): "This issue is tied to the Soviet Union; improving diplomatic relations to avert misunderstandings is a matter that brooks no delay." This comment highlights the importance to China of resolving the conflict in Xinjiang through diplomatic channels.[7] On January 7, 1945, after receiving the news that the airfield at Ghulja had fallen, Wu Zhongxin and Commander Zhu Shaoliang of the 8th Military District sent a joint telegram to Nationalist Party leader Chiang Kai-shek: "The military situation in Xinjiang has reached a critical stage: its success or failure rests on logistical support and diplomatic relations with the Soviet Union."[8]

Wu Zhongxin expressed the following views with respect to the connection between Sino-Soviet diplomatic relations and the conflict in Xinjiang: "I would say that diplomatic relations between Xinjiang and the Soviet Union are certainly not a simple matter of diplomacy between Xinjiang Province and the Soviet Union: the focal points are Chongqing and Moscow. Thus the Soviet attitude toward Xinjiang is sufficient to represent the Soviet Union's national policy toward the whole of China. If the foreign ministries of China and the Soviet Union can discuss a means of engaging in truly amicable cooperation, Xinjiang's relationship with the Soviet Union will undoubtedly be improved."[9]

At the time, the Nationalist government was "loath for the conflict on the Sino-Soviet border to impact the allied states' diplomatic relationship with the Soviet Union, out of consideration for the larger picture of the Allies' anti-fascist strategies."[10] Owing to its reluctance to stir up anti-Soviet sentiment amongst its citizens, the Nationalist government went so far as to conceal the "Yining [Ghulja] Incident" (*Yining shijian* 伊寧事件) from the wider world.[11] It is evident that the Nationalist government was inclined to seek a resolution to the East Turkestan independence movement through diplomatic negotiations with the Soviet Union.

On December 3, 1944, Director Bu Daoming of the West Asia Bureau of the Ministry of Foreign Affairs arrived in Urumqi by command of Chiang Kai-shek to engage in talks with the Soviet Consul General Georgiy Maksimovich Pushkin with regard to "matters of economic cooperation, as well as cooperation in maintaining order in the border region."[12] During the negotiations, which began on December 5, Bu Daoming probed, "With regard to this incident at Yining, of which Your Excellency is already aware, presumably Your Excellency is also aware of the motivations and reasons for this eruption of violence?" However, Pushkin responded by steadfastly denying any connection between the Soviet Union and the Second East Turkestan Independence Movement:

> It would appear that the news I have received is the same as what Your Excellency has heard. Our office has had no contact with the consul in Yining: in the past few days, three attempts were made to send a message to the consul at Yining by means of the Chinese telegraph office, and each time the cable failed. I have just been informed by Moscow that Chinese troops fired several dozen rounds of artillery at the consulate in Yining, and part of the building was destroyed; the consular secretary was killed in the explosion, and another staff member was injured. The Minister of Foreign Affairs of the USSR has lodged a protest with the Chinese embassy, and the USSR is currently preparing to evacuate the women and children from the consulate. Furthermore, the USSR has notified the Chinese embassy that previous plans to transport 500 American trucks to China through the

USSR have been postponed due to the unrest in Yining. I have also learned that there are some four hundred thousand residents in the Yining District: aside from the Han minority (including government officials) and approximately 7,000 naturalized White Russians, the remainder are all of Kazakh and Hui ethnicity. This rebellion seems to have the nature of a popular rebellion, and it would appear that the White Russians are not the primary force behind the rebellion; I have heard recently that a republic has already been established in the district. As for the motivations and reasons for the unrest, I have no knowledge of this.[13]

Wu Zhongxin offered the following analysis of the consul general's comments: "Recently we suffered setbacks in the Battle of Hunan–Guangxi [against the Japanese] and the front has been moved back to Dushan; the Soviet Union values strength, and must certainly look down upon our country."[14] Soon thereafter, to preserve peace between China and the Soviet Union and for the sake of security in Xinjiang, T. V. Soong, then the Minister of Foreign Affairs and the President of the Executive Yuan of the Nationalist government, submitted a "Proposal Regarding Sino-Soviet Trade and Economic Cooperation in Xinjiang Province" to the chargé d'affaires of the Soviet embassy in China, in the hope of placing economic constraints on the Soviet Union's role in manufacturing unrest in Xinjiang; however, the Soviet embassy gave no response to the proposal.[15]

In the Name of "National Revolution"

The Soviet Union did not formally acknowledge its relationship with the East Turkestan independence movement until Mao Zedong's visit to Moscow in 1949, after the founding of the People's Republic of China. Shi Zhe, who served at the time as Mao Zedong's Russian translator, later recalled the encounter in his memoirs:

> During one of the discussions, Stalin spontaneously mentioned that, during the Sheng Shicai era, they helped the people of Xinjiang establish armed forces and trained cadres to resist the forces of the Nationalist Party; a fairly large arsenal had also been established over there, stockpiling some weapons and ammunition; he had now decided to transfer all of this to the Chinese, and hoped that the Chinese would assign someone to be responsible for coordination and receipt by personnel. The Chairman immediately authorized Premier Zhou to handle the matter.[16]

However, in the period of 1944–1945, the Soviet Union refused to acknowledge any association with the East Turkestan independence movement. This approach was likely calculated to preserve the notion that the Second East Turkestan Independence Movement was a "national revolution." During this period, the Soviet Union thus loudly proclaimed the Second East Turkestan Independence Movement to be a "national revolution" spontaneously organized by the Turkic Muslim peoples of Xinjiang, whilst scheming to manufacture said "revolution."

First, all efforts were made to select Turkic Muslims from Soviet Central Asia to serve as Soviet advisors in the East Turkestan Republic's government and military. Since they resembled the Turkic-Islamic peoples of Xinjiang with respect to their race, language and customs, outsiders could not recognize that they were in fact Soviet nationals. For instance, the Soviet advisor to Tarbagatay District was a Uyghur from Soviet Central Asia, while the advisor to Altay District was a Soviet Kazakh: they experienced no language barrier in communication with the local Turkic Muslims, and in Xinjiang, where the household registration system was as yet incomplete, they were indistinguishable in appearance and customs from the indigenous Turkic Muslims of Xinjiang, for those without prior knowledge.

Second, Soviet nationals were instructed to masquerade as White Russians living in China; Soviet Red Army troops even crossed into Xinjiang to pose as a military unit composed of White Russians. Many White Russians had fled to Xinjiang following the October Revolution of 1917. Although China later dubbed those White Russians who obtained Chinese citizenship as "naturalized persons" (*guihua zu* 歸化族), many retained dual nationality, or were of unconfirmed nationality. In an interview with the author, a former commander of the East Turkestan National Army headquarters confirmed that the contingent of the National Army known as the "Tarbagatay Naturalized Army," which Ivan Polinov led from Tarbagatay District to the front lines at Jinghe in August 1945, were in fact Soviet Red Army troops. The interviewee remarked that he himself could have claimed to be an indigenous Turkic Muslim from Xinjiang, a White Russian, or a Soviet national, with no documents or evidence to gainsay him; the three groups were indistinguishable based on appearance alone. These circumstances not only facilitated the Soviet Union's efforts to deny its involvement in the Second East Turkestan Independence Movement: today, they constitute a great barrier to research on the nature and evolution of the movement.

Finally, the senior position in each branch of the government was granted to elite members of the local ethnic communities, while Soviet personnel merely served as advisors, or at most as first deputy commissioner, as in Tarbagatay and Altay. The climbing rank of Soviet figures in the Tarbagatay and Altay district governments reveals the Soviet Union's designs upon real power in the region. However, the positions of president of the East Turkestan Republic and district commissioner in Tarbagatay and Altay went neither to the Soviet advisors, nor to Xinjiang's indigenous pro-Soviet Turkic-Islamic intellectuals, but rather to the elite members of the local communities. This approach was not only advantageous in mobilizing the people to join the independence movement, but also served to preserve the notion that the movement was spontaneously launched by the indigenous peoples in the name of a national revolution.[17]

Given the Soviet Union's painstaking efforts to proclaim, manufacture and actively maintain the image of the East Turkestan independence movement as a "national revolution," it is clear that the Soviet Union had pinned all its hopes for control over Xinjiang on the movement. Ishii Akira, who produced a detailed study of the Soviet Union's post-war national security system, notes that one important feature of the system was "the pursuit of ever-larger secure spaces beyond its borders."[18] The Soviet Union's initial objective in Xinjiang was quite clear: to exploit the forces of the East Turkestan independence movement, in the name of a "national revolution" by the Xinjiang region's indigenous peoples, to carve an independent nation-state out of China in the style of other Soviet satellite states (such as the Mongolian People's Republic), and thus maintain its dominant position in Xinjiang. In an interview with the author, a former staff member of the East Turkestan National Army headquarters concurred with this characterization.

8.2 The Shift in Soviet Policy

An Artificial Ceasefire and Stalemate

In early September 1945, on the heels of its victories in capturing Altay District as well as the Jinghe and Usu regions, the armed forces of the East

Turkestan Republic halted on the western bank of Manas River in a stalemate with the Chinese government troops, which stood on the eastern bank. Although some argue that a stalemate was reached due to the equal strength of the opposing forces, in actuality, after the battle at Jinghe and Usu, the East Turkestan vanguard pursuing the routed Chinese forces had already crossed Manas River, reaching Manas Town on the eastern bank of the river. The former commander of the East Turkestan National Army headquarters even affirmed in an interview with the author, "The Three Districts Revolutionary Army had in fact captured Manas Town."

Furthermore, in the view of military experts, the Manas River does not provide natural cover for defensive fortifications.[19] In other words, in the absence of orders to withdraw to the western bank, the East Turkestan forces absolutely had the capability to cross the river and break through the defensive line established by the Chinese government forces on the eastern bank.

Ismailow Mahmut, a soldier in the East Turkestan National Army who witnessed this battlefield stalemate, recalled in his memoirs:

> When we reached the western bank of the Manas River, the government forces stationed at Manas Town and the government troops who fled from the battle at Jinghe and Usu together retreated in the direction of Urumqi. At Manas Town, our scouts entered the city and communicated with the local residents to reconnoiter on the enemy situation. Later our troops received orders that we were not to cross the river, so the Nationalist Party troops returned to Manas from Kutubi, and rebuilt their defensive system at Manas.[20]

By September, the East Turkestan Republic had amassed a contingent of some ten thousand soldiers at the front lines at Manas,[21] and had constructed defensive fortifications running 55 kilometers along the western bank of the Manas River, and extending back 60 kilometers.[22] At the same time, to support the Taxkorgan Rebellion initiated by the Uyghur, Kyrgyz and Tajik peoples of southern Xinjiang, 300 soldiers were sent to the Taxkorgan region via Soviet territories.[23] It is clear that the East Turkestan Republic had ample forces to commit to this position and elsewhere: thus the decision to settle into a stalemate on the opposing banks of the Manas River could only have originated from the East Turkestan side.

The Manas River was approximately 532 kilometers away from Ghulja, the heart of the East Turkestan Republic, but lay only 137 kilometers distant from Xinjiang's provincial capital of Urumqi.[24] On September 13, Zhu Shaoliang, the ranking commander of the Nationalist government forces in Xinjiang, submitted a report on the military situation to Nationalist government representative Zhang Zhizhong, noting that the East Turkestan forces could reach Urumqi in two days' time from their position on the western bank of the Manas River, and that an attack on Urumqi could be launched at any time. Urumqi had only six battalions to stand in defense of the city, and the reinforcements dispatched to Xinjiang, including the 5th Cavalry Army and the 1st Company of the 46th Division, would not reach the city for at least another eight to ten days.[25]

In fact, armed groups associated with the East Turkestan Republic had been active on Urumqi's periphery since September 1945, and some guerrilla bands had even reached positions no more than seven or eight kilometers distant from the city center.[26] This state of affairs had prompted the Han merchants of Urumqi to flee toward China's interior provinces, and the price of local goods had soared; the idea of relocating the seat of the government had even been proposed on the agenda of the Xinjiang Provincial Government, and fear was rampant amongst the population of Urumqi.[27]

The former commander of the East Turkestan National Army headquarters mentioned above gave the following statement on the situation at Manas: "If the Three Districts Revolutionary Army had continued its advance, it would have certainly been able to capture Urumqi. At the time, our forces were not only positioned in the Manas region, but also in the regions of Urumqi and Kucha, intercepting all intelligence on the government forces." If the East Turkestan forces had taken Manas, the gateway to Urumqi would have been thrown wide open: the only question is why they did not take action.

A radio technician who served in the Chinese army in the battle at Jinghe and Usu also questioned these circumstances: "At the time, if the armed forces of the Three Districts Revolution had continued their pursuit, they would have likely been able to reach Urumqi in one fell swoop, yet the Three Districts army halted its advance after reaching the western bank of the Manas River. So the 46th Division of the government army, which had been stationed at Kucha, rushed to Manas Town to build up the defensive system, leaving the two sides in a stalemate."[28]

The suspension of the attack and the standoff with government forces at Manas River signaled the abandonment of East Turkestan's efforts to attack and capture Xinjiang's provincial capital of Urumqi. Yet, as discussed above, capturing Urumqi and liberating the entire territory of Xinjiang (East Turkestan) was the ultimate objective in the East Turkestan Republic's battle plan for the Three-Front War. So who gave the order for the East Turkestan forces to call off their attack, on the brink of victory? What was the aim in giving such an order?

It is certain that this order did not originate from Ilhan Tora, the president of the East Turkestan Republic. Tora had consistently called for the overthrow of Han rule, the ejection of the Han Chinese from Xinjiang, and the liberation of Urumqi.[29] The "Resolution on the Matter of Military Supplies," dated May 5, 1945, transcribes Ilhan Tora's statements at a meeting of the government council: "Though we still remain in Ghulja, the things we have done are for the cause of all the people of East Turkestan. From this point forward, we shall advance toward southern Xinjiang and eastern Xinjiang, and capture Urumqi. We must undertake the task of supplying the forces advancing toward Urumqi." After launching the Three-Front War, Tora also appointed Education Minister Saypidin Azizi, a native of Atush County near Kashgar, as "Commander of the Kashgar Regiment."[30] We can see that, although Ilhan Tora did not hold any real power over the armed forces of the East Turkestan Republic, he repeatedly advocated the liberation of the entire territory of Xinjiang.

The Impact of Shifting Global Circumstances on Soviet Policies

The command for the East Turkestan forces to halt their advance at the Manas River in fact originated from the Soviet Union. The former commander of the East Turkestan National Army headquarters stated, "After we had crossed the Manas River, we suddenly received orders that we were not permitted to cross the river. The orders were reportedly issued by the Soviet national Polinov, who was then the commander-in-chief of the National Army. So the troops that had already crossed the river returned to the western bank, and all the Soviet weapons we carried were confiscated and replaced with Chinese-made weapons."

With respect to the Soviet Union's true intentions, the commander speculated: "Although Stalin promised at first that he would recognize the East Turkestan Republic as an independent country if we captured Urumqi, when the time came he realized that it was simply impossible for Xinjiang to be independent of China, so he no longer wished for the attack on Urumqi to be carried out."

This conjecture is not without basis in fact. The dramatic changes occurring around the world after 1945 had a major impact on the Soviet Union's international strategies. At the Yalta Conference in February 1945, the United States and Great Britain pressed the Soviet Union for an early entry into the war against Japan, and agreed that the Soviet Union's claims on China would be reconsidered after it joined the attack on Japan, thus sacrificing China's interests in exchange for the Soviet Union's cooperation. The "Agreement Regarding Japan" stated: "The status quo in Outer Mongolia . . . shall be preserved. . . . The commercial port of Dairen [Dalian] shall be internationalized, the pre-eminent interests of the Soviet Union in this port being safeguarded, and the lease of Port Arthur as a naval base of the U.S.S.R. restored. . . . The Chinese-Eastern Railroad and the South Manchurian Railroad, which provide an outlet to Dairen, shall be jointly operated by the establishment of a joint Soviet-Chinese company, it being understood that the pre-eminent interests of the Soviet Union shall be safeguarded."[31]

After Germany's surrender on May 8, 1945, the Chinese Nationalist government sent T. V. Soong, then the President of the Executive Yuan and Minister of Foreign Affairs, to the Soviet Union to sign the Treaty of Friendship and Alliance between the Republic of China and the U.S.S.R., and urge the Soviet Union to commit troops to the war against Japan, in accordance with the wishes of President Truman of the United States. Soong arrived in Moscow on June 3 to begin the negotiations. The two sides initially refused to make concessions regarding the question of independence for Outer Mongolia; with Chiang Kai-shek's approval, Soong ultimately yielded, reaching an agreement under which the Soviet Union pledged not to interfere in China's "internal affairs"; acknowledged the Nationalist government's full sovereignty over the "Three Eastern Provinces" (Manchuria); and agreed that the Nationalist government, "as the central government of China," would be the sole object of Soviet support in China. It was also agreed that the question of independence for Outer Mongolia would be decided in a plebiscite after the conclusion of the war.[32]

The Sino-Soviet Treaty of Friendship was signed on August 14, 1945, by Foreign Minister Molotov of the Soviet Union and Wang Shijie, then newly appointed as the Minister of Foreign Affairs of the Nationalist government. Molotov also sent a diplomatic note to Wang during this period, referred to as the "Letter from Molotov, People's Commissar for Foreign Affairs of the Soviet Federative Socialist Republic, to Foreign Minister Wang of the National Government of the Republic of China." One passage in the letter made reference to the matter of Xinjiang: "Regarding the recent events in Xinjiang, the Soviet Government confirms that, as stated in Article V of the Treaty of Friendship and Alliance, it has no intention of interfering in the internal affairs of China."[33]

The Treaty of Friendship and the above passage in Molotov's diplomatic letter reveal that, as of August 1945, the Soviet Union had already decided to sacrifice the East Turkestan Republic for the sake of more important national interests, not only pledging to cease all aid to the East Turkestan Republic, but also tacitly recognizing the Chinese Nationalist government's right to suppress the East Turkestan independence movement as a matter of internal governance.

The Ceasefire and Xinjiang's Underground Resources

However, it is noteworthy that, although the Sino-Soviet Treaty of Friendship was concluded on August 14, the advance of the East Turkestan forces continued into early September, after the capture of Usu County on the Central Front and Altay District on the Northern Front. What significance did the capture of Usu and Altay bear in relation to the halt of the East Turkestan forces? In other words, why did the Soviet Union choose the capture of Usu and Altay as the stopping point for the advance of the East Turkestan army?

In researching the motives behind this decision, the author discovered a document entitled "Resolution of the Interim Government of the East Turkestan Republic Regarding Usu County, Jinghe County and the Maytagh Oil Fields." This document reveals that the Maytagh oil fields and refinery were located in Usu County, to the east of Manas. The resolution is dated September 15, 1945, meaning that it was issued only one week after the capture of Usu, and calls for production to be resumed at the oil fields as quickly as possible. The circumstances suggest that the East

Turkestan army's continued eastward push to capture Usu, thus absorbing the territory west of the Manas River into the republic's sphere of influence, was motivated by an effort to gain control over the Maytagh oil fields.

The Maytagh oil fields were the Soviet Union's single most important economic project in Xinjiang in the first half of the 20th century. The Soviet Union had begun excavations at the oil fields in 1935, and officially commenced operations in 1939. On the basis of a verbal agreement with Sheng Shicai, the Soviet Union exerted unilateral control over the operations and profits from the Maytagh oil fields until early 1942. Weng Wenhao, the Minister of Economic Affairs of the Nationalist government, observed in 1942 that the Maytagh oil fields were equipped with the Soviet Union's most advanced extraction equipment, with an estimated monthly output of twenty to thirty thousand gallons and great leeway for increased production in the future. At the time, 140 Russian personnel were assigned to the oil fields, along with their family members, bringing the total number of Russian nationals in the area to 200. However, the Soviet Union was forced to abandon the oil fields due to the deterioration of relations with Sheng Shicai.[34]

Resolution No. 111, passed by the Interim Government Council of the East Turkestan Republic on October 15, reveals the administrative system implemented at the Maytagh oil fields after their capture by East Turkestan forces:

(1) Oil production has important military significance in the current period of wartime. Administration of oil industry tasks is therefore assigned to the Army Logistics Department.

(2) The Ministry of Military Affairs of the East Turkestan Republic shall be responsible for resolving the matter of the experts and workers required for the oil industry.

(3) The Ministry of Military Affairs shall step in to resolve the issue of supplies for workers and personnel in the oil industry.

(4) Regarding the matter of the transfer of oil output to the Ministry of Industry and Commerce, the leaders of the Supply Department shall make the decision after requesting instructions from the leaders of the Ministry of Military Affairs.

(5) The Ministry of Military Affairs shall be responsible for making arrangements with respect to gasoline output, and will supply a

certain amount of gasoline to national organizations, the Ministry of Finance, the Ministry of Industry and Commerce, and other pertinent organizations.

This resolution shows that oil production was to be placed under the administration of the Ministry of Military Affairs. As discussed above, the Ministry of Military Affairs of the East Turkestan Republic was in fact controlled by agents of the Soviet Union. It can therefore be inferred that oil production at the Maytagh oil fields was effectively under the charge of the Soviet Union. If this were not so, the language in the resolution referring to the allocation of technicians and supplies for the oil fields by the Ministry of Military Affairs, which was utterly bereft of such resources, would be entirely meaningless.

Based on the annual budget of the East Turkestan Republic in 1946, we can see that the Maytagh oil fields represented the republic's single greatest revenue item. The Soviet Union thus controlled enormous profits proceeding from the oil fields (Table 8.1).

Resolution No. 241 of the Interim Government of the East Turkestan Republic, dated March 14, 1946, reveals that the republic's total expenditures under the 1946 annual budget amounted to 2,790,388,000 *tangga*; military expenses alone accounted for 67.3% of this sum, or approximately 1,879,106,000 *tangga* (Table 8.2). It may be presumed that expenditures on the military were even greater in 1945 when the republic was in an active state of war, likely resulting in an even larger deficit.

The military deficit occasioned by the war was redressed through financial assistance by the Soviet Union. However, the Soviet Union's military aid did not come without strings attached. According to a staff member who served in the general headquarters of the National Army, after the ceasefire, the East Turkestan Republic repaid the Soviet Union in kind with agricultural products, animal products and raw materials. Abilmit Hajiyow, the first Secretary-General of Tarbagatay District, observed in his memoirs that a large amount of raw materials were shipped to the Soviet Union through Tarbagatay in repayment for the military aid.[35] Based on this observation and the geographical location of the Maytagh oil fields in Tarbagatay District, we can surmise that at least some of the oil produced at Maytagh under the management of the East Turkestan military was transported to the Soviet Union as recompense for its military support.

Table 8.1   1946 Budget Statement for Separately Budgeted Organizations, Formulated by the Planning Bureau of the Ministry of Finance (Unit: *tangga*, currency issued in the East Turkestan Republic)

Organization Name	Annual Income	Production Expenses	Net Revenue
Ministry of Agriculture, Irrigation and Land	17,510,500	17,510,500	0
Post and Telegraphs	4,459,200	20,046,049	−15,586,849
Government Employee Store	25,400,350	179,977,500	−154,577,150
Maytagh Oil Fields	183,640,000	138,447,680	45,192,320
Unknown	8,100,000	7,979,500	110,500
Transportation	6,254,800	2,635,910	3,618,890
Court System	4,785,000	6,341,570	−1,556,570
Bureau of Commerce	412,916,860	29,452,184	383,464,676
Total	663,066,710	402,400,893	260,665,817

Source: Compiled on the basis of "Resolution No. 269 of the Interim Government of the East Turkestan Republic," dated April 20, 1946.

Table 8.2   Expenditures of the East Turkestan Republic under the 1946 Annual Budget (Unit: *tangga*)

Item	Amount
Military Spending	1,879,106,000
Administrative Spending	584,949,000
Redress of Deficit for Government Employee Store	196,333,000
Interest on Treasury Bonds	60,000,000
Road Construction Spending	50,000,000
Spending on Commodities	20,000,000
Total Expenditure in 1946	2,790,388,000
Total Revenue in 1946	2,679,031,000
Deficit	101,357,000

Source: Compiled by the author on the basis of "Resolution No. 241 of the Interim Government of the East Turkestan Republic," dated March 14, 1946.

Oil was not the only prize: much of the wealth of underground resources that had been discovered in Xinjiang at the time was clustered in the Ili, Tarbagatay and Altay districts.[36] On November 26, 1940, Sheng Shicai and Ivan Bakulin, then the Soviet Consul General in Urumqi, had signed a secret treaty—the "Concession Agreement," which stated that, "The Government of Xinjiang grants the Government of the U.S.S.R. the pre-eminent right to explore, prospect and exploit tin and its useful mineral by-products within the territory of Xinjiang." The treaty also recognized the Soviet Union's unconditional right to exploit the tungsten and lead mines in Koktokay, Altay District, and stipulated that, "The term of this treaty shall be fifty years as of the date of signing."[37] However, the Soviet Union was stripped of the above privileges following the collapse of its relationship with Sheng Shicai.

These underground resources were all located west of the Manas River: the fact that the East Turkestan forces advanced only as far as Usu County on the Central Front and Altay District on the Northern Front supports the theory that the expansion of the East Turkestan Republic served to further the Soviet Union's objective of gaining control over Xinjiang's mineral resources.

8.3 The Soviet Union and the Xinjiang Peace Talks

The Republic's Loss of Political Agency

From a political perspective, the support provided to the Interim Government of the East Turkestan Republic was not without its costs. Some Russian scholars argue that not a single member of East Turkestan's government, including Ilhan Tora, was capable of making decisions without the aid and counsel of the Soviet Union's diplomats and advisors, either on the military front or with respect to nation-building efforts.[38] This innate weakness of the Interim Government was vividly on display in the ultimate decision to call a truce and join in talks with the Nationalist government.

After the Nationalist troops' defeat in the battle at Usu and Jinghe, acting in his role as head of the Military Affairs Commission, Chiang Kai-shek dispatched Deputy Commander and Chief of Staff Guo Jijiao of the

8th Military District to Urumqi on September 10, to assist Commander Zhu Shaoliang in redeploying the government forces in Xinjiang.[39] Political Director Zhang Zhizhong of the Military Affairs Commission also arrived in Urumqi on September 13 to survey the situation in Xinjiang and seek a feasible resolution.

However, since the redeployment of the Chinese government forces was necessarily delayed until the arrival of the 5th Cavalry Army from Qinghai Province, the Nationalist government's hopes of retrieving the situation in Xinjiang were pinned on its diplomatic negotiations with the Soviet Union.[40] Zhang Zhizhong requested a meeting with the acting Soviet Consul General in Urumqi, Evseef Konstantin Mihailovic, immediately upon his arrival in the city. In his memoirs, Zhang provided the following description of his conversation with Mihailovic, which was scheduled for the very next day, on the 14th:

> I met with Evseef on September 14 to ask his opinion, and he stated that this was an internal matter of China's, and that the Soviet Union would not interfere in China's internal affairs. In his personal view, it would be best to find a peaceful resolution to these events. At the time, I said that I agreed with his views, and asked if he would be willing to act on our behalf by clearing the path to a peaceful resolution, first and foremost by causing Yining [Ghulja] to cease its military operations, to allow both sides to send representatives to engage in talks. He answered that he would pass on my suggestion to Moscow, and stated that he was personally willing to help from the sidelines, but that he could not act without instructions from his country's government. He also said that it would be best if the Chinese government broached the matter with the Soviet government, which would be relatively easy and effective.[41]

On September 17, Soviet Ambassador to China Apollon Petrov sent the following memorandum to the Chinese Ministry of Foreign Affairs:

> The Soviet Consul in Ghulja has reported to the Soviet government that some Muslims who profess to be representatives of the insurgent peoples of Xinjiang approached the Consul and suggested that the Russians step in as mediators and assume responsibility for settling the conflict which has arisen between them and the Chinese authorities; they also stated that the insurgent peoples had no intention of seceding from China, and that their aim was to achieve autonomy in those parts of Xinjiang where Muslims

constitute a majority of the population, specifically the Ghulja, Tarbagatay, Altay, and Kashgar regions. The representatives also enumerated the oppressions imposed upon them by the authorities of Xinjiang Province in the past. The Soviet government has an abiding interest in stability and order in those regions of Xinjiang contiguous to its borders, and if the Chinese government is willing, I intend to depute the Consul in Ghulja to provide all possible aid to the Chinese government to amicably settle the situation which has arisen in Xinjiang.[42]

After requesting instructions from Chiang Kai-shek, the Nationalist Ministry of Foreign Affairs replied to the Soviet government to express its gratitude, as well as its hope that the Soviet government would convey a message to the Xinjiang "insurgents" by way of the Soviet Consul in Ghulja: namely, that the Nationalist government invited them to send representatives to Urumqi to join in talks with the Chinese representative Zhang Zhizhong to seek a peaceful resolution.[43]

However, Ambassador Petrov's claim that representatives of the East Turkestan Republic requested the peace talks is rather suspect. What we can confirm is that, on October 2, 1945, the Interim Government Council of the East Turkestan Republic issued Resolution No. 100, responding to the Chinese government's call for negotiations. Below is an extract from the resolution:

> There is no doubt that truth is on our side, and that victory belongs to us. But we are compassionate, and seeing the blood that has been shed since November, from a humanitarian perspective, the Republic's future cannot be resolved solely by means of bloodshed, nor can we fail to consider negotiations with the Nationalist government. Therefore, the Interim Government of East Turkestan has passed the following resolutions: 1. We propose that the Chinese government adopt non-violent means, such as negotiations, to resolve the matter of the independence of East Turkestan. 2. If the Chinese government consents to the negotiations, the Interim Government of the East Turkestan Republic has resolved to send a delegation composed of Rahimjan Sabir Ghaji, Abdullah Tora, Ahmatjan Kasimi and others to negotiate on behalf of the East Turkestan Republic. 3. The delegation of the East Turkestan Republic shall seek independence in the negotiations, and all other matters shall be resolved on this basis.[44]

It should be noted that the Interim Government clearly states in this resolution that "the independence of East Turkestan" would be regarded as the fundamental premise of the peace talks. The "delegation of the East Turkestan Republic" arrived in Urumqi on October 12: Zhang Zhizhong recalled in his memoirs, "When they arrived, they all wore emblems of the 'East Turkestan Republic,' and they told the reception staff that they came as representatives of the government of the East Turkestan Republic to engage in negotiations with representatives of the Chinese government; they would produce identifying documents at the meetings, and the Chinese government representatives were also to submit verifying documents."[45]

Their status as a "state" delegation in the talks with representatives of the Chinese Nationalist government was unquestionably an important issue that could determine the fate of the East Turkestan independence movement. It is clear that the demands of the "delegation of the East Turkestan Republic" were consistent with the proposals for the peace talks as formulated in Resolution No. 100 of the Interim Government; significantly, both diverged substantially from the memorandum sent by the Soviet government to the Chinese Nationalist government on September 17.

According to the memorandum sent by Ambassador Petrov, the Soviet Union had been asked by the people of the rebel districts of Xinjiang to intervene as their representative; this was the basis for the Chinese government's authorization of the Soviet Consul in Ghulja to send representatives of Xinjiang's insurgent population to Urumqi. Zhang Zhizhong therefore communicated to acting Consul General Mihailovic that there would be no possibility of putting on talks with the delegation from the East Turkestan Republic. The East Turkestan representatives were ultimately "persuaded" by Mihailovic to abandon their claim to being a "state delegation": instead, they entered the talks with Zhang Zhizhong on October 17 under the title of "Representatives of the People of the Ghulja Region," or "Representatives of Ghulja."[46]

From a theoretical perspective, the East Turkestan delegation's abandonment of the "state" designation and acceptance of the term "representatives of the people" signaled not only surrender with respect to the terms as stated in Resolution No. 100 of the Interim Government Council, but also renunciation of East Turkestan's status and "independence" as a "state." Based on the proceedings of the peace talks, it is clear that the Soviet Union single-handedly engineered and propelled the East Turkestan representatives' engagement in the negotiations, and that this entire sequence of events proceeded in accordance with the Soviet Union's plans. The aspiring state entity which had sought to appear in the guise of the "East Turkestan Republic" thus lost all political agency in the midst of this important political process.

Personnel Changes within the "Republic" and Shifting Soviet Policies

The most prominent member of the East Turkestan Republic delegation at the peace talks was Ahmatjan Kasimi. Kasimi had not previously been well-known within the East Turkestan Republic, and of the three delegates sent to the peace talks, he was the youngest.[47] Yet Zhang Zhizhong came away with the impression that Kasimi was in fact the true spokesman and true leader of the East Turkestan Republic.[48]

The head of the delegation was the government council member Rahimjan Sabir Ghaji, yet Ahmatjan Kasimi served as its de facto leader: this dual power structure within the East Turkestan delegation was tied to Kasimi's rapid ascension within the republic's political circles.

The author met with Ahmatjan Kasimi's surviving family members and other figures involved in the East Turkestan independence movement on several occasions for interviews on his career. According to their statements, Ahmatjan Kasimi was an ordinary employee of the Ghulja Newspaper Office when the rebellion broke out in November 1944. In February 1945, Kasimi was appointed as the Secretary-General of the Secretariat by recommendation of an official in the Ministry of Education, and participated in the drafting of a number of laws and other documents,[49] until his political talents were discovered by Ilhan Tora.[50] Resolution No. 47 of the Interim Government Council, dated April 3, 1945, stated that, "The rank of lieutenant colonel shall be bestowed upon Minister of Military Affairs Ahmatjan Kasimi." Given that the National Army of the East Turkestan Republic was founded in April 1945 and that the former Minister of Military Affairs, Zunon Tayof, was transferred around this time to the position of Deputy Commander of the army, it is apparent that Ahmatjan Kasimi was elevated to a ministerial position in the space of only two months, thus rising into the leadership ranks of the East Turkestan Republic.

Ahmatjan Kasimi's rapid political ascension was closely tied to the start of the peace talks. After his appointment as a member of the peace delegation on October 2, 1945, Kasimi was also named as a member of the Interim Government Council under Resolution No. 103, dated October 9; under Resolution 144, dated October 22, Kasimi was promoted with unprecedented speed to the rank of colonel,[51] and appointed as a member of the five-person Military Affairs Council, the supreme organ in charge of "war proceedings, defense, withdrawal, the mobilization of troops, and the equipping of the armed forces"; and under Resolution No. 200 of the Interim Government Council, dated January 13, 1946, Kasimi was granted the "Republic's highest decoration"—the "Medal of Liberation."[52]

Ahmatjan Kasimi (1914–1949)

Ahmatjan Kasimi's political authority was primarily manifested through his ties to pro-Soviet Uyghur intellectuals. According to Saypidin Azizi, Abdulkerim Abbasow held Kasimi in high regard. Azizi also stated that he himself had been "greatly enlightened by Ahmajtan Kasimi."[53] However, unlike Ilhan Tora, Kasimi did not wield any religious authority; and unlike Abdulkerim Abbasow, Kasimi initially had no great accomplishments in leading the national revolution. His rapid success in climbing the rungs of leadership within the East Turkestan Republic and establishing his political authority within the Soviet-controlled Ministry of Military Affairs suggests that his meteoric rise was tied to his long-term association with the Soviet Union.

From left: Abdulkerim Abbasow, Ahmatjan Kasimi, Rahimjan Sabir Ghaji, Saypidin Azizi

Ahmatjan Kasimi was born to a Uyghur family in Ghulja in 1914. His father died when he was 11 years old, and after his mother remarried, Kasimi was sent to live with his uncle in Soviet Kazakhstan. After graduating from secondary school in Kazakhstan, Kasimi studied political economics at Lenin University in Kazan, where he joined the Leninist Young Communist League (*Komsomol*);[54] in 1938, he was admitted to the Communist University of the Toilers of the East (*Kommunističeskij Universitet trudjaščichsja Vostoka*) in Moscow.[55] However, the question of whether or not Kasimi became a member of the Soviet Communist Party was evaded both in interviews with the author as well as in Uyghur sources on Ahmatjan Kasimi's experiences in the Soviet Union.

Ahmatjan Kasimi returned to Xinjiang in August 1941, reportedly in response to his yearning for his family and his "fatherland."[56] But the period in which he chose to return home coincided precisely with the break in relations between Sheng Shicai and the Soviet Union, and he was soon arrested by the Xinjiang Provincial Government.[57] The alleged reason for his detention was involvement in "revolutionary activities."[58] However, there is no record of the substance or nature of Kasimi's "revolution," even in Uyghur sources.

As discussed above, the Soviet forces in the East Turkestan Republic were primarily concentrated within its military system; interestingly, Ahmatjan Kasimi was the longest-serving Minister of Military Affairs in the East Turkestan Interim Government. This suggests that Kasimi was likely associated with the Soviet agents within the government of East Turkestan.[59] Given that "pro-Sovietism" was a central political doctrine of the Interim Government of the East Turkestan Republic, having Soviet backing was a key symbol of political legitimacy. Amongst pro-Soviet Uyghur intellectuals, Soviet support also became an important measure for gauging an individual's political authority: this is likely part of the reason why the pro-Soviet intellectuals within the government of East Turkestan fell in line behind Ahmatjan Kasimi.

According to Abdulkerim Abbasow's close friend Wen Feiran, he once heard Abbasow say that the Soviet advisors had plans to use Ilhan Tora's secretary and "Soviet Communist Party member Ahmatjan Kasimi" to replace Tora as president of the Interim Government of the East Turkestan Republic.[60] The Soviet Union's objective was undoubtedly to strengthen its influence over the East Turkestan government, to ensure that the Soviet Union's wishes would be more effectively realized through the republic's policy-making process. In fact, through his participation in the Xinjiang Peace Talks, Ahmatjan Kasimi's political status soared to the level of the highest authorities of the East Turkestan Republic. In other words, the changes to Kasimi's personal circumstances mirrored the Soviet Union's shifting policies on the "East Turkestan Republic."

Signing of the "Eleven Articles of Peace"

The East Turkestan Republic had ceased all combat operations against the Chinese government forces in the wake of opening peace negotiations. After more than thirty rounds of discussion, on January 2, 1946, the delegation from the Interim Government of the East Turkestan Republic and Chinese Nationalist government representative Zhang Zhizhong signed the "Articles for a Peaceful Resolution to the Armed Conflict between the Representatives of the Central Government and the Representatives of the Insurgent Population of Xinjiang,"[61] or the "Eleven Articles of Peace" (*Shiyi tiao heping tiaokuan* 十一條和平條款), the pertinent sections of which are as follows:

(1) The government grants to the people of Xinjiang the right to elect indigenous persons of the same faith as administrative officials:

(2) Complete freedom of religion shall be granted to the people;

(3) The official documents of administrative and judicial organs shall be written both in the Chinese language and in the Muslim language;

(4) Education in the primary school and secondary school stages shall be carried out in the native language, and the Chinese language shall be a required subject in the secondary school stage;

(5) Freedom of development shall be guaranteed for ethnic cultures;

(6) Freedom of the press, assembly and speech shall be guaranteed;

(7) Rates of taxation shall be determined on the basis of the productivity of the people;

(8) Freedom in domestic and international trade shall be guaranteed to merchants;

(9) A Coalition Government (*Birlaxma Hukumat*) shall be formed in Xinjiang Province; of the 25 council members, 10 persons shall be

appointed by the central government, 15 persons shall be nominated by each district of Xinjiang, and 6 persons shall be nominated by the "Yining [Ghulja] Party";

(10) The organization of ethnic militias shall be permitted, and these shall be reformed as part of the government armed forces (the specifics of which shall be discussed in separate talks);

(11) Both Parties shall immediately release all detained persons to the other Party.[62]

If considered in the light of the policies of a multi-ethnic state toward its minority population, the "Eleven Articles of Peace" certainly include a fair number of political privileges for minorities. However, if the peace talks were to be regarded the culmination of the East Turkestan independence movement, it must be acknowledged that the content of the "Eleven Articles of Peace" ran counter to the aims of the movement as originally articulated—the overthrow of Chinese rule in Xinjiang, and independence for East Turkestan. In other words, the signing of the "Articles of Peace" in fact signified the failure of the Second East Turkestan Independence Movement. The members of the "Delegation of the Interim Government of the East Turkestan Republic" who were sent to Urumqi to join the talks, and ultimately signed the peace agreement in the name of the "Representatives of the Insurgent Peoples of Xinjiang," would have been well aware of this point.

On January 10, 1946, the East Turkestan delegation flew back to Ghulja on an Aeroflot plane. At the airport in Urumqi, the delegation leader Rahimjan Sabir Ghaji delivered these profound parting words to their escort of Xinjiang Provincial Government officials: "These peace talks have been very smooth, and very successful, yet I fear the people of Ili and the military will be dissatisfied; we must explain to them the central government's determination and desire to strive for peace, and hope that a satisfactory resolution may be reached."[63]

The acting Soviet Consul General in Urumqi, Evseef Konstantin Mihailovic, played an enormous role in bringing the talks to such a conclusion. The negotiations began with a draft proposed by Zhang Zhizhong: the two parties argued over the details, before eventually coming to terms through concessions from both sides. The East Turkestan delegation suspended the talks on two occasions and returned to Ghulja in response to feeling constrained in their decision-making; each time, they returned to Urumqi bearing their demands to resume the talks.[64] Mihailovic was highly active behind the scenes, playing an important role in pushing the two sides to make concessions and seek compromises. Mihailovic also fully exploited his position as acting Consul General, at times standing on the side of the East Turkestan delegation and demanding concessions from Zhang Zhizhong; yet Zhang Zhizhong also maintained close ties with Mihailovic, and took great pains to ensure Mihailovic was aware that his role was no more than that of an "intermediary."

By Zhang Zhizhong's account, the proposals to reform the National Army of East Turkestan as part of the government armed forces, issue government documents in minority languages, and increase the percentage of indigenous representatives among government personnel were offered as concessions to the "Ghulja representatives"; but Zhang also met with acting Consul General Mihailovic on four occasions after encountering difficulties during the talks. On the first occasion, he asked that the Soviet Union seek to persuade the East Turkestan delegation to abandon their claim to being a "state delegation"; at the second meeting, Zhang and Mihailovic reached an agreement that independence from China would not be treated as a premise of the negotiations; on the third occasion, Zhang sought Mihailovic's affirmation that the "Representatives of the People of Ghulja" would agree to peace upon reaching an accord with the Nationalist government representatives; and at the fourth meeting, Zhang asked Mihailovic to pressure the "Ghulja Representatives" to withdraw their "Three Demands," which consisted of the abolishment of the government police force, a complete exodus of the government military forces who had entered Xinjiang to suppress the national liberation movement, and the formation of a local police force by the region's indigenous Muslim inhabitants.[65]

The establishment of the Mongolian People's Republic was formally recognized on January 5, 1946, just three days after the signing of the "Eleven Articles of Peace."

Summary

The Soviet Union actively participated in the development of the East Turkestan independence movement in Xinjiang, and provided strong support to its proponents. After the deterioration of relations with Sheng Shicai in 1942, the Soviet Union had changed its tactics, seeking to exploit the forces of the East Turkestan independence movement to maintain its control over Xinjiang by supporting the "national revolution," thus retaining Xinjiang within the Soviet Union's sphere of influence. In his exploration of Soviet archives, the historian Li Sheng discovered that policies on the "East Turkestan Republic" and problems arising therefrom were all reported to Lavrentiy Beria, the head of the People's Commissariat for Internal Affairs (NKVD); some reports were even sent to Stalin himself.[66] It is clear that issues related to Xinjiang commanded great attention from the Soviet government during this time period.

However, as the Second World War drew to a close, the United States and Britain forced China to make concessions to persuade the Soviet Union to make an early entry into the war against Japan, including recognition of Outer Mongolia's independence, and acknowledgment of the Soviet Union's special interests in northeastern China. In return for these greater and more tangible benefits, the Soviet Union conceded that the conflict in Xinjiang was an internal matter in China, withdrew its recognition of the East Turkestan Republic's right to secede from China, and suspended its support for the East Turkestan Republic. It is clear that, from the Soviet Union's perspective, the East Turkestan Republic was merely a chess piece on the board of international politics and global strategy.

There is no doubt that the Soviet Union's support played a key role in the formation, survival and development of the East Turkestan independence movement. The Soviet Union's motives for providing such support, which would determine the fate of the fledgling nation, should therefore have been a matter of great concern to the proponents of the independence movement. However, under the leadership of Ilhan Tora, the Interim Government of the East Turkestan Republic set the overthrow of Chinese rule as its most important task, and failed to devote sufficient attention to this question. The republic's reliance on Soviet aid to achieve independence from China thus dealt a mortal blow to the Second East Turkestan Independence Movement. The events after September 1945 are quite illustrative of the fact that the Soviet Union's motives and ultimate objectives in aiding the East Turkestan independence movement certainly were not to support the independence of the Turkic Muslim peoples of Xinjiang.

Due to a shift in the Soviet Union's policies on China, the Interim Government of the East Turkestan Republic was forced to abandon what could have been an easy victory—the capture of Urumqi, the capital of Xinjiang—and agree to peace talks with the Chinese Nationalist government. This was followed by the signing of a peace agreement in the name of the "Representatives of the Insurgent Peoples of Xinjiang," and ultimately by the abandonment of the dream of establishing an independent nation. The facts illustrate that the national independence movement, having entrusted its fate to a greater power in the hope of achieving its dreams with the support of said power, ultimately fell victim to changing global circumstances, and was reduced to a pawn in the game of international politics between great nations: this has been true for many peoples, in many different periods of history.

Chapter 9

"National Independence" or "National Liberation"
The Fall of the East Turkestan Republic

From the previous chapters, we can see that the political evolution of the East Turkestan Republic can be divided into five stages:

(1) **Founding of the Regime** (August to November 1944);

(2) **First Expansion Phase** (December 1944 to June 1945: Expansion within Ili District);

(3) **Second Expansion Phase** (July to September 1945: Expansion to Tarbagatay District and Altay District);

(4) **Stalemate** (September 1945 to January 1946: From the ceasefire to the signing of the peace agreement);

(5) **Decline** (January to June 1946: From the signing of the peace agreement to the dissolution of the "East Turkestan Republic").

The East Turkestan Republic and the Second East Turkestan Independence Movement essentially embarked on a downward trend beginning in January 1946, with the signing of the "Eleven Articles of Peace." What actions did the disparate political forces within the republic take during this period? What political struggles arose or could have arisen from the interaction between these political forces? How did events unfold after the signing of the peace agreement? In addition, what role did the Soviet Union play in these affairs, and how did it exercise its political influence? This chapter analyzes the above questions in an attempt to clarify the political processes behind the decline of the East Turkestan Republic.

9.1 A Schism over the Objective of "National Revolution"

The Republic's Internal Disputes Regarding the Peace Talks

From the perspective of the Interim Government of the East Turkestan Republic, the peace negotiations with the Chinese government did not begin smoothly. First, serious opposition to joining the talks emerged from within the East Turkestan regime. A faction of government council members led by President Ilhan Tora strongly opposed the peace talks: at a meeting of the Interim Government Council, Tora fiercely condemned the peace negotiations as, "An action betraying the achievements of the revolution," "an action betraying the interests of the Uyghur people," and "an action to court the favor of the Chinese."[1]

During this period, the Interim Government of the East Turkestan Republic passed a number of resolutions emphasizing the nature of the "East Turkestan Republic" as an independent state. For instance, Resolution No. 110, dated October 15, 1945, declared that November 7 would henceforth be "Memorial Day for the East Turkestan Revolution"; Resolution No. 113, dated October 22, stated that "November 12, the day on which the flag of the brutal Chinese government was burned and the banner of the Islamic Republic was raised," would henceforth be "Founding Day"; Resolution No. 249, dated March 28, 1946, stated that April 8 would be "Memorial Day for the Birth of the National Army."

A number of administrative systems were also rapidly instituted by means of government resolutions. The civil servant wage system was formulated under Resolution No. 185, dated January 5, 1946; national taxes and tax rates were determined under Resolution No. 197, dated January 12; Resolution No. 199, dated January 13, declared the establishment of the National Theater Troupe; Resolution No. 203, also dated January 13, announced the establishment of the state administrative system; Resolution No. 231, dated February 29, marked the founding of the Women's Association (this date is provided in reference materials); while Resolution No. 235, dated March 5, instituted standards for military promotions, and banned the circulation of Chinese currency in the East Turkestan markets. This flood of resolutions suggests that the Interim Government of East Turkestan had previously been remiss in the establishment of administrative systems, and was now rushing to take action; this was likely an attempt by the forces opposing the peace talks to distract from and obstruct the negotiations.

On April 4, 1946, the official newspaper of the East Turkestan Republic—*Free East Turkestan* (*Azatlik Xarkiy Turkistan*)—published a fiercely worded editorial entitled "Negotiations in Progress": "If the Chinese government fails to hand over all power to us in compliance with our terms, and continues to implement the policies of the colonialist system, then we must continue to fight. If our objectives are not achieved, we vow to fight on, through bloody sacrifice and war, to liberate the whole of East Turkestan and found our own eternal state." This essay was clearly written in response to the "Eleven Articles of Peace."[2]

However, Abdulkerim Abbasow, Ahmatjan Kasimi and the other pro-Soviet intellectuals seated on the council endorsed the peace talks and strongly condemned Ilhan Tora's views,[3] effecting a shift in public discourse. On April 7, *Free East Turkestan* published another editorial entitled "We Hope the Negotiations Conclude Successfully," which emphasized the importance of the peace talks: "Now that the armed struggle has been suspended, the political struggle is under way: the negotiations will go on for some time, and the question of peaceful liberation is the object of the talks."[4]

The editorial "All for Victory" in the April 17 edition of *Free East Turkestan* represented even more of a watershed moment, as it explicitly argued that the peace talks were consistent with the objective of "national revolution": "All that we have done was not to oppose the Han people, but

Abdulkerim Abbasow and Ahmatjan Kasimi

rather to oppose the despotic government of the colonialists. Thus the objective in establishing the East Turkestan Republic, on the foundation of brilliant victory in our revolution, was to oppose all dark forces, uphold humanitarian principles, and allow all peoples to achieve liberation."[5] It is also worth noting that this was the first public declaration by the East Turkestan Republic stating that the Han Chinese people were not the enemy in the East Turkestan independence movement; this was indisputably a major turning point in the history of the Second East Turkestan Independence Movement.

On May 25, 1946, Ahmatjan Kasimi delivered a "Report on the Results of the Peace Talks" to the Interim Government Council of the East Turkestan Republic, roundly condemning arguments in opposition to the peace talks and bringing all debate on the matter to an end. Below is an excerpt from the report:

> Now, when we ask this question, we must consider the overall circumstances and the specific situation we face. On the one hand, if the long and bloody struggle for the freedom and autonomy of the East Turkestan Republic continues, then the war must go on, and the people will suffer great harm. Or, seeing that the Second World War has now drawn to a close, the method of peaceful negotiations may be adopted to resolve the conflict, and immediately bring the war to an end. In sum, there are two means of resolution: (1) Resolution by means of an armed struggle; (2) Resolution through discussion on the basis of peaceful negotiations.
>
> Seeing that Mr. Chiang Kai-shek, the head of the Nationalist central government, has pledged in his speeches about the border region and to the peoples of the border region that full autonomy will be granted to the peoples of the border region, our people naturally believe in the possibility of resolving the conflict without bloodshed. Considering the overall circumstances at present, the conflict should be resolved on the basis of peaceful negotiations. In other words, we may adopt the second method to resolve these issues, and there is no need to use the first method.[6]

Growing Dissension Regarding the Objectives of the National Movement

The conflict that arose between Ilhan Tora and Abdulkerim Abbasow, Ahmatjan Kasimi, and the other pro-Soviet intellectuals revolving around engagement in the peace talks was rooted in different understandings of the goals of the national movement.

There is no doubt that, prior to the start of the peace talks, both sides of the debate shared the goals of overthrowing Chinese rule, and establishing East Turkestan (Xinjiang) as a nation-state of Turkic-Islamic peoples, independent of China. For instance, Resolution No. 24 of the Interim Government Council, dated February 24, 1945, declared that, "The most important objectives of the revolution for the liberation of East Turkestan are to topple the brutal rule of the Han Chinese, exterminate the savage Nationalist armies, and achieve the wish that our people have cherished for centuries: driving out the Han colonizers, and establishing a strong and prosperous state that cares for the people, with true equality for all ethnicities."

Since both factions of the government had common goals during this period, references to overthrowing Chinese rule and driving out the Chinese (or Han) rulers as the most fundamental tasks of the republic can be seen in the "Nine Political Precepts," as well as many other early government documents. Under the East Turkestan Republic, those who aided the "Han regime" had previously been punished as political offenders.[7] Article 289 of the "Supplemental Articles to the Provisional Penal Code," promulgated on August 13, 1945, went so far as to legally sanction discrimination and persecution of Han Chinese: "During the period of revolutionary war, in criminal investigations into members of the military who commit the crime of looting the property of Han residents, the sentence stipulated by the law may be reduced by one quarter, one half, or as much as three quarters."

The Mongolian People's Republic stood as the model for the ideal of founding a nation-state. In January 1946, council member Ahmatjan Kasimi delivered the following speech on independence for Outer Mongolia:

> Mongolia is our country's close neighbor to the northeast: it comprises 1.5 million square kilometers of land and has a population of nearly 1 million: until 1921, it was a semi-colony of the European states, and a colony of the despotic Chinese government. The Mongolian people have now driven out the Chinese colonialists, and the establishment of the Mongolian People's Republic was declared in 1924. However, the despotic Chinese government, which refused to allow the Mongolian people to live in freedom and

liberty, did not acknowledge the independence of the Mongolian people. After the Second World War, due to the victory of the democratic nations and the policies regarding oppression of the people adopted by the Soviet government, which has always pursued truly democratic policies around the world, the despotic Chinese government was compelled to recognize the independence of the Mongolian People's Republic. We the people of East Turkestan are boundlessly gratified that our neighbors the Mongolian people, with whom we share historical ties and a common destiny, have achieved independence.[8]

These shared political objectives became the foundation for the coexistence of the two major political factions within the regime of the East Turkestan Republic in its early period. However, once the peace talks began, and particularly after the signing of the "Eleven Articles of Peace" in January 1946, the pro-Soviet intellectuals abandoned the goal of achieving independence. The signing of the peace agreement was a de facto "acknowledgment that the entire province was the sovereign territory of China."[9] This sharp reversal not only gave rise to intra-regime opposition and conflict with Ilhan Tora's faction, but also fomented ideological confusion amongst the general population. Ahmatjan Kasimi gave the following account of the latter situation:

> When the revolution began, it was begun for the sake of national independence for East Turkestan. The purpose and direction of the revolution was "national independence." But since the signing of the peace agreement, the purpose and direction of the revolution have changed somewhat in shape. This is a matter that our younger generation and some teachers in the outlying regions do not understand. They link "freedom," "liberation" and "national independence" together, believing that only a place with "national independence" can have "freedom," and that places without "national independence" do not have freedom. When the peace agreement was signed, we gained freedom, but abandoned "independence," so this is what happened. As a result, this gave rise to the question of "how there can be freedom without national independence."[10]

Ilhan Tora's faction and the great number of supporters amongst the general population who joined in the East Turkestan Independence Movement naturally believed that the ultimate objective of the independence movement was in fact to achieve national independence. When the movement began, the pro-Soviet intellectuals identified themselves as leaders of an oppressed people seeking "national liberation": yet once the peace talks commenced, the goal of "national liberation" was redefined as "ethnic equality." Ahmatjan Kasimi declared, "Our movement is a national liberation movement, and it is also a movement to oppose one people ruling over another people. The objective of this movement is to seek equality with other peoples."[11] He stated further, "We do not seek to rule over others, nor will we permit others to rule over us."[12]

By recasting the objective of "national liberation" as "ethnic equality," "national independence" was thus no longer the only means by which it could be achieved. As Ahmatjan Kasimi noted: "If the Han government which governs us can set aside its colonialist policies and truly implement equal and democratic policies, then the people can still attain political liberties and rights without national independence."[13] The realization of ethnic "autonomy" within a multi-ethnic state thus came to be regarded as one means of achieving "national liberation": "If all of the rights described in the peace agreement are granted to the people, we will be satisfied. If we are granted these rights, we will be able to have autonomy, and thus we will achieve perpetual freedom."[14]

"National liberation" was thus redefined as "ethnic equality": and "ethnic equality" could be achieved through "autonomy" within the bounds of a multi-ethnic state. This reasoning served as an ideological toehold allowing the pro-Soviet intellectuals within the East Turkestan regime to abandon their former goal of "national independence" and engage in peace talks with the Chinese government, following the policy shift enacted by the Soviet Union.

However, the "autonomy" proposed by the pro-Soviet leaders in the East Turkestan regime in fact fell short of the concept of "ethnic" autonomy. Ahmatjan Kasimi stated, "The autonomy we demand is not merely a matter of a Uyghur holding administrative power over the entire province, or allowing the Turkic-Islamic peoples to hold power; rather, it is a matter of creating absolute equality for all peoples, and achieving democratic politics. If the ethnic autonomy we seek is regarded merely as pursuing the interests of one people or one ethnic group, that is wrong."[15] Kasimi firmly denied the possibility of combining nationalism with democracy, arguing that nationalist ideas "in the era of democratic politics" were in service of imperialist and colonialist systems. "Nationalism and democracy cannot

An inspection by Ahmatjan Kasimi

coexist: one is either a democrat, fighting for the liberation of one's people on the battlefront of democracy; or a nationalist, preserving colonialist systems and enslaving one's people on the battlefront of imperialism. There is no middle road."[16]

Ahmatjan Kasimi argued that "nationalism" had merely been a transitional stage, and that the shifting objectives of the "national revolution" were an inevitability: "If our people are discriminated against, oppressed, and wholly deprived of the right to survive, this will cause us to become narrow-minded nationalists; but if our people gain freedom and equality, this narrow-minded nationalism will be swept away."[17] In short, the pro-Soviet intellectuals within the East Turkestan regime maintained that the national liberation movement had entered a new stage following the commencement of the peace negotiations with the Chinese government, which would herald the establishment of a democratic political system. They also held that the institution of democratic systems following the conclusion of the peace agreement would require the complete abandonment of radical nationalist ideas—including "national independence." It is clear that the pro-Soviet faction's dismissal of nationalism as a "transitional stage" was completely at odds with the views of Ilhan Tora's faction, which regarded "national independence" as the ultimate objective of the national movement; conflict between the two sides was thus unavoidable.

9.2 From the "Revolutionary Youth League" to the "Revolutionary Party"

The "Revolutionary Youth League"

Impacted by the Soviet Union's shifting policies, the Interim Government of the East Turkestan Republic experienced a major political upheaval. This process was marked by two key events: the founding of the "East Turkestan Revolutionary Youth League" and the establishment of the "East Turkestan Revolutionary Party" by the regime's pro-Soviet intellectuals,

Chapter 9: "National Independence" or "National Liberation" | 233

under the leadership of Ahmatjan Kasimi. Below we will attempt to reconstruct these events based on the "Constitution of the East Turkestan Revolutionary Youth League" and the "Charter of the East Turkestan Revolutionary Party," as well as the recollections of important members of the league and the party, and explore the reasons why these political organizations came into being, and the significance thereof.

The "East Turkestan Revolutionary Youth League" (*Xarkiy Turkistan Inkilawi Yaxlar Taxkilati*, hereafter abbreviated as the "Youth League") was founded on November 15, 1945, at the first meeting of the East Turkestan Youth Congress.[18] The reasons for the founding of the Youth League were described thusly in a resolution of the Youth Congress:

> November 15, 1945: We the assembly of youths, having heard the instructions of His Excellency the President of our Republic, Supreme Commander Ilhan Tora, have gained a more profound understanding that the responsibilities faced today in the revolution to liberate Xinjiang Province, and the task of ensuring that our young state is forever perpetuated, rest in large part on our young shoulders; at the same time, we have heard that we youths must deeply understand our glorious country, carry out all of our country's commands, and rectify our moral character; at the same time, we must engage in wide-ranging studies, understanding and learning [source text illegible] development, politics, and scientific knowledge; making tremendous efforts and enthusiastically working toward the path of establishing the most advanced, civilized, [source text illegible] free, and happy country on this foundation is the responsibility we bear as youths. . . . In order to complete the tasks of this struggle, with the approval of the government, we shall unite and organize the youths of East Turkestan to establish the East Turkestan Youth League.[19]

This passage reveals that the Youth League was founded by the Youth Congress, the East Turkestan Republic's largest association for youth mobilization. The Youth League instituted strict rules and regulations,[20] and adhered to rigorous standards for the accession of new members.[21] The league also operated under a tightly organized system (Figure 9.1), making it a quasi-party organization with a strong capacity for popular mobilization.

The resolution of the Youth Congress seems to indicate that the Youth League was founded at the direction of the Interim Government, and

Figure 9.1 Organizational Structure of the "East Turkestan Revolutionary Youth League"

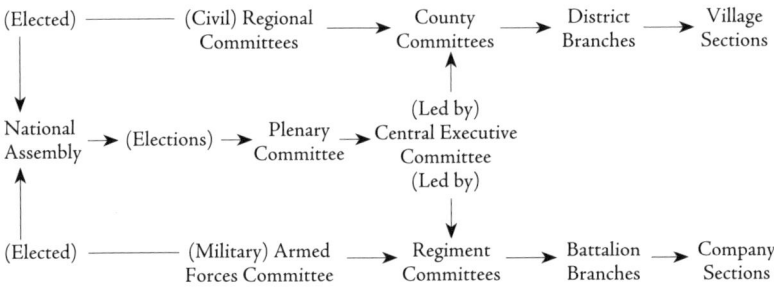

Source: Compiled by the author on the basis of "Plenary Resolution No. 1 of the Ili Youth Congress" and "Provisional Constitution of the East Turkestan Revolutionary Youth League."

operated under the leadership of Ilhan Tora and his government.[22] In reality, the Youth League was not established by resolution of the Interim Government: Instead, it was planned, sponsored and led by the council member, Minister of Communications, and Political Director of the National Army, Abdulkerim Abbasow. This was confirmed in the memoirs of several members of the Youth League's Central Executive Committee.[23] According to Wen Feiran, who had close ties to Abdulkerim Abbasow, Abbasow even considered raiding the bank treasuries to cover the Youth League's operating expenses, but ultimately settled for printing counterfeit notes, at Wen's persuasion.[24] The veracity of this statement is of course unconfirmed: however, the "Youth League Constitution" states in Article 54 that, "The operating expenses of the League shall be defrayed through membership fees," indicating that the league was to rely on its own financial resources, rather than the support of the Interim Government.

The Youth League was in fact controlled by the pro-Soviet intellectuals, and maintained at a certain distance from the Interim Government of the East Turkestan Republic. The league chair and deputy chair were both Uyghur intellectuals, while Uyghur and Uzbek intellectuals constituted the majority on the eleven-member Central Executive Committee (Table 9.1).

The Youth League's political positions were also by no means in alignment with the "Nine Political Precepts" of the East Turkestan Interim

Table 9.1 Members of the Central Executive Committee under the First Session of the "East Turkestan Revolutionary Youth League"

Title	Name	Background
Chair	Abdulkerim Abbasow	Government council member, Minister of Communications, Political Director of the National Army; Uyghur intellectual and graduate of the Advanced Studies Department at Xinjiang College
Deputy Chair	Saydulla Saypullayow	Uyghur intellectual; studied abroad in the Soviet Union
Executive Committee Members	Saypidin Azizi	Minister of Education; Uyghur intellectual; studied abroad in the Soviet Union
	Anwar Hanbaba	Uzbek intellectual; studied abroad in the Soviet Union
	Abdulla Zakirow	Uyghur, born in Ghulja; background unknown
	Nabijan	Deputy Minister of Internal Affairs; Uzbek and citizen of the Soviet Union
	Asilhan Xakirow	Unknown
	Bukara Tixika Nibayow	Unknown
	Alim Aytowarow	Unknown
	Irikqi Yonqi	Unknown
	Popow	Unknown

Source: Compiled by the author on the basis of Materials on the Three Districts Revolution in Ili Prefecture *(1991), pp. 450–459, and* "Plenary Resolution No. 1 of the Ili Youth Congress."

Government. This is demonstrated in the section of the "Youth League Constitution" defining the league's "Tasks":

> Chapter 2: Tasks; Article 5: The Revolutionary Youth League shall work to maintain and strengthen the victories of the November Revolution, for which the people of East Turkestan, particularly the youths, shed their blood. To achieve this goal: (1) We shall improve the political consciousness of the people of East Turkestan, support a regime of the people

founded upon democratic centralist policies, and fight for justice everywhere. (2) We shall strengthen the unity of all the peoples living in East Turkestan, and fight to guarantee their equality. (3) We shall mobilize the youths as a uniting force, and resolutely fight against all the reactionary zealots hindering the establishment of the fatherland and the expansion of the democratic system, as well as the remnants of the despotic regime. (4) We shall fight to develop true democratic education and improve literacy in our country. (5) We shall improve the political consciousness of the soldiers in the National Revolutionary Army, and strengthen their sense of responsibility toward the fatherland. We shall continuously prepare them to fight for true democracy and turn them into warriors sacrificing themselves for the liberation of the people. (6) We shall make them become the champions for social, economic and cultural development. (7) We shall carry out various efforts to improve literacy amongst the masses. (8) We shall fight to help improve the lives of workers, laborers and farmers. (9) We shall resolutely support and fight to protect the principle of equality for all religions, cultures, and ethnic groups.[25]

Similar content is also found in "Chapter 1: General Principles."[26] In comparison with the "Nine Political Precepts" of the Interim Government, the first key difference is that almost none of the Youth League's tasks are directed outward: instead, the tasks focus on social, economic and political issues such as promoting the republic's domestic socioeconomic development, improving standards of living, supporting literacy and education, and establishing a democratic system. This list of concerns might lead one to believe that the Youth League was founded merely to resolve the domestic problems of the East Turkestan Republic.

Official newspaper of the Youth League

With respect to political issues, the Youth League proposes "building a democratic system," "cultivating people with democratic spirit," "strengthening the people's political consciousness," "guaranteeing equal rights for all peoples," and so on. The use of political catchphrases like "democracy," "democratic system," and "democratic centralism" show that the Youth League was attempting to mirror the tone of the "global democratic camp" led by the Soviet Union (in contrast with the "imperialistic camp"). However, other slogans such as "equality for all religions," "developing democratic education and culture," "opposing despotic government," and "cultivating youths of service in social, economic and cultural development," coupled with the league's calls for democratization and government based on popular constituencies, give the clear impression that the Youth League's political platform was designed to challenge Ilhan Tora's religion-based authority.

From "National Revolution" to the "Second Revolution"

The leader and sponsor of the Youth League, Abdulkerim Abbasow, had been a key figure behind the formation of the "National Freedom Group" in the early days of the independence movement. By the time he established the Youth League, Abbasow had reportedly already come to believe that, "National revolution is not our only revolution."[27] According to three former members of the Youth League's Central Executive Committee, Abbasow's aims in founding the Youth League were to "defend and expand the achievements of the revolution";[28] "carry out ideological education and political education of the young";[29] "concentrate the influence of intellectuals," and "strive for victory in the democratic revolution, and teach New Democracy to the young."[30]

The "New Democratic Revolution" (*Xin minzhu zhuyi geming* 新民主主義革命) was a theory proposed by Mao Zedong in 1940 with respect to the Chinese Communist Revolution. The theory held that the Chinese revolution, which sought to overthrow foreign imperialist oppression and domestic feudal rule, could be divided into two stages: The first stage was the "Old Democratic Revolution" led by the capitalist class, with the aim of establishing a capitalist society; the second stage was the "New Democratic Revolution" led by the proletariat class, under which all classes united to found a New Democratic society; the "New Democratic Revolution" consisted of a class struggle by the revolutionary classes against the traditional social elite.

The term "democratic revolution" does not in fact appear in the "Youth League Constitution." However, Abdulkerim Abbasow's memoirs indicate that he had opportunities to be exposed to the concept of "New Democracy"; he had attended the high school attached to Xinjiang College, and was fluent in Chinese.[31] Saydulla Saypullayow, the Deputy Chair of the Youth League, also remarked on Abbasow's espousal of this concept.[32] It is therefore possible that East Turkestan's pro-Soviet intellectuals, led by Abdulkerim Abbasow, drew on the theory of the New Democratic Revolution in establishing the Youth League. Within the framework of the East Turkestan Republic, the targets of a class revolution would have naturally been the traditional social elites and elite religious figures within ethnic society; that is, the class represented by Ilhan Tora.

Abdulkerim Abbasow's status as a leading light in the East Turkestan Republic meant that his ideological reversal also signaled a shift in thinking amongst the republic's pro-Soviet intellectuals. This transformation was likely connected to the changing internal and external environment faced by the East Turkestan Republic during this period.

As discussed above, the most important characteristic of the internal political structure of the East Turkestan Republic was its dual system, which allowed for the coexistence of the regime's two political factions: the traditional faction, composed of religious leaders and elite members of Turkic-Islamic society, represented by Ilhan Tora; and the Soviet faction, composed of pro-Soviet intellectuals of Uyghur, Tatar and other Turkic-Islamic ethnicities as well as Soviet nationals, represented by Abdulkerim Abbasow. Saypidin Azizi noted that, under this system, "The causes of radical, revolutionary intellectuals could not successfully be advanced. Within the headquarters of the Three Districts Revolutionary Government, the feudal ruling class, landowning class, and religious class completely stymied their actions and proposals. The religious faction interfered in all matters. Because Ilhan Tora was himself a religious figure, he judged all matters according to the religious value system."[33]

However, the system was also designed to forward the "national revolution," and mobilize the population to join the "national war." Once the Soviet Union abandoned its policy of supporting national revolution in

Xinjiang, pushing the East Turkestan regime to engage in peace talks with the Chinese government and ultimately bringing the national war to a halt, the urgency and necessity of a "national revolution" faded. This shift meant that the East Turkestan Republic's dual political structure, built to accommodate both the pro-Soviet intellectuals and Ilhan Tora's traditional faction, suddenly lost all value. As the grounds for the intellectuals' long-held tolerance toward Tora and the traditional social elites evaporated, their long-simmering discontent abruptly burst into the open. Abdulkerim Abbasow's objective in establishing the Youth League was to unite intellectuals and youths to found an independent, class-based political party, and launch a "Second Revolution" to expel Ilhan Tora and his faction of traditional social elites and religious figures from the leadership of the East Turkestan Independence Movement.[34]

There is no sign that Ahmatjan Kasimi was involved in the establishment of the Youth League. It is therefore clear that Abdulkerim Abbasow's efforts to found this class-based political party and Ahmatjan Kasimi's forwarding of the peace talks with the Chinese government evolved along different lines. However, common ground may be found in the shifting ideological trajectories of these two figures in terms of their understanding of the "national revolution." In 1949, Abdulkerim Abbasow offered the following commentary on the national movement: "During the imperialist era, two national movements rose up: a revolutionary national movement, and a reactionary national movement. The struggle of the downtrodden people of the colonies and semi-colonies against imperialist oppression was a revolutionary, progressive national movement. . . . Nominally calling for 'national autonomy,' 'national self-determination,' and other pretty slogans while in reality strengthening and consolidating imperialist rule over the colonies and semi-colonies, and striking a heavy blow against the people's liberation—this was a reactionary national movement."[35] Approaching the national movement from the perspective of Lenin's theories on class and imperialism, Abbasow by this point denied the legitimacy of a national movement to seek independence from China, which had itself been reduced to a semi-colonized state.

The pro-Soviet intellectuals' political shift from "national revolution" to "class revolution" coincided with the easing of their nationalistic enmity toward the Han Chinese. In February 1946, Abdulkerim Abbasow married a Han Chinese woman, Lü Suxin. Abbasow deliberately took advantage of the occasion by picking up his new Han bride in the car assigned to Ilhan Tora, who responded to the incident with frustration:

> To save the Muslims, Allah has granted us a man of great talent: he is Abdulkerim Abbasow. But it is a great pity that he has already been half stolen away by the Han race. If he is wholly stolen away by the Han race, he will become our enemy.[36]

The "East Turkestan Revolutionary Party"

The East Turkestan Revolutionary Party (*Xarkiy Turkistan Inkilawi Partiyisi*, hereafter abbreviated as the "Revolutionary Party") was secretly founded on April 26, 1946.[37] Sources differ as to the official name of the Revolutionary Party.[38] However, the author obtained a photocopy of the party constitution written in Abdulkerim Abbasow's own hand, with the title *Constitution of the East Turkestan Revolutionary Party* (*Xarkiy Turkistan Inkilawi Partiyisining Nizamnamisi*). Chapter 1 of the constitution, "On the Name of the Party," reads as follows: "Our party is established with a base of the most progressive intellectuals; in line with the international situation at present and East Turkestan's current stage of historical development, the name of the party shall be set as the East Turkestan Revolutionary Party."[39] The party's formal name was thus *Xarkiy Turkistan Inkilawi Partiyisi*, abbreviated in Uyghur as X.T.I.P.

Constitution of the East Turkestan Revolutionary Party, handwritten by Abdulkerim Abbasow

Table 9.2   Principal Members of the Central Executive Committee of the East Turkestan Revolutionary Party

Name	Position in the Party
Abdulkerim Abbasow	Chairman
Saydulla Saypullayow	Minister for Rural Areas
Saypidin Azizi	Minister of Communication
Asat Ishakow	Minister of Organization
Abdulla Zakirow	Secretary-General
Anwar Hanbaba	Minister of Commerce
Mamatimin Iminow	Minister of Military Affairs

Source: Compiled by the author on the basis of: Saypidin Azizi, "Aslima II" (Recollections II), pp. 112–113; and Anwar Hanbaba, "Abdukirim Abasow Hakkida Aslima" (On Abdulkerim Abbasow), p. 36.

The Revolutionary Party was in fact established on the foundation of the Youth League.[40] The seven-member Central Executive Committee of the Revolutionary Party included five members from the Youth League's central committee, led by Abdulkerim Abbasow as chairman (Table 9.2). After the Revolutionary Party was founded, the Youth League became the party's Youth Division.[41] Article 8 of the Revolutionary Party's constitution affirmed that the party was to serve as the institutional guide for the Youth League, "Raising the young to become fighters, patriots and internationalists."

The East Turkestan Revolutionary Youth League had in fact already made great strides in terms of its organizational development;[42] such being the case, why was it necessary to found a revolutionary party in addition to the Youth League? According to Anwar Hanbaba, who served at the time as a member of the central committees of both the Youth League and the Revolutionary Party, the Youth League had little in the way of resources or power, and was very limited in some respects; Abdulkerim Abbasow therefore decided to found a political party to guide the revolution.[43] The aim in establishing the Revolutionary Party was to form a more cohesive political organization in comparison with the Youth League, to seize the initiative in the revolution, and provide leadership in the East Turkestan Independence Movement.

What were the limitations of the Youth League? The answer to this question can be found in the memoirs of the principal figures in the East Turkestan Revolutionary Party, as well as documents on the party's guiding principles. According to Saypidin Azizi, who served at the time as a Youth League committee member as well as a committee member and Minister of Communications of the Revolutionary Party, the league's efforts to teach and disseminate Marxist and socialist theory and the concept of class struggle met with obstruction by religious figures.

Azizi also noted that the constitution of the Revolutionary Party was inspired by the constitutions of the Soviet Communist Party and the Chinese Communist Party.[44] Saydulla Saypullayow, a party committee member and Minister for Rural Areas, remarked that the Revolutionary Party's constitution "drew on the Chinese Communist Party's theory of New Democracy, and was drafted in accordance with the actual local circumstances."[45] This account is corroborated in the party constitution.

> Chapter 2: Party Members; Article 2: In line with the guiding principles of Third International [3-*intirnatsional*], those who become party members must unconditionally observe and execute all resolutions of Third International and this party, must not be delinquent on party membership dues, and must strive to adhere to the party line, at the cost of life and property; Article 3: This party is the party of the revolution, and will fight disinterestedly and unreservedly for the liberation and independence of all peoples, and for political, economic and social equality for the entire proletariat. As party members, we must make unstinting sacrifices and struggle to fight for the correct revolutionary ideals and the supreme spirit of internationalism [*intirnatsionlchiliq roh*].[46]

Code names were implemented for each of the seven members of the Revolutionary Party's central executive committee: in selecting their code names, the seven committee members deliberately chose initials that would spell out the word *Lininchi* or "Leninist" (in the Uyghur script, *ch* is one letter). This further supports the idea that the Revolutionary Party was organized in the style of a communist political party (see Table 9.2). It is clear that the Revolutionary Party was rooted in the radical shift in political consciousness experienced by East Turkestan's pro-Soviet intellectuals; it was thus completely different in nature from the East Turkestan Republic, which crystallized out of the "national revolution." The founding of the Revolutionary Party thus signaled the total disintegration of the two-faction coalition that had formed the government of the East Turkestan Republic.

Unlike the Youth League, the Revolutionary Party was not known to the general public, or even to the government of the East Turkestan Republic.[47] In an interview with the author, an individual who joined the National Army in 1946 confirmed that many of the military service members at the time, including himself, were unaware that the Revolutionary Party even existed.[48] Saypidin Azizi gave the following explanation for the secrecy: "It was necessary not only to avoid being attacked and destroyed by religious figures and reactionaries within the government, but also to conceal it from the Soviet advisors."[49]

When the organization was first founded, Abdulkerim Abbasow reportedly called it the "Marxist Study Group"; he later established a "Philosophical Study Group." Contemporary accounts state that Abbasow's plan had been to reach out to intellectuals using communist ideas. However, the Soviet advisors believed that the "time was not yet ripe" to pursue "education in the theory of class struggle" and "education in the theory of socialist revolution" within the East Turkestan Republic, and ordered that these organizations be disbanded. To avoid being labeled and persecuted as an "anti-Soviet," Abdulkerim Abbasow ultimately had no choice but to establish the Revolutionary Party in secret.[50]

The Soviet opposition toward the establishment of the Revolutionary Party was rooted in the Soviet Union's efforts at the time to push the East Turkestan Republic to engage in the peace talks with the Chinese government: if it had been discovered at this delicate point that a communist party had been established in the East Turkestan Republic, the Chinese Nationalist government might have believed this engagement to be insincere, or might even have used this as grounds to accuse the Soviet Union of having designs on the territory of Xinjiang. A mysterious Soviet figure who frequently visited Ghulja did eventually grant approval to the Revolutionary Party, but continued to demand that the organization keep its existence secret.[51]

9.3 Fall of the Republic

Second Phase of the Peace Talks

In March 1946, while on a tour to inspect the Chinese Communist armed forces and the Nationalist armies, accompanied by Zhou Enlai and Ma Xie'er, Zhang Zhizhong received a message from the "Representatives of the People of Ili" forwarded by the Soviet Embassy, asking when Zhang Zhizhong could return to Urumqi: "We shall regard Minister Zhang Zhizhong's failure to appear as tantamount to abandoning the peace negotiations."[52] Zhang's secretary Yu Zhanbang opined that this approach by the Ili side was likely prompted by the arrival of three Nationalist government armies in Xinjiang in November 1945 and the threat that these posed.[53]

In light of these circumstances, Zhang Zhizhong's pending appointment as "Head of the Military Affairs Commission and Commander of the Northeast Field Headquarters" was suspended; instead, he was appointed as "Commander of the Northwest Field Headquarters" on March 28, 1946. The Nationalist government promptly announced on March 29 that Wu Zhongxin was to be relieved of the position of governor of Xinjiang and replaced by Zhang Zhizhong, who returned to Urumqi on April 4 to begin the second phase of the peace talks with the East Turkestan representatives.[54]

The second round of negotiations primarily revolved around the matter of absorbing the army of the East Turkestan Republic—the National Army—into the Chinese government forces. Since these military developments were closely implicated in the question of political dominance in the Xinjiang region after the ceasefire, the two parties in the negotiations fiercely wrangled over the number of units to be allowed and where they would be stationed. The East Turkestan representatives initially demanded that 13 regiments be reformed under the Chinese Nationalist army, including two pairs of regiments stationed at Kashgar and Ghulja, the regiments at Aksu, Kucha, Karasahr, Urumqi, Usu, Altay, Tarbagatay, and Dorbiljin, and the joint regiment at Suiding and Huiyuan. However, Zhang Zhizhong insisted that no more than 4 regiments could be reformed, and that their garrisons could not be located outside the zone controlled by the East Turkestan Republic at that time.[55]

Zhang Zhizhong's responded to this intractable disagreement by approaching Savelyev, the newly appointed Soviet Consul General in Urumqi, and requesting that he step in as mediator. However, unlike his predecessor, Acting Consul General Evseef Konstantin Mihailovic, who had generally supported Zhang Zhizhong in the first phase of the negotiations, Savelyev sought at every turn to defend the interests of the East Turkestan Republic. He recommended that Zhang Zhizhong allow at least 6 regiments of the National Army to be reformed, and held that they should be permitted to establish garrisons outside East Turkestan's zone of control.

On April 21, Rahimjan Sabir Ghaji, the chief delegate of the East Turkestan Republic, flew back to Ghulja to submit a report to the republic's Interim Government. Zhang Zhizhong stated in his memoirs that he met with Sabir Ghaji prior to his departure and communicated that 6 regiments could be reformed, but that this was the furthest concession he was willing to make; Zhang also expressed his hopes that a list of personnel who would be joining the Xinjiang Provincial Coalition Government would soon be forthcoming. However, following his return to Urumqi on the 25th, in talks on the 26th, Sabir Ghaji made a counter-demand for the redesignation of 10 regiments, and further called for troops to be stationed at Kashgar and Aksu. Zhang Zhizhong categorically refused, explaining his sentiments to the true power behind the East Turkestan delegation, Ahmatjan Kasimi: "I came on a mission for peace, and I am confident that I have exhausted my greatest efforts for peace. I bear full responsibility, and if peace cannot be achieved, I must take the blame, and resign."[56]

The Soviet Consulate's Plans

On May 1, Consul General Savelyev proposed the "Final Mediated Plan," under which 7 regiments of the National Army would be reformed as part of the Chinese government forces, and one regiment apiece would be stationed in Urumqi and Kashgar. Savelyev had also informed Zhang Zhizhong during an earlier visit by the latter to the Soviet consulate in Urumqi that the Soviet Union would no longer serve as mediator if he rejected this plan.[57]

In talks on May 3, the East Turkestan delegation proposed a new plan. The key points were as follows: (1) 7 regiments of the National Army would be reformed and one regiment apiece would be stationed at Urumqi, Kashgar and Aksu; (2) A commander-in-chief with unified command over the reformed National Army troops would be installed, and would concurrently serve as Deputy Commissioner for Military Affairs in Xinjiang Province; this individual would be selected by recommendation of the East Turkestan Republic; (3) The armed forces of the Chinese government would be prohibited from entering the three districts of Ili, Tarbagatay and Altay; (4) The political police would be disbanded, and police organizations for each region would be formed by the local residents; (5) The number of Chinese government forces in Xinjiang would be reduced to the levels as of January 1944.[58]

It should be noted that the plan proposed by the East Turkestan delegation was essentially consistent with the "Final Mediated Plan" put forward by Consul General Savelyev. This suggests that the East Turkestan delegation either agreed with the Soviet consulate's recommendations, or had cooperated with the consulate to formulate the plan. In short, these circumstances clearly demonstrate that the Soviet Union continued to manipulate the East Turkestan delegation to the peace talks via its consulate in Urumqi.

However, it is a little-known fact that the Interim Government Council of the East Turkestan Republic had previously resolved to accept Zhang Zhizhong's proposal for the reformation of 6 regiments. On April 22, or the second day after Rahimjan Sabir Ghaji returned to Ghulja from Urumqi, the Interim Government issued Resolution No. 271, which read:

> Having heard from Rahimjan Sabir Ghaji with regard to the situation of the negotiations with the Nationalist Government, the following resolution is hereby issued:
>
> I. On the matter of military forces, in accordance with the agreement reached between the Nationalist Party and our representatives, the National Army forces shall number 12,700, and shall be formed into 6 regiments.
>
> With regard to the council and departments of the Provincial Government, appointments shall be made in accordance with the personnel designations below:
>
> (1) Xinjiang Provincial Government Council Member and Deputy Governor: Ahmatjan Kasimi;

(2) Provincial Government Council Member and Deputy Commissioner of Civil Affairs: Rahimjan Sabir Ghaji;

(3) Altay Representative and Provincial Government Council Member: Dalalkan Sugurbayow;

(4) Provincial Government Council Member (and Altay District Commissioner): Osman Islam;

(5) Provincial Government Council Member (and Ili District Commissioner): Ilhan Tora;

(6) Provincial Government Council Member (and Commissioner of Kashgar): Isakbek Munonow;

(7) Provincial Government Council Member and Deputy Secretary-General: Abdulkerim Abbasow;

(8) Provincial Government Council Member and Education Commissioner: Saypidin Azizi.

II. Our representatives Rahimjan Sabir Ghaji, Ahmatjan Kasimi, and Abdullah Tora are authorized to sign the above agreement reached with the Nationalist Government.

Despite having settled on the reformation of 6 regiments by resolution of the Interim Government, upon Sabir Ghaji's return to Urumqi, he and the other delegates amended their demand to 10 regiments; this was later reduced to 7 regiments, the exact number proposed in the recommendations by the Soviet consulate in Urumqi. These circumstances can only indicate that the East Turkestan delegation to the talks was acquiescent to the proposals of the Soviet consul general.

Zhang Zhizhong inspecting the National Army

Zhang Zhizhong believed that the Soviet consulate's withdrawal of its erstwhile support for the Chinese side in the negotiations arose from the Soviet Union's need to push back against the Chinese Nationalist government's anti-Soviet policies.[59] The Nationalist government was deeply mired in conflict with the Soviet Union during this period over the Manchuria question and the issue of the Chinese Communist Party, and was pursuing an increasingly "pro-American, anti-Soviet" agenda. Thus, unlike in the earlier stage of the peace talks, during which the Soviet Union had actively aided the Chinese government in its efforts to dissolve the East Turkestan Republic, once the peace agreement was signed, the Soviet Union devoted itself to preserving and expanding the "East Turkestan Republic" (for instance, by demanding that National Army forces be stationed outside the zone controlled by the former East Turkestan Republic). The aim was to preserve the Soviet Union's influence over Xinjiang, even after the dissolution of the East Turkestan Republic.

Zhang Zhizhong rejected the plans proposed by the East Turkestan delegation and the Soviet consulate, instead offering a counter-proposal while continuing to communicate with Consul General Savelyev. The proceedings of the talks during this period are difficult to determine due to a lack of sources. In the final outcome, the East Turkestan delegation agreed to Zhang Zhizhong's plan in principle: however, according to an account by Tao Tianbai, Zhang's secretary at the time, Zhang Zhizhong did make concessions on several issues, including the disbanding of the political police force in Xinjiang Province and the formation of local police organizations; the latter decisions were also to be publicly announced in the form of the *Minutes of the Talks*. In addition, the number of East Turkestan members on the Provincial Government Council of the coalition government was to be increased from six to eight, among other items.[60] The two parties signed the "Draft Second Addendum to the Peace Terms" late in the evening on May 22, 1946 (the formal document was signed on June 6).

The key content of the "Second Addendum to the Peace Terms" is as follows:

(1) The people's militias which participated in the incidents shall be reformed into 6 regiments, numbering 11,000 to 12,000 persons.

(2) The commanding officer shall be nominated by the Three Districts

area, and shall concurrently serve as Deputy Commander of Public Security in Xinjiang Province.

(3) The National Army forces shall be stationed in the three districts of Ili, Tarbagatay and Altay, and shall be responsible for maintaining peace and order.

(4) The commanding officer of the National Army forces and the Government shall jointly form peace-keeping contingents in Kashgar and Aksu.

(5) The weapons and equipment of the National Army forces shall be provided by the Government.

(6) The commanding officer of the National Army forces shall be responsible to the Government for implementing the reformation of the National Army forces.[61]

The Final Days of Ilhan Tora's Political Life

As the East Turkestan delegation and the Chinese representatives prepared to sign the "Second Addendum to the Peace Terms," East Turkestan's Soviet advisors, including Ivan Polinov, the commander-in-chief of the National Army, and Mansur Apandi, the First Deputy Commissioner of Tarbagatay District, decamped en masse to the Soviet Union.[62] At the same time, Ilhan Tora's life on the political stage in Xinjiang drew to a close.

When the peace talks first began, Ilhan Tora had experienced a brief period of strengthened political authority within the Interim Government of the East Turkestan Republic. Tora was granted the title of Marshal of the Armed Force under Resolution No. 114, dated October 22, 1945; under Resolution 193, dated January 9, 1946, Tora was awarded the highest decoration instituted up to that point in East Turkestan—the "Medal of the East Turkestan Republic."[63] Resolution No. 193 reads as follows:

> To commend Ilhan Tora, the organizer and leader of the East Turkestan Revolution, for his great contributions during the revolutionary era, the Government of the East Turkestan Republic hereby issues the following resolution:
>
> The Distinguished Medal of the East Turkestan Republic is hereby conferred upon the organizer and leader of the East Turkestan Revolution, the Chairman of the Freedom Group, and President of the Republican Government, Ilhan Tora, for winning liberation, equality and happy new

lives for all the peoples of East Turkestan, who suffered centuries of oppression; for inspiring, correctly leading, and bravely commanding the revolutionary struggle to defend the dignity of the fatherland, our people, and our religion; and for making great, historical contributions, unvanquished.

However, Ilhan Tora signaled in a letter to Kazakh leader Osman Islam of the Altay District, dated April 1946, that he would soon flee from Xinjiang to the Soviet Union; at the letter's close, he also expressed his fear of being expelled from East Turkestan by pro-Soviet forces: "Qorqit escaped his tomb and spent 40 years roaming east and west, until he was finally thrown into the grave vault that had been dug all those years ago."[64] (Note: Qorqit was a famous diviner of popular legend.) In other words, Ilhan Tora was well aware at this point that he would soon be forsaken by the pro-Soviet intellectual faction within the government of the East Turkestan Republic, and that his days in power were numbered.

On June 4, 1946, the East Turkestan Republic provided a list of personnel who were to join the Provincial Government Council, along with the specific positions they would hold. On June 18, the Chinese Nationalist government formally announced the appointments to the Coalition Government of Xinjiang Province.

It is a little-known fact that, by the time of this announcement, which named Ilhan Tora as both a council member and as Ili District Commissioner, Tora was no longer even in Xinjiang. On June 6, 1946, the day on which the "Second Addendum to the Peace Terms" was formally signed, President Ilhan Tora of the East Turkestan Republic and several of his most trusted followers were escorted to Almaty, Kazakhstan, by representatives of the Soviet consulate in Ghulja.[65] His detention was confirmed by several involved parties in interviews with the author. One individual who was close to Ahmatjan Kasimi gave the following statement during an interview:

> Ahmatjan Kasimi, Abdulkerim Abbasow, Saypullayow and others of the Uyghur intellectuals wrote an anonymous letter to Ilhan Tora demanding that he leave Ghulja immediately, and fired it into Ilhan Tora's residence using a bow and arrow. After Ilhan Tora read it, he hastily demanded to meet with the Soviet consul in Ghulja. The Soviet consul advised him to temporarily take refuge in the Soviet Union, and mobilized two trucks to

take him and his family to the Soviet Union that very day. After arriving in the Soviet Union, Ilhan Tora was immediately put under house arrest. The intellectuals had originally planned to assassinate Ilhan Tora if he did not leave Ghulja, so one could say that having him escorted away and put under house arrest was the best outcome for them.

Soviet Consulate in Ghulja

On June 27, the Interim Government Council of the East Turkestan Republic issued its final resolution—Resolution No. 324, which stated that, as of June 28, the "Interim Government of the East Turkestan Republic" would be reformed as the Ili District Council, while the staff of the Altay District Government and the Tarbagatay District Government would be reassigned to the Xinjiang Provincial Government. With this, the curtains closed on the history of the East Turkestan Republic. Interestingly, the conclusion of the Xinjiang Peace Talks and the fall of the East Turkestan Republic roughly coincided with the collapse of the peace negotiations between the Chinese Communist Party and the Nationalist government: on June 26, civil war broke out once more in China.[66]

Summary

Progress in the peace talks was accompanied by fierce internal strife between the pro-Soviet intellectuals led by Abdulkerim Abbasow and the traditional social elites who gathered behind Ilhan Tora, with each faction adopting different political tactics to gain the upper hand. The political decline of the East Turkestan Republic set the stage for a series of developments: the start of the Xinjiang Peace Talks; the political elevation of Ahmatjan Kasimi as a delegate to the peace talks; the victory of the "Second Revolution" proposed by the pro-Soviet intellectuals; the fall of Ilhan Tora; and the self-initiated dissolution of the East Turkestan Republic.

Superficially, the decline of the East Turkestan Republic seems to be directly linked to the peace talks with the Chinese government. However, Soviet policy played a decisive role both in forwarding the Xinjiang Peace

Talks and in the waxing and waning of the different political factions within the republic's government. In this sense, the conflict within the East Turkestan regime and the ultimate collapse of the republic unfolded in accordance with the Soviet Union's designs.

In the period from 1945–1946, China was simultaneously engaged in two efforts for peace, both mediated by foreign powers. The first was the Marshall Mission, an attempt to reconcile the Nationalist government and the Chinese Communist Party through American mediation (the "Nationalist–Communist Peace Talks"). The second was the peace negotiations between the Nationalist government and the rebel Turkic-Islamic peoples of Xinjiang Province (the "East Turkestan Republic"), mediated by the Soviet Union (the "Xinjiang Peace Talks"). Interestingly, the representative of the Nationalist government in both efforts was Zhang Zhizhong, who was "marked . . . as a moderate man who favored compromise."[67] Moreover, Zhang's opponents in both sets of negotiations were political forces closely aligned with the Soviet Union. However, the two efforts for peace had very different outcomes: In the Nationalist–Communist Peace Talks, the Chinese Communist Party rejected the recommendations of the Soviet Union, but won great victories thereafter and gained control over the entire territory of China only three years later;[68] while in the Xinjiang Peace Talks, the East Turkestan representatives acted on the Soviet Union's instructions, embarking on the path to their own downfall. It is clear that the Soviet Union acted completely in accordance with its own interests in each set of talks. The different outcomes of the peace negotiations in China during this period reflect the self-serving nature of the Soviet Union's support for "revolutions" in other countries.

CHAPTER 10

IDEALS VERSUS REALITY
A Detailed Analysis of the Second East Turkestan Independence Movement

There is no doubt that the rise and development of the East Turkestan independence movement, particularly the ineffaceable history of the Second East Turkestan Independence Movement and the East Turkestan Republic, have had an enormous and indelible impact on both the future of Turkic-Islamic society in China, as well as the course of China's modern political development as a multi-ethnic state. However, despite its duration and the scale on which it unfolded, the Second East Turkestan Independence Movement was ultimately unsuccessful. What insights does this outcome offer to posterity? Today, as Chinese society continues to be roiled by the idea of independence for East Turkestan, analysis of this issue can aid in deepening our understanding of the true substance of the East Turkestan Independence Movement.

The leading players in the Second East Turkestan Independence Movement and the political history of the East Turkestan Republic were a group of Uyghur intellectuals with modern school education and pro-Soviet leanings: the movement thus had a dual nature as both a national revolution and a social revolution. However, the intellectuals had a weak popular base within Uyghur communities and among other ethnic groups in the Xinjiang region at the time, and could expect few people to directly identify with their leadership. Internally, the intellectual class therefore sought to perpetuate the ideals of the First East Turkestan Independence Movement while pursuing an alliance with traditional ethnic elites and religious figures; externally, they also solicited support from the Soviet Union, despite its ulterior motives. However, faced with the grim reality of war, inflexible traditional communities, and an uncongenial international political situation, not only was the nature of the East Turkestan Independence Movement as a national revolution distorted, the ideals of the social revolution championed by the pro-Soviet intellectuals were never fulfilled. This can be perceived through the following aspects of the movement.

10.1 The Will of the Soviet Union and the Undemocratic Political System

Article 2 of the 1945 version of the "Nine Political Precepts" (issued on January 5, 1945, in the form of "Resolution No. 4 of the Interim Government Council of the East Turkestan Republic") defines the political system of the East Turkestan Republic as follows: "A truly free and independent republic, established on the foundation of equality for all peoples within the borders of East Turkestan." However, although the Interim Government of East Turkestan paid lip service to the ideas of popular sovereignty and a republican system, the politics of East Turkestan in fact featured many undemocratic elements.

In the East Turkestan Republic, the general public was in actuality excluded from the policy-making process. To be sure, citizens' voting rights were officially recognized in the *Provisional Regulations on Criminal Procedure of the East Turkestan Republic* and the *Provisional Penal Code of the East Turkestan Republic*, both promulgated on May 13, 1945: "All men and women, of every ethnicity, residing within the national territories of the East Turkestan Republic, are citizens of the state"; "All persons who are citizens of the state [or "All men and women, of every ethnicity," as per the *Provisional Regulations*] have the right to vote." In addition, the members of the highest authority of the East Turkestan Republic—the Interim Government Council—were elected in accordance with democratic procedures at the mass rally held on November 12, 1944. However, even this, the sole democratic election in the history of the East Turkestan Republic, was not based on a representative vote. The undeveloped election system meant that the general population had almost no opportunities to voice opinions on the policies of the East Turkestan Republic. This was also an important factor enabling the Soviet Union to gain control over East Turkestan politics.

The policy-making process in the East Turkestan Republic had a strong flavor of backroom politics. Allusions to this process in the government resolutions suggest that important policies and personnel appointments were determined through discussion by the Interim Government Council. However, beneath the surface veneer of the council resolutions, backroom politics dominated by Soviet influences (including pro-Soviet intellectuals) played a key role. As discussed in previous chapters, the major political decisions faced by the republic, including its earliest personnel appointments, the military advance from Ili into the Tarbagatay and Altay districts, and engagement in peace talks with the Chinese Nationalist government, were already decided prior to their submission to the Interim Government Council for discussion; confirmation in the form of a government resolution was merely a formality. Two separate policy-making systems existed within the leadership ranks of the East Turkestan Republic: one superficial, and one substantive. Although religious leaders and traditional ethnic elites played a major role in promoting social unity and popular mobilization for the war effort in the East Turkestan Republic, they had no real voice with regard to formulating policy.

The political system of the East Turkestan Republic was by no means a socialist system: the two versions of the "Nine Political Precepts," which functioned as the state constitution, contain no language referencing socialist or communist ideas. However, due to the East Turkestan Republic's

Leaders of the East Turkestan Republic
(First row, from right: Abdulkerim Abbasow, Rahimjan Sabir Ghaji, Dalalkan Sugurbayow, Ahmatjan Kasimi, Anwar Musabayow, and Saypidin Azizi)

general dependence on the Soviet Union, some aspects of its political power structure were clearly imitative of the Soviet Union.

Political power in the East Turkestan Republic was highly concentrated in the hands of the Interim Government Council. Based on "Resolution No. 1 of the Interim Government Council of the East Turkestan Republic," it is clear that the Interim Government Council was the supreme authority on all matters administrative, legislative, judicial and religious; all ministries were subordinate to the council (see Figure 6.1, p. 153). Though a Supervisory Committee was also established, it was merely another organ of the government, and its function was simply to "promote the correct implementation of government directives by the various departments of the government."[1] The East Turkestan Republic was not a parliamentary system, nor did it feature a congress or some other such institution that could express the will of the people. In sum, there is no doubt that the principle of separation of powers did not take firm root. The East Turkestan Republic did bear a certain resemblance to the contemporary soviet republics of the U.S.S.R. in that all legislative, administrative and judicial powers were held by the Interim Government Council.

Many of the Turkic-Islamic residents of the East Turkestan Republic bore a certain antipathy toward the Soviet Union due to its oppressive policies toward the Turkic-Islamic peoples residing within its own territories, and toward Islam in general. Some leaders of the national movement accepted Soviet support in their struggle against the Chinese regime, but once their initial objectives had been achieved, the imperialistic and despotic actions of Soviet forces within the East Turkestan Republic's political zone of control inspired feelings of discontent among many; the Kazakh leader of Altay District, Osman Islam, was one such example.

Osman Islam was the first to lead the Kazakh nomads of Altay District to rebel against the government; he was referred to by the Kazakhs as "Osman Batyr," or "the hero Osman." However, when the government of Altay District was formed following its absorption into the East Turkestan Republic's sphere of influence, the important positions like commander of the Altay Cavalry Regiment, Chief of Police, and county magistrate for the various counties, went not to Osman's trusted followers, but instead to Soviet nationals or pro-Soviet Kazakhs. As a result, although Osman himself was appointed as Altay District Commissioner, he was unwilling to step forward to take up his post. Once the peace talks with the Chinese Nationalist government began in October 1945, the Soviet Union also forcibly confiscated the weapons it had previously given to the Kazakh rebel forces, to avoid giving the Chinese government a pretext to interfere in East Turkestan's internal affairs. This incident inspired fierce resentment on the part of Osman Islam.[2]

Osman Islam

Osman's anti-Soviet sentiments chiefly revolved around his Islamic faith. A Kazakh religious figure who fled from the Soviet Union to Xinjiang in the 1930s told Osman that, "The Soviet Union is destroying religion"; this incident reportedly had a great impact on Osman's ideas.[3] The anti-Soviet leanings of Soviet Kazakhs also played a part in Osman's antipathy toward the Soviet Union. According to Osman's own statements, the Kazakh people of Xinjiang held a grudge against the Soviet Union for its brutal suppression of Kazakhs in the Republic of Kazakhstan.[4] When Altay District was annexed by the East Turkestan Republic, many of Osman's followers therefore quickly surrendered to the Chinese Nationalist government.[5]

Once the peace talks began, the Soviet advisors ensconced in the various departments of the Altay District government and the Altay Cavalry Regiment withdrew.[6] On November 4, 1945, Osman Islam finally came to Chenghua to take up his position as Altay District Commissioner.[7] Following his installation as commissioner, Osman reportedly enforced Sharia law, ordering that: "Those who do not go to mosque [*namazni okumigan*] shall be sentenced to 50 lashes; those who do not observe Ramadan [*roza tutmigan*] shall be sentenced to 100 lashes; those who disregard the prohibition against alcohol [*harak iqkan*] shall be sentenced to 30 lashes."[8] The substantial shift in Osman's policies before and after his installation in the government quickly led to conflict with pro-Soviet Kazakh leaders. On March 19, 1946, Osman left Chenghua and returned to Koktokay County to reorganize his own forces.[9] From May 1946 onward, Osman independently levied taxes in Qinggil, Koktokay, Burultokay and other counties, declaring that he no longer recognized the authority of the East Turkestan Republic.[10]

In May 1946, relying on a 1940 agreement with Sheng Shicai, a Soviet tungsten mining team entered Osman Islam's base of operations—Koktokay County—to begin excavations.[11] Osman called for the mining team to be forcibly expelled: "We shall not leave open any path to aggressors against our territory and our religion."[12] However, Osman's approach was strongly opposed by Dalalkan Sugurbayow, the pro-Soviet Deputy Altay District Commissioner and commander of the Altay Cavalry Regiment. Faced with a conflict between two of their leaders, influential figures from the Kazakh tribes of Altay District gathered at Quw Oy (Osman's place of residence) to discuss strategy, but were ultimately unable to reach a consensus. The Kazakh people of Altay District were thus split into two factions, respectively favoring the Chinese Nationalist government and the Soviet Union.[13]

As discussed in previous chapters, support from a greater nation is often essential to the success of independence movements by minority peoples; however, this must proceed under the principle that said people are not deprived of their political agency. The reason is very simple: on the international political stage, every great nation is fundamentally acting in service of its own national interests. It should be particularly noted here that, apart from the Soviet Union, the East Turkestan Republic did not have any form of contact with other countries, and did not seek any kind of diplomatic recognition. East Turkestan's dreams of achieving independence were wholly entrusted to the Soviet Union, allowing the Soviet Union to unreservedly exploit the East Turkestan Independence Movement in pursuit of its own interests.

The republic's reliance on the Soviet Union gave the latter an influential voice among the forces involved in the Second East Turkestan Independence Movement, thereby weakening the political agency of the indigenous Turkic-Islamic peoples. After the founding of the East Turkestan Republic, due to the great influence wielded by the Soviet Union, the republic's systems of power became burdened by a number of undemocratic elements, and the objectives of the independence movement were clouded. When the Soviet Union began revising its policies toward Xinjiang in the latter half of 1945, pro-Soviet intellectuals in the leadership ranks of the East Turkestan Republic deferred to the will of the Soviet Union, enthusiastically endorsed the peace talks with the Chinese Nationalist government, and abandoned the objectives of achieving national independence and founding a nation-state; thus did the Second East Turkestan Independence Movement meet its inescapable historical fate, which had been building since the initial decision to rely completely on the Soviet Union for aid. In this sense, it was the pro-Soviet intellectuals, who had been the first to launch the movement and had played a key role on the regional political stage until the very end, who ultimately buried the fruit of the Second East Turkestan Independence Movement—the "East Turkestan Republic."

10.2 Conflict between Modern Objectives and Traditional Society

The Interim Government of the East Turkestan Republic placed great emphasis on education. "Resolution No. 108 of the Interim Government Council of the East Turkestan Republic," dated October 15, 1945, offered the following discourse on the importance of education:

> The most important task we face at present is to thoroughly topple the colonial rule of the Han government, and liberate the entire nation. The second important task is to develop the cause of education. This is because cultural education is the driving force that shall spur our nation's military, political and economic development. In the past, the bloodthirsty Han rulers enacted reactionary education, to train running dogs for their own reactionary rule. As a result, the majority of the people of East Turkestan were deprived of a normal education, and many school-aged children were unable to enroll at school. Since the outbreak of the revolution against the Han government, we have continuously achieved victory. Now, as the entire nation is on the brink of liberation, the paramount task we face is to rapidly develop the cause of cultural education, to cultivate the young, the future masters of our nation.

The linking of education with national liberation and the establishment of the nation-state was a key feature of East Turkestan's ideas on education: we can see here the sense of crisis engendered by the Chinese government's attempts to eradicate ethnic culture through its policies of cultural assimilation. "One cause for which our countrymen took up arms to fight against the Han government was the colonialists' adoption of ruthless policies toward the education of the people of East Turkestan."[14] The establishment of the Bureau of Language and Literature under the Ministry of

Education and the creation of an award for outstanding ethnic literary works were likely rooted in the same considerations.[15]

The Interim Government of the East Turkestan Republic devoted particular efforts to training educators. Resolution No. 29 (March 5, 1945), the Interim Government's August 1st order, Resolution No. 78 (August 2), and Resolution No. 108 (October 15) repeatedly ordered that educators who had left their positions during wartime to become soldiers, government officials, or merchants were to return to their former posts. In March and December of 1945 and May 1946, the Interim Government Council issued resolutions calling for the establishment of teacher training courses.[16] The council also issued a special resolution ordering that school campuses converted to military barracks were to revert to their former purpose.[17]

Education in the East Turkestan Republic was not traditional Islamic education, but rather modern school education. From the curriculum for a middle school teacher training course, we can see that middle school classes included language and literature, physics, mathematics, and so on.[18] A seven-year compulsory education system was to be established for urban areas, and a four-year system was to be implemented for rural areas, with free tuition during said periods. Though the systems may never have been put into effect, in concept at least, they predated the compulsory education system formulated by the Chinese government.

The education program drafted by the government of the East Turkestan Republic was patterned after the modern school education system of the Soviet Union, and adopted the Soviet Union's ten-year schooling system. Due to a lack of textbooks, East Turkestan's Uyghur, Uzbek, Kazakh and Tatar schools reportedly used old textbooks from Soviet Central Asia produced prior to the region's ban on the use of the Arabic script.[19]

The East Turkestan Republic also established a modern legal system. A series of legal statutes were formulated, including: *Organizational Structure of County Courts and Provisional Rules of Proceedings of the East Turkestan Republic* (April 18, 1945); *Provisional Regulations on Criminal Procedure of the East Turkestan Republic* and the *Provisional Penal Code of the East Turkestan Republic* (May 13, 1945); *Provisional Regulations on Economic Procedural Law of the Supreme Court* (June 6, 1945); *Provisional Regulations on the Penal Code of the East Turkestan Republic* (August 23, 1945), and so on.

The *Provisional Regulations on Criminal Procedure* defined and established the tripartite modern judicial system, including the police, prosecution, and the courts (Articles 14 and 38), and underlined principles emphasizing evidence (Articles 22 and 33) and impartial justice (Articles 45 and 46). *Organizational Structure of County Courts and Provisional Rules of Proceedings of the East Turkestan Republic* also outlined the election system for court justices (Article 2) and the people's assessor system (Article 4). The *Provisional Regulations on the Penal Code* contained 260 regulations on matters of criminal law, including a description of the attorney system.

The *Provisional Penal Code* divided criminal offenses into several categories, including political offenses, larceny, malfeasance, failure to obey government orders, forging of documents, crimes against the person, and sexual assault against females. It established the principle of determining punishment according to the degree of harm caused by the assailant; the method of punishment was generally imprisonment, with the aim of rehabilitation. Although capital punishment existed in the East Turkestan Republic, only the Supreme Court had the authority to pass a sentence of execution; prisoners sentenced to death had the right to submit an appeal within 72 hours.[20]

The most important aspect of East Turkestan's legal system was its exclusion of religious practices from criminal trials. "Resolution No. 258 of the Interim Government Council of the East Turkestan Republic," dated April 10, 1946, prescribed the subjects to be studied in training courses for attorneys and political representatives, including "national policies, judicial power and duty, the history of East Turkestan, international trends, criminal law and the concrete application of criminal punishment, judicial procedure, and civil procedure." It is clear that the laws of the East Turkestan Republic were not based on the Sharia law of Islam. Article 5 of the *Provisional Regulations on Economic Procedural Law of the Supreme Court* stated: "With regard to legal cases arising between Kazakh compatriots, if pertaining to homicide, an investigation for liability must proceed in accordance with the law. Independent attempts at resolution such as reaching an agreement between the two local parties or demanding a blood debt are prohibited." In other words, an important principle of Islamic law—*Qisas*, or "retaliation in kind"—was banned under the judicial system of the East Turkestan Republic.

Article 1 of "Resolution of the Interim Government of the East Turkestan Republic on Religion," dated March 1946, stated: "The right of freedom of religion shall be protected for all denominations. Registration shall be granted to all religious associations within the borders of the East Turkestan Republic, without exception." Thus, despite President Ilhan Tora's status as an Islamic leader and the many aspects of Islam that permeated the political sphere, the East Turkestan Republic ultimately rejected the identity of a politicoreligious Islamic nation.

The East Turkestan Republic's ability to pursue its goals for social modernization was founded upon the pro-Soviet intellectuals, who served as the leading political force in the republic. Ilhan Tora reportedly made repeated calls for the Quran to serve as the basic law of the land, forming an Islamic political system guided by Sharia law; however, his efforts were met with strong opposition by the pro-Soviet intellectuals, and were ultimately unsuccessful.[21]

Yet the indissoluble nature of the traditional social framework during this era meant that the intellectuals' methods for promoting social unity and popular mobilization were not equal to their ambitions. The East Turkestan Republic therefore avoided an overt declaration of its secular principles, and the traditional socioeconomic system was preserved. The "Nine Political Precepts," released on January 5, 1945, stated that, "Banks, the postal service, forests, and all underground deposits shall revert to state ownership." However, none of the council's resolutions touched upon the matter of land ownership. Article 4 of "Resolution No. 234 of the Interim Government Council of the East Turkestan Republic" reveals that the traditional rural leadership positions (such as the *Ming bash*, or "leader of a thousand households"; and *Yuz bash*, or "leader of a hundred households") were perpetuated by the Interim Government of the East Turkestan Republic, along with the old social structures.

> On the matter of national grain levies in Ghulja City and County: Publicity and education work on the issue of grain levies in Ghulja City and Ghulja County for the general population of farmers has not been well-performed. A forum for all *Ming bash*, *Yuz bash* and other distinguished figures among the people was convened under the leadership of the President of the Government and Supreme Commander Ilhan Tora: at the forum, the importance and urgency of grain levy work was emphasized. In order to

quickly complete the grain levy work, apart from *Ming bash*, *Yuz bash* and other figures from the rural areas, counties also received aid from officials transferred from national organizations (such as the Ministry of Finance, Ministry of Internal Affairs and other organizations), who were embedded in rural areas to carry out publicity and education for the general population of farmers.[22]

To ensure social order, the East Turkestan Republic recognized the right of the Islamic system to exert control over society. For instance, although "Resolution No. 231 of the Interim Government Council of the East Turkestan Republic," dated February 29, 1946, grants permission for the establishment of a Women's Association, several requirements related to religious beliefs are appended: "(3) The Ministry of Religious Affairs and the Ministry of Education shall be responsible for supervision and management; ... (5) Muslim women are strictly prohibited from watching films or plays together with men; ... (6) Women's apparel must conform to the customs and habits of each ethnic people." Under "Resolution No. 277 of the Interim Government Council of the East Turkestan Republic," the sale of alcohol was also banned.

Under East Turkestan's judicial system, general courts existed alongside Islamic courts, demonstrating the limitations of the social revolution pursued by intellectuals in that era. Criminal cases were, by requirement, tried in the general courts, and the religious courts never became a mainstream part of the judicial system.[23] However, issues related to inheritance, marital disputes, orphans and widows, religious matters, and other civil cases all fell under the purview of the religious courts. Islamic beliefs were even interjected into school education. The Ministry of Finance set aside special funding to build school facilities and print teaching materials,[24] but nearly all of this funding was sourced from religious taxes, including the *ushr* tax levied by the Ministry of Religious Affairs, as well as the *zakat* taxes levied by the Ministry of Religious Affairs and the Ministry of Education.[25]

10.3 Uyghur-Centrism in the Republic

Xinjiang was home to five Turkic-Islamic peoples, including the Uyghurs, Kazakhs, Kyrgyz, Uzbeks, and Tatars. Under the regime of the East Turkestan Republic, each of these ethnic groups had their own representatives. For instance, President Ilhan Tora was Uzbek; Vice President Hakimbek Hoja was Uyghur; Minister of Education Habib Yuqi was Tatar; Isakbek Munonow, the Deputy Commander of the National Army, was Kyrgyz; and Ubulhari Tora, the Minister of Nomadic Pasturing, was Kazakh. Although one Mongol also sat on the government council, this individual was not appointed to any actual government position, and merely played an ornamental role in service of "ethnic equality." Based on the ethnic composition of the Interim Government Council, it is clear that the East Turkestan Republic sought to establish a nation-state centered on the Turkic-Islamic peoples.

However, there were clear disparities in political status among the different ethnic groups, despite their shared Turkic-Islamic identity.

The total population residing within the borders of the East Turkestan Republic was 705,168; Kazakhs represented 52.1%, while Uyghurs represented 25.3% of the overall population (Table 10.1). However, the government of the East Turkestan Republic was by no means reflective of this demographic composition. At the time of its founding on November 12, 1944, the 17 members of the Interim Government Council (*Wakitlik hokumiti azasi*) included 10 Uyghurs, 2 Russians, 2 Tatars, 1 Uzbek, 1 Kazakh and 1 Mongol (see Table 6.1, p. 150). Based on their representative numbers and the positions they held, it is clear that Uyghurs dominated the Interim Government of the East Turkestan Republic.

The Uzbek and Tatar populations in Xinjiang had always been small in number. According to the 1944 census completed by the Xinjiang Bureau of Civil Affairs, at the time, Uzbeks accounted for 0.26% of the total population, while Tatars accounted for 0.14%.[26] The president of the East Turkestan Republic was nevertheless Uzbek, and the two Tatar council members also held important positions in the government. In contrast, despite the fact that the Kazakh people comprised more than half of the region's total population, they were represented by only one council member, who was appointed as Minister of Nomadic Pasturing. Given this lack of representation, we can imagine that the Kazakhs played little to no role in deciding the major policies of the East Turkestan Republic.

After its founding on November 12, 1944, and the initial round of appointments, a total of nine new council members were appointed to the Interim Government of the East Turkestan Republic (Table 10.2). Aside

Table 10.1   Population of the East Turkestan Republic and Regional Representation of the Kazakh and Uyghur Peoples

	Total Population	Kazakhs (Share of Inhabitants)	Uyghurs (Share of Inhabitants)
Ili District	471,686	210,672 (44.7%)	165,416 (35.1%)
Tarbagatay District	170,442	103,180 (60.5%)	10,515 (6.2%)
Altay District	63,040	53,352 (84.6%)	2,596 (4.1%)
Total	705,168	367,204 (52.1%)	178,527 (25.3%)

Source: Compiled by the author on the basis of Zhang Dajun, Seventy Years of Upheaval in Xinjiang, *p. 6327; Zhou Dongjiao,* Ten Years in Xinjiang, *p. 312.*

Table 10.2   Interim Government Council Members Appointed after November 12, 1944

Name	Ethnicity	Position	Position Prior to Revolution	Resolution Naming Appointment
Wakax Haji	Tatar	Deputy Chair of the Supervisory Committee	Unknown	"Resolution No. 33 of the Interim Government Council of the East Turkestan Republic," dated Mar. 13, 1945
Ivan Polinov	Russian	Commander of the National Army	Soviet Military Officer	"Resolution No. 79 of the Interim Government Council of the East Turkestan Republic," dated Aug. 9, 1945
Isakbek Munonow	Kyrgyz	Deputy Commander of the National Army	In exile in the Soviet Union	Same as above

Table 10.2 (continued)

Name	Ethnicity	Position	Position Prior to Revolution	Resolution Naming Appointment
Jabukbay Aklakeqi	Kazakh	None	*Ming bash*	"Resolution No. 84 of the Interim Government Council of the East Turkestan Republic," dated Aug. 22, 1945
Osman Islam	Kazakh	Altay District Commissioner	Nomadic leader	"Resolution of the Interim Government Council of the East Turkestan Republic Regarding Altay District," dated September 23, 1945
Dalalkan Sugurbayow	Kazakh	Commander of the Altay Cavalry Regiment	In exile in the Soviet Union	Same as above
Alim	Kazakh	None	Prince of the Second Rank	Same as above
Ahmatjan Kasimi	Uyghur	Minister of Military Affairs in the Interim Government	Studied abroad in the Soviet Union	"Resolution No. 103 of the Interim Government Council of the East Turkestan Republic," dated Oct. 19, 1945
Basbay Qulak	Kazakh	Tarbagatay District Commissioner	Large landowner	"Resolution No. 216 of the Interim Government Council of the East Turkestan Republic," dated Jan. 29, 1946

Source: Compiled by the author on the basis of the resolutions of the Interim Government Council of the East Turkestan Republic.

from the Tatar Wakax Haji, who was appointed as Deputy Chair of the Supervisory Committee; the Soviet national Ivan Polinov and the Kyrgyz nomad Isakbek Munonow, both of whom led armies from the Soviet Union; and the Uyghur Ahmatjan Kasimi, who was appointed as a delegate in the peace talks, another five Kazakh council members joined the Interim Government as the Tarbagatay and Altay districts were absorbed into the East Turkestan Republic's sphere of influence. However, of these five individuals, one was unable to take up the position, while another three were government and military leaders in their respective districts; as for the remaining figure, despite his presence in the East Turkestan Republic's capital city of Ghulja, he was not assigned to any actual positions. In sum, not a single Kazakh was able to truly gain access to the leadership ranks controlling the formulation of policy in the East Turkestan Republic.[27]

Within the East Turkestan Republic, in comparison to the elevated political status of Uyghurs, Uzbeks, and Tatars, Kazakhs had the lowest status, for two reasons:

First, it should be noted that the Kazakhs lacked the enthusiasm shown by the Uyghurs, Uzbeks and Tatars for the East Turkestan Independence Movement. Historically, the Altay and Ili districts had been separate administrative areas. Ghulja, the heart of Ili District, had never before served as the administrative center for Altay District.[28] The Uyghur people primarily resided in Ili District, while the Kazakhs were clustered in the Altay and Tarbagatay districts. Prior to the revolution, the Kazakhs had not embraced the concept of East Turkestan. The First East Turkestan Independence Movement of the 1930s had been a movement by and for the Uyghur peoples of Xinjiang. Altay District, the northern region of Xinjiang primarily populated by Kazakhs, was not included in the conceptual scope of "East Turkestan" until the republic's founding during the Second East Turkestan Independence Movement. In reality, despite merging forces with the East Turkestan Republic, the Kazakh nomads of Altay District did not establish any formal administrative ties with the republican government in Ili District.[29]

However, the most important reason for the lack of ties between the two sides was the ethnic bias harbored by Uyghurs, Uzbeks and Tatars against the Kazakh people. Since the Uyghur, Uzbek and Tatar peoples were economically focused on oasis agriculture and trade, they were ethnically and culturally quite similar.[30] However, the Kazakh people traditionally relied on nomadic pasturing, and the majority of their population were nomadic herders. Thus, although these groups all identified as Turkic-Islamic peoples, there was in fact a wide cultural gap between the Kazakhs and the Uyghurs, Uzbeks and Tatars. The latter three groups often deliberately sought to differentiate themselves both culturally and economically from the Kazakhs, who observed completely different cultural customs, and were organized under a different social structure.[31] This bias was reflected in the administration of the East Turkestan Republic.

"Resolution No. 262 of the Interim Government Council of the East Turkestan Republic" declares sternly: "(1) The Planning Department of the Ministry of Finance has approved the budget of 321,360 *tangga* formulated by Altay District; (2) The respective offices of Altay District shall conduct strict reviews with regard to the above sum, at all levels. For spending amounts and expenditures approved by this Ministry, payment processing for all expenses shall be promptly completed by the head of the organization and the officer in charge of accounting at the district's National Bank; (3) Unlawful squandering of state capital and assets (referring to expenditures by personnel exceeding the budgetary amounts approved by the government) shall be strictly handled in accordance with the law." The budget referred to in this passage is the 1946 budget. The Altay District had previously been ordered to issue "Victory Bonds" valued at 50 million *tangga* under "Resolution No. 85 of the Interim Government Council of the East Turkestan Republic," dated August 22, 1945; the contrast between this sum and the meager 1946 budget for Altay District authorized by the East Turkestan Republic reveals the Interim Government's economic exploitation of the Kazakh nomads.

Letif Mustafa, the head of the Altay District Bureau of Finance, was in Ghulja at the point when Resolution No. 262 was released. He may in fact have been responsible for transporting the cash allocated to Altay in the 1946 budget back to his district. However, it should be noted that Mustafa's visit to Ghulja may have been a critical factor in East Turkestan's imminent schism with the Kazakh people of Altay District. Not long after his return to Chenghua in May, Mustafa sought refuge at Osman Islam's encampment; soon thereafter, Osman began independently levying taxes in

Qinggil County, Koktokay County and Burultokay County. By right, this tax revenue belonged to the East Turkestan Republic, yet opposition against the Interim Government in Ghulja emerged from within the Altay District Government at Chenghua. The political wrangling over Altay tax revenue reflects the fierce resentment harbored by the region's Kazakh residents against the extortionary fiscal policies of the East Turkestan Interim Government.[32]

10.4 Economy of the East Turkestan Republic

Based on the 1946 national budget, we can see that the East Turkestan Republic's greatest source of revenue was trade with the Soviet Union (Table 10.3). As discussed above, shipments of oil from the Maytagh oil fields in repayment for Soviet military aid represented the principal line item in the budget, but the income from this trading arrangement appeared only on paper, and did not involve any actual revenue. Although the East Turkestan Republic also exported domestic livestock and other products to the Soviet Union,[33] given the self-serving nature of the Soviet Union's involvement in East Turkestan, it is unlikely that the republic profited much by the exchange.[34] Lacking modern industry and saddled with immense military expenditures, the East Turkestan Republic turned to confiscation of Han property, imposition of heavy taxes, issuance of deficit bonds and paper currency, collection of donations, and levies for unpaid, forced labor as its only options to sustain its financial income.

The expropriation of property belonging to the old regime and the region's Han Chinese inhabitants primarily occurred during the early stages of the revolution.[35] "Resolution No. 9 of the Interim Government Council of the East Turkestan Republic," dated January 16, 1945, declared:

> (1) The military and bureaucratic institutions established by the Han government imposed tyranny upon the people: they relied on pillaging of the people's property and bribery to accrue wealth. The property of these bandits was assuredly not earned by their own blood and sweat, but rather through the industrious labor of the people of East Turkestan. The Interim Government of the East Turkestan Republic shall resolutely confiscate these ill-gotten gains and place them in the national treasuries; (2) In the Ili region, although it has already been two months since the old regime

Table 10.3 Revenue Items in the 1946 Budget of the East Turkestan Republic
(Unit: one thousand *tangga*)

Item	Amount
Income from foreign trade	736,957
Pasturing Tax	545,000
Commercial Tax	402,517
Land Tax	146,170
Tobacco Tax	14,694
Stamp Tax	2,000
Livestock Slaughter Tax	4,968
Taxes turned over by Tarbagatay District	424,228
Revenue from the Ministry of Education	73,980
Revenue from the Ministry of Religious Affairs	64,359
Income from donations	50,000
Oil field revenue	45,000
Revenue from the National Bank	25,000
Revenue from the Ministry of Agriculture	8,875
Revenue from the Newspaper Office	8,561
Revenue from the Ministry of Health	7,432
Revenue from the Supreme Court	5,575
Revenue from the Postal Service	5,000
Revenue from Printing Factories	4,709
Revenue from the transportation industry	4,244
Fines	3,643
Revenue from pharmacies	3,000
Total Revenue	2,585,912
Total Expenditures	2,780,388
Deficit	194,476

Source: Compiled by the author on the basis of "Government Resolution No. 241 of the Interim Government Council of the East Turkestan Republic," dated March 14, 1946.

was overthrown and the government of the people's republic was founded, the reactionary partisans who supported the Han government continue to disregard the communications and announcements of the new government, and persist in taking up arms to oppose the new government of the people, in an attempt to restore the old regime. The government has determined that the property of these individuals shall be confiscated and expropriated, without exception; (3) In order to quickly implement the above two resolutions, the Ministry of Finance is instructed to take responsibility for their enforcement; (4) With regard to all property belonging to owners who committed suicide or died during the revolution or which, being ownerless, has reverted to the state, aside from one part which shall be given to their offspring as living expenses, and one part which shall be transferred to the Spoils of War Office by authorization of the Ministry of Finance, the remainder shall all be transferred to the government's fiscal revenue account.

However, income from the confiscation of property belonging to the old regime and the Han Chinese inhabitants was limited. We can see in the 1946 annual budget that tax revenue represented the principal income for that year. The tax rates set by the Interim Government of the East Turkestan Republic were also rather high. For instance, "Resolution No. 82 of the Interim Government Council of the East Turkestan Republic," dated August 19, 1945, set the land tax as 12% of the total harvest.[36] Resolution No. 210, dated January 22, 1946, declared that: "When collecting taxes left unpaid during the era of the Chinese regime, the Ministry of Finance, the Ministry of Land, Irrigation and Agriculture, and the county governments must submit a list of persons in truly straitened economic circumstances to the central government" (Chapter 8, Article 3). This passage indicates that the Interim Government of the East Turkestan Republic even sought to collect back taxes accrued prior to the revolution against the old regime, though some consideration was given to those in distressed circumstances. Resolution No. 197, dated January 12, 1946, stipulated that the general commercial tax was to be 2% of total circulating capital in each three-month period; if goods were resold in another district, an additional 2% tax would be levied on total circulating capital; the international trade duty was 7.5% of the cost of goods, while the livestock sales tax was 6% of cost, and the land sales tax was 10% of cost; these taxes far exceeded the 2.5% tax on annual income described in Islamic law.

The Interim Government of the East Turkestan Republic also adopted other measures to raise funds from the general population. For instance, exorbitant registration fees were collected on all means of conveyance, from horses to automobiles, "for the purpose of administration of transportation."[37] "Revenue stamps" (which doubled as postage stamps) were issued in July 1945.[38] In addition, state-owned land and lands where the landowner was not present were leased for cultivation by farmers, subject to land rent amounting to as much as two thirds of the harvest.[39]

After the founding of the Interim Government of the East Turkestan Republic, the circulation of paper currency issued by Xinjiang Commercial Bank—referred to as "provincial bank notes"—was still permitted for some time. In response to sharp inflation of commodity prices in Xinjiang Province in July 1945, the Interim Government decided to endorse the provincial bank notes with the seal of the Bank of the East Turkestan Republic.[40] While circulating the stamped provincial bank notes, between January 1945 and late May 1946, the Ministry of Finance of the East Turkestan Republic simultaneously issued "National Bank Bonds of the Ministry of Finance of the East Turkestan Republic" valued at 320.2 million *tangga*. As of late May 1946, the Tarbagatay District Bank had also issued "Tarbagatay Bank Bonds" valued at 5 million *tangga*, and the Altay Commission for the Issuance of Paper Currency had issued an unknown quantity of "Altay Bank Bonds." "Resolution No. 83 of the Interim Government Council of the East Turkestan Republic," dated August 20, 1945, announced the issuance of paper currency in the amount of 100 million *tangga* to remedy a shortfall in meeting military expenditures. It is clear that the East Turkestan Republic's issuance of paper currency was not based on market demand for money, but merely served as a means for the government to foist its fiscal deficit upon the general population.[41]

Paper currency issued in the East Turkestan Republic

Other such measures included the issuance of deficit bonds and private borrowing. The government of the East Turkestan Republic successively issued 200 million *tangga* in no-interest treasury bonds and 300 million *tangga* in interest-bearing treasury bonds, for a total sum of 500 million *tangga*.[42] A Treasury Bond Issuance Committee presided over by President Ilhan Tora was created for each issuance of treasury bonds,[43] and the Ministry of Internal Affairs was called upon to render assistance.[44] In practice, the involvement of the Ministry of Internal Affairs, which controlled the police and the judiciary, resulted in the compulsory purchase of treasury bonds. These circumstances highlight the importance of treasury bonds to East Turkestan's economy.

The East Turkestan Republic also engaged in active fundraising efforts via the Ministry of Religious Affairs and the Ministry of Education. These efforts proceeded under the auspices of the *ushr* (one-tenth tax) and *zakat* (religious tithe), which were intended to support *jihad* and promote the development of ethnic cultural education.[45] Based on the amount of revenue collected by the Ministry of Religious Affairs and the Ministry of Education under the 1946 budget, private donations occupied an important place in the economy of the East Turkestan Republic. Resolution No. 71 of the Interim Government Council, dated July 26, 1945, stated that each county magistrate was required to aid in the collection of the *ushr* tax and other fundraising efforts (Article 5); Resolution No. 206, released on January 16, 1946, also announced the establishment of the "Committee for the Promotion of Donations."

The general population was also frequently asked to provide unpaid labor in the name of the "fatherland." Cobblers and tailors across East Turkestan were drafted in several mobilization campaigns to create military uniforms for the army.[46] Resolution No. 118 of the Interim Government Council, dated October 27, 1945, ordered that: "Tailors and cobblers throughout East Turkestan shall be mobilized to active duty in the army within one month; their assignments are to be determined by the Army Logistics Department. Those who complete their assignments may be released in advance to return home; individuals who do not comply with mobilization shall be regarded as enemies of the Fatherland, and shall be dealt with in accordance with military law."

Resolution No. 142 of the Interim Government Council, dated

December 2, 1945, stated that: "The nation's finances are currently in extremely straitened circumstances, thus the Ministry of Finance has established the 'Committee for the Recovery of Loans,' to recall in full all funds loaned to the general population." Similar orders for the return of lending funds were repeated on several occasions in the council resolutions.[47] East Turkestan residents were also compelled to repay all loans borrowed from the banks during the era of the previous government.[48] It is clear that the Interim Government of the East Turkestan Republic resorted to practically any means to increase its fiscal revenue.

The Interim Government of the East Turkestan Republic strictly monitored all fiscal spending,[49] and even prevailed upon government employees to engage in agricultural production.[50] Despite these efforts, the Interim Government's financial situation remained dire: it entirely lacked the wherewithal to provide public services, while the ration system put in place for military families was on the brink of collapse;[51] the government even had difficulty paying the salaries of the state's civil servants.[52]

The worsening economic situation in the East Turkestan Republic became increasingly conspicuous as time went by. Resolution No. 19 of the Interim Government Council, dated February 3, 1945, set the monthly salary for low-ranking military officers at 500 *tangga*; however, according to the wage schedule described in Resolution No. 185, dated January 5, 1946, first month's wages for even an ordinary factory worker had climbed to 3,500 *tangga*, indicating an inflation rate of at least 700% in a one-year period.

The "Report on Revenue and Expenditure in the Three Districts of the East Turkestan Republic as of June 1, 1946" prepared by the Ministry of Finance revealed that: "The government has 337,039,083 *tangga* in capital, 16,080,000 *tangga* in loans, and 477,000,000 *tangga* in treasury bond debt. At this time, the East Turkestan Republic completely lacks any surplus capital. There is also no possibility of accumulating assets within two years' time. As of June 1, the amount in the ledgers is entirely borrowed from the citizenry." It is clear that, at the point when the peace agreement with the Chinese Nationalist government was signed, the financial administration of the East Turkestan Republic was in fact on the verge of bankruptcy.

10.5 The Historical Significance of the East Turkestan Republic

On July 1, 1946, Ahmatjan Kasimi, Abdulkerim Abbasow, Saypidin Azizi and the Kyrgyz leader Isakbek Munonow arrived in Urumqi to accept positions in the Xinjiang Province Coalition Government as Deputy Governor, Deputy Secretary-General, Commissioner of Education, and Deputy Commander of the Xinjiang Police, respectively; other Uyghur intellectuals also assumed positions in the Coalition Government. The National Army of East Turkestan was reformed as part of the Xinjiang provincial forces, retaining 13,500 soldiers. However, on May 19, 1947, Zhang Zhizhong resigned as governor of Xinjiang Province, nominating as his successor the pro-Chinese Uyghur intellectual Masud Sabri. Ahmatjan Kasimi and other representatives of the Ili, Tarbagatay and Altay districts who opposed Sabri's succession as provincial governor left Urumqi in August 1947 and returned to Ghulja to form their own political organization known as the "Three Districts Economic Commission," which sought to autonomously govern the Three Districts region; this marked the collapse of the Xinjiang Province Coalition Government.

On August 14, 1949, Deng Liqun, secretary to the Chinese Communist Party delegation then visiting Moscow, traveled to Ghulja with the aid of the Soviet Union to meet with Ahmatjan Kasimi as a CCP liaison, and establish the "Liqun Radio Station" to enable daily contact with the CCP Central Committee. On August 25, Ahmatjan Kasimi, Abdulkerim Abbasow, Isakbek Munonow, Dalalkan Sugurbayow and other Uyghur, Kyrgyz and Kazakh leaders of the Three Districts boarded a Soviet plane bound for Beijing to attend a "New Political Consultative Conference" convened by the Chinese Communist Party. However, the plane crashed in Soviet territory, resulting in the death of all its passengers (a thought-provoking turn of events). Saypidin Azizi, who had been elected as a representative in the new Communist government of China, arrived in Beijing on September 15 and expressed his fealty to the Chinese Communist Party leaders. The People's Liberation Army advanced into Xinjiang soon thereafter, reaching the Three Districts region in December 1949: the staging grounds of the Second East Turkestan Independence Movement were thus absorbed into the People's Republic of China.

Saypidin Azizi presents a gift to Mao Zedong while attending the 1ˢᵗ National Political Consultative Conference of the People's Republic of China

Back row, from left: Ahmatjan Kasimi, Abdulkerim Abbasow
Front row, from left: Isakbek Munonow, Saypidin Azizi

The short-lived nature of the Islamic Republic of East Turkestan, which was founded on November 12, 1933, and lasted for only 85 days, meant that it did not have time to formulate any concrete cultural, educational, social or economic policies, or establish a set power structure or political system; it also lacked a true military, police force, and other apparatuses of state power, and failed to establish a clear ruling relationship between its leaders and its citizens. Thus, in terms of its political structure, the "Islamic Republic of East Turkestan" failed to meet the standards of a modern "nation-state."

However, the East Turkestan Republic, founded in 1944, was possessed of a powerful military and police force, relatively organized legal and administrative systems, and systematic educational, cultural, social and economic policies; the republic also exercised effective administrative control over its sovereign territories, performing the functions of a state power in several regions. Had it not emerged during such a precarious

Report on the tragedy that befell Ahmatjan Kasimi and his fellow travelers

period in the final stages of the Second World War, the East Turkestan Republic could very well have followed in Mongolia's footsteps to win its independence from China.

There is no question that the two East Turkestan independence movements that emerged in the 1930s and 1940s left an important mark on the history of the Xinjiang region, and even on the history of China as a whole. The Second East Turkestan Independence Movement, which gave rise to the East Turkestan Republic, represents the region's largest independence movement in the period from the 1930s to the present, with the longest duration and the most participation by the local Turkic-Islamic ethnic groups. The participants in the First East Turkestan Independence Movement of the 1930s were limited to the Uyghurs and a small Kyrgyz minority, but the Second East Turkestan Independence Movement mobilized all the Turkic-Islamic peoples of Xinjiang, drawing in the Uyghurs as well as the Kazakhs, Uzbeks, Tatars and Kyrgyz.

Of course, one important factor allowing the movement to achieve this unprecedented pan-ethnic mobilization was the support of the Soviet Union. Nevertheless, it should be acknowledged that Soviet support could not have been the only reason why the Second East Turkestan Independence Movement was able to unite so many of the region's Turkic-Islamic inhabitants under its banner. The movement's appeal to the idea of Islamic *jihad* against *kafir* ("non-believers") was in fact the essential factor that bound together Xinjiang's disparate peoples. The cohesiveness, vitality and drive of this religiously motivated national movement not only threatened China's national unity, but also tested the Chinese civilization and the inclusiveness of the Chinese state. In modern Chinese politics, effacing the impact of the East Turkestan independence movement has become a touchstone for political success.

Ethnic conflict in Xinjiang did not wholly disappear after the region was incorporated into the People's Republic of China. The region was witness to the "Mijit Rebellion" of 1972 in Kashgar; the "Uqkun Partiyer [Prairie Fire Party] Incident" of 1981 in Jiashi (Peyziwat) County; the "October 30 Incident" in Kashgar in 1981;[53] and the "Baren Riot" of 1990 in Akto County. Notably, the instigators of these events all voiced slogans calling for East Turkestan independence and Islamic *jihad*. Such unrest represents a challenge not only to the Chinese government's policies on Xinjiang, but also to its ethnic, religious and diplomatic policies, as well as its strategies for national economic development.

The East Turkestan independence movement in fact served as a point of reference as China sought to formulate its basic policy on ethnic matters: the "system of regional national autonomy." The Ili Kazakh Autonomous Prefecture, established in 1954, encompasses the Ili, Tarbagatay and Altay districts, coinciding with the territories of the former East Turkestan Republic; it is China's only autonomous ethnic prefecture with jurisdiction over three separate districts. The Xinjiang Uyghur Autonomous Region, established in 1955, was also the first provincial-level autonomous region formed after the founding of the People's Republic of China in 1949.

The Xinjiang Uyghur Autonomous Region was deliberately organized in counterpoint to the East Turkestan independence movement. Premier Zhou Enlai made the following comments on the formation of the Xinjiang Uyghur Autonomous Region in 1957: "Prior to liberation, some reactionaries engaged in divisive activities revolving around East Turkestan; this was exploited by the imperialists. For this reason, when the Xinjiang Uyghur Autonomous Region was established, we did not approve the use of the name Uyghurstan. . . . The party and the government ultimately decided to establish the Xinjiang Uyghur Autonomous Region, and the comrades in Xinjiang agreed. . . . The issue of the name may seem trivial, but it was very important to the issue of regional national autonomy in China; this also carries a sense of ethnic cooperation."[54] The Xinjiang Uyghur Autonomous Region later became a model for the resolution of ethnic matters in China, arguably because it assuaged calls for "independence" by offering "autonomy," thus warding off the looming crisis of territorial disintegration.

After the Cultural Revolution ended, easing the tensions stirred by a series of political campaigns, the East Turkestan independence movement resurfaced. In the 1980s, Chinese officials banned the use of terms such as "East Turkestan," "Turkestan," and "Turkic peoples," in an effort to prevent the spread of such ideas. However, this list of banned phrases did not quash thoughts of independence.[55] The widespread, violent riots that broke out in Yining (Ghulja) in February 1997 and Urumqi in July 2009 have demonstrated that Uyghur communities still gravitate strongly toward the idea of independence for East Turkestan.[56]

Unlike the wars and social upheaval that roiled the Xinjiang region in previous centuries, the series of movements for East Turkestan independence in the 20th century were driven by Uyghur intellectuals exposed to a modern education or modern social influences, indicating that intellectuals' pursuit of the political right of self-determination has been an important factor perpetuating the ideas of the East Turkestan independence movement. The many incidents that have taken place in Xinjiang since the 1980s illustrate that some Uyghur intellectuals still embrace the independence movements of the past, particularly the glory of the Second East Turkestan Independence Movement, despite the lessons offered by these movements with regard to the thorniness of the path to national autonomy and independence, and the ease with which independence movements can be exploited as tools of international politics. In recent years, organizations of Uyghur intellectuals in exile have actively solicited support from the international community, gradually internationalizing the idea of "East Turkestan independence." This trend evokes the Second East Turkestan Independence Movement's historical reliance on, and ultimate abandonment by outside forces from the Soviet Union.

However, what China must consider is why many Uyghur intellectuals continue to dedicate their lives to the political ideal of independence, despite the painful history of the Uyghur people. The reason is in fact quite simple: through its policies toward the Uyghur minority, the Chinese government has consistently failed to give the general Uyghur population, and Uyghur elites in particular, the perception that they will receive equal treatment in the "People's Republic of China."

The Chinese government's policies on minority ethnic groups do guarantee ethnic equality, at least on paper. However, the power structure in the Xinjiang Uyghur Autonomous Region, under which the region's highest-ranking position of Communist Party Secretary is invariably filled by Han Chinese officials, exposes the lack of trust in the minority population and minority elites in particular, as well as their unequal status. The Chinese government has also undeniably made efforts to support the economic development of minority regions, but it must be noted that, under the status quo of effective inequality for minority ethnic groups, regional economic development has not signaled improvements in the economic wealth and status of the minority population. The so-called "Great Western Development Strategy" (*Xibu da kaifa* 西部大開發) has transformed minority regions into sources for raw materials under a capitalist production system, and the flow of Han Chinese people and capital from the interior provinces into Xinjiang has further widened the economic gap between minority groups and the Han population. These trifold inequalities—within the privileged ranks of the Chinese Communist Party, between ethnic groups, and with regard to economics and production relations—have naturally led to resentment and resistance among Uyghur intellectuals and the general Uyghur population, who seek equality, freedom and other political rights. In recent years, the Chinese government has imposed ever more stringent measures to control, repress and extinguish national consciousness by expunging ethnic culture. However, in the age of globalized information, even the tightest blockade on information or the most fearsome authoritarian rule cannot prevent the people from yearning for and pursuing equality, freedom, human rights, democracy, and other universal values. In laying to rest the upheaval in the west, it is therefore of primary importance that the Uyghur elite and the general Uyghur population are granted the sense that their human rights as well as their political rights of freedom and equality are truly guaranteed.

Postscript

This book is a revised and expanded version of the doctoral dissertation I submitted to the Graduate School of Arts and Sciences at the University of Tokyo for my degree in Area Studies. The original dissertation was published in December 1995 by the University of Tokyo Press under the title *A Study of the "East Turkestan Republic": Islam and Ethnic Conflict in China* (Higashi Torukisutan kyōwakoku kenkyū: Chūgoku no Isuramu to minzoku mondai); it was awarded Japan's 18th Suntory Prize for Social Sciences and Humanities in 1996, and its 3rd edition was published in 2009.

The East Turkestan independence movement is a weighty topic. I encountered many difficulties in collecting the materials, and the task of deciphering primary sources handwritten using several writing systems was daunting; more importantly, tackling this sensitive topic required its own type of courage. The reason why I selected this topic as the subject of my doctoral dissertation at the time was chiefly because I had lived in the Xinjiang Uyghur Autonomous Region for twelve years before enrolling at Minzu University of China in 1978. During my time there, I personally witnessed the complexity and gravity of ethnic tensions in Xinjiang: the ties between colleagues, party members, neighbors, and even members of the same religion (such as the Uyghurs and the Hui people) all crumbled against the barriers of "race." I learned from these personal experiences that the East Turkestan independence movement still simmers beneath the surface in China, and will one day return to haunt it. As I stated in the introduction to this book, "Faithfully reconstructing the true circumstances of the East Turkestan independence movement and, in particular, accurately understanding and evaluating the nature of the Second East Turkestan Independence Movement can help provide insights into the simmering ethnic tensions that have given rise to events such as the 2009 Urumqi riots, and could also have profound significance in the efforts to chart China's future as a multi-ethnic state."

When the Urumqi riots broke on July 5, 2009, I was in the office of Professor Yao Xinzhong at King's College London conducting a research interview. Coincidentally, the University of Tokyo Press had just confirmed the publication of the 3rd edition of my original dissertation, and before I left for London, Japan's Wedge Magazine had arranged for me to write a piece on ethnic tensions in Xinjiang for its opinion column. I was therefore able to sample the media response to the riots in several different countries just after they occurred. What concerned me was the lack of contextual knowledge: it seemed that many journalists and other authors were not only unaware of the connection between the events in Urumqi and the East Turkestan independence movement, but also scarcely aware of the movement's existence. This brought home to me the limitations of having published my study on the history of Xinjiang in Japanese. Fortunately, when I contacted Gan Qi, the director of The Chinese University Press, she immediately offered her support to publish a Chinese edition. Professor Yang Shu, the director of the Institute for Central Asian Studies at Lanzhou University, was able to provide an unofficial Chinese translation prepared by the institute, which served as the first draft for this book. I would like to express my heartfelt gratitude to Director Gan Qi and Professor Yang Shu. The manuscript was of course revised and expanded, and any errors in this book are my own.

At the suggestion of Mr. Xie Maosong, the sections in this book regarding the influence of pan-Turkism and pan-Islamism in early modern Uyghur society were supplemented and rewritten on the basis of a review of the latest research. I feel very deeply that it is necessary to elucidate the relationship between Islam and Uyghur society in order to understand how the East Turkestan independence movement unfolded so rapidly in the first half of the 20th century. While the violent protests by Uyghur communities against Chinese rule in that period at times exhibited the characteristics of a national resistance, they also exhibited strong overtones of

Islamism; ultimately, these two currents of necessity converged into one movement.

However, it should be noted that this phenomenon did not emerge out of nothing in the 20th century. In fact, it first surfaced in the mid-18th century as the Qing Dynasty extended its rule over Uyghur-inhabited regions, causing the Uyghur and Chinese societies to become intertwined. Chapter 1 of this work, "The '*Ummah*' and 'China': The Qing Dynasty's Rule over Uyghur Society in Xinjiang," was added to address this history. From the day the Qing Dynasty imposed its rule over the region, its inhabitants were placed under the power of a people they regarded as "heathens"; this is an important factor to be considered in evaluating the governing policies enacted by all the succeeding Chinese regimes. Through this chapter, we are able not only to examine the special policies formulated by the Qing Dynasty to address the relationship between Uyghur communities and Islam, but also to perceive the connections between the rise of ethnic conflict in early modern China and the structure of the pre-modern state.

I am deeply grateful to my mentor, Professor Yamauchi Masayuki of the Graduate School of Arts and Sciences at the University of Tokyo, who made it possible for this research to be published. Meeting Professor Yamauchi and receiving his guidance has been the greatest fortune in my life. On April 1, 1989, despite having never been enrolled previously at a Japanese university, I was admitted directly to the Master's program at the Graduate School of the University of Tokyo. At first my proficiency in Japanese was very low, and I was unfamiliar with the teaching system at Japanese universities; moreover, I was untrained in any kind of research methods. In addition, only a few days after I enrolled, a popular movement calling for democratization spread like wildfire across China, and on June 4, the student protesters were suppressed by the military; needless to say, I found it very difficult to focus on my studies. Yet Professor Yamauchi always encouraged me, and showed me through his actions that I would only be able to promote social progress by producing exceptional research. During the five years that I spent in the Master's and PhD programs at the University of Tokyo, Professor Yamauchi helped me to gain a profound understanding of the true essence of learning and the significance of scholarship through his all-embracing academic prowess, encompassing all things past and present, across all national borders. I was also fortunate to have benefited from the guidance of several other professors, including Namiki Yoritosi, Ishii Akira, and Takahashi Mitsuru, particularly Professor Ishii, who applied for funding without my knowledge to have my doctoral dissertation published by the University of Tokyo Press, for which I am sincerely grateful today.

I am also eternally indebted to my mentor Professor Wang Fuhan, whom I met in 1978 when I was admitted to Minzu University of China. Professor Wang knew ancient Chinese literature, history and philosophy like the palm of his hand, and he could recite from memory everything from the Four Books and the Five Classics to Tang and Song poetry; he had earned the veneration of countless students, yet he treated me as if I were his own child. This August it will have been 12 years since he passed away, but I still meet him in my dreams, to listen to his lectures and his thoughtful attentions. I would also like to thank my mother for enduring the many years I spent apart from her while pursuing my studies, and my elder sister and two younger brothers for taking on the responsibility of caring for our mother in my stead. Among the many people who have supported me in my life and encouraged me to press ever forward, there is one whom I cannot fail to mention: my wife, Kadowaki Katsuyo. Every day when I return home from my labors, my wife is patiently waiting for me, and many of my ponderings stem from our evening discussions. I thank fate for bringing me to the doorstep of such a thoughtful and insightful woman.

The publication of this book in English was made possible thanks to Director Gan Qi and chief editors Lin Ying and Ye Minlei of The Chinese University Press, as well as my two editors, Brian Yu and Lin Xiao, who have supported me for many years; I would like to take this opportunity to thank them again, and also to thank Ms. Carissa Fletcher for her excellent translation. This book was sponsored by the Suntory Foundation under its Support for Overseas Publication program, and also supported by the Mitsubishi Foundation's Research Grants in the Humanities, on "A Study of Uyghur Diaspora in Democratic Countries." I would like to express my sincere gratitude here for their support.

Wang Ke
2017

Timeline of Important Events

Year	Month	Event
1931	March	The "Kumul Rebellion" is launched by the Uyghur inhabitants of the Kumul region in eastern Xinjiang.
1933	April	The "April 12 Coup" is staged in Urumqi (Dihua); Sheng Shicai becomes the Xinjiang Frontier Defense Commissioner (*Xinjiang bianfang duban* 新疆邊防督辦).
	May	Sheng Shicai reveals his Communist leanings to the Soviet consul-general in Urumqi.
	November	The "Islamic Republic of East Turkestan" is founded on November 12.
	December	The Soviet Red Army dispatches troops to Xinjiang. Ma Zhongying's forces retreat to southern Xinjiang.
1934	April	The Islamic Republic of East Turkestan collapses.
	Spring–Summer	Sheng Shicai consolidates his rule with Soviet support, gradually forming a dual power structure within the regime.
1937	Summer	Sheng Shicai carries out his First Great Purge, eliminating Soviet agents and local ethnic political leaders.
1940		Sheng Shicai carries out his Second Great Purge, targeting local ethnic leaders, Soviet agents, and Chinese Communist Party forces.
1942	August	Sheng Shicai pivots toward the Chinese Nationalist government, and seeks to drive Soviet and Chinese Communist Party forces out of the Xinjiang government.
1943		Pro-Soviet Uyghur intellectuals found an underground organization in Ghulja (Yining).
	December	The "Altay Kazakh National Restoration Committee" is established.

286 | Timeline of Important Events

Year	Month	Event
1944	April	The "National Freedom Group" is founded in Ghulja on April 9.
	June	The "Imir Command Post" is established in Soviet territory. Dalalkan Sugurbayow arrives in Altay District, accompanied by Soviet and Mongolian advisors, and joins forces with the armed Kazakh rebel organization led by Osman Islam.
	July	On July 8, the Jiminay rebel faction is established in Altay District. On July 10, the Imir Command Post orders the rebel nationalist forces in Tarbagatay District to form an alliance.
	August	On August 11, Sheng Shicai arrests the representatives of the Chinese Nationalist government in the "August Coup." On August 14, a rebel guerrilla force is formed by the Turkic-Islamic inhabitants of Nilka County in Ili District. The National Freedom Group in Ghulja temporarily suspends its activities. On August 29, the Nationalist government announces that Sheng Shicai has been removed from his position, and Wu Zhongxin is appointed governor of Xinjiang.
	September	On September 11, Sheng Shicai departs from Xinjiang.
	October	On October 4, Wu Zhongxin becomes governor of Xinjiang Province. On October 6, Wu Zhongxin releases several hundred political prisoners arrested during Sheng Shicai's purges. On October 7, the Nilka rebel guerrillas capture Nilka County Town. In late October, the "Altay Revolutionary Interim Government" is founded and merges with the armed rebel forces in Jiminay.
	November	The Ghulja National Freedom Group resumes operations. On November 7, the "Ghulja Uprising" erupts. On November 12, the "Interim Government of the East Turkestan Republic" is founded, and the first version of the "Nine Political Precepts" is issued. On November 15, Zhu Shaoliang, commander of China's 8th Military District, decides to send the first wave of reinforcements to Ghulja. On November 16, Ivan Polinov and the Nilka guerrillas arrive at Ghulja leading forces from the Soviet Union. Soviet advisors are installed within each rebel organization and each department of the East Turkestan government.

Year	Month	Event
1944	November–December	The forces of the East Turkestan Republic capture most of Ili District.
	December	On December 5, the Soviet Consulate in Urumqi (Dihua) denies that the Soviet Union had any involvement in the "Ghulja Uprising." The first wave of reinforcements from the Chinese Nationalist army is defeated in battle at Ghulja.
1945	January	On January 4, the Interim Government of the East Turkestan Republic issues the second version of the "Nine Political Precepts." On January 7, the Interim Government establishes the Ministry of Military Affairs. On January 9, the Chinese Nationalist army sends its second wave of reinforcements. On January 19, the second wave of reinforcements is defeated on the battlefield. Between January 28–30, the Chinese Nationalist garrison at Ghulja is annihilated. The "Bank Notes of the Ministry of Finance of the East Turkestan Republic" are issued.
	February	On February 3, the "Military Service Law" is instituted under "Resolution No. 19 of the Interim Government Council of the East Turkestan Republic." The forces of the Altay Revolutionary Interim Government capture Jiminay County Town.
	March	On March 13, East Turkestan's military and government personnel are reorganized under "Resolution No. 33 of the Interim Government Council of the East Turkestan Republic."
	April	On April 8, the Interim Government of the East Turkestan Republic forms the National Army, with forces totaling 15,000 soldiers. On April 13, Chiang Ching-kuo (son of Chiang Kai-shek) arrives in Urumqi as Chiang Kai-shek's representative, to speak with the Soviet Consul General at Urumqi. The Chinese Nationalist army reorganizes its defensive line, concentrating its forces at Usu and Jinghe.
	May	On May 13, the Interim Government of the East Turkestan Republic issues its *Provisional Regulations on Criminal Procedure*.

Year	Month	Event
1945	June	The forces of the Altay Revolutionary Interim Government capture Qinggil, Koktokay, and Jiminay counties. On June 30, the Chinese and Soviet governments begin talks at Moscow.
	July	On July 5, the Imir Command Post requests that the East Turkestan National Army launch an attack on Tarbagatay District. The National Army begins a "Three-Front War," capturing Tarbagatay on the Northern Front.
	August–September	The East Turkestan National Army captures Bay Town and Aksu Old Town in southern Xinjiang.
	August	On August 14, the "Sino-Soviet Treaty of Friendship" is signed.
	September	On September 2–7, the forces of the Altay Revolutionary Interim Government join up with the National Army detachment in Altay to capture Chenghua County Town. On September 4–8, the National Army captures Jinghe under the command of Ivan Polinov. On September 5–8, National Army forces led by Deputy Commander Isakbek Munonow capture Usu. In early September, the East Turkestan National Army and Chinese Nationalist army settle into a stalemate on opposite banks of the Manas River. On September 14, Zhang Zhizhong speaks with the Soviet Consul General in Urumqi and requests that the Soviet Union intervene. On September 17, the Soviet ambassador to China delivers a message to the Chinese Nationalist government from the "Representatives of the Peoples of Xinjiang," who also request Soviet intervention.
	October	On October 2, under "Resolution No. 100 of the Interim Government Council of the East Turkestan Republic," East Turkestan decides to join in the Peace Talks. On October 17, the "Representatives of the Peoples of Xinjiang" enter into negotiations with Zhang Zhizhong at Urumqi.
	December	On December 5, the "East Turkestan Revolutionary Youth League" is founded.

Year	Month	Event
1946	January	On January 2, the "Eleven Articles of Peace" and the First Addendum are signed.
	March	On March 19, Altay District Commissioner Osman Islam decamps from Chenghua County Town. On March 29, Zhang Zhizhong is appointed as Commander of the Northwest Field Headquarters and governor of the Xinjiang provincial government.
	April	On April 5, the Peace Talks enter their second stage. On April 26, the "East Turkestan Revolutionary Party" is founded.
	May	The Kazakh tribes of Altay District gather for a rally at Quw Oy; Osman Islam and Dalalkan Sugurbayow mount a resistance against the operations of a Soviet tungsten mining team in Altay. On May 22, the Draft Second Addendum to the "Eleven Articles of Peace" is signed.
	June	On June 6, the Second Addendum to the "Eleven Articles of Peace" is formally signed. Ilhan Tora is sent under escort to the Soviet Union. On June 18, the Chinese Nationalist government announces personnel appointments for the Coalition Government of Xinjiang Province. On June 27, the East Turkestan Republic is dissolved under "Resolution No. 324 of the Interim Government Council of the East Turkestan Republic."
	July	On July 1, the Coalition Government of Xinjiang Province is founded. Ahmatjan Kasimi is appointed as Deputy Governor, and Abdulkerim Abbasow is appointed as Deputy Secretary-General.
	November–December	Ahmatjan Kasimi presents a "Proposal for the Autonomy of East Turkestan" at the National Congress of the Chinese Nationalist government. Abdulkerim Abbasow secretly engages in talks with representatives of the Chinese Communist Party.
1947	May	On May 19, Zhang Zhizhong resigns as governor of the Xinjiang Coalition Government, and nominates the pro-Chinese Uyghur Masud Sabri as his successor.
	August	The Three Districts ("East Turkestan") representatives in the Xinjiang Coalition Government all return to Ghulja.

Year	Month	Event
1949	August	On August 14, Chinese Communist Party representative Deng Liqun returns to Ghulja from Moscow. On August 25, Ahmatjan Kasimi, Abdulkerim Abbasow, Isakbek Munonow, Dalalkan Sugurbayow and other Uyghur, Kazakh and Kyrgyz leaders of the "Three Districts" are all killed while en route to Beijing aboard a Soviet plane.
	September	On September 15, Saypidin Azizi arrives in Beijing and expresses his fealty to the leaders of the Chinese Communist Party.
	December	The Chinese People's Liberation Army is stationed in Ghulja.

NOTES

Introduction

1. Xu Yuqi (ed.), *Xinjiang san qu geming shi* (History of the Three Districts Revolution in Xinjiang) (Beijing: Minzu chubanshe, 1998).
2. The Uyghur author Turgun Almas was said to have written three works between 1986 and October 1989, including *The Uyghur People* (Uygurlar), *Ancient Uyghur Literary History*, and *History of the Huns*. Almas' works were banned in China after their publication, and he was rumored to have been placed under house arrest. For information on the content of his works, this book primarily referred to: Emet Molla Turdi, "'Weiwu'er ren' deng san ben shu de zhuyao wenti jiqi sixiang genyuan" (Key issues in *Uygurlar* and the two other works and their intellectual roots), Xinjiang Academy of Social Sciences, *Xiyu yanjiu* (Studies of the Western Regions), 1991 special edition, *Weihu zuguo tongyi, fandui minzu fenlie* (Defending national unity, opposing ethnonational disintegration), pp. 23–26; Awut Tohti, "Weiwu'er ze shi Zhonghua minzu de yige chengyuan" (The Uyghurs are members of the Chinese race), ibid., pp. 15–22.
3. Nakada Yoshinobu, "Inei jihen to Shinkyō no minzoku undō" (The I-Ning Affair and the national movement in Sinkiang) [伊寧事変と新疆の民族運動], Tōyō gakuhō (Journal of the Research Department of the Toyo Bunko) [東洋学報].
4. Wang Dagang, "20 shiji yilai zhongwai xuezhe dui xiandai Xinjiang zhi yanjiu" (Studies of modern Xinjiang by Chinese and foreign scholars since the 20th century), Institute of Modern History, Academia Sinica, *Jindai Zhongguo yanjiu tongxun* (Newsletter for Modern Chinese History), no. 13 (1992), p. 121.

Chapter 1

1. Miao Pusheng and Tian Weijiang (eds.), *Xinjiang shigang* (Historical survey of Xinjiang) (Urumqi: Xinjiang renmin chubanshe, 2004), p. 323.
2. Yasushi Shinmen [新免康], "Henkyo-teki min to Chūgoku" (The border peoples and China) [边境的民と中国], in *Ajia kara kangaeru* (Studies of Asia and China) [アジアから考える], vol. 3: *Shūen kara no rekishi* (History of the Chinese periphery) [周縁からの歴史] (Tokyo: University of Tokyo Press, 1994), p. 104.
3. Song Yun, *Qinding Xinjiang shilüe* (Imperial survey of knowledge on the new borderland), vols. 3 and 12 (Shanghai: Shanghai Jishan shuju, lithographic edition, orig. published in 1894; Taipei: Wenhai Press, 1966).
4. Although this region is now known in some quarters as East Turkestan, between the 18th century and the early 20th century, this term was not in fact used by any Uyghur person or Qing official to refer to that region.
5. [Qing] Fuheng et al., *Qinding pingding Zhunga'er fanglüe* (Imperial military annals of the pacification of the Dzungars), original work, vol. 10 (Taipei: Taiwan Commercial Press, orig. published in 1772).
6. Ibid., original work, vol. 14.
7. *Da Qing Gaozong Chun (Qianlong) huangdi shilu* (Veritable Records of the Great Qing Emperor Gaozong Chun [Qianlong]), vol. 555 (Taipei: Hualian Publishing House, 1964); Song Yun, *Qinding Xinjiang shilüe*, vol. 1.
8. Yuan Dahua (auth.), Wang Shunan and Wang Xuezeng (eds.), *Xinjiang tuzhi* (Atlas of Xinjiang), vol. 10, Imperial Chapter 1 (Shanghai: Shanghai guji chubanshe, orig. published 1911, 1992 edition).
9. Fuheng et al., *Qinding pingding Zhunga'er fanglüe*, vols. 39, 44.
10. *Da Qing Shizong Xian (Yongzheng) huangdi shilu* (Veritable Records of the Great Qing Emperor Shizong Xian [Yongzheng]), vol. 96 (Taipei: Hualian Publishing House, 1964).
11. Kazutada Kataoka [片岡一忠], *Shinchō Shinkyō tōchi kenkyū* (Study of the Qing Dynasty's administration of Xinjiang) [清朝新疆統治研究] (Tokyo: Yūzankaku, 1991), p. 65.
12. *Da Qing Gaozong Chun (Qianlong) huangdi shilu*, vol. 666.
13. Chinese Border History and Geography Research Center of the Chinese Academy of Sciences (ed.), *Qinding Huijiang zeli* (Imperial code of the Muslim borderland), vol. 5, in *Zhongguo bianjiang shidi ziliao congkan* (Collected materials on Chinese border history and geography), comprehensive edition (Beijing: China National Microfilming Center for Library Resources, published in 1988).
14. Chinese Border History and Geography Research Center of the Chinese Academy of Sciences (ed.), *Qianlong chao Lifanyuan zeli* (Code of the Board for the Administration of Outlying Regions in the Qianlong Reign), Qing Border Reception Bureau, in *Zhongguo bianjiang shidi ziliao congkan*, 1988.
15. Chinese Border History and Geography Research Center of the Chinese Academy

of Sciences (ed.), *Qinding Huijiang zeli*, vols. 1 and 2.
16 Song Yun, *Qinding Xinjiang shilüe*, vol. 8.
17 Tōru Saguchi [佐口透], "Shinkyouiguru shakai no nogyo mondai, 1760–1820" (Agricultural problems in Xinjiang Uyghur society, 1760–1820) [新疆ウイグル社会の農業問題], *Shigaku zasshi* (Journal of Historical Science) [史学雑誌], vol. 59, no. 12 (1959), pp. 28–29.
18 Tong Yufen, *Zhongguo Xinjiang de renkou yu huanjing* (The population and environment of Xinjiang, China) (Beijing: Shijie zhishi chubanshe, 2006), p. 84.
19 Lin Enxian, *Qingchao zai Xinjiang de Han Hui geli zhengce* (The Qing Dynasty's policy of Han-Muslim segregation in Xinjiang) (Taipei: Taiwan Commercial Press, 1988), p. 104.
20 Tōru Saguchi, "Shinkyouiguru shakai no nogyo mondai, 1760–1820," pp. 25–26.
21 Masami Hamada [濱田正美], "'Shio no gimu' to 'seisen' tono aida de" (Between the 'Duty of Salt' and 'Jihād') ["塩の義務"と"聖戦"との間で], *Tōyōshi Kenkyū* (Journal of Oriental Researches) [東洋史研究], vol. 52, no. 2 (1993), pp. 131–136.
22 Chinese Border History and Geography Research Center of the Chinese Academy of Sciences (ed.), *Qinding Huijiang zeli*, vol. 6: "It is prohibited for low-ranking officers and soldiers of the Green Banners in the relief garrisons and criminals deported as slaves to take a Muslim woman to wife without authorization."
23 Lin Enxian, *Qingchao zai Xinjiang de Han Hui geli zhengce*, p. 170.
24 *Da Qing Gaozong Chun (Qianlong) huangdi shilu*, vol. 746; Lin Enxian, *Qingchao zai Xinjiang de Han Hui geli zhengce*, p. 207.
25 Hua Li, *Qingdai Xinjiang nongye kaifa shi* (History of agricultural development in Xinjiang during the Qing Dynasty) (Harbin: Heilongjiang jiaoyu chubanshe, 1995), pp. 134, 164.
26 Lin Enxian, *Qingchao zai Xinjiang de Han Hui geli zhengce*, p. 221.
27 *Da Qing Gaozong Chun (Qianlong) huangdi shilu*, vols. 610, 612.
28 Lin Enxian, *Qingchao zai Xinjiang de Han Hui geli zhengce*, p. 150.
29 Song Yun, *Qinding Xinjiang shilüe*, vol. 8.
30 Su-er-de, *Huijiang zhi* (Treatise on the Muslim borderland), vol. 3 (written in the 37th Year of the Qianlong Reign [1772]).
31 Lin Enxian, *Qingchao zai Xinjiang de Han Hui geli zhengce*, p. 302.
32 Ibid., p. 228.
33 *Da Qing Gaozong Chun (Qianlong) huangdi shilu*, vol. 983.
34 The Qing Dynasty implemented a "fiefdom system" in southwestern China, which resembled the "beg system" in that the local elite were employed to govern over the ethnic communities. However, the regions in which the fiefdom system was instituted fell under the jurisdiction of the Ministry of Personnel and the Ministry of War, while the "Muslim borderland," where the beg system was implemented, fell under the jurisdiction of the Board for the Administration of Outlying Regions and the Ministry of War, giving the two systems completely different positions

within the national political framework.
35 *Da Qing Shengzu Ren (Kangxi) huangdi shilu* (Veritable Records of the Great Qing Emperor Shengzu Ren [Kangxi]), vol. 2 (Taipei: Hualian Publishing House, 1964). Zhao Yuntian, *Zhongguo bianjiang minzu guanli jigou yange shi* (Evolutionary history of the institutions for the administration of China's borderland ethnic groups) (Beijing: Zhongguo shehui kexue chubanshe, 1993), p. 301.
36 *Da Qing Gaozong Chun (Qianlong) huangdi shilu*, vol. 571.
37 Lin Enxian, *Qingchao zai Xinjiang de Han Hui geli zhengce*, pp. 71–85.
38 Song Yun, *Qinding Xinjiang shilüe*, vol. 3.
39 Ibid.; Chinese Border History and Geography Research Center of the Chinese Academy of Sciences (ed.), *Qinding Huijiang zeli*, vol. 8.
40 Zuo Zongtang, *Zuo Zongtang quanji* (Complete works of Zuo Zongtang), draft memorial, vol. 53 (Shanghai: Shanghai shudian, 1986).
41 John K. Fairbank and Kwang-Ching Liu (eds.), *The Cambridge History of China*, vol. 10: *Late Ch'ing 1800–1911*, Part I (Cambridge: Cambridge University Press, 1978), p. 366.
42 Ibid., p. 359.
43 Feng Jiasheng, Cheng Suluo, Mu Guangwen (eds.), *Nawenyi gong zouyi* (Memorials of Nawenyi) [Nayancheng], vol. 77, *Weiwu'erzu shiliao jianbian* (Selected materials on the Uyghurs), Part II (Beijing: Minzu chubanshe, 1981).
44 Hori Sunao, "Shinchō no Kaikyō tōchi ni tsuite no 2, 3 no mondai: Yārukando no ichi shiryō no kentō wo tsūjite" (Some problems on Ch'ing rule over Hui-chiang: Based on a document about Yarkand in the 19th century) [清朝的回疆統治について の二,三問題—ヤールカンドの一史料の検討を通じて], *Shigaku zasshi*, vol. 88, no. 3 (1979), pp. 16–18.
45 Fairbank and Liu, *Late Ch'ing*, p. 374.
46 Ethnic Research Institute of the Xinjiang Academy of Social Sciences (ed.), *Xinjiang jianshi* (A concise history of Xinjiang), Book 2 (Urumqi: Xinjiang renmin chubanshe, 1980), p. 110.
47 Li Sheng, *Zhongguo Xinjiang lishi yu xianzhuang* (The history and current conditions of Xinjiang, China) (Urumqi: Xinjiang renmin chubanshe, 2006), Japanese edition, p. 99.
48 Molla Musa Sayrami, *Tārīkh-i Khāmīdī* (History of Hāmīdī) (Beijing: Millatla Nasriyati, 1988), p. 362.
49 Ibid., pp. 497–503.
50 According to *Tārīkh-i Khāmīdī* and other Uyghur sources, in an effort to put down the rebellion, Yaqub Beg slaughtered 50,000 Uyghurs in Hotan, poisoned Katti Khan Törä and Kiçik Khan Törä of the White Mountaineers, and threw Wali Khan Khoja down a well and buried him alive.
51 Demetrius C. Boulger, *The Life of Yakoob Beg: Athalik Ghazi, and Badaulet; Ameer of Kashgar* (London: Wm. H. Allen and CO., 1878), pp. 212–232.
52 Guo Songtao, with selected annotations by Lu Yulin, *Shixi jicheng—Guo Songtao ji*

(Diary of a diplomatic mission to the West—Collected works by Guo Songtao) (Shenyang: Liaoning renmin chubanshe, 1994), p. 123.
53 Baoyun et al., *Choubian yiwu shimo* (Story of the debate on tribal affairs) (Tongzhi Reign), vol. 9 (photocopy of the Palace Museum manuscript, Taipei: Wenhai Press, 1971).
54 Zuo Zongtang, *Zuo Zongtang quanji*, draft memorial, vol. 46.
55 Yuan Dahua, Wang Shuya and Wang Xueceng (eds.), *Xinjiang tuzhi*, vol. 116. However, *Tārīkh-ī Khāmīdī* (Molla Musa Sayrami, pp. 490–491), cited above, and other Uyghur sources argue that Yaqub Beg was poisoned by the Uyghur Niyaz Beg.

Chapter 2

1 Demetrius C. Boulger, *The Life of Yakoob Beg, Athalik Ghazi, and Badaulet; Ameer of Kashgar* (London: Wm. H. Allen and CO., 1878), p. 1.
2 Molla Musa Sayrami, *Tārīkh-ī Khāmīdī* (History of Hāmīdī) (Beijing: Millatla Nasriyati, 1988), p. 47. This work primarily addresses Uyghur history in the era between the Kucha uprising of 1864 and the establishment of Xinjiang Province in 1884.
3 Zhao Ruisheng (trans.), "Beijing zhengfu shidai zhi Xinjiang yiyuan" (Xinjiang legislators in the era of the Beijing government), *Tianshan yuekan* (Tianshan Monthly), vol. 1, no. 3 (1934), pp. 33–37.
4 Shinmen Yasushi, "Shinkyo musurimu hanran (1931–34 nen) to himitsu soshiki" (The Xinjiang Muslim rebellion [1931–1934] and secret organizations) [新疆ムスリム反乱（1931–34 年）と秘密組織], *Shigaku zasshi* (Journal of Historical Science) [史学雑誌], vol. 99, no. 12 (1990), p. 12.
5 According to Miao Pusheng and Tian Weijiang (eds.), Xinjiang shigang (Historical survey of Xinjiang) (Urumqi: Xinjiang renmin chubanshe, 2004), pp. 420–421, the British diplomatic personnel stationed at the Kashgar Consulate attended the founding ceremony of the Islamic Republic of East Turkestan, and when J. W. Thomson-Glover assumed the post of British consul-general in Kashgar, he recommended that Britain offer its sympathy and aid to the fledgling republic.
6 Guo Weiping, "Nanjiang shijian yu diguo zhuyi qinlüe Xinjiang zhi fenxi" (Analysis of the southern Xinjiang incident and imperialist encroachment upon Xinjiang), *Xibei wenti yanjiuhui huikan* (Journal of the Society for Northwestern Affairs), vol. 1, no. 1 (1934), p. 51.
7 "Furthermore, Russian citizens shall be permitted to trade in Ili, Tarbagatay, Kashgar, Urumqi, and the cities of the Northern and Southern Circuits beyond the passes, duty free"—Article 12 of the Treaty of Ili, also known as the Chonghou Treaty (for the Qing diplomat in charge of negotiations) or the Treaty of Livadia, concluded on October 2, 1879. This article incited broad outrage within the government and amongst the public for ceding too much national sovereignty, and

Wanyan Chonghou was discharged and arrested. The Qing government sent Zeng Jize to negotiate revisions to the treaty: in the revised treaty, known as the Treaty of Saint Petersburg, concluded on February 24, 1881, the text was rephrased as, "provisionally duty free."

8   Shinmen Yasushi, "Shinkyo musurimu hanran (1931–34 nen) to himitsu soshiki," p. 12.

9   Ibrayim Niyaz, "Atux Nahiye Iksahkantida yekinkizaman panni muaripining dunyaga kilixi" (The birth of a modern school education in Iksak Township, Atush County), *Xinjiang Tarih Matiriyalliri* (Xinjiang Historical Materials), 13 (1984), p. 90.

10 On the establishment of Jadidist schools, see the following texts: Ibrayim Niyaz, "Atux Nahiye Iksahkantida yekinkizaman panni muaripining dunyaga kilixi," pp. 83–94; Ibrahim Mugit, "Marhum maripatparwar Mahsut Mukiyit togursida aslima" (Recollections of the late Enlightener Mahsut Mukiyit), *Xinjiang Tarih Matiriyalliri* 13 (1984), pp. 100–115; Xawkat Abdurihim, "Kaxkarda panni maktaplarning xakillinixi wa tarakkiyati tohursida" (On the origins and development of school education in Kashgar), *Xinjiang Tarih Matiriyalliri* 13 (1984), pp. 95–99. See also Tahir and Yang Renzhi, "Tacheng funü jiaoyu de xianqu" (Pioneers in women's education in Tacheng), *Yili wenshi ziliao* (Historical and cultural materials on Ili), vol. 4 (1988), pp. 142–144, for records on a Tatar figure who accepted a teaching position at a Jadidist school in the Turpan region in 1914; and Abdukadir Abdullah, "Qitai minzu jiaoyu jinxi tan" (Discussion of the past and present of minority education in Qitai), *Qitai wenshi ziliao* (Historical and cultural materials on Qitai), vol. 11 (1987), pp. 125–128, for records on a Tatar figure invited to teach at a Jadidist school in Guchung (Qitai) in 1916.

11 Ibrahim Mugit, "Marhum maripatparwar Mahsut Mukiyit togursida aslima," pp. 104–105.

12 Ibrayim Niyaz, "Atux Nahiye Iksahkantida yekinkizaman panni muaripining dunyaga kilixi," pp. 83–94. The Musabayow family of Atush were a rich and powerful clan renowned throughout Xinjiang. The above source also describes the later establishment of another school in Ili by the elder brother Husayn Musabayow. However, the local elementary school in Iksak celebrated its 100th anniversary in 1985, which is inconsistent with the putative founding year of 1883, indicating that the actual years in which the earlier Uyghur Jadidist schools were founded are indeterminate. On this point, see Ooishi Shin'ichiro, "Kashugaru ni okeru jadido undo—musabayofu-ka to shin hōshiki kyōiku" (The Kashgar Jadidist movement—the Musabayow family and new-style education) [カシュガルにおけるシャディード运动—ムーサー・バヨフ家と新方式教育], *Tōyō gakuhō* (Journal of the Research Department of the Toyo Bunko) [東洋学報], vol. 78, no. 1 (1996), p. 21.

13 Yamauchi Masayuki, *Surutan Gariefu no yume: Isuramu sekai to Roshia Kakumei* (Sultan Galiev's dream: the Islamic world and the Russian revolution) [スルタンガ

リエフの夢：イスラム世界とロシア革命] (Tokyo: University of Tokyo Press, 1986), p. 92.
14 Burhan Shahidi, "Fan Yisilan zhuyi he fan Tujue zhiyi zai Xinjiang de xingwang" (The rise and fall of pan-Islamism and pan-Turkism in Xinjiang), *Wenshi ziliao xuanji* (Selected cultural and historical materials), vol. 79 (1982), p. 110.
15 Ibrayim Niyaz, "Atux Nahiye Iksahkantida yekinkizaman panni muaripining dunyaga kilixi," p. 85.
16 Xawkat Abdurihim, "Kaxkarda panni maktaplarning xakillinixi wa tarakkiyati tohursida," pp. 95–99; Ooishi Shin'ichiro, "Kashugaru ni okeru jadido undo—musabayofu-ka to shin hōshiki kyōiku," p. 21.
17 Ooishi Shin'ichiro, "Kashugaru ni okeru jadido undo—musabayofu-ka to shin hōshiki kyōiku," p. 21.
18 Burhan Shahidi, "Fan Yisilan zhuyi he fan Tujue zhiyi zai Xinjiang de xingwang," p. 110. In the original text, the term "pan-Turkism" was written using the characters 土耳其 (*Tuerqi*, "Turkey") rather than 突厥 (*Tujue*, "Turks"), signifying a geographical reference to Turkey rather than to the Turkic peoples.
19 Tominaga Osamu, *Kaikyōto minzoku undō no shomondai* (Several issues related to Muslim national movements) (Tokyo: Institute for East Asian Studies, 1941), p. 51.
20 Yamauchi Masayuki, *Surutan Gariefu no yume: Isuramu sekai to Roshia Kakumei*, pp. 90–91.
21 Abdukadir Haji, "1933 yildin 1937 yilgiqa Kaxkar Hotan Aksularda bulup otkan wakalar" (Events in Kashgar, Hotan, and Aksu in the years 1933–1937), *Xinjiang Tarih Matiriyalliri* 17 (1986), p. 7.
22 Pan Zuhuan, "Jin Shuren dengtai he Hami shibian de qianyin houguo" (The ascension of Jin Shuren and the causes and consequences of the Hami Rebellion), Historical and Cultural Materials Research Committee of the Xinjiang Uyghur Autonomous Region Committee of the Chinese People's Political Consultative Conference (ed.), *Xinjiang wenshi ziliao xuanji* (Selected cultural and historical materials on Xinjiang), vol. 5 (1980), p. 11.
23 Of the 14 individuals present at the military conference for the Kumul Rebellion, 6 were *dorga*, and 4 were *mirab*. Aysa Niyaz, "Kumul dihanlar kozhulingiha dair bazi masililar tohursida aslima" (Recollections of the Kumul peasant rebellion), *Xinjiang Tarih Matiriyalliri* 12 (1983), p. 13. *Dorga* was the title of a village headman subordinate to the khanate, while the *mirab* were water management officials. The supreme commanders of the Kumul Rebellion, Yolbars Khan and Khoja Niyaz, rose from common stock to become high ministers of the khanate, demonstrating the link between the rebellion's organizers and figures associated with the khanate, who were set to lose power if the khanate was abolished. The farmers participating in the rebellion thus had no common ground with its leaders.
24 Today, Han Chinese represent 65% of the total population in the Kumul (Hami) region; we may therefore infer that the Han Chinese population in that region was

relatively high even in the 1930s. Yang Lipu, *Xinjiang Weiwuer zizhi qu dili* (Geography of the Xinjiang Uyghur Autonomous Region) (Urumqi: Xinjiang renmin chubanshe, 1987), p. 237.

25 See the section on "Activities of the People of Southern Xinjiang," in Xu Chun and Zhao Ruisheng, "Xinjiang minbian jishi" (Record of popular revolts in Xinjiang), *Bianduo* (Border News), vol. 2, no. 1 (1934); reprinted in: Institute of Ethnology and Anthropology, Chinese Academy of Social Sciences (ed.), *Xinjiang de geming yundong yu baoluan shijian (1911–1949)* (Revolutionary movements and rebellions in Xinjiang [1911–1949]) (Letterpress edition, 1961), p. 73.

26 Guo Weiping, "Nanjiang shijian yu diguo zhuyi qinlüe Xinjiang zhi fenxi," p. 51.

27 Ibid., p. 48.

28 He Yangling, "Posui de Xinjiang" (A fragmented Xinjiang), *Xin Zhonghua zazhi* (New China Magazine), vol. 2, no. 8 (1934), pp. 29–39.

29 Hai Weiliang, "Guoren zhuyi budao de nanjiang" (Southern Xinjiang, unnoticed by the Chinese people), *Xinya xiya* (New Asia), vol. 7, no. 6 (1934), p. 57.

30 See Guo Weiping, "Nanjiang shijian yu diguo zhuyi qinlüe Xinjiang zhi fenxi," p. 50. Aside from the 1934 essay by Guo Weiping, the "Founding Principles" of the Islamic Republic of East Turkestan were also published in: Zeng Wenwu, *Zhongguo jingying xiyu shi* (History of China's administration of the Western regions) (Shanghai: Shangwu yinshuguan, 1936, reprint by the Xinjiang Local Historical Records Office); in the journal *Fandi zhanxian* (Frontlines of Anti-Imperialism) (vol. 7, no. 3, year unknown); and in: Institute of Ethnology and Anthropology, Chinese Academy of Social Sciences (ed.), *Xinjiang de geming yundong yu baoluan shijian (1911–1949)*. However, the content printed in *Fandi zhanxian* differs widely from the other publications.

31 The passage of the "Founding Principles" cited here stems from *Fandi zhanxian*, vol. 7, no. 3.

32 Shinmen Yasushi, "Shinkyo musurimu hanran (1931–34 nen) to himitsu soshiki," p. 14.

33 Muhemmet Yakup Bughra, "Guanyu Hetian qiyi" (On the Hotan uprising), *Xinjiang wenshi ziliao xuanji*, vol. 18 (1987), pp. 76–81.

34 Guo Weiping, "Nanjiang shijian yu diguo zhuyi qinlüe Xinjiang zhi fenxi," p. 51.

35 Ibid., p. 48.

36 Hai Weiliang, "Guoren zhuyi budao de nanjiang," p. 54.

37 Wang Ke, "Seiritsu-ki no kindai Uiguru shakai o meguru kokusai kankei oyobi shinkyōshō no secchi" (International relations with respect to modern Uyghur society and the establishment of Xinjiang Province) [成立期の近代ウイグル社会を巡る国際関係及び新疆省の設置], *Dongying qiusuo* (Exploring Japan), no. 4 (1991), p. 22.

38 Zeng Wenwu, *Zhongguo jingying xiyu shi*, pp. 626, 640.

39 Hori Sunao, "Ichi hachi—ni rei seiki Uiguru jinkō shiron" [一八－二〇世紀ウイグル人口試論] (Discussion of the Uyghur population from the 18th to 20th centuries),

Shilin (Historical Review), vol. 60, no. 4 (1977), p. 114.
40 Zeng Wenwu, *Zhongguo jingying xiyu shi*, p. 640.
41 Xinjiang Archives Office, "Yang Zengxin tongzhi Xinjiang shiqi guanzhi biao" (Roster of officials in the era of Yang Zengxin's rule over Xinjiang), *Xinjiang wenshi ziliao xuanji*, vol. 11 (1982), p. 126; Xinjiang Archives Office, "Jin Shuren tongzhi Xinjiang shiqi guanzhi biao" (Roster of officials in the era of Jin Shuren's rule overXinjiang), *Xinjiang wenshi ziliao xuanji*, vol. 14 (1985), p. 146. See also Part 2, Section 1, Chapter 4, "Provincial-Level Government Offices and Official Positions," in Zhang Dajun, *Xinjiang fengbao qishi nian* (Seventy years of upheaval in Xinjiang) (Taipei: Lanxi chuban youxian gongsi, 1980), for records on provincial-level bureaucrats.
42 Yang Zengxin was quite partial to the following couplet, written by his subordinate Wang Shuzhan: "Disputes in the affairs of the Central Plains are of no concern; The frontier government has the beautiful scenery of Utopia," hanging the lines before the new-built Frontier Garrison. This couplet reflects both Yang's state of mind, and his strategy for governing Xinjiang. For details, see Wang Zichun, "Yang Zengxin yiwen" (Anecdotes of Yang Zengxin), *Xinjiang wenshi ziliao xuanji*, vol. 3 (1979), p. 79.
43 Gu Bao, "Nanjiang noncun de jingji jiegou yu jieji qingkuang" (Economic structure and class composition of rural southern Xinjiang), *Nanjiang nongcun shehui* (Rural society in southern Xinjiang) (Urumqi: Xinjiang renmin chubanshe, 1953), p. 110.
44 Zhang Dajun, *Xinjiang fengbao qishi nian*. See Part 2, Section 1, Chapter 4, "Provincial-Level Government Offices and Official Positions," for the roster of official personnel in the administrative districts and at the county level.
45 See "Activities of the People of Southern Xinjiang," in Xu Chun and Zhao Ruisheng, "Xinjiang minbian jishi." The passage appears in the conclusion to the essay, reprinted in: Institute of Ethnology and Anthropology, Chinese Academy of Social Sciences (ed.), *Xinjiang de geming yundong yu baoluan shijian (1911–1949)* (Mimeographed edition), pp. 6–19. This passage was omitted from the letterpress edition of *Xinjiang de geming yundong yu baoluan shijian (1911–1949)*, cited above.
46 Zhao Ruisheng (trans.), "Beijing zhengfu shidai zhi Xinjiang yiyuan," pp. 33–35.
47 Zhang Dajun, *Xinjiang fengbao qishi nian*; see page 987 for a list of the National Assembly members elected in Xinjiang, and pages 964–965 for a list of the Xinjiang representatives elected to the bicameral parliament.
48 Chen Huisheng, "Yang Zengxin zhuzheng Xinjiang shi de gongye jiaotong" (Industry and transportation in the era of Yang Zengxin's rule of China), *Xinjiang lishi yanjiu* (Historical studies of Xinjiang), vol. 1 (1987), pp. 54–56.
49 Tong Bao, "Yang Zengxin shidai zaji" (Notes on the era of Yang Zengxin), *Xinjiang wenshi ziliao xuanji*, vol. 3 (1979), pp. 58–59.
50 Zhao Ruisheng (trans.), "Beijing zhengfu shidai zhi Xinjiang yiyuan," p. 35.
51 Chen Yanqi, "Yang Zenxin shi ruhe huanjie Xinjiang caizheng weiji de" (How Yang Zengxin mitigated Xinjiang's financial crisis), *Xinjiang shehui kexue* (Xinjiang

Social Sciences), vol. 1 (1989), p. 100.
52 Ibid., pp. 100–110.
53 Ibid., pp. 64–65.
54 Dong Qingxuan, *Xinjiang jin erbai nian qian zhibi tulun* (Atlas of Xinjiang currency for nearly two hundred years), "Zhibi" (Paper currency) (Editorial board of *Xinjiang jinrong* [Xinjiang Finance], 1986), pp. 8–18. Chen Yanqi, "Yang Zenxin shi ruhe huanjie Xinjiang caizheng weiji de," p. 108.
55 Chen Yanqi, "Yang Zenxin shi ruhe huanjie Xinjiang caizheng weiji de," pp. 102–103.
56 Hawir Tumor, "Har kaysi tarih dawirlardiki hiyanatqilik wa uning xakilliri" (Corruption and negligence in every era and their forms), *Xinjiang Tarih Matiriyalliri* 13 (1984), pp. 140–146.
57 Chen Huisheng, "Yang Zengxin tongzhi Xinjiang shiqi de caizheng jinyong" (Fiscal administration and finances in the era of Yang Zengxin's rule of Xinjiang), *Xinjiang lishi yanjiu*, vol. 3 (1985), p. 113.
58 Chai Hengsen, "Qingmo zhi Yang, Jin tongzhi shiqi de fushui zhidu yu xianzhang" (The taxation system and county leaders from the late Qing to the eras under the rule of Yang and Jin), *Xinjiang wenshi ziliao xuanji*, vol. 10 (1981), pp. 106–109.
59 For this reason, many Uyghurs refused to enroll their children in school. For details, see Chai Hengsen, "Qingmo zhi Yang, Jin tongzhi shiqi de Xinjiang jiaoyu zhidu" (The Xinjiang education system from the late Qing to the eras under the rule of Yang and Jin), *Xinjiang wenshi ziliao xuanji*, vol. 10 (1981), p. 126.
60 Wang Guangzhi (trans.), *Kashigeer* (Kashgar) (Institute of Ethnology and Anthropology, Chinese Academy of Social Sciences, mimeographed edition; publication date unknown), p. 112.
61 Abdurixit Hoja Ahmat, "Qakilih nayisining 1926 yildin 1936 yilhiqa bolhan 10 yillik tarihidin aslima" (Historical events in Kargilik in the decade from 1926 to 1936), *Xinjiang Tarih Matiriyalliri* 12 (1983), pp. 205–207.
62 Fu Zhufu, "Xinjiang minzu wenti" (Ethnic issues in Xinjiang), *Tianshan yuekan*, vol. 1, no. 3 (1934), p. 3.
63 See Chai Hengsen, "Qingmo zhi Yang, Jin tongzhi shiqi de fushui zhidu yu xianzhang"; Political Affairs Department of the Asia Development Board, *So ren no mitaru Shinkyōjijō—Shinkyō no sovu-ēeto-ka ni tsuite* (Soviet observations on Xinjiang affairs—Xinjiang's sovereignty) [ソ聯の観たる新疆事情—新疆のソヴェート化について] (Tokyo: Political Affairs Department, Asia Development Board, Japan, 1940), p. 60.
64 Hori Sunao, "Ichi hachi—ni rei seiki Uiguru jinkō shiron," p. 114.
65 Publicity Department, Xinjiang Branch of the Chinese Communist Party Central Committee, "Jiashi xian gumoke cun diaocha" (Survey of Gumoke Village, Jiashi County), *Nanjiang nongcun shehui*, p. 76; Chen Gonghong, "Nanjiang de shuili qingkuang" (Circumstances of water irrigation in southern Xinjiang), *Nanjiang nongcun shehui*, pp. 121–122.

66 O. T. Crosby, *Tibet and Turkestan; A Journey through Old Lands and a Study of New Conditions* (New York: Putnams, 1905), cited in Zhang Zhiyi, *Xinjiang zhi jingji* (Economy of Xinjiang) (Zhonghua shuju, 1945), p. 38. According to the report "Xinjiang fazhan jieshui nongye" (The development of water-efficient agriculture in Xinjiang) published on June 8, 1990 in *Renmin ribao* (People's Daily), yearly average rainfall in southern Xinjiang is only 145 millimeters. Ni Chao: *Xinjiang zhi shuili* (Irrigation in Xinjiang) (Shangwu yinshuguan, 1948, p. 8) also points out that average rainfall is even lower in the regions where the majority of the Uyghurs live: the Kashgar region receives 82 millimeters, while the Hotan region receives only 47 millimeters.
67 Political Affairs Department of the Asia Development Board, *So ren no mitaru Shinkyōjijō—Shinkyō no sovu-ēeto-ka ni tsuite*, p. 8.
68 Office of the National People's Congress Ethnic Affairs Committee, "Nanjiang Shufu xian Tuoguzhake qu di liu xiang diaocha cailiao" (Survey data on the No. 6 Township of Toguzak District, Shufu County, southern Xinjiang), *Xinjiang Weiwuer zizhi qu ruogan diaocha cailiao bian* (Selected survey data on the Xinjiang Uyghur Autonomous Region) (unpublished, 1956), pp. 29–30.
69 Wang Guangzhi (trans.), *Kashigeer*, p. 116.
70 Saguchi Tōru, *Jūhachi–Jūkuseiki higashi Torukisutan shakaishi kenkyū* (Study of the social history of East Turkestan in the 18th and 19th centuries) [十八－十九世紀東トルキスタン社会史研究] (Yoshikawa Kobunkan Publishing House, 1963), p. 111.
71 Gu Bao, "Nanjiang nongcun de fengjian boxue zhidu" (Feudal systems of exploitation in rural southern Xinjiang), *Nanjiang nongcun shehui*, pp. 142–147.
72 Chen Gonghong, "Nanjiang de shuili qingkuang," p. 122.
73 Ibid., pp. 123–126.
74 Office of the National People's Congress Ethnic Affairs Committee, "Nanjiang Shufu xian Tuoguzhake qu di liu xiang diaocha cailiao," p. 121.
75 Gu Bao, "Shufu xian yi qu san xiang jiefang qian de fengjian jituan yu zhengzhi zuzhi" (Feudal groups and political organizations in No. 3 Township, District 1, Shufu County before liberation), *Nanjiang nongcun shehui*, p. 187; Office of the National People's Congress Ethnic Affairs Committee, "Nanjiang Shufu xian Tuoguzhake qu di liu xiang diaocha cailiao," p. 29.
76 Gu Bao, "Shufu xian yi qu san xiang jiefang qian de fengjian jituan yu zhengzhi zuzhi," p. 188.
77 Wang Guangzhi (trans.), *Kashigeer*, p. 114.
78 Deng Liqun, Gu Bao, "Nanjiang de wahafu di wenti" (The issue of *waqf* land in southern Xinjiang), *Nanjiang nongcun shehui*, pp. 102–104; Publicity Department, Xinjiang Branch of the Chinese Communist Party Central Committee, "Akesu di yi qu di wu xiang diaocha" (Survey of No. 5 Township, District 1, Aksu), *Nanjiang nongcun shehui*, pp. 49–50.
79 Ibid., p. 50.

80 Office of the National People's Congress Ethnic Affairs Committee, "Nanjiang Shufu xian Tuoguzhake qu di liu xiang diaocha cailiao"; Gu Bao, "Shufu xian yi qu san xiang jiefang qian de fengjian jituan yu zhengzhi zuzhi," pp. 150–151.
81 Wang Guangzhi (trans.), *Kashigeer*, p. 102; Gu Bao, "Shufu xian yi qu san xiang jiefang qian de fengjian jituan yu zhengzhi zuzhi," p. 113.
82 Gu Bao, "Shufu xian yi qu san xiang jiefang qian de fengjian jituan yu zhengzhi zuzhi," p. 113.
83 Husayn Musabayow of the Musabayow family also founded a Jadidist school in Ili. See Ibrayim Niyaz, "Atux Nahiye Iksahkantida yekinkizaman panni muaripining dunyaga kilixi."

Chapter 3

1 Du Zhongyuan, *Sheng Shicai yu xin Xinjiang* (Sheng Shicai and new Xinjiang) (Chongqing, Guilin, Shanghai, Hong Kong, Xi'an, Kunming, Chengdu, Changsha, Lanzhou, Guiyang: Shenghuo shudian, 1939), p. 73.
2 Chen Jiying, *Xinjiang niaokan* (A bird's-eye view of Xinjiang) (Hong Kong: Shangwu yinshuguan, 1941), pp. 20–21.
3 Nakada Yoshinobu, "Shinkyo uiguru jichiku to nihonjin" (The Xinjiang Uyghur Autonomous Region and the Japanese) [新疆ウイグル自治区と日本人] (I), *Ajia Afurika shiryō tsūhō* (Materials on Asia and Africa) [アジア・アフリカ資料通報], vol. 21, no. 5 (1983), p. 33.
4 Oobayashi Yogo, "Shinkyō o otozureta nihonjin" (The Japanese who visited Xinjiang) [新疆を訪れた日本人] (I), *Aichi daigaku kokusai mondai kenkyujo kiyo* (Journal of the Aichi University Institute of International Affairs) [愛知大学国際問題研究所紀要], no. 54 (1974), pp. 156–157.
5 Ibid., pp. 151–154.
6 Ibid., pp. 144–145.
7 Kaneko Tamio, *Chūō Ajia ni haitta Nihonjin* (The Japanese in Central Asia) [中央アジアに入った日本人] (Tokyo: Chūō Kōronsha, 1992). The works published by Hino Tsutomu after returning to Japan include: "Iri ryokōdan" (Travels in Ili) [伊犁旅行談] (I and II), *Chigaku zasshi* (Journal of Geography) [地学雑誌], nos. 241 and 243 (1911); "Chainīzutorukisutan ni okeru jūmin to sono fūshū" (The inhabitants of Chinese Turkistan and their customs) [チャイニーズトルキスタンに於ける住民と其の風習] (I and II), *Jinruigaku zasshi* (Journal of the Anthropological Society of Nippon), vol. 29, nos. 1 and 3 (1914); and *Iri kikō* (Journey to Ili) (Tokyo: Hakubunkan, 1909).
8 Nakada Yoshinobu, "Shinkyo uiguru jichiku to nihonjin" (II), *Ajia Afurika shiryō tsūhō*, vol. 21, no. 6 (1983), p. 36.
9 Yuan Dahua (auth.), Wang Shunan and Wang Xuezeng (eds.), *Xinjiang tuzhi* (Atlas of Xinjiang), vol. 10, Imperial Chapter 1 (Shanghai: Shanghai guji

chubanshe, orig. published in 1911, 1992 edition). Tong Bao, Han Xiliang, "Xinhai geming zai Xinjiang de jianwen" (Details on the 1911 Revolution in Xinjiang), Historical and Cultural Materials Research Committee of the Xinjiang Uyghur Autonomous Region Committee of the Chinese People's Political Consultative Conference (ed.), *Xinjiang wenshi ziliao xuanji* (Selected cultural and historical materials on Xinjiang), vol. 1 (1979), p. 38.

10 Saitō Suejirō (1867–1921) graduated from the Army War College of Japan in 1897 (Meiji 30), and in August 1899, he was dispatched to Hangzhou as a member of the General Staff; after returning to Japan in April 1904, he was appointed as Commissioner of the Manchukuo military administration (subordinate to the Second Army); in August 1906, he was appointed to the staff of the Korea Garrison Army; and in 1907, he assumed the post of Imperial Administrator for the Governor-General of Korea (Jiandao Chief of Police). From August 1913 to August 1914, Saitō served as the Assistant Military Attaché to the legation in China; in July 1915, he was appointed as Commander of the China Garrison Army; in May 1916, he was re-appointed as the Assistant Military Attaché to the legation in China; in April 1919, he was assigned as the commander of the 11th Division; and in February 1921, he died in battle at Vladivostok. See Association for Studies of Modern Japanese History (Nihon Kindai Shiryō Kenkyūkai) (ed.), *Nihon rikukaigun no seido, soshiki, jinji* (Institutions, organizations, and personnel of the Japanese Navy and Army) [日本陸海軍の制度・組織・人事] (Tokyo: University of Tokyo Press, 1971), p. 33.

11 "Riku, hi, ni gatsu muika, Sanbō sōchō ate, Zai Pekin Saitō shōshō-hatsu, shihoku den ichi roku gō" (Army, classified, February 6, General Chief of Staff, sent by Major-General Saitō from Beijing, North China telegram no. 16) [陸・秘，二月六日・参謀総長宛・在北京斎藤少将発・支北電一六号], Diplomatic Archives of the Ministry of Foreign Affairs of Japan, Dept. 1, Category 2, Entry 1, Item 29, in the archive *Kiyokuni kakumei dōran-go dō kuni henkyō ni tai suru Roshia no taido nami kōdō ichi-ken* (Correspondence on attitude and actions vis-à-vis Russia at the Qing state's borders following the upheaval of the country's revolution) [清国革命動乱後同国辺境ニ対スル露国ノ態度並行動一件].

12 The Ili Rebellion broke out on January 7, 1912, and the Ili General Zhi Rui was executed on the 8th. See Wei Changhong, *Xinhai geming zai Xinjiang* (The 1911 Revolution in Xinjiang) (Urumqi: Xinjiang renmin chubanshe, 1981), pp. 43–57.

13 Oobayashi Yogo, "Shinkyō o otozureta nihonjin" (I), p. 150.

14 Ibid., p. 151.

15 Nakada Yoshinobu, "Shinkyo uiguru jichiku to nihonjin" (II). This work states that Uehara Taichi was captured in February 1911, and released in February 1913. However, the telegram cited in Note 11 (Diplomatic Archives of the Ministry of Foreign Affairs of Japan, Dept. 1, Category 2, Entry 1, Item 29) indicates that Uehara Taichi remained in Ili until at least February 1912.

16 "Mongoru oyobu Shinkyōchihō chōhō kikan haichi no kudan" (Archive on

intelligence reports and agency arrangements in the Mongolia and Xinjiang regions) [蒙古及新疆地方諜報機関配置の件], *Rikugun-shō dai nikki* (Diaries of the Ministry of War) [陸軍省大日記], 1918, "Hi dai nikki" (Classified diaries) Book 1 of 4; see also Wang Ke, "Riben qin Hua zhanzheng yu 'Huijiao gongzuo'" (The Japanese war of aggression against China and "Islam work"), *Lishi yanjiu* (Historical Research), no. 5 (2009), pp. 87–105 (the full text was reprinted in *Zhongguo renmin daxue baokan fuyin ziliao: jindai shi yanjiu* [Reprint series of Renmin University of China: studies of modern history], 2010, no. 1).

17 Nakada Yoshinobu, "Shinkyo uiguru jichiku to nihonjin" (II), pp. 35–36.
18 "Riku, hi, ni gatsu muika, Sanbō sōchō ate, Zai Pekin Saitō shōshō-hatsu, shihoku den ichi roku gō," Diplomatic Archives of the Ministry of Foreign Affairs of Japan, Dept. 1, Category 2, Entry 1, Item 29, in the archive *Kiyokuni kakumei dōran-go dō kuni henkyō ni tai suru Roshia no taido nami kōdō ichi-ken*.
19 Foreign Service Training Institute of the Ministry of Foreign Affairs of Japan (ed.), *Kenshū sankō shiryō: Manshū jihen no kenkyū* (Training reference materials: studies of the Mukden Incident) [研修参考資料・満洲事変の研究] (Tokyo: Foreign Service Training Institute, 1967), p. 14.
20 Foreign Service Training Institute (ed.), *Kokusai renmei shina chōsa iinkai hōkokusho ni taisuru teikoku seifu ikensho* (Opinion papers of the imperial government on the report of the League of Nations China Inquiry Commission) (Lytton Commission) [国際連盟支那調査委員会報告書ニ対スル帝国政府意見書] (Tokyo: Foreign Service Training Institute, 1967), p. 164.
21 Ibid., p. 15.
22 "Abe seimu kyokuchō kō tai Shina (Man-mō) seisaku gaiyō · shina ni-seki suru gaikō seisaku no tsuna-ryō · Taishō gan'nen kō" (Summary of policies on China (Manchuria–Mongolia) drafted by Director Abe of the Political Affairs Bureau · Outline of Diplomatic Policies on China · drafted in Taishō 1) [1912] [阿部政務局長稿対支那（満蒙）政策概要・支那ニ関スル外交政策ノ綱領・大正元年稿], Diplomatic Archives of the Ministry of Foreign Affairs of Japan, Dept. 1, Category 2, Entry 1, Item 27, Matsumoto minutes, in the archive *Uchida gaimu daijin no tai Shina (Man-mō) seisaku ni-seki shi Ijūin kōshi heno kunrei* (Directives of Foreign Minister Uchida to Ambassador Ijuin Regarding Policies on China (Manchuria–Mongolia)) [内田外務大臣ノ対支那（満蒙）政策ニ関シ伊集院公使ヘノ訓令].
23 However, the criticism that this policy drew from the military, the opposition party, and various politicians is believed to be the reason behind the assassination of Political Affairs Director Abe Moritarō on September 5, 1913; at the time, Abe was responsible for handling the China problem. See Kurihara Ken, *Tai Man-Mō seisakushi no ichimen: Nichi-Ro sengo yori Taishōki ni itaru* (A look at the history of policies on Manchuria and Mongolia: From the Russo-Japanese War to the Taishō period) [対満蒙政策史の一面：日露戦後より大正期にいたる] (Tokyo: Hara Shobo, 1966), Chapter 4, "The Assassination of Director Abe of the Political Affairs Bureau of the Foreign Ministry and the China (Manchuria–Mongolia) Problem."

24 Zhao Diangao, "Xinjiang zhi guoji wenti ji qi qiantu" (Xinjiang's international problems and its prospects), *Xin yaxiya* (New Asia), vol. 7, no. 6 (1934), p. 39.
25 Nakada Yoshinobu, "Shinkyo uiguru jichiku to nihonjin" (II), *Ajia Afurika shiryō tsO*, vol. 21, no. 6 (1983), pp. 31–36.
26 Foreign Service Training Institute (ed.), *Kenshū sankō shiryō: Manshū jihen no kenkyū*, p. 15.
27 "Shinkyō seikyō hō jijō kankei zassan" (Notes on the political situation in Xinjiang and the connections between events) [新疆政況並事情関係雑纂], document in the Diplomatic Archives of the Ministry of Foreign Affairs of Japan, Dept. A, Category 6, Entry 1, Item 3-4.
28 "Kō · kimitsu · dai ichi kyū hachi roku gō · Shōwa ichi rei-nen ichi rei tsuki ni yokka · Zai Manshū-koku tokumei zen-ken taishi Minami Jirō · Gaimu daijin Hirota Kōki-dono · 'Sorenpō no Shinkyō sekka no jōkyō ni tsuite' hō 'Seihoku Kyōsan-gun oyo sōhi-gun taisei yōzu'" (Official · Top-Secret · No. 1986 · October 24, Shōwa 10 [1936] · Sent by Minami Jirō, Ambassador Extraordinary and Plenipotentiary to Manchukuo to Foreign Minister Hirota Kōki: 'On the situation of the Soviet red-ification of Xinjiang' and 'Maps of the positions of the Northwestern Communist Army and the 'Bandit-Suppression' Army') [公・機密・第一九八六号・昭和一〇年一〇月二四日・在満州国特命全権大使南次郎・外務大臣広田広毅殿・「ソ連邦ノ新疆赤化ノ状況ニ就テ」並「西北共産軍及剿匪軍態勢要図」送付ノ件], document in the Diplomatic Archives of the Ministry of Foreign Affairs of Japan, Dept. A, Category 2, Entry 2, Item 0, C/R 1-3, in the archive *So Shi Mō Kyō kankei* (Relationships between the Soviet Union, China, Mongolia and Xinjiang) [蘇支蒙疆関係].
29 "Kimitsu · kō · dai san ichi shi gō · Shōwa ichi rei-nen hachigatsu ni mikka · Zai sovu-i-eto renpō toku inochi zenken taishi Ōta Tamekichi · Gaimu daijin Hirota Kōki-dono · Saikin niokeru so' renpō to Shinkyō tono kankei ni-seki shi hōkoku" (Top-Secret · Official · No. 314 · August 23, Shōwa 10 [1936] · Sent by Ōta Tamekichi, Ambassador Extraordinary and Plenipotentiary to Foreign Minister Hirota Kōki: Latest report on relations between the Soviet Union and Xinjiang) [機密・公・第三一四号・昭和一〇年八月二三日・在ソヴィエト聯邦特命全権大使大田為吉・外務大臣広田広毅殿・最近ニ於ケル「ソ」聯邦ト新疆トノ関係ニ関シ報告ノ件], document in the Diplomatic Archives of the Ministry of Foreign Affairs of Japan, Dept. A, Category 2, Entry 2, Item 0, C/R 1-3, in the archive *So Shi Mō Kyō kankei*.
30 "Toku gōgai · Shōwa ichi rei-nen jūnigatsu tsuitachi · Zai novuoshibirisuku Nihon ryōjikan · Shinkyō jissa ni-seki suru iken" (Special Issue · December 1, Shōwa 10 [1936] · Japanese Consulate in Novosibirsk · Recommendations regarding a field investigation of Xinjiang) [特号外・昭和一〇年一二月一日・在ノヴオシビリスク日本領事館・新疆実査ニ関スル意見], Diplomatic Archives of the Ministry of Foreign Affairs of Japan, Dept. A, Category 2, Entry 2, Item 0, C/R 1-3, in the archive *So Shi Mō Kyō kankei*.

31 Sheng Shicai, *Shi nian Xinjiang huiyi lu* (Memoirs of a Decade in Xinjiang), serially printed in Taiwan's *Zili wanbao* (Independence Evening Post) from Apr. 2–Dec. 11, 1952 (Sept. 30, Oct. 7).
32 Yang Boqing, "Ma Zhongying ru Xin suijun jianwen" (Embedded news on Ma Zhongying's invasion of Xinjiang), *Wenshi ziliao xuanji* (Selected cultural and historical materials), vol. 27 (1986 reprint), pp. 106–107.
33 Wu Zhiping, "Buchong 'Ma Zhongying ru Xin suijun jianwen'" (Supplement to 'Embedded news on Ma Zhongying's invasion of Xinjiang'), *Wenshi ziliao xuanji*, vol. 34 (1986 reprint), pp. 275–276.
34 Sven Anders Hedin, *The Silk Road: Ten Thousand Miles Through Central Asia* (New York: E. P. Dutton and Company, 1938), p. 298.
35 Song Chun, *Zhongguo Guomindang shi* (History of the Chinese Nationalist Party) (Changchun: Jilin wenshi chubanshe, 1990), pp. 382–383.
36 Li Xiuye, "Su jun jinru Dongbei qianhou" (Circumstances of the Soviet Army's arrival in the northeast), *Wenshi ziliao xuanji*, supplement vol. 1 (1986), p. 143.
37 Liu Tangling, "Fu Su caigou kang Ri wuqi de huiyi" (Memoir of traveling to the Soviet Union to purchase weapons for the resistance against Japan), *Xinjiang wenshi ziliao xuanji*, vol. 24 (1992), p. 14.
38 Zou Taofen, "Xuyan" (Preface), in Du Zhongyuan, *Sheng Shicai yu xin Xinjiang* (Chongqing: Shenghuo shudian, 1939), p. 2.
39 Chen Jiying, *Xinjiang niaokan*, p. 8; Du Zhongyuan, *Sheng Shicai yu xin Xinjiang*, p. 33.
40 Eric Teichman, *Journey to Turkistan* (London: Hodder and Stoughton, 1937), p. 105. *Tupan* is an alternate spelling of the title 督辦 (*duban*), "provincial governor."
41 Chen Jiying, "Sheng Shicai xiaozhuan" (A biography of Sheng Shicai), in *Xinjiang niaokan*, pp. 8–10. However, the "Biography of Mr. Sheng Jinyong" compiled by the Sheng Shicai Funerary Committee in 1970 states that Sheng Shicai traveled to Japan after graduating from the Shanghai Wusong Public School with a major in political economics in 1915. See Sheng Shicai Funerary Committee (ed.), "Sheng Jinyong xiansheng xingshu," in Zhang Dajun, *Xinjiang fengbao qishi nian* (Seventy years of upheaval in Xinjiang) (Taiwan: Lanxi chuban youxian gongsi, 1980), pp. 3174–3177.
42 Miyachi Masato, *Kokusai seijika no kindai Nihon* (International politics and modern Japan) [国際政治下の近代日本] (Tokyo: Yamakawa Shuppansha, 1987), p. 161.
43 Du Zhongyuan, *Sheng Shicai yu xin Xinjiang*, p. 32.
44 Du Zhongyuan describes the organization Sheng Shicai represented as an exchange students' association (Du Zhongyuan, *Sheng Shicai yu xin Xinjiang*, p. 32), while Chen Jiying describes it as a Liaoning native-place association (Chen Jiying, *Xinjiang niaokan*, p. 8).
45 Sheng Shicai Funerary Committee (ed.), "Sheng Jinyong xiansheng xingshu," in Zhang Dajun, *Xinjiang fengbao qishi nian*, pp. 3174.

46 Du Zhongyuan, *Sheng Shicai yu xin Xinjiang*, pp. 32–33; Chen Jiying, *Xinjiang niaokan*, p. 8.
47 Zhou Dongjiao, "Sheng Shicai shi zenyang qude Xinjiang tongzhiquan de" (How Sheng Shicai achieved his rule over Xinjiang), *Wenshi ziliao xuanji*, vol. 46 (1964), p. 211.
48 There is another theory that Sheng Shicai's wife was Guo Songling's niece. See Bai Zhensheng and Koibuchi Shin'ichi (eds.), *Xinjiang xiandai zhengzhi shehui shilüe* (Outline of Xinjiang's modern sociopolitical history) (Beijing: Zhongguo shehui kexue chubanshe, 1992), p. 210.
49 Du Zhongyuan, *Sheng Shicai yu xin Xinjiang*, p. 33.
50 The Japanese government initially adopted a neutral stance with regard to this conflict. However, the Japanese Kwantung Army believed that Guo Songling sought to oppose Japan and allow Soviet forces to enter Manchuria and Mongolia; it therefore adopted a policy to "support Zhang and exclude Guo," hindering the operations of Guo Songling's forces throughout the region. There are reports that the Kwantung Army secretly aided Zhang Zuolin's forces by replenishing their supply of ammunition and assisting in operational planning, and that a number of Japanese soldiers disguised themselves as Chinese and participated directly in the battle alongside Zhang's troops. On December 1, Shigeru Yoshida, who was then the Japanese Consul-General in Fengtian, sent a telegram to the Japanese Foreign Ministry, which read: "I believe that in order to defend our position in Manchuria, aiding Zhang Zuolin, who is in difficult straits, will not be unprofitable." After Guo Songling defeated Zhang Zuolin at Lianshan and captured Fengtian, the Japanese government abandoned its position of non-interference. Following consultation between the government and the army headquarters, on December 10, warnings were sent to both Guo and Zhang in the name of the Kwantung Army Commander Shirakawa Yoshinori, declaring that Japan would not stand idly by as havoc was wreaked upon the Manchuria Railway and the surrounding area. The unspoken implication was that Japan would not countenance the defeat of the pro-Japanese Zhang Zuolin. Left in a weakened position, Guo's army was defeated by Zhang's forces on December 23. See *Nihon gaikō bunsho* (Documents on Japanese foreign policy) [日本外交文書], Taishō 14 (1926), bk. 2 (vol. 2) (Tokyo: Diplomatic Archives of the Ministry of Foreign Affairs of Japan, 1983), including documents No. 904, No. 913, No. 950, No. 997, No. 1018, No. 1019, No. 1056, No. 1057, and No. 1068.
51 Zhou Dongjiao, "Sheng Shicai shi zenyang qude Xinjiang tongzhiquan de," p. 211.
52 Sheng Shicai would later play a key role in funneling Soviet aid into China's interior for the war against Japan. After the Marco Polo Bridge Incident of July 7, 1937, the Nationalist government established the Central Transportation Committee in Lanzhou for the purpose of receiving Soviet aid. Sheng Shicai personally served as the chairman of the Xinjiang Branch Committee (Xu Taihe, "Zai Zhongyunhui shouzhan suiding qinli ji" [A record of first-hand experiences

in Shuiding, the first station of the Central Transportation Committee], *Xinjiang wenshi ziliao xuanji*, vol. 24 [1994], p. 46); for each local branch committee along the route, he appointed the highest-ranking administrative official and the chief of public security as the director and assistant director (Fu Dazheng, "Ji Sun ke shicha Manasi Zhongyunhui qichezhan" [A record of Sun Ke's inspection of the Manas Central Transportation Committee Bus Station], *Xinjiang wenshi ziliao xuanji*, vol. 24 [1992], p. 64); and he even personally appointed the ordinary receptionists (Zhou Hengshun, "Zai Qijiaojing nanwang de rizi li" [Unforgettable days at Qijiaojing], *Xinjiang wenshi ziliao xuanji*, vol. 24 [1992], p. 102). In the face of Xinjiang's impending financial collapse, Sheng's sole aim was to continue funding the Central Transportation Committee, no matter the cost (Yang Zaiming, "Kangzhan shiqi de Zhongyunhui" [The Central Transportation Committee in the era of the War of Resistance], *Xinjiang wenshi ziliao xuanji*, vol. 24 [1992], p. 35). Sheng explicitly instructed the ranking administrative officials in counties along the route that their primary task was to complete the work of the Central Transportation Committee, declaring that their work as military quartermasters would be their greatest contribution to the War of Resistance against Japan (Wu Shuhe, "Yiqie weile kang Ri, yiqie weile qianxian" [Everything to resist Japan, everything for the front lines], *Xinjiang wenshi ziliao xuanji*, vol. 24 [1992], p. 94). In addition to building a Soviet-supported fighter plane assembly plant in the Hami (Kumul) region, a massive amount of Soviet matériel was transported along the Xinjiang route to Lanzhou in China's interior in the space of approximately one year from 1937 to the summer of 1938, including: 985 fighter planes, 82 tanks, 1,300 artillery pieces, and 1,400 machine guns (Wang Deyu, "Xinjiang Zhongyunhui zhi wo wen wo jian" [My experiences of the Central Transportation Committee in Xinjiang], *Xinjiang wenshi ziliao xuanji*, vol. 24 [1992], p. 55; Yang Zaiming, "Kangzhan shiqi de Zhongyunhui," p. 37).

53 "Jūichigatsu ni itsuka · Zai Amatsu Arita sōryōji Yori ·Shidehara gaimu daijin'ate (denpō) · Li Jinglin no hisho Zhang Tonglin ga Feng Guo mitsuyaku nitsuki setsumei no kudan" (November 25 · From Consul-General Arita in Tianjin to Foreign Minister Shidehara [Telegram] · Notes on the secret agreement between Li Jinglin's secretary Zhang Tongli, Feng, and Guo) [一一月二十五日・在天津有田総領事ヨリ・幣原外務大臣宛（電報）・李景林ノ秘書張同礼ガ馮郭密約ニツキ説明ノ件], *Nihon gaikō bunsho*, Taishō 14 (1926), bk. 2 (vol. 2), Document No. 885.

54 "Jūgatsu ichi mikka · Kara Han tai Feng Yuxiang mitsuyaku taikō narumono nyūshu nitsuki hōkoku no kudan" (October 13 · From Yoshizawa, Envoy to China, to Foreign Minister Shidehara [Telegram] · Report on acquiring an outline of the secret treaty between Karakhan and Feng Yuxiang) [一〇月一三日・在中国芳沢公使ヨリ・幣原外務大臣宛（電報）・カラハン対馮玉祥密約大綱ナルモノ入手ニツキ報告ノ件], *Nihon gaikō bunsho*, Taishō 14 (1926), bk. 2 (vol. 2), Document No. 785.

55 Regarding the appellation "King of Xinjiang for a decade," see Zhang Dajun, *Xinjiang fengbao qishi nian*, p. 3153.

56 Lang Daoheng, "'Xinjiang ribao' de pianduan" (Excerpts from the "Xinjiang Daily"), *Xinjiang wenshi ziliao*, vol. 6 (1990), pp. 177–178.
57 The Naturalized Army was originally formed in 1931 by Jin Shuren, then the Governor of Xinjiang and the General of Border Defenses, to suppress a Uyghur uprising in the Kumul region. The army was composed primarily of White Russians who had emigrated to Xinjiang following Russia's October Revolution. Some of the White Russian soldiers were naturalized Chinese citizens, while others had not obtained citizenship.
58 Zhou Dongjiao, "Sheng Shicai shi zenyang qude Xinjiang tongzhiquan de," p. 218.
59 Zhou Dongjiao, *Xinjiang shi nian* (Ten years in Xinjiang) (Stencil mimeograph edition; the date of publication is unknown, but the postscript was written in 1948), p. 11.
60 This disadvantage was due to the fact that the Naturalized Army had only 200 soldiers (ibid., p. 12), while the Northeast Army (*Dongbei jun* 東北軍), which also joined the coup, suffered from lax discipline and weak combat effectiveness (Wu Aichen [translated into Japanese by Yanai Katsumi], *Shinkyō kiyu* (Travels in Xinjiang) [Tokyo: Koa Shokyoku, 1943], p. 291).
61 Yulbars Khan, *Yaole boshi huiyi lu* (Memoirs of Yulbars Khan) (Taipei: Taiwan zhuanji wenxue chubanshe, 1969), pp. 157–159.
62 According to Zhou Dongjiao (*Xinjiang shi nian*, p. 12), the coup leader Chen Zhong traveled to Ulanbay alongside the commander of the Naturalized Army on the 13th to persuade Sheng Shicai to their side. However, according to Gong Bicheng ("Sheng Shicai ru Xin duoqu zhengquan de jingguo" [Events of Sheng Shicai's arrival in Xinjiang and seizure of power], *Wenshi ziliao xuanji*, vol. 46 [1964]), Li Xiaotian himself traveled by plane to persuade Sheng Shicai. In addition, Jin Shuren's bodyguard claimed in his memoirs that he personally delivered Jin Shuren's orders to Sheng Shicai (Liu Yinglin, "Xinjiang 'Si yi er' zhengbian zhong de yixie wenti" [Some questions regarding Xinjiang's "April 12" coup], *Xinjiang wenshi ziliao xuanji*, vol. 11 [1982], p. 69).
63 Zhou Dongjiao, "Sheng Shicai shi zenyang qude Xinjiang tongzhiquan de," pp. 218–219.
64 Gong Bicheng, "Wo zhidao de Tao Mingyue" (The Tao Mingyue that I knew), *Xinjiang wenshi ziliao xuanji*, vol. 5 (1980), p. 7; Wu Aichen (translated into Japanese by Yanai Katsumi), *Shinkyō kiyu* (Travels in Xinjiang), p. 255.
65 Cai Jinsong, Cai Ying, "Yi jiu san san nian Nanjing Guomindang zhengfu he Sheng Shicai zhengduo Xinjiang tongzhiquan de douzheng" (The Nanjing Nationalist government in 1933 and Sheng Shicai's struggle to seize power in Xinjiang), *Xinjiang lishi yanjiu* (Historical studies of Xinjiang), no. 1 (1985), p. 73; Chen Feng, "Huang Musong, Luo Wengan xianhou zai Xin de huodong" (Activities of Huang Musong and Luo Wengan in Xinjiang), *Xinjiang wenshi ziliao xuanji*, vol. 6 (1980), p. 104.
66 Tao Mingyue and Gong Bicheng, who had independently set out for Nanjing to

report on these events, met with Huang Musong en route and decided to return with him to Urumqi. See Wu Aichen, *Shinkyō kiyu*, p. 248.
67 Du Zhongyuan, *Sheng Shicai yu xin Xinjiang*, p. 34; Zhou Dongjiao, *Xinjiang shi nian*, p. 20.
68 Sheng Shicai, "Mubian suoyi" (Trivial memories of the pastureland frontier), *Wushi nian zhenghai fengyun—Tianshan nanbei* (Fifty years of political upheaval—the northern and southern Tianshan Mountains) (Taipei: Chunqiu chubanshe, 1967), pp. 76–77. However, according to memoirs by other individuals, Sheng Shicai only learned of the secret collaboration between Chen Zhong, Tao Mingyue, Li Xiaotian, Huang Musong, and the others after deciphering a coded telegram with the aid of the Japanese spy Ōnishi Tadashi (Wu Aichen, "Du 'Ma Zhongying ru Xin jianwen' buzheng" [Corrections on reading "News of Ma Zhongying's invasion of Xinjiang"], *Wenshi ziliao xuanji*, vol. 34 [1989 reprint], pp. 277–279). Zhou Dongjiao states that Sheng Shicai returned unexpectedly to Urumqi on June 25, and that he assassinated Chen Zhong, Tao Mingyue, and Li Xiaotian at the emergency meeting on June 26 and put Huang Musong under house arrest, staging what was known as the "Second Coup" (Zhou Dongjiao, *Xinjiang shi nian*, pp. 16–17).
69 Zhou Dongjiao, *Xinjiang shi nian*, p. 11; Institute of History of the Xinjiang Academy of Social Sciences, *Xinjiang jianshi* (Concise history of Xinjiang), vol. 3 (Urumqi: Xinjiang renmin chubanshe, 1987), pp. 195–197.
70 Yulbars Khan, *Yaole boshi huiyi lu*, p. 156.
71 According to Gao Wentian ("Ma Zhongying lian ci jin Jiang ji gongzhan Qitai de jingguo" [Events of Ma Zhongying's two invasions of Xinjiang and capture of Qitai], *Changji wenshi ziliao xuanji* [Selected cultural and historical materials on Changji], vol. 3 [1985], p. 5), Ma Zhongying appointed Yulbars Khan and Hoja Niyaz as brigade commanders upon arriving in Hami (Kumul), and Hoja Niyaz was assigned to the vanguard, indicating a military alliance between Ma Zhongying and the Uyghur rebellion. In addition, according to several memoirs by local residents, including: Yin Zonglin and Wang Dexiang, "Ma Zhongying ju Qitai shi ba tian jianwen" (Experiences during Ma Zhongying's eighteen-day occupation of Qitai), *Changji wenshi ziliao xuanji*, vol. 3 (1985), pp. 47–51; Wu Ying, Ding Wanfu, Mi Wanlong, Shen Deyun, and Ding Fuhai, "Ma Yinghai qibing lü" (Ma Yinghai's cavalry brigade), *Changji shi wenshi ziliao* (Cultural and historical materials of Changji City), vol. 2 (1985), pp. 13–33; Ma Sheng and Cui Wanshou, "Ma Zhongying de qing madui" (Ma Zhongying's Young Cavalrymen), *Changji wenshi ziliao xuanji*, vol. 3 (1985), pp. 40–41, Ma Zhongying's forces adhered strictly to military discipline, and did not mistreat or massacre the local inhabitants. Ma Zhongying's army was therefore able to absorb a substantial number of new recruits from the local Hui communities. For instance, both Ma Yinghai's cavalry brigade and the Young Cavalrymen replenished their forces with local Hui inhabitants. For more on Ma Zhongying's efforts to make common cause with Uyghur

rebel factions, see Yulbars Khan, *Yaole boshi huiyi lu*, pp. 156–157. A number of sources contain records on Ma Zhongying's victories in the region near Urumqi; this book primarily makes reference to Zhang Shengbao, "Ma Zhongying weigong Qitai cheng" (Ma Zhongying's siege of Qitai City), *Changji wenshi ziliao xuanji*, vol. 2 (1985), pp. 31–34.

72 Sven Anders Hedin, *The Silk Road: Ten Thousand Miles Through Central Asia*, p. 2.
73 Wu Aichen, *Shinkyō kiyu*, p. 253; Yulbars Khan, *Yaole boshi huiyi lu*, p. 159; Yang Guoliang, "Ji Sheng, Ma Ziniquan zhanyi" (Recalling the events of the Battle of Ziniquan between Sheng and Ma), *Fukang wenshi ziliao* (Historical and cultural materials on Fukang), vol. 1 (1985), pp. 51–56.
74 Sheng Shicai, "Mubian suoyi," p. 75; Burhan Shahidi, *Xinjiang wushi nian* (Fifty years in Xinjiang) (Beijing: Wenshi ziliao chubanshe, 1984), p. 187.
75 Han Zhenhua, "Lun Xinjiang nanbu zhi weiji" (On the crisis in southern Xinjiang), *Xin Qinghai* (New Qinghai), no. 10 (1933), p. 122.
76 "Zhang Peiyuan zhi Yan Huiqing dashi dian" (Telegram from Zhang Peiyuan to Ambassador Yan Huiqing) reads as follows: "After visiting Minister Luo, I turned to the coded telegram orders from the central loyalists, which gave orders for Peiyuan to lead an army into Urumqi, to dispose of Sheng Shicai and clean up northern Xinjiang, eliminating the root of the troubles; they also gave orders for Ma Zhongying to cooperate and rapidly engage in all-out war, to rescue the people from their suffering, defend the national territories, and so on. At that time, Wusu and Suilai dispatched troops to detain the traitor Sheng's secret purchase of a large amount of arms and ammunition . . . now a brigade of the Headquarters cavalry has stationed heavy forces in Suilai, Wusu and Tacheng, cutting off the traitor Sheng's transportation; a rapid resolution and an early victory are expected." Document No. 4853, in the collection of the Xinjiang Institute of History: see Cai Jinsong, Cai Ying, "Yi jiu san san nian Nanjing Guomindang zhengfu he Sheng Shicai zhengduo Xinjiang tongzhiquan de douzheng," p. 79.
77 Du Zhongyuan, *Sheng Shicai yu xin Xinjiang*, p. 29.
78 Chen Jiying, *Xinjiang niaokan*, pp. 18–21.
79 Huang Fensheng, *Bianjiang zhengjiao zhi yanjiu* (A study of border politics and religion) (Shanghai: Shangwu chubanshe, 1946, 1966 edition), p. 118.
80 During the 1930s, prior to the coining of the ethnonym "Uyghur," there was no unified term describing the Uyghur ethnic group. When the Qing Dynasty conquered southern Xinjiang in the mid-18th century, it referred to the local inhabitants, who were all of Islamic faith, as *Huizi* (回子 , "Muslims"). Later, to distinguish them from the Muslims of China's interior province, the Uyghurs, who wore turbans, were referred to as *chantou Hui* (纏頭回) or *chan Hui* (纏回), meaning "turbaned Muslims."
81 Du Zhongyuan, *Sheng Shicai yu xin Xinjiang*, pp. 73–74.
82 Chen Feng, "Zhang Peiyuan, Ma Zhongying lianhe fan Sheng shibai jingguo" (Events of the defeat of the anti-Sheng alliance between Zhang Peiyuan and Ma

Zhongying), *Xinjiang wenshi ziliao xuanji*, vol. 6 (1980), p. 122.
83 Zhou Jianjin, "Ma Zhongying weikun Dihua shi xiangxi yingji A'ertai jun de qingkuang" (Ma Zhongying's interception of the Altay Army in the west while besieging Dihua [Urumqi]), *Xinjiang wenshi ziliao xuanji*, vol. 11 (1982), pp. 40–46.
84 This battle was waged on a massive scale: the fighter planes, tanks, armored cars, and artillery directly invested by the Soviet Union figure largely in the memoirs of the participants on the battlefield. This book primarily makes reference to: Mi Wankui, Su Deyan, Ma Sheng, Ma Yi and Ma Yonggui, "Toutunhe zuji zhan" (The holding operation at Toutunhe), *Changji wenshi ziliao xuanji*, vol. 3 (1985), pp. 21–24; Ma Yi, "Toutunhe zhanyi qinli ji" (A record of personal experiences at the Battle of Toutunhe), *Changji wenshi ziliao xuanji*, vol. 3 (1985), pp. 37–39; Jin Guozhen, "Wo canjia de jici zhanyi shikuang gaiyao" (A true outline of the several battles I participated in) *Xinjiang wenshi ziliao xuanji*, vol. 14 (1984), pp. 53–74; Jin Guozhen, "Yi jiu san san nian dong zhi yi jiu san si nian chun baowei Dihua shengcheng zhanyi de qianhou qingkuang" (Circumstances before and after the battle to defend the provincial capital of Dihua [Urumqi] from winter 1933 to spring 1934), *Xinjiang wenshi ziliao xuanji*, vol. 20 (1986), pp. 35–44; Dai Liangzuo, "Toutunhe zhi zhan de riqi he bingli zhuangbei" (Dates, troop strength and equipment at the battle of Toutunhe), *Changji wenshi ziliao xuanji*, vol. 3 (1985), pp. 81–83.
85 Sheng Shicai referred again to this matter in an essay published in Taiwan's *Zili wanbao* (Independence Evening Post) (page 3) on November 14, 1952, but his comments were again an obvious lie. In his second memoir, *Trivial Memories of the Pastureland Frontier*, Sheng admitted that the Soviet consul general in Urumqi visited him unexpectedly just prior to the arrival of the Soviet Red Armies in Xinjiang, to notify him that Stalin had decided to send troops to Xinjiang, and request that he prepare supply materials for the Soviet armies. Sheng Shicai, "Mubian suoyi," p. 82.
86 Burhan Shahidi, *Xinjiang wushi nian*, pp. 209–210; see also Chapter 2 of this work.
87 Aysa Niyaz, "Kumul dihanlar kozhulingiha dair bazi masililar tohursida aslima" (Recollections of the Kumul peasant rebellion), *Xinjiang Tarih Matiriyalliri* (Xinjiang Historical Materials) 12 (1983), pp. 69–71.
88 Hawir Tomur, "Hoja Niyaz Togrisida Aslima" (Recollections of Hoja Niyaz), *Xinjiang Tarih Matiriyalliri* 12 (1983), pp. 23–24.
89 Liu Yinglin, "Yaole boshi duoqu ha zhen jingbei siling de jingguo" (How Yulbars Khan seized control as the Garrison Commander of Hami Township), *Xinjiang wenshi ziliao xuanji*, vol. 6 (1980), pp. 168–169.
90 Ma Xiaoshi, "Ma Zhongying tuizou nan Jiang yihou" (After Ma Zhongying's retreat to southern Xinjiang), *Xinjiang wenshi ziliao xuanji*, vol. 1 (1979), pp. 49–50.
91 Wang Mengyang, "Ma Zhongying shibian shimo" (The whole story of events

surrounding Ma Zhongying), *Xinjiang wenshi ziliao xuanji*, vol. 5 (1980), pp. 148–149.
92 Burhan Shahidi, *Xinjiang wushi nian*, pp. 197–226.
93 A number of local memoirs found in local county and district collections of historical materials in northern Xinjiang make reference to the activities of Ma Zhongying's subordinate Ma Heying in the northern Kazakh region. See Da Lu, "1933 nian Manasi fasheng de ji jian shi" (Several events that occurred in Manas in 1933), *Changji wenshi ziliao xuanji*, vol. 3 (1985), pp. 30–34; Nai Weng, "Ma Heying zai Manasi qianhou" (When Ma Heying was in Manas), *Changji wenshi ziliao xuanji*, vol. 3 (1985), pp. 63–74; Chen Zhilan, An Weiting, "Ma Heying zai Hutubi de fumie" (The destruction of Ma Heying at Hutubi), *Changji wenshi ziliao xuanji*, vol. 3 (1985), pp. 26–29; Hamidi, "Ma Heying zhi si" (The death of Ma Heying), *Changji wenshi ziliao xuanji*, vol. 2 (1987), pp. 34–54; and so on.
94 On March 13, 1934, Sven Hedin witnessed an attack by Soviet aircraft on Ma Zhongying's forces at Korla; on March 17, he witnessed the Soviet army's pursuit of Ma Zhongying's troops. Sven Anders Hedin, *The Silk Road: Ten Thousand Miles Through Central Asia*, p. 298. Tungan or "Dungan" was a term used in the former Soviet Union to describe Chinese Hui Muslims; here the term refers to Ma Zhongying's Hui army.
95 Eric Teichman, *Journey to Turkistan*, p. 105.
96 Ibid., p. 25. For details on how Teichman's journey across Xinjiang transitioned from the planning stage to its final execution, see "Yingren Taikeman youli Xinjiang an" (Archive on the British Teichman's journey across Xinjiang), vols. 1 and 2, Archive No. 366.3/0001, in the collection of the Diplomatic Archives of the Ministry of Foreign Affairs of the Republic of China, which are held in the archives of the Institute of Modern History, Academia Sinica, Taiwan.

Chapter 4

1 During his 1935 visit to Xinjiang, Eric Teichman, a consular officer at the British Embassy in China, offered the following observations of the relationship between Sheng Shicai and Li Rong, then the President or Chairman of the Provincial Government: "The *Chu-hsi*, or 'Chairmen,' of the Provincial Governments are in effect nothing but the former governors under another name. Li *Chu-hsi* (Mr. Li Jung, the Chairman) should therefore have been the superior of Sheng *Tupan* (General Sheng, the Frontier Defence Commissioner); but this was another case where things Chinese must be assessed and judged by the facts rather than the names; and, while General Sheng was omnipotent, Mr. Li gave rather the impression of a figure-head." Eric Teichman, *Journey to Turkistan* (London: Hodder and Stoughton, 1937), p. 104.
2 Jin Guoxiang, "Xinjiang lujun junguan xuexiao xiaoshi" (History of the Xinjiang

Army Military Academy), Historical and Cultural Materials Research Committee of the Xinjiang Uyghur Autonomous Region Committee of the Chinese People's Political Consultative Conference (ed.), *Xinjiang wenshi ziliao xuanji* (Selected cultural and historical materials on Xinjiang), vol. 22 (1987), pp. 113–128. Li Liansheng, "Wo zai Xinjiang zhanche dui" (I was in the Xinjiang tank brigade), *Fukang wenshi ziliao* (Cultural and historical materials on Fukang), vol. 2 (1986), pp. 53–55.

3   Huang Musong, *Xinjiang gaishu* (Overview of Xinjiang) (Taipei: Taiwan wenhai chubanshe youxian gongsi, 1977), p. 2.

4   The Xinjiang Provincial Government reorganized its financial administration in 1934 and formulated a currency reform plan to withdraw all paper currency province-wide within 18 months, to achieve "the abolishment of the *tael* and introduction of the *yuan*." Xinjiang therefore requested that the central government issue 14 million yuan in central bank notes, but the request was ultimately denied. See Anonymous, "Shinkyō no zaisei konran" (Financial turmoil in Xinjiang) [新疆の財政混乱], *Dai Ajia Shugi* (Pan-Asiatic Journal) [大亜細亜主义], vol. 2, October issue (1934), p. 26. Sven Hedin also described the financial troubles Xinjiang faced in 1934: "When I first visited the capital of Sinkiang, in the spring of 1928, one had got 2½ Urumchi paper taels for a silver dollar. . . . On June 16, 1934, 240 Urumchi taels were to be had for a dollar!" "As a rule this press printed 700,000 taels (or *liang*, in the Turki *sär*) daily. For the festivities in April twenty millions had been printed. In 1928 there were only one-tael notes . . . but now 5,000 and 10,000 tael notes were printed, which further accelerated the fall in the exchange. People who had collected their notes and kept them for some time suddenly found themselves ruined." Sven Anders Hedin, *The Silk Road: Ten Thousand Miles Through Central Asia* (New York: E. P. Dutton and Company, 1938), p. 154. Sven also observed that, "Food prices rose fantastically. Thus on March 9, at Bugur, 100 catties of wheat flour cost 75 Urumchi taels; on May 22, at Tikkenlik, 550 taels; and on June 26, at Urumchi, 5,000 taels. Later the price rose to 14,000 Urumchi taels, and no one could afford to buy bread. On June 2, at Korla, an egg cost half a tael; three days later, at Toksun, 5 taels; and at the end of June, at Urumchi, 30 taels. Fruit, usually so cheap, rose in price and grew scarcer and scarcer." Sven Anders Hedin, *The Silk Road: Ten Thousand Miles Through Central Asia*, p. 159.

5   Zhou Dongjiao, *Xinjiang shi nian* (Ten years in Xinjiang) (Stencil mimeograph edition, 1948), p. 27.

6   Andrew D. W. Forbes, *Warlords and Muslims in Chinese Central Asia: A Political History of Republican Sinkiang 1911–1949* (Cambridge: Cambridge University Press, 1986), p. 136. Alexander Svanidze was the younger brother of Ekaterina Svanidze (nicknamed Kato), Stalin's first wife.

7   Xinjiang Opening Up Strategic Study Task Group (ed.), *Xinjiang dui Su jingmao wenti yanjiu* (Study of Xinjiang's economic and trade issues with the Soviet Union) (Urumqi: Xinjiang daxue chubanshe,1987), pp. 276–277.

8   The "Abundant Xinjiang Native Products Company" (裕新土特產公司 Yu Xin tutechan gongsi) monopolized foreign trade in Xinjiang during Sheng Shicai's era, buying up all agricultural and livestock products for export to the Soviet Union via ubiquitous branch companies, and importing industrial products from the Soviet Union into Xinjiang. The head of the Xinjiang Department of Finance concurrently served as the board chairman, and the president of the company was also appointed by the Xinjiang Provincial Government. The provincial government initially contributed 30% of the total capital, organizing the company in the form of a public-private partnership. After 1937, the Xinjiang government recalled all private shares, monopolizing the profits from Xinjiang-Soviet trade.
9   Zhou Dongjiao, "Sheng Shicai zai Xinjiang de tongzhi" (Sheng Shicai's rule over Xinjiang), *Xinjiang wenshi ziliao xuanji*, vol. 6 (1980), p. 24.
10 Zhou Dongjiao, *Xinjiang shi nian*, p. 24; Gong Bicheng, "Huiyi Xinsui gongsi" (Remembering the Xinsui Company), *Xinjiang wenshi ziliao xuanji*, vol. 4 (1979), pp. 143–146.
11 Du Zhongyuan, *Sheng Shicai yu xin Xinjiang* (Sheng Shicai and new Xinjiang) (Chongqing, Guilin, Shanghai, Hong Kong, Xi'an, Kunming, Chengdu, Changsha, Lanzhou, Guiyang: Shenghuo shudian, 1939), p. 29.
12 Zhou Dongjiao, *Xinjiang shi nian*, p. 23.
13 Sven Anders Hedin, *The Silk Road: Ten Thousand Miles Through Central Asia*, pp. 143, 198; Eric Teichman, *Journey to Turkistan*, p. 23.
14 Zhou Dongjiao, *Xinjiang shi nian*, p. 27–28.
15 Ibid.
16 In that era, Xinjiang's local administrative system was divided into three tiers: the province (with the president of the government as the provincial head), administrative regions (controlled by a senior administrator), and counties (led by county magistrates).
17 Zhao Jingyuan, "Xinjiang shibian jiqi shanhou" (Events in Xinjiang and their aftermath), *Xin Zhonghua zazhi* (New China Magazine), vol. 1, no. 10 (1933), pp. 4–5.
18 Chai Jisen, "Yu Xiusong zai Dihua de geming huodong" (Yu Xiusong's revolutionary activities in Dihua), *Wulumuqi wenshi ziliao* (Historical and cultural materials on Urumqi), vol. 7 (1984), p. 2.
19 Lang Daoheng, "'Xinjiang ribao' de pianduan" (Extracts from the "Xinjiang Daily"), *Xinjiang wenshi ziliao xuanji*, vol. 6 (1980), p. 175.
20 He Yuzhu, Kang Binglin, "Guanyu 'Xinjiang minzhong fandi lianhehui' ji qita" (On the "Xinjiang People's Anti-Imperialist Federation" and other matters), *Xinjiang wenshi ziliao xuanji*, vol. 14 (1984), pp. 38–41.
21 Chen Peisheng, "Xin de gangwei" (A new position), *Xinjiang wenshi ziliao xuanji*, vol. 19 (1991), p. 15.
22 Sun Hanwen, "Xinjiang minzu niaokan" (A bird's-eye view of the ethnic peoples of Xinjiang), *Xin yaxiya* (New Asia), vol. 12, no. 1 (1936), p. 36.
23 Wen Feiran, "Xinjiang kang-Ri minzu tongyi zhanxian de xingcheng yu polie"

(Formation and collapse of the Xinjiang People's United Front for Resistance Against Japan), *Xinjiang wenshi ziliao xuanji*, vol. 8 (1981), p. 3.

24 Wang Shoucheng (an alias used by Yu Xiusong, 1899–1938) had been an activist in the Chinese Communist Party since its early stages. In 1925, he was sent to the Soviet Union as a supervisor for CCP exchange students in Russia; he returned to Xinjiang in 1935. He served as the secretary-general of Xinjiang's Anti-Imperialist Federation, while concurrently holding the positions of head of the Political Training Office of the Frontier Defense Commissioner's Office, president of Xinjiang College, and principal of Xinjiang No. 1 Secondary School. In 1936, Wang married Sheng Shicai's younger sister, Sheng Shitong. On December 1937, Wang was arrested by Sheng Shicai under accusations of being a Trotskyite; in June 1938, he was sent under escort to the Soviet Union, and executed. See Luo Zhengjing, "Gongchan zhuyi de kaituozhe—Yu Xiusong lieshi" (Pioneer of Communism—the martyr Yu Xiusong), *Xinjiang lieshi zhuan* (Biographies of Xinjiang martyrs), vol. 2 (Urumqi: Xinjiang renmin chubanshe, 1986).

25 Luo Zhengjing, "Gongchan zhuyi de kaituozhe—Yu Xiusong lieshi." According to He Yuzhu and Kang Binglin ("Guanyu 'Xinjiang minzhong fandi lianhehui' ji qita," p. 43), prior to the establishment of the Society for the Promotion of Uyghur Culture in summer 1935, it was Wang Shoucheng and He Yuzhu who formulated this program revolving around ethnic culture and the "Six-Point Policy."

26 With respect to the development of ethnic school education in Xinjiang from 1935–1938, according to Du Zhongyuan, the Xinjiang Provincial Department of Education established 10 schools at the junior secondary school level or higher, 215 primary schools, and 50 adult schools (literacy schools). In addition, the Society for the Promotion of Uyghur Culture founded more than 1,980 local Uyghur schools, accommodating 129,649 students (Du Zhongyuan, *Sheng Shicai yu xin Xinjiang*, pp. 81–88). This era was also termed "the golden age for ethnic education in Xinjiang." For more details on the above, see Zhao Xinya, "Huiyi Xinjiang meng ha xuexiao chuangjian pianduan" (Incomplete memoirs on the founding of Mongolian and Kazakh schools in Xinjiang), *Xinjiang wenshi ziliao xuanji*, vol. 20 (1985); Liu Dehe, "Xinjiang gezu wenhua cujinhui jixu" (Narration of the cultural promotion societies of Xinjiang's various ethnic groups), *Xinjiang wenshi ziliao xuanji*, vol. 22 (1987); Guo Chenghua, "Kang-Ri zhanzheng shiqi Manasi xian de wenminghua jiaoyu" (Civilizing education in Manas County during the era of the War of Resistance against Japan), *Changji wenshi ziliao xuanji* (Selected cultural and historical materials on Changji), vol. 4 (1986); Zhao Yan'an, Zhang Dingbao, "Qitai xian jiaoyu jinxi" (Education in Qitai County, past and present), *Changji wenshi ziliao xuanji*, vol. 1 (1984); Yao Shijun, *Jimusa'er xian jiaoyu fazhan guancha* (Observations on educational development in Jimsar County) (Part 1), *Changji wenshi ziliao xuanji*, vol. 5 (1986); Qi Shoushan, "Huiyi Qiande xian Minguo shiqi de jiaoyu" (Recollections on education in Qiande County during the Republican era), *Miquan wenshi* (History and culture of

Miquan), vol. 1 (1987); and so on.
27 Wang Shoucheng, "Guanyu xin zhengfu minzu zhengce de baogao" (Report on the new government's ethnic policies), *Wulumuqi wenshi ziliao*, vol. 8 (1985, 2nd edition).
28 Luo Zhengjing, "Gongchan zhuyi de kaituozhe—Yu Xiusong lieshi," p. 24.
29 Beginning in 1934, Sheng Shicai sent 100 students each year to study abroad at the Soviet Union's National University of Central Asia in Tashkent; the composition of the students was 40% Han Chinese, Hui and Manchu; 40% Uyghur; 10% Mongolian; and 10% Kazakh. See Chai Hengsen, "Sheng Shicai xuansong liuxuesheng de qianqian houhou" (Details of Sheng Shicai's selection of study abroad students), *Xinjiang wenshi ziliao xuanji*, vol. 20 (1985), pp. 55–57.
30 Yulbars Khan, *Yaole boshi huiyi lu* (Memoirs of Yulbars Khan) (Taipei: Taiwan zhuanji wenxue chubanshe, 1969), p. 115.
31 Anonymous, "Nanjiang shibian zhi zhenxiang" (The true facts of the events in southern Xinjiang), *Dongfang zazhi* (Oriental Magazine), vol. 31, no. 6 (1934), p. 71.
32 Hosuyin Haji, "1933–34 yillardiki Kaxkar Halik Hozgilangliri wa Kirgizlar Bilan Bolgan Munasiwiti" (Connection between the mass uprising in Kashgar in 1933–1934 and the Kyrgyz people), *Xinjiang Tarih Matiriyalliri* (Xinjiang Historical Materials) 12 (1983), p. 131.
33 According to Liu Dehe, his brother Liu De'en was serving at the time as the Chinese deputy consul in Tashkent; he took photographs of the arrival of the Islamic delegation from East Turkestan and the local welcoming ceremony, and used these to lodge a protest with the Soviet government. Liu Dehe, "Ma Hushan, Muhuti zai nan Jiang panluan de jingguo" (Course of the armed rebellion by Ma Hushan and Muhiti in southern Xinjiang), *Xinjiang wenshi ziliao xuanji*, vol. 6 (1980), pp. 148–149.
34 Li Huiying, "Wo suo zhidao de Zhang Peiyuan de jiashi" (The family affairs of Zhang Peiyuan, according to my knowledge), *Xinjiang wenshi ziliao xuanji*, vol. 18 (1987), pp. 135–136; Asia Development Board, "(Hi) Soren no Shina henkyō shinryaku · kōa shiryō" ([Classified] The Soviet Union's invasion of China's border region: materials of the Asia Development Board) [（秘）ソ連の支那辺疆侵略・興亜資料] (Compiled by the Political Affairs Office), no. 5 (1939), pp. 84–85.
35 Institute of History of the Xinjiang Academy of Social Sciences, *Xinjiang jianshi* (Concise history of Xinjiang), vol. 3 (Urumqi: Xinjiang renmin chubanshe, 1987), p. 207.
36 Burhan Shahidi, *Xinjiang wushi nian* (Fifty years in Xinjiang) (Beijing: Wenshi ziliao chubanshe, 1984), pp. 188–189.
37 Sakamoto Koretada, *Chūgoku no henkyō to shōsū minzokumondai* (China's frontiers and problems with ethnic minorities) [中国の辺境と少数民族問題], Tokyo: Institute of Asian Economic Affairs, 1970, pp. 98–99.
38 Murata Shirō, "Henkyō sekka no kiki" (The crisis of frontier redification) [辺境赤化の危機], *Dai Ajia Shugi*, vol. 3, no. 2 (1935), p. 22.

39 Tanaka Kanae, "Henkyō ni okeru Ei Ro hotoke no kakuchiku" (The struggle between Britain, France and the Soviet Union for hegemony in the border regions) [辺疆における英露佛の角逐], *Dai Ajia Shugi*, vol. 3, no. 6 (1935), p. 60.

40 Sheng Shicai, *Shi nian Xinjiang huiyi lu* (Memoirs of a Decade in Xinjiang), Taiwan: *Zili wanbao* (Independence Evening Post) (Oct. 29, 1952).

41 Wen Feiran, "Xinjiang kang-Ri minzu tongyi zhanxian de xingcheng yu polie," pp. 21–22.

42 "Charter of the Xinjiang People's Anti-Imperialist Federation. Chapter 1: The Federation's Tasks. Article 1: The Xinjiang People's Anti-Imperialist Federation is a political organization spontaneously organized by the people; it shall adhere to the nationalism of President Sun, lead all the people of Xinjiang, establish Xinjiang as a permanent territory of China, and determinedly resist the imperialists who would sow discord in the peace amongst ethnic peoples and scheme for opportunities to make seizures." Zhang Dajun, *Xinjiang fengbao qishi nian* (Seventy years of upheaval in Xinjiang) (Taiwan: Lanxi chuban youxian gongsi, 1980), p. 3572.

43 Zhang Dajun, *Xinjiang fengbao qishi nian*, p. 3432.

44 Ishikawa Tadao, *Kokusai seiji to Chūkyō* (International Politics and the Chinese Communist Party) [国際政治と中共] (Tokyo: Yūshindō, 1986), p. 18.

45 Kasahara Masaaki, "Soren no Shinkyō shinshutsu no dōki (1931–1934)" (Motivations for the Soviet Union's Advances into Xinjiang [1931–1934]), *Kōbe-gai dai ronsō* (Collected papers of Kobe Municipal College of Foreign Affairs) (1961), pp. 93–104.

46 Andrew D. W. Forbes, *Warlords and Muslims in Chinese Central Asia: A Political History of Republican Sinkiang 1911–1949*, p. 136.

47 Eric Teichman, *Journey to Turkistan*, pp. 188–190.

48 Huang Musong, *Xinjiang gaishu*, p. 1.

49 Sven Anders Hedin, *The Silk Road: Ten Thousand Miles Through Central Asia*, p. 200.

50 Andrew D. W. Forbes, Warlords and Muslims in Chinese Central, p. 137; Lars-Erik Nyman, "Sinkiang 1934–1943: Dark Decade for a Pivotal Puppet," *Cahiers du Monde Russe et Soviétique*, vol. XXII (1), Jan.–Mar. (1991), p. 100.

51 Chen Peisheng, "Xin de gangwei," p. 4.

52 He Yuzhu, Kang Binglin, "Guanyu 'Xinjiang minzhong fandi lianhehui' ji qita," p. 41.

53 Burhan Shahidi, *Xinjiang wushi nian*, pp. 267–268.

54 Murata Shirō, "Henkyō sekka no kiki," p. 22.

55 Zhang Yiwu had studied abroad at the Advanced Gunnery School (Russian name unknown) in Moscow. See Zhou Dongjiao, "Sheng Shicai shi zenyang qude Xinjiang tongzhiquan de" (How Sheng Shicai achieved his rule over Xinjiang), *Wenshi ziliao xuanji*, vol. 46 (1964), p. 238; Wen Feiran, "Sheng Shicai tewu kongzhi xia de Xinjiang" (Xinjiang under the control of Sheng Shicai's secret agents), *Xinjiang wenshi ziliao xuanji*, vol. 7 (1981), pp. 2–3. Wang Lixiang (an

alias used by Zeng Youfu) had served in an intelligence organization in Outer Mongolia before being repatriated to Xinjiang by the Soviet Union. Zhou Dongjiao, *Xinjiang shi nian*, p. 68.
56 Lars-Erik Nyman, "Sinkiang 1934–1943: Dark Decade for a Pivotal Puppet," p. 98.
57 Institute of History of the Xinjiang Academy of Social Sciences, *Xinjiang jianshi*, vol. 3 (1987), p. 236.
58 Zhou Dongjiao, *Xinjiang shi nian*, p. 68.
59 Asia Development Board, "(Hi) Soren no Shina henkyō shinryaku· kōa shiryō," no. 5, pp. 85–86.
60 Zhang Dajun, *Xinjiang fengbao qishi nian*, p. 3708.
61 Hewir Tumor, "Hoja Niyaz Haji Togrisida Aslima" (Recollections of Hoja Niyaz), *Xinjiang Tarih Matiriyalliri* 12 (1983), pp. 25–26.
62 Ma Xiaoshi, "Ma Zhongying tuizou nan Jiang yihou" (After Ma Zhongying's retreat to southern Xinjiang), *Xinjiang wenshi ziliao xuanji*, vol. 1 (1979), pp. 49–50.
63 Ibid., p. 55.
64 Sheng Shicai, "Mubian suoyi" (Trivial memories of the pastureland frontier), *Wushi nian zhenghai fengyun—Tianshan nanbei* (Fifty years of political upheaval—the northern and southern Tianshan Mountains) (Taipei: Chunqiu chubanshe, 1967), p. 76.
65 When Sheng Shicai met the Soviet consul-general in Urumqi for the first time in May 1933, he presented the consul-general with a number of Marxist-Leninist works from his personal collection, including *Das Kapital* and the *Communist Manifesto*. However, as Zhang Yiwu revealed to Burhan Shahidi, most of these books were confiscated items, serving merely as ornamentation in a show put on for the Soviet consul-general. Burhan Shahidi, *Xinjiang wushi nian*, p. 188.
66 Wen Feiran, "Xinjiang kang-Ri minzu tongyi zhanxian de xingcheng yu polie," p. 21.
67 Sheng Shicai once told his subordinates that, if he had not received the Soviet Union's support in 1933, he would have had no choice but to abandon Xinjiang to central China. At that time, a pro-Soviet approach represented Sheng Shicai's only means of preserving his rule over Xinjiang. Burhan Shahidi, *Xinjiang wushi nian*, p. 188.
68 Party History Work Committee, Xinjiang Committee of the Chinese Communist Party, *Xin minzhu zhuyi geming shiqi Zhongguo gongchandang suo zai Xinjiang huodong jishi* (A record of the Chinese Communist Party's activities in Xinjiang during the era of the New Democratic Revolution) (Beijing: Jiefangjun chubanshe, 1985).
69 Chen Peisheng, "Xin de gangwei," p. 15.
70 In April 1937, the remaining forces of Regiment 268 of the Chinese Red West Road Army retreated across the eastern border of Xinjiang following their defeat

by a Hui warlord in Gansu; Sheng Shicai sent out troops to the eastern frontier to guide them into Urumqi, where they established the "New Barracks" (*Xin bingying* 新兵營). Yin Yuheng, "Yingjie Xizheng Hongjun lai Xinjiang huiyi pianduan" (Brief memoirs on welcoming the West March Red Army into Xinjiang), *Xinjiang wenshi ziliao xuanji*, vol. 11 (1982), pp. 2–4. When the "Ma Hushan Rebellion" broke out, the Xinjiang Provincial Army decamped to the front lines, and the Chinese Red Army became the sole defensive force in eastern Xinjiang warding off attacks on Urumqi by Yulbars Khan. Wen Feiran, "Xinjiang kang-Ri minzu tongyi zhanxian de xingcheng yu polie," p. 7.

71 Hu Xiaoguang, "Balu jun zhu Xinjiang banshi chu" (Xinjiang Station of the 8th Route Army), *Wulumuqi shi wenshi ziliao* (Historical and cultural materials on Urumqi City), vol. 3 (1982), p. 10.

72 Zhu Peimin, "Xinjiang kangri minzu tongyi zhanxian de xingcheng jiqi tedian" (The formation and characteristics of the Xinjiang People's United Front for Resistance Against Japan), *Jindai shi yanjiu* (Modern Chinese history studies), no. 5 (1988), p. 189.

73 See Luo Zhengjing, "Gongchan zhuyi de kaituozhe—Yu Xiusong lieshi," p. 25.

74 Institute of History of the Xinjiang Academy of Social Sciences, *Xinjiang jianshi* (Concise history of Xinjiang), vol. 2 (1980), p. 237.

75 Robert C. North, *Moscow and Chinese Communists* (Stanford: Stanford University Press, 2nd edition, 1963), p. 183.

76 Burhan Shahidi, *Xinjiang wushi nian*, p. 268.

77 Wen Feiran, "Xinjiang kang-Ri minzu tongyi zhanxian de xingcheng yu polie," p. 8.

78 Lars-Erik Nyman, "Sinkiang 1934–1943: Dark Decade for a Pivotal Puppet," p. 100.

79 According to Uyghur eyewitnesses, the Soviet planes and tanks and the Kyrgyz cavalry pursued Ma Hushan's forces deep into the Hotan region. Mamtimin Tohti, "Ma Husan Kuxunlirining Hotan Halkiga Salhan Zorawanlihi wa Buzhunqilih Ixliridin Aslima" (On the oppression and exploitation of the people of the Hotan region by Ma Hushan's army), *Xinjiang Tarih Matiriyalliri* 17 (1986), p. 158.

80 Hewir Tumor, "Hoja Niyaz Haji Togrisida Aslima," pp. 29–31; Liu Dehe, "Ma Hushan, Muhuti zai nan Jiang panluan de jingguo," p. 153.

81 Bay Ezizi, "Zhuisu Mamuti shizhang er shi nian" (Following Division Commander Muhiti for twenty years), *Xinjiang wenshi ziliao xuanji*, vol. 6 (1980), p. 142.

82 Hewir Tumor, "Hoja Niyaz Haji Togrisida Aslima," pp. 29–31; Liu Dehe, "Ma Hushan, Muhuti zai nan Jiang panluan de jingguo," p. 163.

83 Zhou Dongjiao, *Xinjiang shi nian*, pp. 75–76; Liu Dehe, "Ma Hushan, Muhuti zai nan Jiang panluan de jingguo," p. 163.

84 Hewir Tumor, "Hoja Niyaz Haji Togrisida Aslima," p. 31.

85 Shi Yuanpu, "Xinjiang mimi shenpan weiyuanhui jiepou" (Analysis of Xinjiang's

secret interrogation commission), *Xinjiang wenshi ziliao xuanji*, vol. 1 (1979), pp. 62–63.
86 Sheng Shicai once told Du Zhongyuan in 1938 that Japan kept a close watch on Xinjiang due to its important position in China's national defenses, establishing intelligence offices in Qinghai, Ningxia, Gansu and other places around Xinjiang's periphery, instigating civil strife in Xinjiang, and buying off Hoja Niyaz for three million yuan via a Tianjin merchant (Du Zhongyuan, *Sheng Shicai yu xin Xinjiang*, pp. 62–63). This story is completely at odds with the grounds given for the arrest of Hoja Niyaz, i.e., that he had initiated contact with Japan.
87 Hewir Tumor, "Hoja Niyaz Haji Togrisida Aslima," pp. 32–33.
88 Chai Hengsen, "Sheng Shicai xuansong liuxuesheng de qianqian houhou," p. 57.
89 According to Sheng Shicai himself, Stalin personally approved his accession to the Communist Party, and issued him with Party Card No. 1859118. Sakamoto Naomichi, *Chūso kokkyō funsō no haikei* (Background on the Sino-Soviet border disputes) [中ソ国境紛争の背景] (Tokyo: Kajima Kenkyūjo Shuppankai, 1970), p. 134; Li Sheng, *Zhongguo Xinjiang lishi yu xianzhuang* (The history and current conditions of Xinjiang, China) (Urumqi: Xinjiang renmin chubanshe, 2006), Japanese edition, p. 119.
90 Owen Lattimore, *Pivot of Asia: Sinkiang and the Inner Asian Frontiers of China and Russia*, Boston: Atlantic Monthly Press, 1950, pp. 71–72.
91 Party History Work Committee, Xinjiang Committee of the Chinese Communist Party, *Xin minzhu zhuyi geming shiqi Zhongguo gongchandang suo zai Xinjiang huodong jishi*, p. 19.
92 Zhao Jianfeng, "Xinjiang quansheng gong'an guanli chu de chansheng he moluo" (The Rise and fall of the Xinjiang Provincial Public Security Administration), *Xinjiang wenshi ziliao xuanji*, vol. 7 (1981), p. 39.
93 Zhou Dongjiao, *Xinjiang shi nian*, pp. 84–86.
94 Zhao Jianfeng, "Xinjiang quansheng gong'an guanli chu de chansheng he moluo," p. 39.
95 Li Mingzhang, "Du Zhongyuan xiansheng lai Xin he Beihai jingguo jianwen" (Mr. Du Zhongyuan's arrival in Xinjiang and the circumstances of his murder), *Xinjiang wenshi ziliao xuanji*, vol. 20 (1985), p. 139.
96 Zhou Dongjiao, *Xinjiang shi nian*, p. 86.
97 Mukax Jakan Ogli, "Xaripkan Ogadayiw Togrisida Aslima" (Recollections of Xaripkan Ogadayiw), *Xinjiang Tarih Matiriyalliri* 18 (1986), pp. 59–60. Shi Yuanpu, "Xinjiang mimi shenpan weiyuanhui jiepou," p. 68.
98 Zhang Dajun, *Xinjiang fengbao qishi nian*, p. 4099.
99 Editorial Team for "A Concise History of the Kyrgyz Minority," *Ke'erkezi zu jianshi* (A concise history of the Kyrgyz minority) (Urumqi: Xinjiang renmin chubanshe, 1985), p. 126; Liu Dehe, "Xinjiang gezu wenhua cujinhui jixu," p. 160; Hosuyin Haji, "1933–34 yillardiki Kaxkar Halik Hozgilangliri wa Kirgizlar Bilan Bolgan Munasiwiti," p. 133.

100 Haji Nabi Waliyuf, "Abah Kari Halpining Tarih Ahwali" (History of the Abah Kari [Clan]), *Xinjiang Tarih Matiriyalliri* 13 (1984), pp. 47–49.
101 Wan Lingyun, "Canjia Sheng Shicai de fushen weiyuanhui de diandi huiyi" (Fragmentary memories of participating in Sheng Shicai's review board), *Xinjiang wenshi ziliao xuanji*, vol. 4 (1979), pp. 166–168.
102 Gao Chongmin, "Huainian Du Zhongyuan tongzhi" (Remembering Comrade Du Zhongyuan), *Xinjiang wenshi ziliao xuanji*, vol. 6 (1980), p. 98.
103 Institute of History of the Xinjiang Academy of Social Sciences, *Xinjiang jianshi*, p. 311.
104 Zhang Bochun, "Nanwang de Yan'an zhi xing" (The unforgettable journey to Yan'an), *Changji wenshi ziliao xuanji*, vol. 1 (1984), p. 1.
105 The Chinese Red Army was divided into three garrisons in Xinjiang. Under the guidance of instructors from the Soviet Union and the Xinjiang Provincial Army, the troops learned how to drive cars, tanks and armored vehicles, and how to operate artillery, aircraft, and radios. Li Zhiming and Wang Chongguo, "Xilu jun zai Xinjiang" (The West Road Army in Xinjiang), *Xinjiang wenshi ziliao xuanji*, vol. 1 (1979), p. 21. The Red Army was also granted special treatment by Sheng Shicai in terms of living conditions. Xiao Xianqing, "Zai Xinjiang xin bingying de ririyeye" (Day and night at the new garrisons in Xinjiang), *Xinjiang wenshi ziliao xuanji*, vol. 20 (1985), pp. 9–11.
106 Zhu Peimin, "Xinjiang kangri minzu tongyi zhanxian de xingcheng jiqi tedian," pp. 187–193.
107 Guo Lin, "Xi'an shibian yu Xinjiang kangri minzu tongyi zhanxian de xingcheng" (The Xi'an incident and the formation of the Xinjiang People's United Front for Resistance Against Japan), *Xinjiang lishi yanjiu* (Historical studies of Xinjiang), no. 1 (1987), p. 72.
108 Zhu Peimin, "Xinjiang kangri minzu tongyi zhanxian de xingcheng jiqi tedian," p. 192.
109 Zhang Shiwan, "Xinjiang xuesheng lianhehui zhaji" (Notes on the Xinjiang Student Federation), *Wulumuqi wenshi ziliao*, vol. 10 (1986), pp. 79–82; Gong Xiuqin, "Kangzhan shiqi de Xinjiang funü xiehui" (The Xinjiang Women's Association during the War of Resistance), *Changji wenshi ziliao xuanji*, vol. 4 (1986), p. 59.
110 Haliq Saq, "Millitaris Shing Sisay Dawrida Har Millat Ziyalilirining Surgun Kilinix Ahwali Tohursida" (Recollections of the warlord Sheng Shicai's persecution of intellectuals of all ethnicities), *Xinjiang Tarih Matiriyalliri* 17 (1986), pp. 159–171.
111 Zhu Peimin, "Xinjiang kangri minzu tongyi zhanxian de xingcheng jiqi tedian," pp. 196–197.
112 The first CCP representative in Xinjiang was Chen Yun, a member of the Political Bureau (January–November 1937); the second was Deng Fa, an alternate member of the Central Political Bureau (January 1938–May 1939); the third was Chen

Tanqiu, a founder of the Chinese Communist Party (May 1939–September 1943; Chen was executed by Sheng Shicai).
113 Zhou Dongjiao, *Xinjiang shi nian*, p. 84; Zhu Peimin, "Xinjiang kangri minzu tongyi zhanxian de xingcheng jiqi tedian," p. 197.
114 Fang Zhichun, *Huiyi Xinjiang jianyu de douzheng* (Remembering my struggle in a Xinjiang prison) (Beijing: Renmin chubanshe, 1982), p. 33.
115 Tang Shenghua, "Huiyi zai Xinjiang xueyuan dushu de rizili" (Remembering my time studying at Xinjiang College), *Changji wenshi ziliao xuanji*, vol. 2 (1985), p. 8.
116 According to the memoirs compiled by Ji He, the secretary to CCP representative Chen Tanqiu, Chen used various tactics to evade Sheng Shicai's surveillance as he secretly made contact with CCP cadres across Xinjiang to guide their work. Ji He, "Chen Tanqiu tongzhi zai Xinjiang" (Comrade Chen Tanqiu in Xinjiang), *Xinjiang wenshi ziliao xuanji*, vol. 8 (1981), p. 29. For details, see Zhu Peimin, "Xinjiang kangri minzu tongyi zhanxian de xingcheng jiqi tedian," p. 198–199.
117 Zhang Dajun, *Xinjiang fengbao qishi nian*, p. 3999.
118 Materials of the Political Department of the Xinjiang Military Zone, *San qu geming qian Xinjiang de jingji he shehui qingkuang* (Xinjiang's socioeconomic conditions prior to the Three Districts Revolution) (Mimeographed edition), p. 4.
119 Zhang Yuansheng, "Kang Ri zhanzheng shiqi zai Kashi gongzuo de Gongchandang yuan" (The Communist Party members working in Kashgar in the era of the War of Resistance against Japan), *Kashi shi wenshi ziliao* (Historical and cultural materials on Kashgar City), vol. 2 (1987), pp. 1–29.
120 Party History Work Committee, Xinjiang Committee of the Chinese Communist Party, *Xin minzhu zhuyi geming shiqi Zhongguo gongchandang suo zai Xinjiang huodong jishi*, p. 36.
121 The Soviet Red Army stationed in Hami withdrew to the Soviet Union in April 1943, in response to demands by Sheng Shicai. In September of the same year, Sheng Shicai executed Chen Tanqiu, the CCP representative in Xinjiang; Mao Zemin, the younger brother of Mao Zedong; and Lin Jilu. Ma Zhaosong, "Cong ruyu dao chuyu" (From imprisonment to release), *Xinjiang wenshi ziliao xuanji*, vol. 10 (1982), p. 3.
122 Sheng Shicai himself claimed that the pivotal moment when he decided to abandon his pro-Soviet policies was in November 1940, when the Soviet Union forced him to sign a secret treaty: the "Xinjiang Tin Mining Concession Treaty." Zhang Dajun, *Xinjiang fengbao qishi nian*, pp. 4030–4031. In May 1942, Vladimir Dekanozov, the Deputy People's Commissar for Foreign Affairs of the Soviet Union, requested to visit Xinjiang to open negotiations with Sheng Shicai regarding oil fields in the region. On receiving this message, Sheng Shicai immediately invited Zhu Shaoliang, the Commander of China's 8th Military District, and Weng Wenhao, the Economic Minister and Chairman of the Resources Committee of the Chinese Nationalist government, to visit Xinjiang to convey the sense that he was part of the Nationalist government. Sun Yueqi, "Kangzhan qijian

liangci qu Xinjiang jilüe" (An account of two visits to Xinjiang during the War of Resistance), *Wenshi ziliao xuanji* (Selected cultural and historical materials), vol. 84 (1986), pp. 139–141. In August, Chiang Kai-shek's wife Soong Mei-ling arrived in Urumqi alongside Wu Zhongxin, the chairman of the Nationalist government's Commission on Mongolia and Tibet, to discuss the reinstatement of Nationalist control over the Urumqi regime. Lu Guisen, "Guofu shiye kaocha tuan jin Xin de jingguo" (Events of the Founding Fathers Industrial Inquiry Commission's arrival in Xinjiang), *Xinjiang wenshi ziliao xuanji*, vol. 20 (1986), p. 69.

Chapter 5

1   At the time, Xinjiang was divided into 10 districts, including Urumqi (Dihua), Hotan, Yarkent (Shache), Kashgar, Aksu, Karasahr (modern-day Yanqi), Kumul (Hami), Altay, Tarbagatay (modern-day Tacheng) and Ili. Ili District had jurisdiction over 11 counties, including Ghulja (Yining), Tekes, Qorghas (modern-day Huocheng), Nilka (Gongha), Tokkuztara (Gongliu), Zhaosu, Wenquan, Bole, Jinghe, Suiding, and Qapqal (Ningxi).
2   Mao Zedong, "Gei Ahemaitijiang de xin" (Letter to Ahmatjan), Aug. 18, 1949. *Kunlun.com: Xinjiang Party-Building Network*, retrieved from http://www.xjkunlun.cn/dswx/dszl/2010/2003786.htm (accessed on June 22, 2017).
3   Ahmatjan Kasimi, "Zai Yining Weiwuer-Hasake-Ke'erkezi renmin julebu de jianghua" (Speech at the Uyghur-Kazakh-Kyrgyz People's Club in Ghulja), Aug. 24, 1946, unpublished.
4   Enclosure No. 1 to Dispatch No. 23, dated September 25, 1945, on the subject "Rebel Objectives in Sinkiang" from the American Consulate, Tihwa. C.I.A XL32642-19. At the time, Robert Ward served as the U.S. consul general in Urumqi. Known in Chinese as Hua Ruide, Ward was referred to by relevant figures in the Urumqi government and military as "Consul Hua," demonstrating a close relationship.
5   The *Diary of Wu Zhongxin* (Wu Zhongxin riji), also referred to as *Diary of the Governor of Xinjiang* (Zhu Xin riji), was a diary kept by Wu Zhongxin during his term as the governor of Xinjiang; the author obtained access to an unpublished photocopy.
6   In 1943, the designation of "administrative district" was changed to "special district," and the title of "senior administrator" was changed to "commissioner."
7   *Wu Zhongxin riji*, Jan. 11, 1945: "Consul Hua recently expressed a desire to hear my significant political measures since March, so as to publicize these in the newspapers of the different nations and elicit worldwide attention and sympathy. I consented to the request, yet the subject was complex, and my promise could not be fulfilled instantly; I repeatedly enjoined Secretary Shen of the provincial government and Minister Shui of the Foreign Affairs Office to promptly provide the

materials. The sole request was that Consul Hua should release to those able to publish, and defer release to those unable to publish, to prevent misunderstandings by the outside world."

8   *Taranchi* is a transliteration of a term in the Mongolian language meaning "people who labor on the land." In the mid-17th century, the Mongol Dzungar tribe founded the Dzungar Khanate, centering on the Ili region of northern Xinjiang. After the Dzungars conquered southern Xinjiang, some of the Uyghur farmers in the region were conscripted as agricultural slaves and sent to the Ili basin, where they were known as *Taranchis*.

9   Urano Tatsuo, *Minzoku dokuritsuron: ajia afurika ni okeru dokuritsu no keika to imi* (Discourse on national independence: the process and significance of independence in Asia and Africa) [民族独立論：アジア・アフリカにおける独立の経過と意味] (Tokyo: Gunshuppan, 1982), p. 31.

10   *Wu Zhongxin riji*, Oct. 4, 1944.

11   Andrew D. W. Forbes, *Warlords and Muslims in Chinese Central Asia: A Political History of Republican Sinkiang 1911–1949* (Cambridge: Cambridge University Press, 1986), p. 167.

12   Ibid., pp. 165–167.

13   Sawdanow Zayir, "Xinjiang Uq Wilayat Inkilawiga Ait Ahwallar Hakkida Aslima" (A look back at the Xinjiang Three Districts Revolution), *Xinjiang Tarih Matiriyalliri* (Xinjiang Historical Materials) 16 (1985), p. 68.

14   Sha Long, "Xinjiang minzu yundong zhenxiang" (The truth of the Xinjiang national movement), *Jiefang ribao* (Liberation daily), Mar. 28, 1946.

15   Haliq Saq, "Millitaris Shing Sisay Dawrida Har Millat Ziyaliliring Surgun Kilinix Ahwali Tohursida" (Recollections of the warlord Sheng Shicai's persecution of intellectuals of all ethnicities), *Xinjiang Tarih Matiriyalliri* 17 (1986), p. 166.

16   The Nationalist government forces began moving into Xinjiang in 1943. The Xinjiang Provincial Party Committee for the Nationalist Party was reestablished in January; in May, Huang Rujin and Lin Jiyong, both of whom had studied abroad in the United States, were sent to Xinjiang. In June, the director of the Central Statistics Bureau led the "Sun Yat-sen Commission for Development" into Xinjiang to make preparations for two contingents of the Nationalist Army to be stationed in Xinjiang. Lu Guilin, "Guofu shiye kaocha tuan jin Xin de jingguo" (Events of the arrival of the Sun Yat-sen Commission for Development in Xinjiang), *Xinjiang wenshi ziliao xuanji* (Selected cultural and historical materials on Xinjiang), vol. 20 (1986), pp. 70–71. Sheng Shicai fiercely opposed the stationing of Nationalist government forces in Xinjiang: to avoid provoking him, the Nationalist government ordered one division of the army to secretly enter Xinjiang disguised as refugees. Du Xuezeng, "Lan Xin gonglu shang de dilei sheng" (The sound of land mines on the Lanzhou–Xinjiang Highway), *Xinjiang wenshi ziliao xuanji*, vol. 10 (1982), pp. 28–30.

17 Li Fanqun, "1944 nian Sheng Shicai zai Xinjiang de zuihou yici da daibu" (Sheng Shicai's last big round of arrests in Xinjiang in 1944), *Wenshi ziliao xuanji* (Selected cultural and historical materials), vol. 46 (1981), pp. 277–282.
18 Huang Jianhua, *Guomindang zhengfu de Xinjiang zhengce yanjiu* (A study of Nationalist government policies on Xinjiang) (Beijing: Minzu chubanshe, 2003), pp. 77–79.
19 *Wu Zhongxin riji*, Aug. 29, 1944.
20 Huo Dianqing, Xie Hai, "Zhengbian Guomindang Dihua shi jingchaju shimo" (Reexamination of events at the Urumqi Police Bureau under the Nationalist Party), *Xinjiang difang zhi* (Xinjiang Local Gazette), vol. 3 (1991), pp. 45–46.
21 Jin Shaoxian, "Yishu Guomindang yuanlao Wu Zhongxin" (Remembering the Nationalist Party veteran Wu Zhongxin), *Wenshi ziliao xuanji*, vol. 18 (1989), p. 93.
22 Andrew D. W. Forbes, *Warlords and Muslims in Chinese Central Asia*, p. 168.
23 *Wu Zhongxin riji*, Dec. 6, 1944.
24 Zeng Xiaolu, "Wu Zhongxin zhuzheng Xinjiang jilüe" (Account of Wu Zhongxin as the head of government in Xinjiang), *Wenshi ziliao xuanji*, vol. 46 (1964), p. 290.
25 Andrew D. W. Forbes, *Warlords and Muslims in Chinese Central Asia*, p. 165.
26 *Wu Zhongxin riji*, Nov. 4, 1944.
27 Ibid., Dec. 2, 1944.
28 Ibid., Dec. 9, 1944.
29 Urano Tatsuo, *Minzoku dokuritsuron*, p. 31.
30 *San qu geming Yili zhou ziliao* (Materials on the Three Districts Revolution in Ili Prefecture) (1991), p. 1. This provisional title refers to an unpublished collection of first-hand materials on the Three Districts Revolution in the Ili region; for convenience's sake, the collection is referred to in this work as *Materials on the Three Districts Revolution in Ili Prefecture*. The 1988 and 1991 versions differ somewhat in terms of their content.
31 Hakim Jappar, "Yaxlarning Uginix Olgisi Abdukirim Abasow" (A model for the young: Abdulkerim Abbasow), *Xinjiang Tarih Matiriyalliri* 26 (1989), p. 197.
32 Anwar Hanbaba, "Abdukirim Abasow Hakkida Aslima" (On Abdulkerim Abbasow), *Xinjiang Tarih Matiriyalliri* 25 (1988), p. 32.
33 Saypidin Azizi, *Tianshan xiongying* (Eagles of the Tianshan Mountains) (Beijing: Zhongguo wenshi chubanshe, 1987), p. 45.
34 You Li, "Abasuofu yinxiang ji" (Impressions of Abbasow), *Wulumuqi wenshi ziliao* (Cultural and historical materials on Urumqi), vol. 9 (1985), p. 40.
35 Abilmit Hajiyow, "Olmas Jangqi, Xanliq Tohpa: Yingi Zhonggo Kurux Yolida Kurban Bolganlar" (Immortal warriors, brilliant achievements: Dedicated to building New China), *Yinge Jiongguo Kurux Yolida Kurban Bolganlar* (Dedicated to building New China) (Urumqi: Xinjiang Halik Naxriyati, 1991), p. 95.
36 Saypidin Azizi, *Tianshan xiongying*, pp. 46–51.

37 Yasin Hudabardi, "Uq Wilayat Inkilawi Haqqida" (On the Three Districts Revolution), *Xinjiang Tarih Matiriyalliri* 16 (1985), p. 25.
38 Hakim Jappar, "Yaxlarning Uginix Olgisi Abdukirim Abasow," p. 197.
39 Saypidin Azizi, *Tianshan xiongying*, pp. 47–49.
40 Ibid., p. 51.
41 Xinjiang Three Districts Revolution History Editing Committee, *Xinjiang san qu geming shi* (History of the Xinjiang Three Districts Revolution) (Beijing: Minzu chubanshe, 1998), p. 36.
42 The commander of the Nilka guerrillas was the Tatar figure Fatih Muslimow; the first band was composed of 300 Kazakhs, led by the Kazakh Akbar and his deputy Sayit; the second band numbered 250, primarily composed of Uyghurs and Mongols, and led by the Uyghur Jani; the third band was primarily composed of White Russians, under the Russian leader Ivan.
43 *Wu Zhongxin riji*, Dec. 12, 1944.
44 Saypidin Azizi, "Aslima II" (Recollections II), *Omur Dastani* (Epic of life) (Beijing: Millatla Naxiriyati, 1990), p. 39.
45 Ibid., p. 38. Kurban Imin Osman, "Uq Wilayat Inkilawining Baxlinix Hakkida Aslima" (A look back at the beginning stages of the Three Districts Revolution), *Xinjiang Tarih Matiriyalliri* 16 (1985), p. 261.
46 "Nileike baodong huiyilu" (Memoirs of the Nilka rebellion) (Handwritten manuscript, anonymous, undated), pp. 20–21. Special thanks to a professor at the School of Ethnology and Sociology at Minzu University of China, who provided the author with access to this manuscript.
47 Kurban Imin Osman, "Uq Wilayat Inkilawining Baxlinix Hakkida Aslima," pp. 261–262; "Nileike baodong huiyilu," pp. 20–21.
48 "Nileike baodong huiyilu," p. 8.
49 Kurban Imin Osman, "Uq Wilayat Inkilawining Baxlinix Hakkida Aslima," p. 261.
50 Zhang Dajun, *Xinjiang fengbao qishi nian* (Seventy years of upheaval in Xinjiang) (Taiwan: Lanxi chuban youxian gongsi, 1980), p. 6258.
51 Saypidin Azizi, "Aslima II," p. 31.
52 Xinjiang Three Districts Revolution History Editing Committee, *Xinjiang san qu geming shi*, p. 39.
53 Kurban Imin Osman, "Uq Wilayat Inkilawining Baxlinix Hakkida Aslima," p. 261.
54 Saypidin Azizi, *Tianshan xiongying*, pp. 46–47.
55 Hakim Jappar, "Yaxlarning Uginix Olgisi Abdukirim Abasow," p. 195.
56 Anwar Hanbaba, "Abdukirim Abasow Hakkida Aslima," p. 31.
57 Yang Zongyu, Li Zhanlin, "Fang Xinjiang san qu geming lingdaoren Abasuofu furen Lü Suxin tongzhi jishi" (Transcript of an interview with Lü Suxin, the wife of Abbasow, leader of the Xinjiang Three Districts Revolution), *Yili wenshi ziliao* (Cultural and historical materials on Ili), vol. 5 (1989), p. 17.

58 "Dong tujuesitan gongheguo linshi zhengfu weiyuanhui di 26 hao jueyi" (Resolution No. 26 of the Committee of the Interim Government of the East Turkestan Republic), Mar. 1, 1945.
59 Xinjiang Three Districts Revolution History Editing Committee, *Xinjiang san qu geming shi*, p. 36.
60 Anwar Hanbaba, "Abdukirim Abasow Hakkida Aslima," p. 32.
61 Zhou Dongjiao, "Xinjiang bianluan jilüe" (Overview of the upheaval in Xinjiang), *Guancha* (Observations), Nov. 30, 1946, p. 10.
62 *Wu Zhongxin riji*, Dec. 21, 1944.
63 Xinjiang Three Districts Revolution History Editing Committee, *Xinjiang san qu geming shi*, p. 37.
64 Saypidin Azizi, *Tianshan xiongying*, p. 67; Institute of History of the Xinjiang Academy of Social Sciences, *Xinjiang jianshi* (Concise history of Xinjiang), vol. 3 (Urumqi: Xinjiang renmin chubanshe, 1987), p. 359; *San qu geming Yili zhou ziliao* (1988), pp. 16–17.
65 For details on the events in Ghulja, see Sawdanow Zayir, "Xinjiang Uq Wilayat Inkilawiga Ait Ahwallar Hakkida Aslima," pp. 13–19; Saypidin Azizi, "Aslima II," pp. 56–63; Chen Li, *Yili shibian jilüe* (An overview of events in Ili) (Taipei: Wenhai chubanshe, 1977 reproduction), pp. 17–19; Zhou Dongjiao, "Xinjiang bianluan jilüe," pp. 12–14.
66 Saypidin Azizi, *Tianshan xiongying*, p. 68. Note: *Haji* are Muslims who have made the pilgrimage to Mecca.
67 Ibid., p. 70.
68 Yasin Hudabardi, "Uq Wilayat Inkilawi Haqqida," pp. 24–25.
69 "Dong Tuerqi gongheguo linshi zhengfu zhuxi Yilihan de jianghua" (Speech by President Ilhan of the Interim Government of the East Turkestan Republic), Nov. 12, 1944, unpublished. This passage was translated verbatim to stay true to the original text.
70 With regard to the flags carried in the Ghulja Uprising, see Deng Liqun, "Guanyu Yili xuangua qizhi wenti gei zhongyang dian" (Telegram to central on the question of the flags flown in Ili) (Oct. 7, 1949). "Two flags have been used in this area: one is the green national flag of East Turkestan, and one is a white Islamic religious banner. When the flags were presented to the troops, all the officers and soldiers swore an oath to sacrifice all rather than allow anyone to take the flag." For the above source, see *San qu geming Yili zhou ziliao* (1991), p. 381; Party History Work Committee of the Xinjiang Uyghur Autonomous Region CCP Committee and Political Department of the Xinjiang Military Zone of the China People's Liberation Army (eds.), *Xinjiang heping jiefang* (Peace and liberation in Xinjiang) (Urumqi: Xinjiang renmin chubanshe, 1990), p. 292.
71 This army commander, left anonymous here, was of Sibe ethnicity; his father served as a Chinese consul in Almaty, so he spent his childhood in the Soviet Union and became proficient in Russian.

72 Yasin Hudabardi, "Uq Wilayat Inkilawi Haqqida," pp. 24–25.
73 "Dong Tuerqi gongheguo linshi zhengfu zhuxi Yilihan de jianghua." As above, the passage is translated verbatim from the original text.
74 *Wu Zhongxin riji*, Nov. 13, 1944; Zhou Dongjiao, "Xinjiang bianluan jilüe," p. 13.
75 An account of the execution of Han prisoners of war is provided in: Saypidin Azizi, *Tianshan xiongying*, pp. 74–75. Records of the massacre of Han civilians and looting of property may be found in: *San qu geming Yili zhou ziliao* (1991), p. 37; *Wu Zhongxin riji* (Nov. 13, 1944), and a number of other sources. Suiding County was reportedly home to 6,000 Han civilians, and except for 5 families, the remainder were all slaughtered. See Chen Li, *Yili shibian jilüe*, p. 18; and Chai Hengsen, "Hanzu renmin de zhiyou—Abasuofu" (A friend to the Han people—Abbasow), *Wulumuqi wenshi ziliao*, vol. 10 (1985), pp. 39–40.
76 Abdulkerim Abbasow, "Muqian de zhengzhi xingshi he women de renwu" (The current political trends and our tasks), May 11, 1945, *Wulumuqi wenshi ziliao* (Historical and cultural materials on Urumqi), vol. 6 (1983).
77 Ahmatjan Kasimi, "Women zai minzu wenti shang de yixie cuowu" (Some of our mistakes with respect to ethnic questions), Jun. 6, 1949, unpublished.
78 Yasin Hudabardi, "Uq Wilayat Inkilawi Haqqida," p. 35.
79 Ismailow Mahmut, "Uq Wilayat Milli Armiya 1-Suydung Piyada Polkining Duniyaga Kilixi wa Uning Bisip Otkan Yoli Togrisida Aslima" (The birth and development of Suiding 1st Infantry Corps of the Three Districts National Army), *Xinjiang Tarih Matiriyalliri* 16 (1985), p. 202.
80 Saypidin Azizi, *Tianshan xiongying*, p. 74.
81 Sawdanow Zayir, *5-korpusning Bisip Otkan Inkilawiy Musapisi* (The revolutionary path of the 5th Army) (Urumqi: Xinjiang Halik Naxriyati, 1989), p. 17.
82 Sawdanow Zayir, "Xinjiang Uq Wilayat Inkilawiga Ait Ahwallar Hakkida Aslima," p. 72.
83 Ibid., p. 71.
84 Kurban Imin Osman, "Uq Wilayatining Baxlinix Hakkida Aslima," p. 283.
85 Xinjiang Three Districts Revolution History Editing Committee, *Xinjiang san qu geming shi*, p. 37.
86 *Wu Zhongxin riji*, Oct. 19, 1944.
87 Saypidin Azizi, "Aslima II," p. 50.
88 Ibid., p. 57.
89 Ibid., p. 55; Sawdanow Zayir, *5-korpusning Bisip Otkan Inkilawiy Musapisi*, p. 14; *San qu geming Yili zhou ziliao* (1991), p. 26.
90 This figure is provided in: *San qu geming Yili zhou ziliao* (1991), p. 15. The detailed breakdown is as follows: The 128th Division included the 383rd Regiment, with 420 soldiers; the 4th Peace-Keeping Regiment, with 961 soldiers; the Air Force Training Squadron, with approximately 500 personnel; the Peace-Keeping Corps, with 285 soldiers; and the 1st Battalion, with 285 soldiers, for a total of 2,551

personnel. However, some of these personnel were unarmed. According to Sawdanow Zayir ("Xinjiang Uq Wilayat Inkilawiga Ait Ahwallar Hakkida Aslima," p. 14) and Saypidin Azizi ("Aslima II," p. 57), the government armed forces in Ghulja city proper numbered only 1,500 during the uprising.

91 Sawdanow Zayir, "Xinjiang Uq Wilayat Inkilawiga Ait Ahwallar Hakkida Aslima," p. 14.
92 *San qu geming Yili zhou ziliao* (1988), pp. 14–15.
93 Saypidin Azizi, "Aslima II," p. 55; Sawdanow Zayir, *5-korpusning Bisip Otkan Inkilawiy Musapisi*, p. 14.
94 *Wu Zhongxin riji*, Nov. 9, 1944.
95 Ibid., Nov. 13, 1944.
96 Xinjiang Three Districts Revolution History Editing Committee, *Xinjiang san qu geming shi*, pp. 38–39.
97 Zhang Dajun, *Xinjiang fengbao qishi nian*, pp. 6269–6270.
98 Yang Zongyu, Li Zhanlin, "Fang Xinjiang san qu geming lingdaoren Abasuofu furen Lü Suxin tongzhi jishi." Wen Feiran's memoirs are included in this text.
99 Li Sheng, *Zhongguo Xinjiang lishi yu xianzhuang* (The history and current conditions of Xinjiang, China) (Urumqi: Xinjiang renmin chubanshe, 2006), Japanese edition, p. 148.
100 Uyghur Saiman, "'Dong Tuerqisitan' geming bao zong bianji Weiwuer Sayiran zai Yining 'Xinmeng' jijifenzi huiyi shang de jianghua" (Speech by Uyghur Saiman, editor-in-chief of the revolutionary newspaper *East Turkestan*, at a meeting of the Ghulja "New Alliance" activists), May 11, 1949, unpublished.
101 Ahmatjan Kasimi, "Zhishi fenzi muqian de renwu he jijiang daolai de xuanju" (The current tasks faced by intellectuals and the upcoming elections), Sept. 25, 1946, unpublished.
102 Li Sheng, *Zhongguo Xinjiang lishi yu xianzhuang*, p. 148.

Chapter 6

1 For details on the "Nine Political Precepts" (*Tokkuz Maddlik Siyasiy Programma*) of November 12, 1944, see *San qu geming Yili zhou ziliao* (Materials on the Three Districts Revolution in Ili Prefecture) (1991), p. 32.
2 "Resolution No. 4 of the Interim Government Council of the East Turkestan Republic," dated January 5, 1945, contains the "Nine Political Precepts," along with other content.
3 Saypidin Azizi, "Aslima II" (Recollections II), *Omur Dastani* (Epic of life) (Beijing: Millatla Naxiriyati, 1990), p. 64. Saypidin Azizi was appointed as Minister of Education under "Resolution No. 33 of the Interim Government Council of the East Turkestan Republic," dated March 13, 1945.
4 Saypidin Azizi, "Aslima II," p. 64.

5   Saypidin Azizi, *Tianshan xiongying* (Eagles of the Tianshan Mountains) (Beijing: Zhongguo wenshi chubanshe, 1987), p. 70.
6   The *Provisional Working Regulations of the Ministry of Internal Affairs of the East Turkestan Republic* were issued in accordance with "Order No. 27 of the Ministry of Internal Affairs of the East Turkestan Republic," dated June 14, 1945.
7   "Resolution No. 8 of the Interim Government Council of the East Turkestan Republic," Jan. 16, 1945.
8   Hakim Jappar, "Yaxlarning Uginix Olgisi Abdukirim Abasow" (A model for the young: Abdulkerim Abbasow), *Xinjiang Tarih Matiriyalliri* (Xinjiang Historical Materials) 26 (1989), p. 199.
9   Xinjiang Three Districts Revolution History Editing Committee, *Xinjiang san qu geming shi* (History of the Xinjiang Three Districts Revolution) (Beijing: Minzu chubanshe, 1998), p. 55. This text claims that Piotr Alexandrov was less than sanguine about the outlook of an impending attack on Ghulja by Chinese government reinforcements, so he loaded the spoils of war he had collected onto a truck and attempted to flee to the Soviet Union.
10 "Resolution No. 33 of the Interim Government Council of the East Turkestan Republic," Mar. 13, 1945.
11 In accordance with "Resolution No. 6 of the Interim Government Council of the East Turkestan Republic" (Jan. 12, 1945), the armed forces of the East Turkestan Republic were divided into four branches, including the Army, Cavalry, Artillery, and Military Engineers; and 14 military ranks were instituted from rank-and-file soldiers to the highest-ranking officers, including Private First Class, Corporal, Sergeant, Warrant Officer, Second Lieutenant, First Lieutenant, Captain, Major, Lieutenant Colonel, Colonel, Junior Adjutant, Senior Adjutant, Major General, and Lieutenant General.
12 The full text of "Resolution No. 7 of the Interim Government Council of the East Turkestan Republic" (Jan. 15, 1945) reads: "All officers and field officers of the armed forces in Ili District shall be appointed by the Government of the East Turkestan Republic, and the formalities shall be observed posthaste for officers and field officers who have not yet been appointed by the government. Full authority is given to Minister Alexandrov of the Minister of Military Affairs of the East Turkestan Republic in this matter." The Minister of Military Affairs had the power to grant promotions and salary increases to officers at the rank of captain or below, while the power to make appointments to the rank of major or above was arrogated to the Interim Government Council.
13 "Resolution No. 26 of the Interim Government Council of the East Turkestan Republic," Mar. 1, 1945.
14 "Resolution No. 33 of the Interim Government Council of the East Turkestan Republic" (Mar. 13, 1945) contains the following passage on Rahimjan Sabir Ghaji's transfer: "(5) In accordance with Government Resolution No. 26 of March 1, 1945, Rahimjan Sabir Ghaji shall assume the position of Minister of Internal

Affairs. . . . (7) Due to his transfer to the Ministry of Internal Affairs, Rahimjan Sabir Ghaji is hereby dismissed from his position as Minister in the Ministry of Military Affairs."

15 Yang Zongyu, Li Zhanlin, "Fang Xinjiang san qu geming lingdaoren Abasuofu furen Lü Suxin tongzhi jishi" (Transcript of an interview with Lü Suxin, the wife of Abbasow, leader of the Xinjiang Three Districts Revolution), *Yili wenshi ziliao* (Cultural and historical materials on Ili), vol. 5 (1989), p. 17.

16 *San qu geming Yili zhou ziliao* (1991), pp. 36–44.

17 Turganow Osman, "Kandah Kilip Uq Wilayat Inkilaniga Katnaxkanligim Togrisida Aslima" (A brief retrospective on how I joined the Three Districts Revolution), *Xinjiang Tarih Matiriyalliri* 16 (1985), p. 247; Ismailow Mahemut, "Uq Wilayat Armiya I-suydung Piyada Polkining Duniyaga Kilixi wa Uning Bisip Otkan yoli Togrisida Aslima" (On the establishment of Suiding 1st Infantry Regiment of the Three Districts National Army and the path it followed), *Xinjiang Tarih Matiriyalliri* 16 (1985), p. 205.

18 The seven regiments of the National Army were as follows: Suiding 1st Infantry Regiment, Ghulja 2nd Infantry Regiment, Ghulja 4th Reserve Infantry Regiment, Tekes 1st Cavalry Regiment, Tekes 2nd Cavalry Regiment, Ertai 3rd Cavalry Regiment, and Tekes Dala 4th Cavalry Regiment (The regiments were given place names as the personnel in each unit were organized by place of origin). The four independent battalions included the Hui Independent Cavalry Battalion, Mongol Independent Cavalry Battalion, Independent Mortar Battalion, and the Independent Garrison Battalion. The independent company was the Usu Independent Company. According to Sawdanow Zayir in *The Revolutionary Path of the 5th Army* and *Materials on the Three Districts Revolution in Ili Prefecture* (1991), the National Army of the East Turkestan Republic numbered some 15,000. Sawdanow Zayir, *5-korpusning Bisip Otkan Inkilawiy Musapisi* (The revolutionary path of the 5th Army) (Urumqi: Xinjiang Halik Naxriyati, 1989), p. 47; *San qu geming Yili zhou ziliao* (1991), p. 82. However, in "Recollections II," Saypidin Azizi places the figure at approximately 12,000 (Saypidin Azizi, "Aslima II," p. 82).

19 Sawdanow Zayir, *5-korpusning Bisip Otkan Inkilawiy Musapisi*, p. 89.

20 Saypidin Azizi, "Aslima II," p. 89.

21 Hakim Jappar, "Yaxlarning Uginix Olgisi Abdukirim Abasow," p. 200.

22 *Wu Zhongxin riji* (Diary of Wu Zhongxin), Dec. 21, 1945.

23 In response to Talhat Musabayow's defection, his property was confiscated by order of "Resolution No. 4 of the Interim Government Council of the East Turkestan Republic" (Jan. 5, 1945).

24 According to the records in *Materials on the Three Districts Revolution in Ili Prefecture* (1991), after Fatih was forced out of the headquarters of the armed forces, he became the magistrate of Nilka County (*San qu geming Yili zhou ziliao* [1991], pp. 433–434). Fatih was later appointed as Ili District Advisor under "Resolution No. 324 of the Interim Government Council of the East Turkestan Republic" (Jun. 27,

1946); he served in this position until the fall of the East Turkestan Republic. After the founding of the People's Republic of China, Fatih fled to the Soviet Union.
25 In *Eagles of the Tianshan Mountains*, Saypidin Azizi states that Ilhan Tora became Marshal of the Armed Forces in February 1945 (Saypidin Azizi, *Tianshan xiongying*, p. 78). However, this title was not granted until June 27, 1945, under "Resolution No. 324 of the Interim Government Council of the East Turkestan Republic." The title Tora assumed in February 1945 was in fact "Supreme Commander of the Army."
26 Saypidin Azizi, *Tianshan xiongying*, p. 78.
27 "Resolution No. 79 of the Interim Government Council of the East Turkestan Republic" (Aug. 9, 1945) stripped Piotr Alexandrov of his position as a member of the Interim Government Council, and simultaneously installed Ivan Polinov as a council member.
28 "Resolution No. 33 of the Interim Government Council of the East Turkestan Republic" (Mar. 13, 1945).
29 Saypidin Azizi, *Tianshan xiongying*, p. 84.
30 Wu Haomin, "Xibozu qibing lian de zhandou shengya" (Exploits of the Sibe Cavalry Company in combat) (manuscript, 1991), p. 24.
31 Saypidin Azizi, "Aslima II," p. 108.
32 Hakim Jappar, "Yaxlarning Uginix Olgisi Abdukirim Abasow," p. 201.
33 Yasin Hudabardi, "Uq Wilayat Inkilawi Haqqida" (On the Three Districts Revolution), *Xinjiang Tarih Matiriyalliri* 16 (1985), p. 18.
34 *Wu Zhongxin riji*, Dec. 3, 1944.
35 Zhang Dajun, *Xinjiang fengbao qishi nian* (Seventy years of upheaval in Xinjiang) (Taiwan: Lanxi chuban youxian gongsi, 1980), p. 6288.
36 The Guozi Ravine is a mountain river valley in the Talichi Mountains near the border of Qorghas County: it runs for a distance of approximately 28 kilometers, bisected by the Urumqi-Ghulja Highway, and features rough terrain. Pine Pass, Ertai Bay, and Ertai are vital strategic points along the ravine.
37 Zunon Tayof, "Bor'ba za svobodu" (On the struggle for freedom), Наука (Nauka), (Glavnaya redaktsiya vostochnoy literatury izdatel'stva, 1974), p. 93.
38 *San qu geming Yili zhou ziliao* (1991), p. 45.
39 *Wu Zhongxin riji*, Feb. 4, 1945.
40 Ibid., Feb. 1, 1945; Zhang Dajun, *Xinjiang fengbao qishi nian*, pp. 6287–6310.
41 Enclosure No. 2 to Dispatch No. 23, dated September 25, 1945, on the subject "Rebel Objectives in Sinkiang" from the American Consulate, Tihwa. C.I.A XL32642-19. In the bulletin, Ilhan Tora is referred to using the title of Supreme Commander of the Army, so we can surmise that the document was circulated in 1945. The text also states, "A very short time had scarcely passed before we had taken Rjulja [Ghulja], Kura, Suiting [Suiding], Chilfanza, and Bortala, and had reached Chingho [Jinghe]." This passage indicates that the document was written

after March 1945.
42 *San qu geming Yili zhou ziliao* (1991), p. 56.
43 Bai Zhensheng and Koibuchi Shin'ichi (eds.), *Xinjiang xiandai zhengzhi shehui shilüe* (Outline of Xinjiang's modern sociopolitical history) (Beijing: Zhongguo shehui kexue chubanshe, 1992), pp. 391–392.
44 Yasin Hudabardi, "Uq Wilayat Inkilawi Haqqida," p. 29.

Chapter 7

1 Saypidin Azizi, "Aslima II" (Recollections II), *Omur Dastani* (Epic of life) (Beijing: Millatla Naxiriyati, 1990), p. 97; Zhou Dongjiao, *Xinjiang shi nian* (Ten years in Xinjiang) (Stencil mimeograph edition, 1948), pp. 207–208. Zhang Dajun provides the following timeline for the National Army's assault on Tarbagatay: on July 18, 1945, the road from Urumqi to Tarbagatay was cut off; on the 20th, the important strongholds of Miao'ergou and Hansantai near the road were captured; a major assault was launched on the 22nd; on the 29th; Dorbiljin was captured; and on the 31st, the Tarbagatay District Commissioner and the garrison commander led the local Chinese government officials and troops in a retreat from Choqak into Soviet territories. On August 2 saw the capture of Hoboksar Town, a key crossing point in the route from Tarbagatay District to Altay District; and on August 22, the Chinese regiment commander stationed in Hoxtolgay Town, the seat of the Hoboksar County Government, abandoned the city and fled to Urumqi. See Zhang Dajun, *Xinjiang fengbao qishi nian* (Seventy years of upheaval in Xinjiang) (Taiwan: Lanxi chuban youxian gongsi, 1980), pp. 6335–6343.

2 Sources give varying accounts of the liberation of Altay District. This chapter relies on *San qu geming Yili zhou ziliao* (Materials on the Three Districts Revolution in Ili Prefecture) (1991), pp. 121–127.

3 With regard to the National Army's advance toward southern Xinjiang, this chapter primarily relies on: Sawdanow Zayir, *5-korpusning Bisip Otkan Inkilawiy Musapisi* (The revolutionary path of the 5th Army) (Urumqi: Xinjiang Halik Naxriyati, 1989), pp. 90–95. Sources vary somewhat as to the dates when each of these places fell. For instance, Chen Li states in *An Overview of Events in Ili* that Bay Town fell on August 11, and that Aksu Old Town was captured on September 6. See Chen Li, *Yili shibian jilüe* (An overview of events in Ili) (Taipei: Wenhai chubanshe, 1977 reproduction), p. 36.

4 According to the account given by Saypidin Azizi in "Aslima II" (pp. 55–89), on the Northern Front, three regiments were deployed to Dorbiljin County, Choqak County and Hoboksar County in Tarbagatay District; in Altay District, one regiment was posted to Burqin County, and two regiments were sent to Chenghua County. On the Central Front, four regiments were posted to Jinghe, along with the 45th Division Headquarters Company, and two regiments were sent to Usu

alongside the 2nd Army Headquarters Company. On the Southern Front, Bay Town and Aksu Old Town each saw the deployment of one regiment.

5   These figures are an estimate based on *Materials on the Three Districts Revolution in Ili Prefecture* (1991), pp. 101–128, and Sawdanow Zayir's *The revolutionary path of the 5th Army*, p. 41. The lists included 1,100 men deployed to Tarbagatay District, 1,846 in Altay District, 3,000 in the battle at Jinghe and Usu, and 220 in Aksu District.

6   For the events of the battle at Jinghe and Usu, this chapter primarily relies on *Materials on the Three Districts Revolution in Ili Prefecture* (1991), pp. 85–96. However, according to the account provided by Chen Li in *An Overview of Events in Ili*, p. 32, the Chinese government forces at Jinghe and Usu included two regiments from the 45th Division, 3 regiments from the 3rd Irregulars Division, two regiments from the 7th Reserve Division, two regiments from the 1st Cavalry Division, one company from the Special Operations Regiment, and one tank company, for a contingent numbering some 20,000 in total. According to Wu Haomin, a soldier in the East Turkestan National Army who participated in the battle at Jinghe and Usu, the political director of the Ili 2nd Infantry Regiment characterized the combat thusly in the aftermath of the battle: "Generals Polinov and Munonow personally took command over the battle at Jinghe and the battle at Usu. Aside from the Ili 2nd Infantry Regiment, the forces committed to the battlefield by our army numbered some 4,000 men, including the 1st Cavalry Company under the personal command of General Munonow, Tekes 1st Cavalry Regiment, and Ili 4th Regiment. Two bomber planes also supported the operation from the air." See Wu Haomin, "Xibozu qibing lian de zhandou shengya" (Exploits of the Sibe Cavalry Company in combat) (manuscript, 1991), p. 37. According to the account by Tong Pei, a radio technician serving with the Chinese government forces, three bomber planes conducted daily runs over the Chinese position, wreaking destruction on the Chinese line and causing a great many casualties among the government forces. See Tong Pei, "Guomindang jundui Wusu kuitui ji" (Account of the rout of Nationalist armed forces at Usu), *Changji wenshi ziliao xuanji* (Selected cultural and historical materials on Changji), vol. 6 (1985), p. 58. Another participant in the battle stated in an interview with the author that the bombers were Soviet planes repainted with the symbols of the East Turkestan Republic.

7   Xinjiang Three Districts Revolution History Editing Committee, *Xinjiang san qu geming shi* (History of the Xinjiang Three Districts Revolution) (Beijing: Minzu chubanshe, 1998), p. 80.

8   Due to the guerrilla warfare being waged around the periphery of Urumqi, Wu Zhongxin, the president of the Xinjiang Provincial Government, believed that an invasion of the city by East Turkestan forces was imminent. Chiang Kai-shek also gave Wu the following instructions: "As for the fortifications near Urumqi, particularly the former aircraft factory and each of the airfields, you must immediately set about shoring up the defenses; it is paramount that there should be no delay"

See *Wu Zhongxin riji* (Diary of Wu Zhongxin), Dec. 3, 1945. Wu Zhongxin reportedly once declared to the troops under his command, with an air of looking death in the eye, that it was a great honor to die in battle in defense of one's country. See Zhang Dajun, *Xinjiang fengbao qishi nian*, p. 6767. In mid-April 1945, Commander Zhu Shaoliang of China's 8th Military District redeployed the military forces in Xinjiang, with the aim of recapturing Ili and supporting the Tarbagatay and Altay Districts; the defenses were also concentrated at Jinghe and Usu to meet the primary objective of defending Urumqi. See *San qu geming Yili zhou ziliao* (1991), p. 84.

9   According to Zhang Dajun, the headquarters of the Chinese government forces at Guchung received intelligence that the Kazakh magistrate Zaraban of Xinjiang's Nanshan District had met with Osman Islam's guerrillas and decided that all the Kazakhs in Guchung County would migrate to Altay District to join Osman's revolution. See Zhang Dajun, *Xinjiang fengbao qishi nian*, pp. 6320–6321.

10 The rebellion in Taxkorgan was instigated by the local Kyrgyz, Tajiks and other Muslim inhabitants of the region. For details on this uprising, see Part 1 of the chapter "Taxkorganidiki Partizan Urux" (Guerrilla warfare in Taxkorgan) in Sawdanow Zayir, *5-korpusning Bisip Otkan Inkilawiy Musapisi*, pp. 102–107; as well as Part 1 of the chapter "Taxkorgan Inkilawiy" (The Taxkorgan Revolution) in Saypidin Azizi, "Aslima II," pp. 136–166.

11 Saypidin Azizi gives the following description of the plan of operations: "Cut off the routes from Urumqi and Jinghe to Tarbagatay District and Altay District; liberate Tarbagatay District and Altay District. Control all the mountain roads from Ili District to southern Xinjiang; liberate Karasahr, Aksu and other places [in southern Xinjiang]. Meet up with the Taxkorgan guerrillas; destroy the road between Kashgar and Hotan; put pressure on Kashgar, Hotan and other places. Boost guerrilla operations at Usu, Manas, Jinghe, Turpan and other places; put pressure on the routes for the Nationalist reactionary army to come to Urumqi; push the front lines forward to the Manas River; and finally liberate Urumqi." See Saypidin Azizi, "Aslima II," p. 85.

12 *San qu geming Yili zhou ziliao* (1991), pp. 89–90.

13 The specific figures were: "(1) Ghulja County, 220 persons; (2) Suiding County, 40 persons; (3) Qorghas County, 40 persons; (4) Bortala County, 50 persons; (5) Wenquan County, 20 persons; (6) Qizil Kol (Tekes County), 40 persons; (7) Zhaosu County, 40 persons; (8) Tekes Dala County, 50 persons; (9) Nilka County, 20 persons; (10) Kunes County, 20 persons." Interim Government of the East Turkestan Republic, "Draft Conscription Order," Jun. 1, 1945.

14 *San qu geming Yili zhou ziliao* (1991), p. 104.

15 In December 1944, the Chinese forces in Xinjiang included central government troops as well as the forces formerly under the command of Sheng Shicai. "Xinjiang now has four divisions of the central army [the 45th division, 46th Division, 128th Division, and the 7th Reserve Division], 26,350 men in all." See *Wu Zhongxin riji*,

Dec. 6, 1944. The Xinjiang Provincial Army formed under Sheng Shicai's regime included six divisions, four peace-keeping regiments, one artillery regiment, one special operations regiment, and one tank battalion, numbering 34,000 in total. (The breakdown is as follows: for the central government forces, the 128th Division numbered approximately 8,000 men; the Xinjiang provincial forces included the 3rd Irregulars Division: 8,000; 1st Cavalry Division: 3,000; 2nd Cavalry Division: 3,000; 11th Cavalry Division: 3,000; 12th Cavalry Division: 3,000; a total of 3,000 men in the four peace-keeping regiments; 3,000 soldiers in the Artillery Regiment; 1,500 personnel in the Special Operations Regiment; and 300 men in the Tank Battalion.) See Chen Li, *Yili shibian jilüe*, p. 15.

16 On January 25, 1945, Chiang Kai-shek commanded the Hui warlord Ma Bufang of Qinghai to send two divisions to Xinjiang (see *Wu Zhongxin riji*, Jan. 25, 1945). Ma Bufang sent a telegram on February 8 informing Wu Zhongxin of the deployment of the 5th Cavalry Army. According to the telegram, the 5th Cavalry Army consisted of "5,618 officers and men, and 6,230 horses." See *San qu geming Yili zhou ziliao* (1991), p. 70. The 5th Cavalry Army had originally been under the command of Ma Bufang's elder brother, Ma Buqing, before being subsumed under Ma Bufang's forces. See Wang Jishan, "Ma Chengxiang zai Xinjiang" (Ma Chengxiang in Xinjiang), *Wulumuqi wenshi ziliao* (Historical and cultural materials on Urumqi), vol. 9 (1985), p. 65.

17 *San qu geming Yili zhou ziliao* (1991), p. 70.

18 The timeline for the arrival of the 5th Cavalry Army in Xinjiang is based on the account in: Han Youwen, "'Bei Tashan shijian' jiqi jingguo" (Events of the "North Tashan Incident"), *Xinjiang wenshi ziliao xuanji* (Selected historical and cultural materials on Xinjiang), vol. 20 (1985), p. 100. The 5th Cavalry Army was cobbled together from the 5th Division and the 1st Irregulars Division; at the time, Han Youwen served as the commander of the 1st Irregulars Division.

19 Wu Haomin, "Xibozu qibing lian de zhandou shengya" (1991).

20 Zhang Dajun, *Xinjiang fengbao qishi nian*, p. 6548: "Su-ka-u-bo (a Soviet Russian Kazakh, given the title of general) leads forces composed of Soviet Russians, Kazakhs, Kyrgyz, Uyghurs and other ethnic groups; the cavalry troop numbers approximately 3,000 men, equipped with rifles and horses, as well as a large supply of heavy machine guns, mortars, small cannon, mountain guns, anti-matériel rifles, and handheld machine guns; each soldier is also equipped with a saber. Known as the *Yiwei* Troop, they are believed to have been formed from the core troops of the Red 8th Army; their whereabouts after the battle at Jinghe are unknown."

21 Isakbek Munonow participated in the First East Turkestan Independence Movement in 1933, yet he later accepted Soviet aid to establish a Kyrgyz troop devoted to stamping out the independence movement. During the 1937 Hotan Rebellion instigated by Ma Zhongying's subordinate Ma Hushan, a troop of Kyrgyz cavalry from the Soviet Union led by Munonow became the vanguard to suppress the uprising, contributing to the preservation of Sheng Shicai's regime. Munonow was

later appointed as the Commissioner of the Governance Board (senior regional administrator) in Ulughqat. In 1940, he became the director of the Xinjiang Society for the Promotion of Kazakh and Kyrgyz Culture, before fleeing to the Soviet Union in 1941. Munonow later trained a band of guerrillas in Soviet territory, and in October 1944, he organized the Taxkorgan Rebellion (Puli Revolution) in southern Xinjiang. On November 16, 1944, Munonow led troops into Ghulja alongside Ivan Polinov; he later made important contributions in the attacks on Hayranbaq Airfield and the efforts to seize Ili District for the East Turkestan Republic. See Saypidin Azizi, "Aslima II," p. 69, and *San qu geming Yili zhou ziliao* (1991), p. 40. On April 8, 1945, Isakbek Munonow was awarded the rank of major general and appointed as the deputy commander of the National Army: alongside the Soviet national Ivan Polinov, who served as commander-in-chief of the National Army with the rank of lieutenant general, Munonow took command in the Three-Front War, and played a major role in the expansion of the East Turkestan Republic. On October 14, 1945, Munonow was promoted to lieutenant general under Resolution No. 107 of the Interim Government Council; and after Polinov returned to the Soviet Union in June 1946, he became the commander-in-chief of the National Army.

22 Saypidin Azizi, "Aslima II," p. 69; *San qu geming Yili zhou ziliao* (1991), p. 40.
23 Li Sheng, *Zhongguo Xinjiang lishi yu xianzhuang* (The history and current conditions of Xinjiang, China) (Urumqi: Xinjiang renmin chubanshe, 2006), Japanese edition, p. 149.
24 In May 1945, the Interim Government of the East Turkestan Republic ordered that all Han residents of Bortala County, Tekes County, Nilka County, and Kunes County in Ili District were to be relocated to Qapqal County, and that all Han residents of Qapqal County, Suiding County, Qorghas County, and Ghulja County were to be relocated to Huiyuan; the Han Chinese would also be permitted to return to China's interior provinces. See *San qu geming Yili zhou ziliao* (1991), p. 87. The push for relocation is also referenced in the bulletin by President Ilhan Tora; see Enclosure No. 2 to Dispatch No. 23, dated September 25, 1945, on the subject "Rebel Objectives in Sinkiang" from the American Consulate, Tihwa. C.I.A XL32642-19.
25 *San qu geming Yili zhou ziliao* (1991), p. 111.
26 The National Army established supply depots in Ghulja, Jinghe, Usu, Sawan, Dorbiljin, Altay, Qorghas, Tekes, Tekes Dala, Suiding, and other places. See "Minzu jun de gongying he houqin gongzuo de qingkuang" (Details on the supply and logistics work of the National Army) (unpublished, unknown author, 1959), pp. 112–114.
27 Saypidin Azizi, "Aslima II," p. 97.
28 Zhang Dajun, *Xinjiang fengbao qishi nian*, p. 6532.
29 The East Turkestan Republic only named three generals. Aside from Lieutenant General Ivan Polinov, the other two figures were Major General Isakbek

Munonow (who was promoted to lieutenant general on October 14, 1945, under "Resolution No. 107 of the Interim Government Council of the East Turkestan Republic"), and Dalalkan Sugurbayow, who was awarded the rank of major general in September 1945.

30 Ivan Polinov was appointed as a council member and Isakbek Munonow as an alternate member under "Resolution No. 79 of the Interim Government Council of the East Turkestan Republic," dated August 9, 1945.
31 Saypidin Azizi, "Aslima II," p. 95.
32 A telegram entitled "On Matters Related to the Trip to Visit Nationalist Party Military and Political Authorities in Urumqi" sent by Deng Liqun to the Central Committee of the Chinese Communist Party on September 11, 1949, read: "To the Central Committee: Regarding my journey to Urumqi, the results of discussions with friends and the Ili authorities are as follows. . . ." "Friends" is a reference to the Soviet consular officials in Ghulja; this passage indicates the influence that the Soviet consulate wielded within the East Turkestan Republic. See Deng Liqun, "Guanyu qu Dihua huijian Guomindang junzheng dangju youguan shiyi," in Party History Work Committee of the Xinjiang Uyghur Autonomous Region CCP Committee and Political Department of the Xinjiang Military Zone of the China People's Liberation Army (eds.), *Xinjiang heping jiefang* (Peace and liberation in Xinjiang) (Urumqi: Xinjiang renmin chubanshe, 1990), p. 225.
33 Saypidin Azizi, "Aslima II," p. 115.
34 Xinjiang Three Districts Revolution History Editing Committee, *Xinjiang san qu geming shi*, p. 44.
35 Ibid., p. 71.
36 *San qu geming Yili zhou ziliao* (1991), p. 84.
37 Zhang Dajun, *Xinjiang fengbao qishi nian*, p. 6526.
38 Xinjiang Three Districts Revolution History Editing Committee, *Xinjiang san qu geming shi*, pp. 79–80.
39 Saypidin Azizi, "Aslima II," p. 95.
40 Zhang Dajun, *Xinjiang fengbao qishi nian*, pp. 6326–6327.
41 Ibid., pp. 6328–6330.
42 Hawir Tomur, "Hoja Niyaz Togrisida Aslima" (Recollections of Hoja Niyaz), *Xinjiang Tarih Matiriyalliri* (Xinjiang Historical Materials) 12 (1983), p. 26. *History of the Xinjiang Three Districts Revolution* states that "Abla Remzanov" was in fact the true name of Mansur Roziyow (Apandi). See Xinjiang Three Districts Revolution History Editing Committee, *Xinjiang san qu geming shi*, p. 28.
43 Hawir Tomur, "Hoja Niyaz Togrisida Aslima," p. 26; Zhang Dajun, *Xinjiang fengbao qishi nian*, p. 3708.
44 Saypidin Azizi, "Aslima II," p. 98.
45 Abilmit Hajiyow, "Uq Wilayat Inkilawining Aldi-kayindiki Tarbagatay" (Tarbagatay before and after the Three Districts Revolution), *Xinjiang Tarih Matiriyalliri* 26 (1989), p. 35.

46 Imir (transliterated in Chinese as 伊米爾 or *Yi-mi-er*) is the name of a river that wends its way from Dorbiljin in Tarbagatay District to Lake Alakol (*Oziro Alakol*) in the Republic of Kazakhstan; part of the river serves as the border between China and the Soviet Union.
47 Abilmit Hajiyow, "Uq Wilayat Inkilawining Aldi-kayindiki Tarbagatay," p. 35.
48 Saypidin Azizi, "Aslima II," p. 479.
49 Abilmit Hajiyow, "Uq Wilayat Inkilawining Aldi-kayindiki Tarbagatay," pp. 8–14.
50 Ibid., p. 15.
51 Ibid., pp. 20–21.
52 Abilmit Hajiyow, "San qu geming zhong Tacheng de dixia huodong he wuzhuang douzheng" (Underground activities and armed conflict in Tarbagatay during the Three Districts Revolution), *Yili wenshi ziliao* (Historical and cultural materials on Ili), vol. 4 (1998), p. 38; *San qu geming Yili zhou ziliao* (1991), p. 93; Abilmit Hajiyow, "Uq Wilayat Inkilawining Aldi-kayindiki Tarbagatay," p. 29.
53 Abilmit Hajiyow, "Uq Wilayat Inkilawining Aldi-kayindiki Tarbagatay," p. 22.
54 Ibid., pp. 28–32.
55 Saypidin Azizi, "Aslima II," pp. 96–98.
56 "Resolution of the Field Meeting of the Interim Government Council of the East Turkestan Republic," Aug. 6, 1945.
57 Zhang Dajun, *Xinjiang fengbao qishi nian*, p. 6341.
58 *San qu geming Yili zhou ziliao* (1991), pp. 106–107.
59 Xinjiang Three Districts Revolution History Editing Committee, *Xinjiang san qu geming shi*, p. 77.
60 "Resolution No. 85 of the Interim Government Council of the East Turkestan Republic," dated August 22, 1945, sets the quotas for the issuance of "Victory Bonds" as 150 million for Ili District, 100 million for Tarbagatay District, and 50 million for Altay District.
61 Altay District is composed of seven counties, including Altay County, Koktokay County, Burqin County, Jiminay County, Kaba County, Burultokay County and Qinggil County. In July 1945, the Kazakh rebel forces controlled Koktokay, Jiminay, Burultokay, and Qinggil.
62 Patihan Sugurbayow was born in 1927; at age 14, he joined his father's guerrilla band. After the founding of the People's Republic of China, he served as the Deputy Governor of Xinjiang Uyghur Autonomous Region from September 1955 to September 1968; he also served as a standing member of the Chinese People's Political Consultative Conference of Xinjiang Uyghur Autonomous Prefecture until his death in 1996. His wife was the daughter of Secretary-General Mankay of Altay Administrative District, who was executed during Sheng Shicai's first great purge of 1937–1938.
63 Kurban Ali Ospanow, "Barikol Wakaliri Tohursida Aslimilar" (The truth about the events in Barköl), *Xinjiang Tarih Matiriyalliri* 18 (1986), p. 128.

64 Burhan Shahidi, *Xinjiang wushi nian* (Fifty years in Xinjiang) (Beijing: Wenshi ziliao chubanshe, 1984), pp. 204–206.
65 This figure is cited from: Su Beihai and Li Xiumei, "Zai Sheng Shicai canku tongzhi xia, Xinjiang Hasake zu taoqian Gansu, Qinghai ji guowai de jingguo" (The experiences of Xinjiang Kazakhs who fled to Gansu, Qinghai and abroad under the brutal rule of Sheng Shicai), in Learning Cultural and Historical Materials Committee of the CPPCC Changji Hui Autonomous Prefecture Committee (ed.), *Changji Hasake zu de bianqian* (Vicissitudes of the Kazakhs in Changji) (Changji: CPPCC Changji Hui Autonomous Prefecture Committee, 1989), pp. 46–65. Other sources vary: the figure is placed at approximately 15,000 in Barköl Kazakh Autonomous County Survey Group (ed.), *Balikun Hasake zizhi xian kaikuang* (Survey of Barköl Kazakh Autonomous County) (Urumqi: Xinjiang renmin chubanshe, 1984), p. 49; in He Junfang, "Minguo shiqi Hasake zu xiang gansu de qianxi" (Kazakh migration into Gansu in the era of the Republic of China), *Xibei shidi* (Historical and Geographical Review of Northwest China), no. 1 (1989), p. 17, the figure is given as 10,579; while in Qi Xiangyang, "Xinjiang Hasake zu dongqian Gan Qing jilüe" (Overview of the eastward migration of Xinjiang Kazakhs into Gansu and Qinghai), *Changji wenshi ziliao xuanji*, vol. 4 (1986), p. 88, the number is placed at 9,455. The Kazakh nomads of Barköl County migrated to Gansu in two great waves during the 1930s: the first wave occurred in 1935–1936, while the second wave spanned the period from late 1938 to early 1939. This book relied on the following sources in reference to the Kazakh migrations: Kurban Ali Ospanow, "Barikol Wakaliri Tohursida Aslimilar," pp. 127–169; Xinjiang Minority Sociohistorical Survey Team of the Institute of Ethnology and Anthropology of the Chinese Academy of Social Sciences (ed.), *Hasake zu jianshi jianzhi hebian* (Combined survey history and atlas of the Kazakh people) (Draft, unpublished, 1963), pp. 42–43; Survey History of the Kazakh People Editing Group (ed.), *Hasake zu jianshi* (Survey history of the Kazakh people), Urumqi: Xinjiang renmin chubanshe, 1987, p. 231; Barköl Kazakh Autonomous County Survey Group, *Balikun Hasake zizhi xian kaikuang*, pp. 46–51; and Kul Bhat, "Hasake zu dongqian Gansu" (Eastward migration of Kazakhs to Gansu), *Qitai xian wenshi ziliao* (Historical and cultural materials on Qitai County), vol. 26 (1990).
66 Kurban Ali Ospanow, "Barikol Wakaliri Tohursida Aslimilar," p. 137.
67 The Kazakh residents of Koktokay County were the first to rise up in the Kazakh uprisings that spread across the Altay region, thus the incidents were referred to as the "Koktokay Rebellion."
68 Peace terms were finally reached in the First Altay Kazakh Rebellion in 1941 under the conditions that Sheng Shicai would release the detained rebels, abolish the police bureaus, give amnesty to the rebel leaders, and cease the confiscation of weapons. See Muqash Jakeugli, "Xaripqan Ogdayup Tohursida Aslima" (Recollections of Xaripqan Ogdayup), *Xinjiang Tarih Matiriyalliri* 18 (1986), pp. 99–100. However, a second wave of uprisings broke out in 1941 after Sheng Shicai failed to

honor the terms of the agreement. The brutal suppression of the uprisings led to internal dissension among the rebels, and another accord was reached with Sheng Shicai under the condition of amnesty for the rebel leaders; in return, the rebels were to surrender their weapons to the regime. See "Koktokai Kozhulingi Tohursida Yadimda Kalhan Bazi Ixlar" (Certain memories of the Koktokay rebellions), *Xinjiang Tarih Matiriyalliri* 18 (1986), pp. 122–124.

69 According to the census conducted by the Xinjiang Provincial Police Headquarters in 1943, the total population of Altay District at the time was 63,040. This included 27,469 Kazakh men and 25,883 Kazakh women. See Chen Chengzhi, "Xinjiang Yili shijian zhi fenxi" (Analysis of the events in Ili, Xinjiang), *Xin Zhonghua* (New China) supplement edition, vol. 4, no. 11 (1946), reprinted in: Institute of Ethnology and Anthropology of the Chinese Academy of Sciences (ed.), *Xinjiang lishi ziliao ji* (Collected historical materials on Xinjiang), vol. 5, 2nd photo-offset edition, pp. 131–138.

70 Zhang Dajun, *Xinjiang fengbao qishi nian*, pp. 5198, 4345.

71 Haji Nabi Walyow, "Abaq Kari Halipning Tarih Ahwali" (Historical events of the Abaq Kari [tribe]), *Xinjiang Tarih Matiriyalliri* 18 (1986), pp. 56–57.

72 Ibid., pp. 58–60.

73 *Materials on the Three Districts Revolution in Ili Prefecture* (1991, p. 427) states that the "Altay Kazakh National Restoration Committee" was founded in mid-December 1943. However, in Kadis Janabil, "Altay Wilayiti Inkilawi Kuruxi wa Dalelhan Sugurbawef" (The revolution struggle in Altay District and Dalalkan Sugurbayow) (*Yingi Junggo Kurux Yolida Kurban Bolganlar* [Dedicated to building New China], Urumqi: Xinjiang Halik Naxiryati, 1991), pp. 152–172, the date is given as April 1944.

74 Shahrux, "Huiyi yeye Dalielihan er san shi" (Remembering two or three deeds of my grandfather Dalalkan), *Yili wenshi ziliao*, vol. 3 (1987), p. 71.

75 In his interview with the author, Patiha Sugurbayow gave the name of the Altay government as the "National Revolutionary Interim Government of Altay." However, the formulation "Altay Revolutionary Interim Government" also appears frequently in the memoirs of witnesses to these events, as seen in: Ashat Makay, "Altay Wakitlik Hukumiti Ning Kuruluxi wa Baxkilar" (The founding of the Altay Revolutionary Interim Government and other matters), *Yingi Junggo Kurux Yolida Kurban Bolganlar* (Urumqi: Xinjiang Halik Naxiryati, 1991), p. 179.

76 In his interview with the author, Patiha Sugurbayow also described how Dalalkan Sugurbayow escaped to the Soviet Union: "Dalalkan first got in contact with the Soviet Consulate in Altay through Hasan, a Soviet Tatar, and secretly entered the consulate in disguise. The Tatar vice-consul then personally formulated a plan for Dalalkan to be hidden inside a bottomless barrel and loaded onto the gas transport truck of the Soviet Underground Resource Survey Team; on October 10, 1941, he crossed the border at Jiminay to enter the Soviet Union." Accounts vary as to the precise date of Dalalkan Sugurbayow's arrival in the Soviet Union. Kadis Janabil

gives the date as September 26, 1941 (Kadis Janabil, "Altay Wilayiti Inkilawi Kuruxi wa Dalelhan Sugurbawef," p. 157), while Dalalkan's granddaughter claims that he reached the Soviet Union in February 1941 (Shahrux, "Huiyi yeye Dalielihan er san shi," p. 71). However, each of these accounts states that Sugurbayow crossed the border at Jiminay with the aid of the Soviet Consulate.

77 Ashat Makay, "Altay Wakitlik Hukumiti Ning Kuruluxi wa Baxkilar," p. 180; Xinjiang Three Districts Revolution History Editing Committee, *Xinjiang san qu geming shi*, pp. 21–22.
78 Xinjiang Three Districts Revolution History Editing Committee, *Xinjiang san qu geming shi*, pp. 21–22.
79 Ibid., p. 76.
80 In his interview with the author, Patiha Sugurbayow clarified that the advisors sent by the Mongolian People's Republic were either Soviet nationals or Kazakhs from Outer Mongolia. On this point, see also: Zhang Guojie, "Cong fan Qing douzheng dao san qu geming—Aleitai lishi diaocha" (From the struggle against the Qing Dynasty to the Three Districts Revolution—Historical survey of Altay), *Xinjiang lishi yanjiu* (Historical studies of Xinjiang), no. 1 (1987), p. 79.
81 Haji Nabi Walyow, "Abaq Kari Halipning Tarih Ahwali," p. 66.
82 In particular, Dalalkan Sugurbayow (himself a tribal leader) often used his authority within the tribal system to mobilize the nomadic herders. Prior to his return to Altay, Sugurbayow wrote letters to all the tribal leaders in Altay, calling upon each tribe for aid (Ashat Makay, "Altay Wakitlik Hukumiti Ning Kuruluxi wa Baxkilar," pp. 175–176). To gather troops and isolate the Chinese government forces, Sugurbayow used his authority as a tribal leader to persuade the Kazakh nomads living in Altay County, Burqin County and Burultokay County to relocate to Qinggil County in September 1944 (Kadis Janabil, "Altay Wilayiti Inkilawi Kuruxi wa Dalelhan Sugurbawef," pp. 160–161). He also stipulated that the members of the Revolutionary Interim Government Council should be leaders representing each county and tribe (Ashat Makay, "Altay Wakitlik Hukumiti Ning Kuruluxi wa Baxkilar," pp. 178–179).
83 The distance between Jiminay Town and the town of Zaysan in Soviet Kazakhstan was only 50 kilometers, with a road running between them. The national border was also marked only by a narrow river. The distance from Qinggil Town to the border of the Mongolian People's Republic was no more than 60 kilometers. Zhou Dongjiao, "Ashan qu gaikuang" (Survey of Altay District), *Xinjiang luncong* (Collected essays on Xinjiang), First Issue (1947); this essay was reprinted in Institute of Ethnology and Anthropology of the Chinese Academy of Sciences (ed.), *Xinjiang lishi ziliao ji*, vol. 5, pp. 343–344.
84 Abilmit Hajiyow, "Uq Wilayat Inkilawining Aldi-kayindiki Tarbagatay," pp. 12–13.
85 Kadis Janabil, "Altay Wilayiti Inkilawi Kuruxi wa Dalelhan Sugurbawef," p. 160.
86 Ashat Makay, "Altay Wakitlik Hukumiti Ning Kuruluxi wa Baxkilar," p. 178.

87 Zhang Guojie, "Cong fan Qing douzheng dao san qu geming—Aleitai lishi diaocha," p. 79.
88 Kadis Janabil, "Altay Wilayiti Inkilawi Kuruxi wa Dalelhan Sugurbawef," p. 163; Ashat Makay, "Altay Wakitlik Hukumiti Ning Kuruluxi wa Baxkilar," p. 185.
89 Ahmatjan, "Zai Yining Weiwuer, Hasake, Ke'erkezi renmin julebu de jianghua" (Speech at the Uyghur, Kazakh & Kyrgyz Club in Ghulja), Aug. 24, 1946, unpublished.
90 Saypidin Azizi, "Aslima II," p. 105.
91 "Resolution of the Interim Government of the East Turkestan Republic Regarding Altay Special District," Sept. 23, 1945.
92 Li Sheng, *Zhongguo Xinjiang lishi yu xianzhuang*, p. 149.

Chapter 8

1 Andrew D. W. Forbes, *Warlords and Muslims in Chinese Central Asia: A Political History of Republican Sinkiang 1911–1949* (Cambridge: Cambridge University Press, 1986), pp. 319–320.
2 In 1942, He Yingqin, Cheng Qian, Xu Yongchang, Zhang Wenbo, He Yuezu, and Zhou Zhirou established a task group by command of Chiang Kai-shek to discuss the recapture of Xinjiang, formulating a "Plan to Restore Sovereignty in Xinjiang." One of the plan's key proposals was as follows: "2. To check the Soviet Union's actions, it is agreed that methods such as allowing British and American Christians to enter Xinjiang to engage in missionary activities shall be utilized. . . . On a deeper level, this issue is a matter of urging the two countries to establish consulates; needless to say, the latter method will achieve results in this respect." On September 28, 1942, the Nationalist government began using the Soviet Union's excessive interest in Xinjiang as grounds for urging the United States to establish a consulate in the region; the United States also began to develop an interest in Xinjiang. Britain and the United States successively established consulates in the region in 1943. Kashima Akio, *Chūso gaikōshi kenkyū: 1937–1946* (Study of Chinese diplomatic history: 1937–1946) [中ソ外交史研究：1937–1946] (Kyoto: Sekai Shisōsha, 1990), pp. 109–110.
3 Jiang Zhongzheng, *Su'e zai Zhongguo* (Soviet Russia in China) (Taipei: Zhongyang wenwushe, 1957), p. 88.
4 John W. Garver, *Chinese-Soviet Relations, 1937–1945: The Diplomacy of Chinese Nationalism* (New York, Oxford: Oxford University Press, 1988), p. 176.
5 Pan Rongli, "Guomindang junshi weiyuanhui pai fu Xinjiang ganbu tuan de zaoyu" (Experiences of the cadre team sent to Xinjiang by the Military Affairs Commission of the Nationalist Party), *Xinjiang wenshi ziliao xuanji* (Selected cultural and historical materials on Xinjiang), vol. 10 (1982), p. 35.
6 John W. Garver, *Chinese-Soviet Relations, 1937–1945*, p. 176.

7   *Wu Zhongxin riji* (Diary of Wu Zhongxin), Nov. 22, 1944.
8   Ibid., Jan. 7, 1945.
9   Ibid., Jan. 15, 1945.
10 Ishii Akira, "Shinkyō o meguru naka so kōshō: 1949–50 nen" (Sino-Soviet negotiations over Xinjiang: 1949–50) [新疆をめぐる中ソ交渉：一九四九 – 五〇年], Faculty of Education of the School of Education at University of Tokyo (ed.), *Kyōiku gakka kiyō* (Journal of the Faculty of Education) [教育学科紀要], no. 14 (1981), p. 63. This paper is also included in: Ishii Akira, *Chuso kankeishi no kenkyu: 1945–1950 nen* (Study of the history of Sino-Soviet diplomatic relations: 1945–1950) [中ソ関係史の研究：1945–1950 年] (Tokyo: University of Tokyo Press, 1990).
11 *Wu Zhongxin riji*, Jan. 23, 1945.
12 Ibid., Dec. 3, 1944.
13 Ibid., Dec. 5, 1944.
14 Ibid.
15 Ishii Akira, "Shinkyō o meguru naka so kōshō: 1949–50 nen," p. 63.
16 Shi Zhe, *Zai lishi juren shenbian* (By the side of a giant of history) (Beijing: Zhongyang wenxian chubanshe, 1991), pp. 450–451.
17 Osman Islam was appointed as the Altay District Commissioner. The majority of the Kazakhs who ascended to positions as government officials were Kazakh tribal leaders. Zhang Guojie, "Cong fan Qing douzheng dao san qu geming—Aleitai lishi diaocha" (From the struggle against the Qing Dynasty to the Three Districts Revolution—Historical survey of Altay), *Xinjiang lishi yanjiu* (Historical studies of Xinjiang), no. 1 (1987), p. 80. In Tarbagatay District, the position of district commissioner was held by elite members of local ethnic communities who had not participated in the underground rebel movement.
18 Ishii Akira, "Chū so kankei ni yoru Ryojun, Dairen mondai" (Sino-Soviet relations with respect to the matters of Port Arthur and Dairen [Dalian]) [中ソ関係による旅順、大連問題], in The Japan Association of International Relations (ed.), *Kokusai seiji* (International politics) [国際政治], no. 95: *Chuso kankei to kokusai kankyo* (Sino-Soviet relations and the international environment) [中ソ関係と国際環境] (Tokyo: Yūhikaku, 1990), p. 46.
19 Zhang Dajun, *Xinjiang fengbao qishi nian* (Seventy years of upheaval in Xinjiang) (Taiwan: Lanxi chuban youxian gongsi, 1980), p. 6556.
20 Ismailow Mahmut, "Uq Wilayat Milli Armiya 1-Suydung Piyada Polkining Duniyaga Kilixi wa Uning Bisip Otkan Yoli Togrisida Aslima" (The birth and development of Suiding 1st Infantry Corps of the Three Districts National Army), *Xinjiang Tarih Matiriyalliri* 16 (1985), pp. 219–220.
21 *San qu geming Yili zhou ziliao* (Materials on the Three Districts Revolution in Ili Prefecture) (1991), pp. 140–141.
22 Sawdanow Zayir, *5-korpusning Bisip Otkan Inkilawiy Musapisi* (The revolutionary path of the 5th Army) (Urumqi: Xinjiang Halik Naxriyati, 1989), p. 81.

23 *San qu geming Yili zhou ziliao* (1991) p. 106.
24 Zhang Dajun, *Xinjiang fengbao qishi nian*, p. 6556.
25 Zhang Zhizhong, *Zhang Zhizhong huiyi lu* (Memoirs of Zhang Zhizhong) (Beijing: Wenshi ziliao chubanshe, 1985), pp. 418–419.
26 Zhang Dajun, *Xinjiang fengbao qishi nian*, pp. 6557–6558.
27 Ibid., pp. 6558–6559; Chen Li, *Yili shibian jilüe* (An overview of events in Ili) (Taipei: Wenhai chubanshe, 1977 reproduction), p. 139.
28 Tong Pei, "Guomindang jundui Wusu kuitui ji" (Account of the rout of Nationalist armed forces at Usu), *Changji wenshi ziliao xuanji* (Selected cultural and historical materials on Changji), vol. 6 (1985), p. 59.
29 *Wu Zhongxin riji*, Feb. 5, 1945.
30 Saypidin Azizi, "Aslima II" (Recollections II), *Omur Dastani* (Epic of life) (Beijing: Millatla Naxiriyati, 1990), p. 90.
31 Edward R. Stettinius, Jr., *Roosevelt and the Russians: The Yalta Conference* (Garden City, N.Y.: Doubleday, 1949), p. 93.
32 Jiang Junzhang, "Song Ziwen Mosike huitan zhuiji" (Retrospective on T. V. Soong's talks at Moscow), *Zhongguo yi zhou* (Week in China), no. 100 (1952). At the time of writing, Jiang Junzhang was a clerk in the editorial office for the *President's Biography* (Zongtong shilüe 總統事略) under the President's Secret Service, and had access to documents pertaining to state secrets. It was fired immediately after the publication of this article. For more details, see Kashima Akio, *Chūso gaikōshi kenkyū: 1937–1946*, pp. 190–192.
33 Ishii Akira, "Shinkyō o meguru naka so kōshō: 1949–50 nen," p. 63. The "Letter from Foreign Minister Wang Shijie of the National Government of the Republic of China to Molotov, People's Commissar for Foreign Affairs of the Soviet Federative Socialist Republic," another memorandum exchanged during the talks, contains the following passage: "The Chinese government expressed its interest in the desire for independence among the people of Outer Mongolia on many occasions; after the defeat of Japan, this desire was affirmed by the people of Outer Mongolia through a plebiscite, and the Chinese government is willing to recognize Outer Mongolia's independence within the existing borders." "Chū so yūkō dōmei jōyaku, kōkan kō bun oyobi fuzoku kyōtei, 1945-nen 8-gatsu 14-nichi" (Effective Sino-Soviet treaty of alliance, exchanged documents and attached agreements, August 14, 1945), in: China Department of the Japan Institute of International Affairs (ed.), *Shin Chūgoku shiryō shūsei* (Anthology of materials on new China), vol. 1 (Tokyo: Nihon Kokusai Mondai Kenkyūjo [Japan Institute of International Affairs], 1963), pp. 104–105.
34 In 1942, Molotov offered Sheng Shicai a greater share of profits in exchange for abandoning the idea of breaking away from the Soviet Union, but his overture was unsuccessful. The Soviet Union then proposed talks regarding a Sino-Soviet petroleum partnership to manage the Maytagh oil fields; this effort also failed due to political one-upmanship on the part of both the Soviets and the Chinese. The

Soviet Union ultimately dismantled its facilities at the oil fields, and began transporting the equipment back across the border. China and the Soviet Union finally reached an agreement in 1942 under which the remaining equipment would be sold to China for 1.7 million USD, and the oil fields would revert to Chinese ownership. Kashima Akio, *Chūso gaikōshi kenkyū*: 1937–1946, pp. 98–111.

35 Abilmit Hajiyow, "Tarbagatay Wilayitining Igilik Terekkiyat Tarihiga Dair Aslima" (Recollections on the economic development of Tarbagatay District), *Xinjiang Tarih Matiriyalliri* 25 (1988), pp. 292–293.
36 Ishii Akira, "Shinkyō o meguru naka so kōshō: 1949–50 nen," p. 69.
37 Chinese Association on Frontier Administration (ed.), *Sheng Shicai zenyang tongzhi Xinjiang* (How Sheng Shicai ruled over Xinjiang) (Taipei: Zhongguo bianzheng xiehui [Chinese Association on Frontier Administration], 1954), pp. 21–27.
38 Li Sheng, *Zhongguo Xinjiang lishi yu xianzhuang* (The history and current conditions of Xinjiang, China) (Urumqi: Xinjiang renmin chubanshe, 2006), Japanese edition, p. 149.
39 Zhang Dajun, *Xinjiang fengbao qishi nian*, pp. 6561–6575.
40 Zhang Zhizhong later described his thinking at the time in his memoirs: "There was not the slightest hope of resolving the incidents in Ili through military operations; the political approach was the only option. An intermediary was necessary for a political resolution, and the most appropriate intermediary was the Soviet Union." Zhang Zhizhong, *Zhang Zhizhong huiyi lu*, p. 419.
41 Ibid.; see also Burhan Shahidi, *Xinjiang wushi nian* (Fifty years in Xinjiang) (Beijing: Wenshi ziliao chubanshe, 1984), p. 268.
42 Zhang Zhizhong, *Zhang Zhizhong huiyi lu*, pp. 420–421.
43 Ibid., p. 421; Burhan Shahidi, *Xinjiang wushi nian*, pp. 286–287.
44 "Resolution No. 100 of the Interim Government Council of the East Turkestan Republic," Oct. 2, 1945.
45 Zhang Zhizhong, *Zhang Zhizhong huiyi lu*, pp. 422–423; Burhan Shahidi, *Xinjiang wushi nian*, p. 287.
46 Zhang Zhizhong, *Zhang Zhizhong huiyi lu*, p. 423; Burhan Shahidi, *Xinjiang wushi nian*, p. 287.
47 As per "Resolution No. 100 of the Interim Government Council of the East Turkestan Republic," the delegation of the East Turkestan Republic was to be composed of three members, with Rahimjan Sabir Ghaji as the head of the delegation. Despite being the youngest member, Ahmatjan Kasimi was not the least qualified, and his signature appears on the final document arising from the peace talks—an addendum to the Articles of Peace, signed in June 1946.
48 Zhang Zhizhong, *Zhang Zhizhong huiyi lu*, p. 449.
49 Tiyupjan Adil, "San qu renmin jing'ai de geming lingdaoren Ahemaitijiang Hasimu" (The beloved revolutionary leader Ahmatjan Kasimi of the people of the Three Districts), *Yili wenshi ziliao* (Historical and cultural materials on Ili), vol. 3 (1987), p. 56.

50 Saypidin Azizi, "Aslima II," pp. 84–86.
51 "Resolution No. 235 of the Interim Government Council of the East Turkestan Republic," dated March 5, 1946, stipulated that lieutenant colonels could only be promoted to colonel after six years of service.
52 Regarding the decorations bestowed by the East Turkestan Republic, four categories were created on March 19, 1946, including the "Medal of the East Turkestan Republic," the "Medal of Liberation," the "Medal of Loyalty," and the "Medal of Independence." The "Medal of the East Turkestan Republic" was only bestowed upon Ilhan Tora (on January 9, 1946), as well as Commander-in-Chief Ivan Polinov and Deputy Commander Isakbek Munonow of the National Army (on March 2, 1946). The "Gold Medal of Liberation," created in May 1945, was also granted to only a handful of recipients. According to the author's research, the recipients of this medal included: President Ilhan Tora; Vice President Hakimbek Hoja (on January 9, 1946); Ahmatjan Kasimi;, council member and Minister of Finance Anwar Musabayow; council member and National Army chief of staff Povel Maskolyov; council member and Altay District Commissioner Osman Islam; council member and Altay Cavalry Regiment commander Dalalkan Sugurbayow; council member Abdullah Jani; Fatih Muslimow, the leader of the Nilka guerrillas; and so on. Ahmatjan Kasimi was the 4th recipient of this medal. "Resolution No. 235 of the Interim Government Council of the East Turkestan Republic," dated March 5, 1946, stipulated that the following privileges would be accorded to recipients of the "Medal of Liberation": (1) Recipients were to be honored by the citizens of the East Turkestan Republic; (2) Recipients could not be arrested without their consent; (3) Recipients who had committed a crime could only be arrested by permission of the Interim Government Council. Other benefits included: (4) A special salary; (5) State sponsorship of their children's tuition expenses; (6) Free tickets to movie theaters; (7) One free international trip each year; (8) Precedence for enjoyment of therapeutic hot springs; and (8) Rights of first purchase for televisions, theater tickets, and plane tickets for work purposes.
53 Saypidin Azizi, "Aslima II," p. 87.
54 Yusupjan Aysa, "Uq Wilayat Rahbiri Ahmatjan Kasim Tohursida Aslima" (On Ahmatjan Kasimi, leader of the Three Districts Revolution), *Xinjiang Tarih Matiriyalliri* 25 (1988), p. 67.
55 The above curriculum vitae for Ahmatjan Kasimi is primarily based on the author's interviews with Kasimi's family members and other figures involved in the East Turkestan Republic. See also Yusupjan Aysa, "Uq Wilayat Rahbiri Ahmatjan Kasim Tohursida Aslima," p. 68; and Tiyupjan Adil, "San qu renmin jing'ai de geming lingdaoren Ahemaitijiang Hasimu," pp. 54–55.
56 Tiyupjan Adil, "San qu renmin jing'ai de geming lingdaoren Ahemaitijiang Hasimu," p. 55; Yusupjan Aysa, "Uq Wilayat Rahbiri Ahmatjan Kasim Tohursida Aslima," pp. 71–72.
57 According to Yusupjan Aysa, Ahmatjan Kasimi was arrested while passing

through Customs (see Yusupjan Aysa, "Uq Wilayat Rahbiri Ahmatjan Kasim Tohursida Aslima," pp. 71–72). The arrest occurred in 1942, and Kasimi was detained in the Urumqi No. 2 Prison (Burhan Shahidi, *Xinjiang wushi nian*, p. 293). He was released in October 1944, just at the point when Sheng Shicai was appointed as Minister of Agriculture and Forestry in the Nationalist government and replaced by Wu Zhongxin as governor of Xinjiang Province (Tiyupjan Adil, "San qu renmin jing'ai de geming lingdaoren Ahemaitijiang Hasimu," p. 55).
58 Burhan Shahidi, *Xinjiang wushi nian*, p. 293.
59 Four individuals served as Minister of Military Affairs of the East Turkestan Republic. Ahmatjan Kasimi held the position for more than one year, from April 1945 to the fall of the East Turkestan Republic, making him the longest-serving Minister of Military Affairs.
60 Yang Zongyu, Li Zhanlin, "Fang Xinjiang san qu geming lingdaoren Abasuofu furen Lü Suxin tongzhi jishi" (Transcript of an interview with Lü Suxin, the wife of Abbasow, leader of the Xinjiang Three Districts Revolution), *Yili wenshi ziliao*, vol. 5 (1989), p. 22.
61 Hawir Tomur, "Xinjiangda *11 bitim* ning Tuzuluxi wa Buzuluxi" (The signing and dissolution of Xinjiang's *Eleven Articles of Peace*), *Xinjiang Tarih Matiriyalliri* 15 (1984), p. 3.
62 Zhang Zhizhong, *Zhang Zhizhong huiyi lu*, pp. 437–441; Burhan Shahidi, *Xinjiang wushi nian*, pp. 288–292; Hawir Tomur, "Xinjiangda *11 bitim* ning Tuzuluxi wa Buzuluxi," pp. 4–9.
63 *San qu geming Yili zhou ziliao* (1991), p. 172.
64 Three conferences were held during the talks. The first conference was held during October 13–22, 1945; the second spanned November 14–27, 1945; and the third ran from December 26, 1945, to January 2, 1946.
65 Zhang Zhizhong, *Zhang Zhizhong huiyi lu*, pp. 423–437.
66 Li Sheng, *Zhongguo Xinjiang lishi yu xianzhuang*, pp. 149–150, 154.

Chapter 9

1 Saypidin Azizi, *Tianshan xiongying* (Eagles of the Tianshan Mountains) (Beijing: Zhongguo wenshi chubanshe, 1987), p. 114.
2 *San qu geming Yili zhou ziliao* (Materials on the Three Districts Revolution in Ili Prefecture) (1991), p. 190.
3 Saypidin Azizi, *Tianshan xiongying*, p. 114.
4 *San qu geming Yili zhou ziliao*, p. 191.
5 Ibid., p. 192.
6 Ahmatjan Kasimi, "Report on the Conclusion of the Peace Talks," May 25, 1946, unpublished.
7 Under "Order No. 82 of the Ministry of Internal Affairs of the Government of the

East Turkestan Republic" (the employee handbook of the East Turkestan Ministry of Internal Affairs), dated September 25, 1945, arrest warrants for the crime of supporting the Chinese regime were to read as follows: "(Name of criminal), having associated closely with officials in the time of the Chinese regime and aided the police in arresting our innocent people, is hereby placed under arrest in accordance with the laws related to 'aiding the Chinese regime.'"

8   Ahmatjan Kasimi, "Our Good News," *Azatlik Xarkiy Turkistan* (Free East Turkestan), Feb. 3, 1946.
9   Ahmatjan Kasimi, "Learning from the Lessons of the Past, and Correcting our Shortcomings: Speech at the Welcome Celebration held at the Tarbagatay People's Club," Jan. 18, 1948, unpublished.
10 Ahmatjan Kasimi, "Speech to the Teachers of the Ghulja Schools at the Ghulja Uyghur, Kazakh, and Kyrgyz Club," Jan. 13, 1949, unpublished.
11 Ahmatjan Kasimi, "The Peace Terms and the Tasks We Now Face," Jul. 16, 1946, unpublished.
12 Ahmatjan Kasimi, "Speech to the Teachers of the Ghulja Schools at the Ghulja Uyghur, Kazakh, and Kyrgyz Club."
13 Ibid.
14 Ahmatjan Kasimi, "The Peace Terms and the Tasks We Now Face."
15 Ahmatjan Kasimi, "Speech at the Mass Rally Held at the Provincial Society for the Promotion of Uyghur Culture Regarding the Constitution Passed by the National Congress and the Recent Situation in Our Province," Feb. 17, 1947, unpublished.
16 Ahmatjan Kasimi, "Our Revolution and Alliance for National Liberation," August 1949, unpublished.
17 Ahmatjan Kasimi, "The Current Tasks Faced by Intellectuals and the Upcoming Elections," Sept. 25, 1946, unpublished.
18 Hakim Jappar, "Yaxlarning Uginix Olgisi Abdukirim Abasow" (A model for the young: Abdulkerim Abbasow), *Xinjiang Tarih Matiriyalliri* 26 (1989), p. 202.
19 "Yili shi quanti qingnian di yi ci dahui jueyi" (Resolution at the first congress of the youths of Ili City) (Dec. 1945), in the section "Geming zuzhu huodong ziliao" (Materials on the activities of revolutionary organizations) in *San qu geming ziliao huibian* (Collected materials on the Three Districts Revolution) (Compiled and translated by the Xinjiang Minority Society & History Survey Group, mimeograph edition), p. 57.
20 The league regulations are described in detail in the "Provisional Constitution of the East Turkestan Revolutionary Youth League." Article 40 reads as follows: "Members must attend all meetings of each League office, at all levels. Modestly accept any task assigned by the League, and execute it unconditionally." See the section "Geming zuzhu huodong ziliao" in *San qu geming ziliao huibian*, p. 65.
21 "Provisional Constitution of the East Turkestan Revolutionary Youth League," Article 9: "Those accepted as candidate League members shall be recommended by two full members; following a review by the grassroots branch, the district or

county and the regional committee shall conduct a review and pass the resolution of the branch presidium; the accepted candidates shall then be presented to the Central Executive Committee for approval." Article 15: "When each candidate member becomes a full member, he or she must take the oath. Branches at all levels shall, within their given scope, conduct the oath under the supervision of their own presidium. The pledge: I willingly and sincerely join the East Turkestan Revolutionary Youth League, and shall unconditionally abide by and execute the League Constitution, unconditionally accept and execute all League resolutions and orders, and engage in the struggle for the cause of the scientific application of the democratic spirit and the development of all ethnic peoples, with no fear of the difficulties. If I break this pledge, I shall willingly bear the League's strictest punishments. Oath-Taker ××××. (Each ethnic group may swear the oath in accordance with their religious customs)."

22 Article 3 of the Youth Congress resolution read: "The Revolutionary Youth League shall be the branch of the government of the East Turkestan Republic directly engaged in fighting."

23 Saypidin Azizi, "Aslima II" (Recollections II), *Omur Dastani* (Epic of life) (Beijing: Millatla Naxiriyati, 1990), p. 108; Saydulla Saypullayow, "Kaysar Jangqi" (Brave warriors), *Xinjiang Tarih Matiriyalliri* (Xinjiang Historical Materials) 25 (1988), p. 10; Anwar Hanbaba, "Abdukirim Abasow Hakkida Aslima" (On Abdulkerim Abbasow), *Xinjiang Tarih Matiriyalliri* 25 (1988), p. 35.

24 Yang Zongyu, Li Zhanlin, "Fang Xinjiang san qu geming lingdaoren Abasuofu furen Lü Suxin tongzhi jishi" (Transcript of an interview with Lü Suxin, the wife of Abbasow, leader of the Xinjiang Three Districts Revolution), *Yili wenshi ziliao* (Cultural materials on Ili), vol. 5 (1989), p. 23.

25 "Provisional Constitution of the East Turkestan Revolutionary Youth League," "Geming zuzhu huodong ziliao," in *San qu geming ziliao huibian*, pp. 59–60.

26 The "General Principles" of the "Provisional Constitution of the East Turkestan Revolutionary Youth League" read as follows: "Chapter 1: General Principles; Article 1: The name of this group is the East Turkestan Revolutionary Youth League. Article 2: The purpose of the East Turkestan Revolutionary Youth League is to unite all youths living in East Turkestan, foster their democratic spirit, and enable them to join the struggle for the bright future, development and scientific advancement of the people of East Turkestan. Article 3: The East Turkestan Revolutionary Youth League is a political organization, which stands on the front lines of democracy to engage in activities for independence. Article 4: In achieving its own purpose, on the basis of a democratic movement of peoples seeking liberation, the East Turkestan Revolutionary Youth League shall rely on the strength and staunch will of its body of members, and the support of other democratic sympathizers." "Geming zuzhu huodong ziliao," in *San qu geming ziliao huibian*, p. 59.

27 Saypidin Azizi, "Aslima II," p. 111.

28 Saydulla Saypullayow, "Kaysar Jangqi," p. 10.
29 Anwar Hanbaba, "Abdukirim Abasow Hakkida Aslima," p. 35.
30 Saypidin Azizi, "Aslima II," p. 109.
31 According to Saypidin Azizi, in the summer of 1945, Abdulkerim Abbasow personally translated Mao Zedong's treatise "Xin minzhu zhuyi lun" (The theory of New Democracy) and explained it to his fellow intellectuals. The treatise was reportedly given to Abdulkerim Abbasow by his former Han Chinese inamorata, Yang Fengyi. Saypidin Azizi, *Tianshan xiongying*, pp. 109–111.
32 Saydulla Saypullayow, "Kaysar Jangqi," p. 13.
33 Saypidin Azizi, "Aslima II," p. 107.
34 Saypidin Azizi states that Abdulkerim Abbasow was the first to use the term "Second Revolution." Saypidin Azizi, *Tianshan xiongying*, p. 83.
35 Abdulkerim Abbasow, "Muqian de zhengzhi xingshi he women de renwu" (The current political trends and our tasks), May 11, 1945, *Wulumuqi wenshi ziliao* (Historical and cultural materials on Urumqi), vol. 6 (1983), pp. 3–4.
36 Regarding Abdulkerim Abbasow's wedding ceremony, see Yang Zongyu, Li Zhanlin, "Fang Xinjiang san qu geming lingdaoren Abasuofu furen Lü Suxin tongzhi jishi," p. 28. Abbasow received an education in Chinese culture from the Advanced Studies Department at Xinjiang College; he also studied with Chinese Communist Party member Lin Jilu. In May 1945, Abbasow received word in Ghulja that Lin Jilu had been executed by Sheng Shicai, and wrote the following poem to mourn his beloved teacher: "Sad news comes from Urumqi / My tears flow like floodwaters. / A mentor's revolutionary courage shall forever inspire me, / His spirit shall forever shine radiantly. / Tending seedlings to grow sturdy and strong, / The banner of justice flies high above Ili District. / Swift steeds gallop forth from the Three Districts toward the race course, / The fire of revolution burns to the foot of the mountains. / All demons shall be driven into the abyss, / And workers and farmers shall unite. / Puffing out our chests and racing toward the battlefield, / Our bloodstained flag shall flare in all directions." See Saypidin Azizi, "Aslima II," pp. 87–88. These circumstances indicate that Abdulkerim Abbasow did not in fact cherish a deep enmity against the Han Chinese. His later dismissal from the position of Minister of Internal Affairs was reportedly due to his issuance of orders for the execution of two soldiers who had raped Han Chinese women.
37 Anonymous, "Minzhu geming dang jianshi" (A brief history of the Democratic Revolutionary Party) (1948), in "Geming zuzhu huodong ziliao," *San qu geming ziliao huibian*, p. 53.
38 Saydulla Saypullayow claimed that the name of the party was the People's Revolutionary Party (*Khalikning Inkilawi Partiyasi*) (see Saydulla Saypullayow, "Kaysar Jangqi," p. 14), while Anwar Hanbaba gave the party's initials as "H.I.P." (see Anwar Hanbaba, "Abdukirim Abasow Hakkida Aslima," p. 36).
39 Abdulkerim Abbasow, *Xarkiy Turkistan Inkilawi Partiyisining Nizamnamisi*

(Constitution of the East Turkestan Revolutionary Party) (Handwritten in Uyghur by Abdulkerim Abbasow, photocopy).

40 Abilmit Hajiyow, "Olmas Jangqi, Xanliq Tohpa: Yingi Zhonggo Kurux Yolida Kurban Bolganlar" (Immortal warriors, brilliant achievements: Dedicated to building New China), *Yinge Jiongguo Kurux Yolida Kurban Bolganlar* (Dedicated to building New China) (Urumqi: Xinjiang Halik Naxriyati, 1991), p. 97.

41 Saydulla Saypullayow, "Kaysar Jangqi," p. 14; Anwar Hanbaba, "Abdukirim Abasow Hakkida Aslima," p. 37.

42 Saypidin Azizi, "Aslima II," p. 109.

43 Anwar Hanbaba, "Abdukirim Abasow Hakkida Aslima," p. 36.

44 Saypidin Azizi, "Aslima II," pp. 109–112.

45 Saydulla Saypullayow, "Kaysar Jangqi," p. 13.

46 Abdulkerim Abbasow, *Xarkiy Turkistan Inkilawi Partiyisining Nizamnamisi*.

47 Abilmit Hajiyow, "Olmas Jangqi, Xanliq Tohpa," p. 54.

48 This interview took place on August 14, 1991. The interviewee joined the National Army in 1946 and was later promoted to director of the regiment's Political Department; in the 1980s, he served as the head of research at the Xinjiang Academy of Social Sciences.

49 Saypidin Azizi, "Aslima II," p. 113.

50 Ibid., pp. 110–113.

51 Ibid., pp. 114–115.

52 Zhang Zhizhong, *Zhang Zhizhong huiyi lu* (Memoirs of Zhang Zhizhong) (Beijing: Wenshi ziliao chubanshe, 1985), p. 446.

53 Yu Zhanbang, *Zhang Zhizhong yu Zhongguo Gongchandang—Zhang Zhizhong jiyao mishu huiyi lu* (Zhang Zhizhong and the Chinese Communist Party—the memoirs of Zhang Zhizhong's confidential secretary) (Beijing: Zhonggong zhongyang dangxiao chubanshe, 1991), p. 122.

54 Zhang Zhizhong, *Zhang Zhizhong huiyi lu*, pp. 445–446.

55 Ibid., pp. 447–448.

56 Ibid., p. 449.

57 Ibid.

58 Ibid., p. 450.

59 Ibid., p. 449.

60 Tao Tianbai, "Zhang Zhizhong yu San qu geming" (Zhang Zhizhong and the Three District Revolution), *Yili wenshi ziliao*, vol. 4 (1988), p. 70.

61 Zhang Zhizhong, *Zhang Zhizhong huiyi lu*, pp. 452–453.

62 *San qu geming Yili zhou ziliao* (1991), pp. 428, 445.

63 Resolution No. 245, dated March 19, 1946, announced, "The Medal of the East Turkestan Republic shall be instituted to commend those who make outstanding contributions to the Republic." On March 20, the medal was conferred on Isakbek Munonow, by order of Resolution No. 246.

64 Patihan Sugurbayow, "Osman Zadi Kandah Adam" (The kind of person Osman

really was), *Ili Tarih Matiriyalliri* (Ili Historical Materials) 6 (1992), p. 123.
65 *San qu geming Yili zhou ziliao* (1991), p. 203.
66 Fu Yao et al. (eds.), *Jiefang zhanzheng jishi* (Chronicle of the war for liberation) (Beijing: Jiefang jun chubanshe, 1987), p. 121.
67 Owen Lattimore, *Pivot of Asia: Sinkiang and the Inner Asian Frontiers of China and Russia*, Boston: Atlantic Monthly Press, 1950, p. 91.
68 Stalin remarked on this in 1948: ". . . after the war [Second World War] we invited Chinese comrades to come to Moscow and we discussed the situation in China. We told them bluntly that we considered the development of the uprising in China had no prospect, and that the Chinese comrades should seek a *modus vivendi* with Chiang Kai-shek, that they should join the Chiang Kai-shek government and dissolve their army. The Chinese comrades agreed here with the views of the Soviet comrades, but went back to China and acted otherwise. They mustered their forces, organized their armies, and now, as we see, they are beating the Chiang Kai-shek army. Now, in the case of China, we admit we were wrong. It proved that the Chinese comrades and not the Soviet comrades were right." Cited in Robert Carver North, *Moscow and Chinese Communists* (Stanford, Calif.: Stanford University Press, 1953), p. 222. Mao Zedong made the following comments on September 24, 1962: "That was the situation in 1945: Stalin wanted to obstruct the Chinese revolution, we could not pursue civil war, we had to cooperate with Chiang Kai-shek, or else the Chinese people risked being destroyed. We did not follow [this order] at the time, and victory was later achieved in the revolution." "Zai ba jie shi zhongquanhui shang de jianghua" (Speech at the 10th Plenary Session of the 8th Central Committee), translated and reprinted in Institute of Modern Chinese History of the University of Tokyo (ed.), *Mō Takutō shisō banzai* (Long live Mao Zedong Thought) [毛沢東思想万歳], vol. 2 (Tokyo: San'ichi Shobō, 1975), p. 52.

Chapter 10

1 "Resolution No. 12 of the Interim Government Council of the East Turkestan Republic," Jan. 25, 1945, Article 3.
2 Patihan Sugurbayow, "Osman Zadi Kandah Adam" (The kind of person Osman really was), *Ili Tarih Matiriyalliri* (Ili Historical Materials) 6 (1992), p. 113.
3 Ibid., p. 115.
4 Song Xilian, "Bei Tashan shijian de shikuang ji jingguo" (The true circumstances and unfolding of the events in the northern Tarbagatay mountains), *Xinjiang wenshi ziliao xuanji* (Selected cultural and historical materials on Xinjiang), vol. 3 (1979), pp. 125–126.
5 On March 12, 1945, Osman Islam's supporter Marat surrendered to the Xinjiang provincial government, and released a "Declaration to my Kazakh Compatriots in

Altay," which was primarily aimed at exposing how "Communists incited our independence." See *San qu geming Yili zhou ziliao* (Materials on the Three Districts Revolution in Ili Prefecture) (1991), pp. 77–78. Osman's tribe members and kin Suleiman and Nurhaizah also surrendered to the Xinjiang government in August 1945. See Letif Mustafa, "Wo suo zhidao de Wusiman" (The Osman I knew), *Xinjiang wenshi ziliao xuanji*, vol. 3 (1979), p. 103.

6   *San qu geming Yili zhou ziliao* (1991), p. 164.
7   Ibid., p. 152.
8   Patihan Sugurbayow, "Osman Zadi Kandah Adam," p. 115.
9   *San qu geming Yili zhou ziliao* (1991), p. 188.
10 Patihan Sugurbayow, "Osman Zadi Kandah Adam," p. 121.
11 Song Xilian, "Bei Tashan shijian de shikuang ji jingguo," p. 124.
12 Patihan Sugurbayow, "Osman Zadi Kandah Adam," p. 125.
13 *San qu geming Yili zhou ziliao* (1991), p. 220.
14 "Resolution No. 29 of the Interim Government Council of the East Turkestan Republic," Mar. 5, 1945.
15 "Resolution No. 229 of the Interim Government Council of the East Turkestan Republic," Feb. 24, 1946.
16 "Resolution No. 29 of the Interim Government Council of the East Turkestan Republic," Mar. 5, 1945; "Resolution No. 153 of the Interim Government Council of the East Turkestan Republic," Dec. 5, 1945; "Resolution No. 283 of the Interim Government Council of the East Turkestan Republic," May 21, 1946.
17 "Resolution No. 78 of the Interim Government Council of the East Turkestan Republic," August 2, 1945, Article 14.
18 "Resolution No. 153 of the Interim Government Council of the East Turkestan Republic," Dec. 5, 1945, Article 2.
19 An Shengwu, "Huiyi jiefang qian Tacheng shi jiaoyu jiankuang" (Memoir on the situation of education in Tacheng City before liberation), *Tacheng shi wenshi ziliao* (Historical and cultural materials on Tacheng City), vol. 2 (1987), p. 3.
20 *Provisional Penal Code of the East Turkestan Republic*, May 13, 1945, Article 38.
21 Yasin Hudabardi, "Uq Wilayat Inkilawi Haqqida" (On the Three Districts Revolution), *Xinjiang Tarih Matiriyalliri* (Xinjiang Historical Materials) 16 (1985), p. 19; Saypidin Azizi, *Tianshan xiongying* (Eagles of the Tianshan Mountains) (Beijing: Zhongguo wenshi chubanshe, 1987), pp. 79, 108.
22 The phrase "Ghulja City" appearing in "Resolution No. 234 of the Interim Government Council of the East Turkestan Republic" is likely meant to refer to Ili District. The passage is transcribed verbatim to remain faithful to the original document.
23 *Provisional Regulations on Economic Procedural Law of the Supreme Court*, Article 1: "Religious courts may pass judgments on inheritance, marital disputes and so on after conducting an investigation"; Article 5: "For disputes on matters related to orphans and widows, and their care and support payments, religious courts shall

be permitted to adjudicate in accordance with custom." The foreword to *Supplemental Articles of the Provisional Penal Code of the East Turkestan Republic* states: "Cases pertaining to religion shall be heard by the Ministry of Religious Affairs and its affiliate organizations. Once a ruling is issued by the Ministry of Religious Affairs and its affiliate organizations, it shall be enforced by the enforcement organs of the police bureaus."

24 "Resolution No. 229 of the Interim Government Council of the East Turkestan Republic," Feb. 24, 1946.

25 Article 3 of "Resolution No. 78 of the Interim Government Council of the East Turkestan Republic," dated August 2, 1945, states that, "All school funding is to be allocated by the Ministry of Finance." "Resolution No. 106 of the Interim Government Council of the East Turkestan Republic," dated October 14, 1945, declares that, "This year's *ushr* and *zakat* must be applied to education spending; the salaries for school teaching and administrative staff and school funding shall be drawn from the *ushr* and *zakat*." This is again explicitly stated in "Resolution No. 196 of the Interim Government Council of the East Turkestan Republic," dated January 12, 1946: "School teacher salaries shall be included in the national budget, and the *ushr* and *zakat* remitted to the Ministry of Finance shall be applied to education." Thus the *ushr* tax collected by the Ministry of Religious Affairs and the general *zakat* tax collected by the Ministry of Religious Affairs and the Ministry of Education were first remitted to the Ministry of Finance for publication, and thereafter applied to education spending for the purpose of maintaining and developing ethnic education in the East Turkestan Republic.

26 At the time of the 1944 census, the total population of Xinjiang was 4,011,330; based on the given percentages, there were only 10,429 Uzbeks and 5,616 Tatars in Xinjiang at that time.

27 Prince Alim was unable to accept the position in the Interim Government Council: at the time, he was the leader of the largest Kazakh clan in Xinjiang, the Käräy. His ancestor had been granted the title of "Duke" by the Qing Dynasty in 1790. Alim himself had been granted the title of "Prince of the Second Rank" by Yuan Shikai in 1912, and he was the highest-ranking Kazakh figure in China. When his appointment to the Interim Government Council of the East Turkestan Republic was announced in September 1945, Prince Alim and his wife were in Urumqi assisting the Xinjiang provincial government. Basbay Qulak, the Tarbagatay District Commissioner, Osman Islam, the Altay District Commissioner, and Dalalkan Sugurbayow, the Commander of the Altay Cavalry Regiment, were unable to assume their positions either due to their local responsibilities. The latter three figures never visited Ghulja up until the fall of the East Turkestan Republic in June 1946, so it is safe to say that they had no influence whatsoever over the formulation of policy by East Turkestan's central government.

28 The province of Xinjiang was formed in 1884, and the region's capital was relocated at that point from Ghulja to Urumqi (Dihua). However, Altay District had

always fallen under the jurisdiction of the ministerial attaché stationed in Kobdo (which currently lies within the territory of the Mongolian People's Republic).

29 Letif Mustafa, a supporter of Osman Islam, was the first Kazakh representative of Altay District. He set out from Chenghua on horseback on January 2, 1946, to report to the East Turkestan government, arriving in Ghulja on February 3, a full month later. *San qu geming Yili zhou ziliao* (1991), p. 171.

30 The Uzbek inhabitants of Kashgar, Ghulja and other places, "lived alongside the Uyghur farmers and learned agricultural production techniques from the Uyghurs; they were also influenced by the Uyghur people in other ways. They generally spoke the Uyghur language, and their folk customs differed little from those of the Uyghurs." Xinjiang Minority Sociohistorical Survey Team of the Institute of Ethnology and Anthropology of the Chinese Academy of Social Sciences (ed.), *Wuzibieke zu jianshi jianzhi hebian* (Combined survey history and atlas of the Uzbek people) (Draft, unpublished, 1963), p. 3. The Tatars also garnered the respect of the Uyghur people because they were generally well-educated and relatively wealthy. Xinjiang Minority Sociohistorical Survey Team of the Institute of Ethnology and Anthropology of the Chinese Academy of Social Sciences (ed.), *Tata'er zu jianshi jianzhi hebian* (Combined survey history and atlas of the Tatar people) (Draft, unpublished, 1963), pp. 28–30.

31 Xinjiang Minority Sociohistorical Survey Team of the Institute of Ethnology and Anthropology of the Chinese Academy of Social Sciences (ed.), *Tata'er zu jianshi jianzhi hebian*, p. 16.

32 Osman Islam's armed resistance against the East Turkestan Republic was not merely rooted in ethnic conflict; Osman's anti-Soviet sentiments were in fact the key motivating factor. See Chapter 8 for more details. Given that Osman Islam began independently levying taxes immediately after Letif Mustafa's return from Ghulja, it may be that the anti-Kazakh economic discrimination Mustafa witnessed while in East Turkestan's capital city was the final straw that spurred Osman to open rebellion against the East Turkestan Republic. *San qu geming Yili zhou ziliao* (1991), p. 200.

33 Article 3 of "Resolution No. 4 of the Interim Government Council of the East Turkestan Republic," dated January 5, 1945, states: "In periods when the state is experiencing financial difficulties, to ensure that the state's economic needs are met, property and livestock may be sold to neighboring countries."

34 Ilhan Tora wrote a letter to the Soviet Consulate in Ghulja dated September 2, 1945, requesting that the Soviet government prohibit Soviet trading companies from dealing in livestock stolen from the border regions of the East Turkestan Republic. "Resolution No. 91 of the Interim Government Council of the East Turkestan Republic," dated September 4, notes that secretive organizations were evading taxes by reselling goods across the border, and orders the Ministry of Internal Affairs to ban such activities.

35 Abilmit Hajiyow, "Tarbagatay Wilayitning Iktisadiy Igilik Tarakkiyat Tarihiga

Dair Aslima" (Historical review of the economic development of Tarbagatay), *Xinjiang Tarih Matiriyalliri* 25 (1988), p. 291.

36   Under the land tax rate set by the East Turkestan government, 6,492,704 kilograms of grain were levied in Ili District in 1945. According to the account given in "Resolution No. 82 of the Interim Government Council of the East Turkestan Republic," dated August 19, 1945, this was approximately 243,476 kilograms less than the total yield under the land tax levied by the Nationalist government, suggesting that the war had led to a reduction in the farming population in Ili District.

37   "Resolution No. 60 of the Interim Government Council of the East Turkestan Republic," dated July 7, 1945, set annual vehicle registration fees as 5,000 *tangga* for trucks, 1,000 *tangga* for horse-drawn carts, and 500 *tangga* for bicycles. Fines equal to the registration fees could also be imposed.

38   A graduated stamp tax was charged based on contract price. A tax of 50 *tangga* was charged for a contract price of 3,000–10,000 *tangga*; for a contract price of 10,000–50,000 *tangga*, the tax was 75 *tangga*; for a contract price of 50,000–100,000 *tangga*, the tax was 100 *tangga*; for a contract price of 100,000–500,000 *tangga*, the tax was 200 *tangga*; and for a contract price of 500,000–1,000,000 *tangga*, the tax was 500 *tangga*. See "Resolution No. 63 of the Interim Government Council of the East Turkestan Republic," dated July 1, 1945.

39   "Resolution of the Interim Government Council of the East Turkestan Republic Regarding Usu County, Jinghe County, and the Maytagh Oil Fields," Sept. 15, 1945.

40   According to "Resolution No. 72 of the Interim Government Council of the East Turkestan Republic," dated July 26, 1945, the period for the use of stamped bank notes was set as one month; however, under "Resolution No. 77 of the Interim Government Council of the East Turkestan Republic," dated September 15, this period was extended to October 1. The use of stamped currency was to be prohibited thereafter. "Resolution No. 99 of the Interim Government Council of the East Turkestan Republic," dated October 2, 1945, announced that unstamped provincial bank notes could be exchanged at a 10% exchange rate after October 3. However, the Ministry of Finance issued an announcement on March 10, 1946, banning the circulation of unstamped currency. This series of contradictory orders indicates that unstamped provincial bank notes remained in circulation despite the ban issued by the Interim Government of the East Turkestan Republic. For a discussion of the types of paper currency issued in the East Turkestan Republic, see Dong Qingxuan, *Xinjiang jin 200 nian qian zhibi tujian* (Illustrated handbook of coins and paper currency in Xinjiang in the last 200 years) (Urumqi: *Xinjiang jinrong* [Xinjiang Finance] Editorial Department, 1986), pp. 47–49.

41   The amount of paper currency issued is unknown. The Bank of the East Turkestan Republic was initially controlled by the Ministry of Finance, but it was made independent of the ministry under "Resolution No. 136 of the Interim Government

Council of the East Turkestan Republic," dated November 20, 1945.

42 "Resolution No. 71 of the Interim Government Council of the East Turkestan Republic," dated July 26, 1945, announced the issuance of 100 million *tangga* in treasury bonds, with a five-year term. "Resolution No. 85 of the Interim Government Council of the East Turkestan Republic," dated August 22, 1945, announced the issuance of 300 million *tangga* in "Victory Bonds," also with a five-year term. "Resolution No. 241 of the Interim Government Council of the East Turkestan Republic," dated March 14, 1946, announced the issuance of 100 million *tangga* in secondary no-interest treasury bonds, with a repayment period of 1951–1961: "1) 100 million *tangga* in secondary no-interest treasury bonds shall be issued, with a repayment period of 1951–1961; 2) The treasury bond issuance shall be fully completed within one month of the release date of the resolution; 3) The state shall establish a special committee to achieve the best results in completing the treasury bond issuance. The head of the Central Issuance Committee shall be President Ilhan Tora."

43 "Resolution No. 85 of the Interim Government Council of the East Turkestan Republic," dated August 22, 1945, declared that Ilhan Tora was to be the chairman of the Treasury Bond Issuance Committee. "Resolution No. 87 of the Interim Government Council of the East Turkestan Republic," dated August 26, 1945, announced soon thereafter that advisors were to be sent to each county to promote the issuance of the treasury bonds.

44 The following passage from "Resolution No. 272 of the Interim Government Council of the East Turkestan Republic," dated April 25, 1946, reveals that the Ministry of Internal Affairs was also to assist in the issuance of the treasury bonds: "1) To accelerate the issuance of treasury bonds, the Ministry of Internal Affairs is ordered to assist the Issuance Committee."

45 "Resolution No. 196 of the Interim Government Council of the East Turkestan Republic," dated January 12, 1946, contains the following passage: "2) It is proposed that educational contributions to the Ministry of Religious Affairs and the Ministry of Education, as well as the *ushr* and *zakat* collected by the Ministry of Religious Affairs, shall be reported to the Ministry of Finance. 3) It is resolved that privately-raised funds shall be turned over to the Ministry of Education and the Ministry of Religious Affairs." This excerpt indicates that the *ushr* was collected by the Ministry of Religious Affairs, while the *zakat* was levied by both the Ministry of Religious Affairs and the Ministry of Education.

46 "Resolution No. 44 of the Interim Government Council of the East Turkestan Republic," dated April 24, 1945, declared that all tailors in the country were to be mobilized to sew military uniforms for the armed forces. "Resolution No. 118 of the Interim Government Council of the East Turkestan Republic," dated October 27, 1945, ordered that, "All tailors in the East Turkestan Republic shall be mobilized to serve the armed forces for one month." A similar passage also appears in "Resolution No. 236 of the Interim Government Council of the East Turkestan

Republic," dated March 6, 1946: "In order to provide uniforms for the soldiers in the Army of the East Turkestan Republic, all tailors and cobblers in the country shall be mobilized."

47 "Resolution No. 36 of the Interim Government Council of the East Turkestan Republic," dated March 18, 1945, ordered that all loans were to be repaid to the banks prior to March 25. According to the resolution, those who failed to make repayment by the March 25 deadline would be subject to a daily fine. The fine was to be equal to 15% interest as of the 31st, 30% interest as of April 5, 50% interest as of April 10, 75% interest as of April 15, and 100% interest as of April 20. The government issued a loan settlement resolution on September 15, 1945, declaring that all loans would be recalled, and issuance of new loans would be suspended. Resolution No. 247 of the Interim Government Council of the East Turkestan Republic," dated March 21, 1946, also declared that all grain allowances extended to farmers in the year 1945 would also be recalled prior to April 15.

48 "Resolution No. 39 of the Interim Government Council of the East Turkestan Republic," Apr. 2, 1945, Article 10.

49 See "Resolution No. 4 of the Interim Government Council of the East Turkestan Republic," Jan. 5, 1945, Article 8; "Resolution No. 36 of the Interim Government Council of the East Turkestan Republic," Apr. 2, 1945, Article 6; and "Resolution No. 67 of the Interim Government Council of the East Turkestan Republic," Jul. 22, 1945, Article 1 and 2. In addition, "Resolution No. 173 of the Interim Government Council of the East Turkestan Republic," dated December 18, 1945, declared that experts were to be sent to each county to investigate and reform fiscal spending. "Resolution No. 269 of the Interim Government Council of the East Turkestan Republic," dated April 20, 1946, stated that: "Illegal expenditure of state funds or expenditure of unbudgeted funds shall be punished in accordance with the law."

50 "Resolution No. 210 of the Interim Government Council of the East Turkestan Republic," Jan. 22, 1946.

51 "Resolution No. 19 of the Interim Government Council of the East Turkestan Republic," dated February 3, 1945, stated that a monthly subsidy of 16 kilograms of grain and 100 *tangga* was to be issued to military family members aged 8 and above. However, the "Resolution Regarding the Matter of Supply for Military Dependents," dated May 5, 1945, declared that henceforth no new military family members would be recognized; for previously recognized military families, the maximum number of subsidy recipients in each family was to be three persons.

52 "Resolution No. 157 of the Interim Government Council of the East Turkestan Republic," dated December 8, 1945, includes a passage on the wages paid to national civil servants, which reveals that the government had already gone into arrears on salaries for civil servants.

53 On December 10, 1981, Wang Enmao, the 1st Communist Party Secretary of the Xinjiang Uyghur Autonomous Region, discussed the "October 30 Incident" that

occurred in Kashgar in 1981 at a grand conference of the Autonomous Region Party Committee: "The discovery of this counterrevolutionary organization, the 'Uyghurstan Youth Meteor Party of Central and Western Asia,' was a victory; this must be thoroughly investigated, and in particular we must use this victory to discover the leaders and planners behind the scenes of this counterrevolutionary party. It must be traced back to the 'Prairie Fire Party' previously discovered in Jiashi [Peyziwat] County and counterrevolutionary organizations in other places." Wang Enmao, "Zai Zizhi qu dang weiyuan changwei kuangda huiyi shang guanyu Kashen wenti de jianghua" (Speech on the trouble in Kashgar at the grand conference of the standing committee of the Autonomous Region Party Committee), Guanche minzu zhengce wenjian xuanbian (Selected documents on the implementation of ethnic minority policies) (Urumqi: Xinjiang renmin chubanshe, 1985), p. 135.

54 Zhou Enlai, "Guanyu Woguo minzu zhengce de jige wenti—1957 nian 8 yue 4 ri zai Qingdao minzu gongzuo zuotanhui shang de jianghua" (Several problems with China's ethnic minority policies: speech at the Qingdao Working Forum on Ethnic Minorities on August 4, 1957), Theoretical Study Group on Ethnic Issues, Institute of Ethnology and Anthropology, Chinese Academy of Social Sciences (ed.), Woguo minzu quyu zizhi wenxian ziliao huibian (Collected sources and materials on the autonomy of China's ethnic minority regions), vol. 1 (Beijing, unpublished).

55 Editing Committee for the Deeds of Xinjiang Revolutionary Martyrs, Department of Civil Affairs of the Xinjiang Uyghur Autonomous Region (ed.), Pingbao yinglie zhuan (Biographies of martyrs in the suppression of the riots) (Urumqi: Xinjiang renmin chubanshe, 1990), p. 18.

56 During the "February 5 Incident" (also known as the Ghulja Massacre), which occurred in Ili in February 1997, riots were sparked by the arrest of a number of Uyghur religious worshippers. During the protests, 7 Han Chinese civilians were killed and 198 were wounded; 50 were seriously injured. A number of Uyghur protesters were killed or wounded as the crowds were dispersed by police. During the "July 5 Incident" of July 2009 in Urumqi, which began as a protest against the murder of Uyghur factory workers in Guangdong Province, official sources state that 156 "innocents" were slain, including 134 Han Chinese, 11 Hui Muslims, 10 Uyghurs, and 1 person of Manchu ethnicity, and 1721 were wounded. Uyghur groups in exile estimate that the Uyghur death toll was much higher, and a number of Uyghur activists were later sentenced to execution.